Christian Modernism
in an Age of Totalitarianism

Historicizing Modernism

Series Editors
Matthew Feldman, Professorial Fellow, Norwegian Study Centre, University of York; and Erik Tonning, Professor of British Literature and Culture, University of Bergen, Norway
Assistant Editor: David Tucker, Associate Lecturer, Goldsmiths College, University of London, UK

Editorial Board
Professor Chris Ackerley, Department of English, University of Otago, New Zealand; Professor Ron Bush, St. John's College, University of Oxford, UK; Dr Finn Fordham, Department of English, Royal Holloway, UK; Professor Steven Matthews, Department of English, University of Reading, UK; Dr Mark Nixon, Department of English, University of Reading, UK; Professor Shane Weller, Reader in Comparative Literature, University of Kent, UK; and Professor Janet Wilson, University of Northampton, UK.

Historicizing Modernism challenges traditional literary interpretations by taking an empirical approach to modernist writing: a direct response to new documentary sources made available over the last decade.
Informed by archival research, and working beyond the usual European/American avant-garde 1900–1945 parameters, this series reassesses established readings of modernist writers by developing fresh views of intellectual contexts and working methods.

Series Titles:
Arun Kolatkar and Literary Modernism in India, Laetitia Zecchini
British Literature and Classical Music, David Deutsch
Broadcasting in the Modernist Era, Matthew Feldman, Henry Mead and Erik Tonning
Charles Henri Ford, Alexander Howard
Chicago and the Making of American Modernism, Michelle E. Moore

Ezra Pound's Adams Cantos, David Ten Eyck
Ezra Pound's Eriugena, Mark Byron
Great War Modernisms and The New Age *Magazine*, Paul Jackson
James Joyce and Absolute Music, Michelle Witen
James Joyce and Catholicism, Chrissie van Mierlo
John Kasper and Ezra Pound, Alec Marsh
Katherine Mansfield and Literary Modernism, Edited by Janet Wilson, Gerri Kimber and Susan Reid
Late Modernism and the English Intelligencer, Alex Latter
The Life and Work of Thomas MacGreevy, Susan Schreibman
Literary Impressionism, Rebecca Bowler
Modern Manuscripts, Dirk Van Hulle
Modernism at the Microphone, Melissa Dinsman
Modernist Lives, Claire Battershill
The Politics of 1930s British Literature, Natasha Periyan
Reading Mina Loy's Autobiographies, Sandeep Parmar
Reframing Yeats, Charles Ivan Armstrong
Samuel Beckett and Arnold Geulincx, David Tucker
Samuel Beckett and the Bible, Iain Bailey
Samuel Beckett and Cinema, Anthony Paraskeva
Samuel Beckett's 'More Pricks than Kicks', John Pilling
Samuel Beckett's German Diaries 1936–1937, Mark Nixon
T. E. Hulme and the Ideological Politics of Early Modernism, Henry Mead
Virginia Woolf's Late Cultural Criticism, Alice Wood

Upcoming Titles
Samuel Beckett and Experimental Psychology, Joshua Powell
Samuel Beckett and Science, Chris Ackerley
Samuel Beckett's German Diaries 1936–1937, Mark Nixon

Editorial Preface to *Historicizing Modernism*

This book series is devoted to the analysis of late nineteenth- to twentieth- century literary modernism within its historical contexts. *Historicizing Modernism* therefore stresses empirical accuracy and the value of primary sources (such as letters, diaries, notes, drafts, marginalia or other archival materials) in developing monographs and edited collections on modernist literature. This may take a number of forms, such as manuscript study and genetic criticism, documenting interrelated historical contexts and ideas, and exploring biographical information. To date, no book series has fully laid claim to this interdisciplinary, source-based territory for modern literature. While the series addresses itself to a range of key authors, it also highlights the importance of non-canonical writers with a view to establishing broader intellectual genealogies of modernism. Furthermore, while the series is weighted towards the English-speaking world, studies of non-Anglophone modernists whose writings are open to fresh historical exploration are also included.

A key aim of the series is to reach beyond the familiar rhetoric of intellectual and artistic "autonomy" employed by many modernists and their critical commentators. Such rhetorical moves can and should themselves be historically situated and reintegrated into the complex continuum of individual literary practices. It is our intent that the series' emphasis upon the contested self-definitions of modernist writers, thinkers, and critics may, in turn, prompt various reconsiderations of the boundaries delimiting the concept "modernism" itself. Indeed, the concept of "historicizing" is itself debated across its volumes, and the series by no means discourages more theoretically informed approaches. On the contrary, the editors hope that the historical specificity encouraged by *Historicizing Modernism* may inspire a range of fundamental critiques along the way.

Matthew Feldman
Erik Tonning

Christian Modernism in an Age of Totalitarianism

T.S. Eliot, Karl Mannheim and the Moot

Jonas Kurlberg
Durham University, UK

BLOOMSBURY ACADEMIC
LONDON • NEW YORK • OXFORD • NEW DELHI • SYDNEY

BLOOMSBURY ACADEMIC
Bloomsbury Publishing Plc
50 Bedford Square, London, WC1B 3DP, UK
1385 Broadway, New York, NY 10018, USA
29 Earlsfort Terrace, Dublin 2, Ireland

BLOOMSBURY, BLOOMSBURY ACADEMIC and the Diana logo
are trademarks of Bloomsbury Publishing Plc

First published in Great Britain 2019
Paperback edition published 2021

Copyright © Jonas Kurlberg, 2019

Jonas Kurlberg has asserted his right under the Copyright, Designs
and Patents Act, 1988, to be identified as Author of this work.

For Legal purposes the Acknowledgements on pp. x-xi constitute
an extension of this copyright page.

Cover design: Eleanor Rose

All rights reserved. No part of this publication may be reproduced or transmitted
in any form or by any means, electronic or mechanical, including photocopying,
recording, or any information storage or retrieval system, without prior
permission in writing from the publishers.

Bloomsbury Publishing Plc does not have any control over, or responsibility for,
any third-party websites referred to or in this book. All internet addresses given
in this book were correct at the time of going to press. The author and publisher
regret any inconvenience caused if addresses have changed or sites have ceased
to exist, but can accept no responsibility for any such changes.

A catalogue record for this book is available from the British Library.

Library of Congress Cataloging-in-Publication Data

ISBN: HB: 978-1-3500-9051-4
PB: 978-1-3502-1157-5
ePDF: 978-1-3500-9052-1
eBook: 978-1-3500-9053-8

Series: Historicizing Modernism

Typeset by Integra Software Services Pvt. Ltd.

To find out more about our authors and books visit www.bloomsbury.com
and sign up for our newsletters.

Contents

List of Abbreviations		ix
Acknowledgements		x
1	Introduction: The Moot and Modernism	1
	Brief overview of the Moot	1
	Political Modernism: Decadence and revival	4
	The Moot as a Modernist experiment	10
	The Moot, Modernism and Christianity	12
	Notes on Sources and Methodology	20
2	The Moot and Civilizational Crisis	29
	Introduction	29
	Christianity and crisis	30
	The Moot and crisis	34
	Conclusion	43
3	The Rebirth of Christendom	49
	Introduction	49
	New beginnings through a New Christendom	50
	Maritain's neo-Thomism, medieval modernism and the Moot	52
	The influence of Jacques Maritain's *True Humanism* on the Moot	55
	Lessons from medieval Christendom	56
	Planning for Freedom	67
	Conclusion: 'Programmatic Modernism', prospects and tensions	73
4	'Why We Hate the Gestapo': Liberalism, Totalitarianism and the Third Way	85
	Introduction	85
	The Church, Community and State conference, and Christian totalitarianism	88
	The Moot on liberalism and democracy	90
	Engaging with the political alternatives	99
	Conclusion	119

5	Conflicts in Light of Modernism: T. S. Eliot and Karl Mannheim in Dialogue	133
	Introduction	133
	Eliot and Mannheim at the Moot	134
	Common ground	136
	Clashes on the transformation of culture	141
	Humanism versus Christian theism	148
	Conclusion	152
6	The Moot as a Revitalisation Movement	161
	Introduction	161
	Creating a Manifesto	164
	Oldham's councils	168
	The Formation of an Order	172
	New education, new man	182
	Channels of dissemination	189
	Revolutionary or reformist?	198
	Conclusion: The Moot's failed revolution	201
7	Conclusion	219
	Modernist interpretive framing	219
	Theoretical gains	221
	Legacy of the Moot	224
Appendix: List of the Moot Members		229
	Regular members	229
	Visitors	232
Archives		234
Bibliography		237
Index		251

List of Abbreviations

BBC	British Broadcasting Corporation
BCC	British Council of Churches
CCFCL	Council on the Christian Faith and the Common Life
CFC	Christian Frontiers Council
CNL	Christian News-Letter
CRD	Conservative Research Department
ICF	Industrial Christian Fellowship
IOE	Institute of Education
MRA	Moral Re-Armament Movement
PEP	Political and Economic Planning
SCM	Student Christian Movement Press

Acknowledgements

Numerous people have contributed to the making of this monograph. I am grateful for the opportunity provided by the editors to be included in the *Historicizing Modernism* series. Both have had a direct influence on the book's content. Erik Tonning supervised my doctoral thesis that provided the bulk of the material for the book. As a supervisor Erik was always available, fast in returning drafts, detailed in his comments and unwavering in his support. He has played a significant role in shaping me as a scholar. Matthew Feldman kindly lent his astute eye to the chapter concerning the Moot and totalitarianism. I am thankful to be able to call them my friends.

I am deeply indebted to Matthew Grimley, who has read most of the chapters and provided me with invaluable input that has strengthened the historical context of the research. I am also grateful to Joseph Sverker for his friendship, for our stimulating theological musings and for his helpful suggestions that have fed into the book. My wife, Nina Kurlberg, has been a constant source of encouragement and has significantly improved the book's readability, patiently hunting down my sloppy mistakes and pushing me to improve my written language.

A number of scholars have given generously of their time. My thanks goes to Ronald Bush for his insights into T. S. Eliot's social criticism. David Kettler engaged with me on the role of Karl Mannheim in the Moot, forcing me to articulate my own understanding. I am grateful for the interest he has taken in the research and for sharing some of his personal archival material with me. My gratitude also goes to Keith Clements, who provided me with interesting details concerning his work on the Moot papers.

I have benefitted from the archival work of Dr David Addyman, who on behalf of the Modernism and Christianity Project collected and organized material from a number of archives across the UK. I wish to thank the librarians who have offered me assistance in my own archival research: Trish Hayes at the BBC Written Archives Centre Caversham; Jeremy McIlwaine at the Bodleian Special Collections through whom I found connections between the Moot and Winston Churchill's cabinet; Sigrid Pohl Perry at the McCormick Library of Special Collections, Northwestern University; Rebecca Webster at the Institute of Education; Tracy Wilkinson at the Archive Centre, King's College, Cambridge; Ann Kenne at Special Collections, University of St Thomas; Anne-Emmanuelle Tankam-Tene at the archives of the World Council of Churches who generously gave me access beyond the opening hours of the archive; Natasha Richmond at Churches Together for permission to consult the William Paton Papers and the Christian Frontier Council at the Church of England Record Centre, and the assistance of their archivist Susan Robin; Melanie Smith at the Lambeth Palace Archives; and finally I am grateful to the T. S. Eliot Estate for granting me permission to consult the T. S. Eliot Papers at Houghton Library, Harvard.

The team at Bloomsbury including David Avital, Clara Herberg, Lucy Brown, Shanmathi Priya and Angelique Neumann have efficiently and graciously guided me through the process from manuscript to print, and have worked hard to turn the manuscript into a publishable volume.

I undertook the research for this book as part of the Modernism and Christianity Project at the Department of Foreign Languages, University of Bergen. My doctoral fellowship was funded partly through the department, but also through the generosity of the Bergen Research Council. In addition, I received funding from the Meltzer Fund enabling a month's archival research at various locations in the United States. The Department of Foreign Languages also provided funding for an extensive stay in Oxford during the spring of 2014.

I dedicate this book to my grandmother Kerstin who passed away in 2017 at the age of 100. While she did not share my interest in intellectual enquiry, or appreciate the benefit of it, she nevertheless faithfully supported me throughout my studies.

1

Introduction: The Moot and Modernism

Brief overview of the Moot

Amidst heightened national and international political tensions, J. H. Oldham, a theologian and leading ecumenist, published a letter for *The Times* in October 1938 predicting the imminent collapse of Western civilization. For Oldham, the threat facing British society was not confined to the rise of Nazi Germany, but ultimately sprang from the cancerous growth of paganism.[1] By then, he had already assembled an exclusive group of intellectuals with the aim of producing a road map for a countervailing Christian cultural revolution. With a great sense of urgency, 'the Moot' gathered regularly for almost a decade to strategize for a new lay Order that would act as a catalyst for a neo-Thomist Christian social and political movement.

As a tool to investigate the Moot, this study examines the hypothesis that the core project of the Moot may be described as a Christian variant of 'Programmatic' or 'Political Modernism'. While the discussion engages a number of theorists, this claim conceptually derives from combining Frank Kermode's coupling of Modernism with historical patterns of 'decadence and renovation', Anthony Wallace's conception of 'revitalization movements' and Roger Griffin's further development of these ideas in his analysis of 'Programmatic Modernism' in his *Modernism and Fascism*.[2]

Apart from making preliminary remarks, and outlining the contours of how the argument will evolve in the coming chapters, the introduction serves to provide an overview of Griffin's theory, how it relates to existing notions of Modernism and what it brings to an analysis of the Moot. It is worth noting at the outset that this conceptual framework is being tested here rather than assumed. Given the variety of archival and other documentation examined in this thesis, it is not to be expected that the hypothesis will necessarily account for every voice or problem within a multifaceted and evolving organization such as the Moot. Indeed, the documents suggest that the Moot failed in important respects to implement the more radical aspects of its 'Modernist' programme.

Prior to this theoretical discussion, a brief overview of the establishment, organizational structure, general aims and principal membership of the Moot itself is in place. The Moot was a direct product of the 1937 Oxford Conference on Church, Community and State, organized by Oldham. The conference gathered 425 Christian intellectuals, churchmen and theologians from around the world to articulate a 'common mind' and provide a Christian sociopolitical response to totalitarianism.[3] In a letter sent to the delegates a few months after the conference, Oldham encouraged the formation of 'cells' that would gather 'for the purposes of discovering what Christian action implies in the concrete situations in which [individuals] have to live and act'.[4] The Moot can be seen as Oldham's attempt to realize this undertaking. Several of the Moot members to be, including Eric Fenn, T. S. Eliot, Walter Moberly, Adolf Löwe, Christopher Dawson, Herbert H. Farmer and Eleanora Iredale, played leading roles in the conference.[5] The fact that many of the members had participated in the conference ensured that its ethos had a lasting influence on the Moot.

The diversity of the Moot's core membership accounts for some of its dynamics. As Eliot wrote in a letter to Oldham, this 'variety is what has given the Moot its zest, and even its cohesion' and made it 'so very fecundating'.[6] The Moot was very much J. H. Oldham's venture, something the members readily recognized.[7] Eliot, for example, repeatedly spoke of the Moot as 'Joe's group' in correspondence with friends.[8] Oldham was, indeed, firmly in control of the agenda and proceedings of the Moot, and during the meetings he was literally at the centre of attention. Since Oldham was by this time half-deaf, the members had to take turns to speak into his hearing aid, which was shuffled around the room. This arrangement no doubt gave the meetings a peculiar character.[9]

Amongst the most regular participants were secular Jew and eminent sociologist Karl Mannheim and his fellow émigré economist Adolf Löwe. To this group also belong educationists Sir Walter Moberly, Sir Fred Clarke and Walter Oakeshott. Poet T. S. Eliot, who was at the time highly engaged in social criticism, was also a regular member. Eliot was instrumental in bringing fellow literary critic John Middleton Murry into the group. Philosopher H. A. Hodges of Reading University produced more written contributions than any other member. Another philosopher was Hector Hetherington, at the time Principal of Glasgow University. The Moot consisted primarily of laypersons, but the ordained were represented by reformed theologian John Baillie of New College,

Edinburgh; Anglo-Catholic clergyman Alec Vidler; and Anglican Gilbert Shaw. Eric Fenn was also ordained but would be appointed Assistant Director of Religious Broadcasting at the BBC in 1939. Three women were members of the Moot: Eleanora Iredale, who had acted as an assistant on several of Oldham's ventures; Cathleen Bliss, who was the assistant editor and later editor (1945) of the Moot-sponsored *Christian News Letter;* and Mary Oldham.

There were also those who only attended two to four meetings but were nevertheless considered members. This group includes Cambridge theologian H. H. Farmer, Presbyterian minister Lex Miller, Daniel Jenkins and Oliver Tomkins – both of whom worked for the Student Christian Movement (SCM) – and Geoffrey Vickers, a lawyer and social activist.[10] Roman Catholic historian Christopher Dawson only attended three meetings but corresponded regularly with the group and had a significant influence on the thought of its members. In the final years of the Moot, scientist and philosopher Michael Polanyi and theologian Donald MacKinnon became key contributors.

Furthermore, Oldham regularly brought in guests who he felt could contribute to the discussion. These include American theologian Reinhold Niebuhr; editor of *New English Weekly* Philip Mairet; theologian and missionary Lesslie Newbigin; William Paton, who was instrumental in the formation of the World Council of Churches; Frank Pekenham, the assistant of William Beveridge; acclaimed historian R. H. Tawney and others. In addition, the group dialogued with a network of prominent Christian thinkers both in Britain and beyond, such as William Temple, C. S. Lewis, Arnold Toynbee, Jacques Maritain and Paul Tillich, to mention a few.[11]

During 1–4 April 1938, the Moot gathered at High Leigh, Hertfordshire, to analyse the state of the Western world. It was to be the first of a total of twenty-four weekends over nearly a decade.[12] The procedures of the Moot typically followed the pattern of two to four discussion papers being circulated amongst members prior to the meetings. Members were then given the opportunity to critique these papers in writing. The comments were also pre-circulated. On a fairly regular basis, Oldham posted articles by non-members either to stimulate the discussion further or because he felt they were informative, but these were not discussed at the meetings.[13] Although all the Moot papers and minutes are marked 'Private and Confidential',[14] the large network Oldham had established through the ecumenical movement was used as an international sounding board for some of the Moot papers.[15]

The meetings themselves usually took place two to four weekends annually at various locations in southern England. The fact that members travelled from as far as Edinburgh (as in John Baillie's case) at their own expense and throughout the war bears witness to the level of commitment many members felt towards the Moot. During the latter part of the war, members were even asked to bring their own food rations.[16] The last Moot weekend took place during 10–13 January 1947. Karl Mannheim's unexpected death a few days later was a major contributing factor to the Moot's discontinuation, but it was also apparent that by then it had run its course.[17]

Political Modernism: Decadence and revival

Modernism and crisis

This monograph sets out to recount the intriguing story of the Moot through the lens of Roger Griffin's 'Programmatic Modernism'. Considering the plural and sometimes conflicting conceptions of Modernism, it is necessary at the outset to lay out some definitional boundaries clarifying how the term will be appropriated.[18]

'Modernism' has primarily been associated with the arts and literature as a label for a range of aesthetic expressions in Western societies roughly from the mid-nineteenth century until around the end of the Second World War. On one level then, the term Modernism, as understood by critics and historians of literature and the arts, points towards the striking fact of the proliferation of experimental and challenging new artistic techniques in this period. Accordingly, Maurice Beebe lists four defining features of 'Modernist' art and literature: formalism; an attitude of detachment and non-commitment or irony; the use of myth as a structuring device; and the progression from impressionism to reflectivity.[19] Nevertheless, this approach, via style and technique alone, does not sufficiently address the extent to which Modernism is rooted in ideological and social concerns. Semantically, of course, 'modern' suggests an opposition to tradition. In his survey of Modernist paradigms, critic Astradur Eysteinsson writes that the 'principal characteristic of modernism is the rage against prevalent tradition'.[20] What unites these diverse movements and personalities is the attempt to overcome a perceived oppressiveness or decadence in the prevailing tradition and culture, though there may be little agreement between Modernists themselves about precisely how the dominant paradigm is to be defined and battled. In his attempt to identify common attributes, Peter Gay speaks of this drive to confront the status quo as 'the lure of heresy'.[21]

Much of the debate surrounding the concept emanates from how to understand this rebellion in its relation to sociopolitical processes of modernization. Again, Eysteinsson writes that Modernism has been understood 'as a kind of aesthetic heroism, which in the face of the chaos of the modern world sees art as the only dependable reality and as an ordering principle of a quasi-religious kind. The unity of art is supposedly a salvation from the shattered order of modern reality.'[22] In this conception, the emphasis is placed on Modernist formalism as seen in the new critical paradigm with its idealization of the autonomy, isolated whole and internal unity of art.[23]

The notion of aesthetic autonomy has, however, resulted in ahistorical readings of Modernism. As Leon Surette writes, '[t]o be "modern" in the Modernist sense is to have transcended history, to have climbed out of history into an unmediated, incorrigible realm of knowledge, and in that sense to have fulfilled history.'[24] Nevertheless, the immediate social and cultural background can hardly be excluded when considering the ubiquitous search for order exhibited in Modernist works, that is, mass society, industrialization, colonial wars, secularization, urbanization and global wars, coupled with a tidal wave of new intellectual ideas such as Darwinian evolution, Marx's stress on economic forces as the key to history, Freudian psychoanalysis and Nietzsche's celebration of the 'will-to-power'. Thus, inescapably, as Malcolm Bradbury and James McFarlane write, '[Modernist art] is the one art that responds to the scenario of our chaos … [and] the art of modernization.'[25] A key feature of Modernism, accordingly, is the search for meaning in the face of the upheaval of *modernity*.

Confronting the Modernist crisis

Eysteinsson accordingly points out the deep-rooted tension between, on the one hand, the Modernists' drive towards escape into some pure ahistorical world of aesthetics and, on the other hand, their implicit and explicit critiques of the destructive social and cultural forces of modernity.[26] As mentioned above, a principal feature of some Modernisms celebrates art as transcendent and autonomous, implying separateness from history itself. It is, nevertheless, difficult to avoid the conclusion that even this supposed transcendence implies a social critique in itself, for it is a radical subversion of the prevalent culture and in some cases a rejection of the Enlightenment project. Despite the objections of some Modernist artists and their critics, with the benefit of hindsight, Modernism increasingly emerges as intimately bound up with social modernity and as directed towards alternative modernities. Raymond Williams suggests that the split between the political and the apolitical – whether opting for 'the formerly aristocratic valuation of art as a sacred realm above money and commerce, or the revolutionary doctrines'[27] – is an expression of an anti-bourgeois sentiment.

Investigating the nexus between Modernism and social modernity thus leads to questions of the nature of the relation between Modernism and politics. The kinship between aesthetic Modernism and politics has been widely explored in Modernist studies. For instance, Kermode writes that in an age of perpetual transition 'the sense of an ending … is as endemic to what we call Modernism as apocalyptic utopianism is to political revolution'.[28] Referring to architecture and design, Christopher Wilk asserts that Modernism in these modes of artistic expression was a driving force for revitalization 'to create a better world, to reinvent the world from scratch; an almost messianic belief in the power and potential of the machine and industrial technology'.[29] In her chapter for *The Cambridge Companion to Modernism,* Sara Blair argues that since the Modernists embraced an inclusive notion of culture as a way of life, their works are inherently political, consciously or not.[30] Another example is Alan Munton's contribution to *The Oxford Handbook on Modernism*, where he concludes that while Modernist writers did not hold prominent positions in party politics, they 'used their particular communities to turn political belief into cultural power'.[31]

Understanding Modernism as rooted in a response to modernity provides a vantage point to understand the attitudes of Modernists to political engagement. It is true that some Modernists overtly rejected political activism. James Joyce's reported outburst, '[d]on't talk to me about politics, I'm only interested in form',[32] echoes Beebe's technically and stylistically grounded definition. Nonetheless, Joyce publicly announced his ideas concerning 'Free State' anarchistic socialism,[33] and Dominic Manganiello contends that 'Joyce's espousal of radical social ideals is more deep-rooted and persistent than is generally acknowledged'.[34] With Kafka and Joyce in mind, Marxist critic Georg Lukács famously denounced Modernists as subversive anti-humanists, who by their solitary projects undermined any possibility of human relationships and, by implication, positive political projects.[35] These arguments now appear outdated, for as Manganiello has argued, there is a recognition that art implies politics.[36]

The feeling of cultural and societal decadence within popular imagination during the early twentieth century was too imposing to ignore. Historian Richard Overy suggests that '[f]or the generation living after the First World War the prospect of imminent crisis, a new Dark Age, became a habitual way of looking at the world'.[37] This sense of crisis partly explains the widespread engagement of Modernist writers in social criticism. For Eliot, there was a moral obligation for the 'man of letters', in his intellectual capacity, to contribute to the formation of society. Although Eliot himself saw inconsistencies between his poetry and social criticism, the correlations are apparent – not least in his emphasis on the role of tradition.[38] Another example can be found in Virginia Woolf's musings on her fellow artists' interest in politics, declaring that 'the artist is affected as powerfully as other citizens when society is in chaos'.[39]

Thus, many Modernists were politically engaged and their sociopolitical views have been extensively recorded. Examples of Modernists' allegiance to radical political ideals can be found both in the leftist camp and more notoriously on the far right. James Joyce has already been mentioned as endorsing a socialist anarchism; other examples can be found among writers of the 'Auden generation' or the 'thirties generation' and their pull towards communism.[40] Eliot's attraction to Charles Maurras, Pound's anti-Semitism and propagation on behalf of Mussolini's Italy, Wyndham Lewis' praise of Hitler[41] and W. B. Yeats' fraternization with the Irish Blueshirts provide some examples of varying degrees of allegiance to right-wing ideas and movements among English-speaking Modernists.[42]

Political Modernism

The above discussion on conceptions of Modernism provides the context in which Roger Griffin's definition must be understood. Griffin's basic premise is that the dynamics of Modernism – construed as 'decadence-and-renovation' – are not limited to the artistic sphere but can be seen in numerous social movements of the time. Amongst other works, Griffin draws upon Frank Kermode's classic lecture series *The Sense of an Ending*, which foregrounds affinities between Modernism and Christian apocalypticism. Kermode traces apocalyptic patterns throughout Western history and notes their intensified persistence in the twentieth century. As such, Kermode understands the twentieth century as an age of endings, an age of crisis aspiring to new beginnings. The two go together, for in apocalypticism, claims Kermode, '[d]ecadence is usually associated with the hope of renovation'.[43] According to Kermode, these apocalyptic elements of 'decadence and renovation' characterize the Modernist mindset.[44]

In Griffin's historiography, then, modernity as decadence is a leitmotif. By the mid-nineteenth century, argues Griffin, the processes of modernization had led the cultural elites of Western Europe to question the Enlightenment myth of progress. Increasingly, modernity had come to be understood as 'a period of decline, decay, and loss'.[45] Late nineteenth-century Western modernity – construed by many as afflicted by disorientation, crisis, upheaval and nihilism – is the condition that triggered the renewal-seeking movements that Griffin describes as Modernist. His central contention is that the creative navigation through this felt *malaise* was not merely the prerogative of the artist, but that 'modernity generated myriad countervailing bids ... to assert a higher vision of reality, to make contact with deeper, eternal "truths" – or even to inaugurate an entirely new epoch'.[46] Thus, in Griffin's 'ideal type' or heuristic shorthand, Modernism is defined as 'the generic term for a wide variety of countervailing palingenetic reactions to the anarchy and cultural decay'[47] of modernity. Accordingly, at the heart of the plural responses embraced under this broadly conceived Modernism lies the endeavour to recreate an eroded 'sacred canopy' – or a set of overarching social meanings – supposedly lost through the demise of Christianity and the rise of industrialization and *laissez faire* liberalism in Europe following the Enlightenment. By arguing that the term can be applied to an array of social, cultural and political phenomena that exhibit the Modernist sensibility, Roger Griffin has thus legitimized a significant broadening in the application of the Modernist tag.

To bring conceptual clarity, Griffin differentiates between two ideal types of Modernism responding to the same predicament. The 'epiphanic' mode of Modernism denotes the ahistorical and individualistic 'cultivation of moments in which there is *Aufbruch* of a purely inner, spiritual kind ...',[48] also described above. It confronts the chaos of modernity by seeking epiphanic moments outside of time through art. Franz Kafka is, according to Griffin, the 'paradigmatic' practitioner of epiphanic Modernism. In contrast, a 'programmatic' mode of Modernism 'expresses itself as a mission to change society, to inaugurate a new epoch, to start time anew' and leads to a 'rhetoric of manifestos and declarations, and encourages the artist/intellectual to collaborate proactively with collective movements for radical change and projects for the transformation of social realities and political systems'.[49] Herein lies the crux of Griffin's thesis. While 'programmatic' can be applied to individual intellectuals and artists (Griffin invokes Nietzsche as an example), Griffin's contention is that political movements such as Nazism and fascism can also be described in such terms. His 'synoptic interpretation' 'presents modernism as capable of not just collaborating with sociopolitical movements, but of expressing itself directly in them unmediated through art and liable to manifest itself in the values and politics of the Right no less than the Left'.[50] This *political* Modernism, then, refers to sociopolitical movements reacting to the social and moral fragmentation of modern societies by seeking to create a new world by revitalizing society through a reappropriation of the mythical past and an appeal to transcendent ideals.[51]

Hence, in addition to the notion of 'decadence and renewal', the use of 'myth' as a source of revitalization is another feature that Griffin has appropriated from the artistic counterpart.[52] Indeed, the artistic Modernists often combined nostalgia for the premodern whilst endorsing Ezra Pound's call 'to make it new' (a citation itself annexed from Confucius). Thus, Modernist literature is littered with allusions to myth as a structuring device, not least in Pound's own use of Dante, Homer and the 'Elusinian mysteries'.[53] In this sense, the Modernist utilization of myth is more a matter of form rather than message, but the practice is nevertheless closely connected to ideas of literary and cultural renewal and rebirth. In contrast, the myths generated by political movements – such as the German and Italian forms of fascism and Bolshevik Communism – directly informed their utopian ideologies, their symbols, art and rituals.

This model of Programmatic Modernism is the analytical framework for Griffin's 'synoptic interpretation' of German Social Nationalism and Italian Fascism. In *Modernism and Fascism*, Griffin seeks to recast the widespread view of fascism as simply 'reactionary' anti-Modernism, arguing instead that the movement was directed towards a future *alternative* Modernism.[54] Considered *political* Modernisms, Mussolini's and Hitler's brands of fascism are narrated as renewal movements capitalizing on the mood of disarray amongst the masses in the interwar era while vowing to usher in a new utopian era of nationalist or racial rebirth. Accordingly, '[fascism] in the inter-war period was the vehicle for realizing the heady sense, not of impotently watching history unfold, but of actually "making history" before a new horizon and a new sky'.[55] In short, Griffin argues that the apocalyptic fabric of Modernism can be traced in these radical sociopolitical movements.[56] Throughout the volume, there is a continuous dialogue between this Programmatic Modernism and the aesthetic Modernism of the arts, architecture and literature. While noting the apparent conflicts – for example, the Nazi crusade against 'degenerate' Modernist art – Griffin contends that:

> it is precisely *because* fascism was an intrinsically modernist phenomenon that it could host some forms of aesthetic modernism as consistent with the revolutionary cause it was pursuing, *and* condemn others as decadent, as well as imparting a modernist dynamic to forms of cultural production normally associated with backward looking 'reaction' and nostalgia for the past.[57]

When applying the framework of Political Modernism to the fascist regimes, then, Griffin contends that they emerge as Modernist states *par excellence*. The fascist state becomes a vehicle of the cleansing of 'decadent' elements of modern society and for the creation of a new society, and ultimately a new man.[58]

The Moot as a Modernist experiment

Thus far, the Moot has predominantly been analysed by scholars assessing the contributions of individual members and the Moot's influence on their work. In this literature, the 'celebrities' feature heavily. Eliot, Mannheim, Polanyi and, to a lesser degree, Oldham, Löwe and Baillie have all been the subjects of such investigations.[59] What has been absent is any systematic analysis of the Moot as a whole. Summaries have been offered by Keith Clements in his biography of Oldham[60] and in Roger Kojecky's thesis *T. S. Eliot's Social Criticism*.[61] While Matthew Grimley has advanced the Moot as an example of a resurgence of medieval concepts of civil society, his narration is limited to the discussion on the role and nature of elites.[62] It can therefore best be described as a thematic treatise on the Moot.

In my study, I will explore how the Moot fits the apocalyptic pattern of 'decadence and renewal' in Griffin's Programmatic Modernism framework. Naturally, the Modernist framework is one angle among many from which the Moot can be viewed, but deliberately employing this analytical framework promises a more systematic treatment of the Moot material as a whole, bringing to light its nature, ethos and rationale.

In the next chapter, I will locate the Moot within the pervasive interwar era discourse of despair over the destructive forces of modernity. Only by grasping the extent of this fear of civilizational collapse can the Moot be comprehended as a movement aspiring to instigate a large-scale cultural 'rebirth'. It will be suggested that in the Moot's diagnosis, the crisis of modern societies was so acute that only a far-reaching overhaul could, in the group's view, save their civilization from an impending apocalyptic disaster.

As an example of this outlook, one could point to Mannheim's injunction at the 7th meeting: 'The "Roman Empire" [i.e. Western civilization] had yet not declined: we were on the brink of catastrophe out of which a new world must be built.'[63] It could be further exemplified by Oldham's letter to *The Times* on 3 October 1937, addressed to the nation:

> May our salvation lie in an attempt to recover our Christian heritage, not in the sense of going back to the past but of discovering in the central affirmations and insights of the Christian faith new spiritual energies to regenerate and vitalise our sick society.[64]

Mobilizing the past as a source of renewal for the present, the statement manifests the quintessential features of Griffin's Programmatic Modernism. Thus, it will be contended that even Christianity can be a source of the 'countervailing palingenetic reactions to the anarchy and cultural decay' that Griffin speaks of in his above-cited ideal type.

The premise of this argument partly rests upon the group's integration of the French Catholic philosopher Jacques Maritain's ideas in *True Humanism* of a new era of Christendom. To mobilize a Catholic thinker as a Modernist figure demands some justification, not least since the anti-Modernism of the Catholic Church – ratified in the 1907 *Lamentabili Sane* and *Pascendi* by Pope Pius X – implies incompatibility. However, the anti-Modernism of the Catholic revival amongst French thinkers in the early part of the twentieth century, with which Maritain was associated, resembled the ambivalence towards modernity itself in much aesthetic Modernism, as discussed above. Stephen Schloesser, in his *Jazz Age Catholicism*, suggests that neoclassic writer Jean Cocteau's 'anti-modernist theory of the avant-garde' provided Maritain with a means of synthesizing 'a traditionally anti-Modernist Catholic metaphysics [Thomism] with the post-war avant-garde'.[65] Thus, Maritain's avant-gardist scholasticism reflects the central features of Griffinite Modernism.

It is also this renewed scholasticism that attracted the Moot. While the fascist palingenesis rested upon the mythical appropriations of either 'Aryan' purity, in the Nazi case, or the past glories of Rome under Mussolini's Italy, the Moot mobilized an adaptation of the medieval Christian order as the basis for their own vision of renewal. The Moot is thus a 'Christian' expression of Modernism precisely in its utilization of *premodern* Christian tradition in its venture to revitalize a decadent modern society. This argument will be developed further in Chapter 3.

The fourth chapter will discuss another advantage of using the 'Programmatic Modernism' lens, that is, it allows for situating the Moot *vis-à-vis* sociopolitical movements of the interwar period. Because of the strong affinity between the Griffinite framework and far-right regimes, the Modernism perspective naturally makes the Moot's intellectual encounter with totalitarianism a central focus of study. The analytic framework thus serves to sharpen the comparison between the Moot's agenda and contemporary totalitarian regimes.

Thereafter, in Chapter 5, the 'Moot as "Programmatic Modernism"' thesis will be tested through a case study of the fascinating interaction between T. S. Eliot and Karl Mannheim. The Political Modernism lens brings to light both their shared scepticism of the sustainability of modern liberal society and their conflicting solutions to the crisis of modernity. I trace Eliot's persistent suspicion of Mannheim's meta-planning to his trust in divine providence.

Finally, in Oldham's eyes, the Moot was not simply a research group – he had something more fundamental in mind. He preferred to speak of the Moot as in the process of forming the nucleus of an Order.[66] Using Anthony Wallace's thesis as a reference point, the final chapter will document the extent to which the Moot deliberately sought to catalyse a revitalization movement.

The Modernist lens, then, sharpens our vision of the issues at stake in the group. This does not, of course, mean that one can expect that the fit will always be complete. The personalities and intellectual influences are complex and diverse, and although it is possible to argue for some loose consensual core ideas of the Moot, there are also many contradictions, tensions and conflicts within the group. While my hypothesis – that the Moot is best understood as trying to develop a 'Programmatic Modernism' based around core ideas of civilizational decadence-and-renewal and directed towards some large-scale form of Christian reshaping of British and ultimately Western culture – does explain much about the group's collective activities, it is also the case that the 'programme' was far from complete, and that there were a range of individual views on all issues discussed. Overall, the analytic model of Programmatic Modernism will be deployed precisely as Griffin intended: heuristically.

The Moot, Modernism and Christianity

Challenges to secularization theories

Training the Modernist lens on the Moot clearly hones the focus and brings new perspectives to the group itself. But narrating the group as a Modernist experiment also provides interesting avenues into debates regarding the relation between Modernism and Christianity. In recent years, the nexus between religion and Modernism has been significantly revised. This can be seen as a consequence of challenges posed to a unidirectional understanding of secularization. Still, the idea of a 'Christian Modernist' experiment will appear as a provocative oxymoron in the dominant Modernist readings, including that of Griffin.

The classical type of secularization theory that assumes the demise of religion as the inevitable outcome of processes of modernization – industrialization, urbanization, rationalization, individualization and Weberian disenchantment – no longer seems persuasive. For the founding fathers of sociology, who lived through rapid changes in religious attitudes amongst the elites of the nineteenth and early twentieth centuries, it appeared as though religion was permanently withering away from the consciousness of modern man and modern society. The heavyweights of early sociology, Emilie Durkheim, Karl Marx and Max Weber, believed that under modernity, the social impact of traditional religion would diminish, undermining the plausibility of religious beliefs and practice. From the 1960s on, this discourse, recounted with slight variations, not only gained momentum within sociology but also became an assumed paradigm within the academia and beyond.[67] However, in the last few decades, classical secularization theory has been challenged and revised on a number of counts.

Firstly, the assumed link between modernization and secularization no longer squares up in the face of the evidence. It was taken for granted that the declining influence of traditional religions manifested in Europe would be replicated elsewhere as modernization gathered pace globally. Peter Berger is one of the 'converts' now arguing that 'the assumption that we live in a secularized world is false'.[68] Already in the 1960s, David Martin expressed his misgivings about the usefulness of the 'secularization' paradigm.[69] Martin pointed out significant regional variation in the impact of secularization[70] and has since consolidated his earlier hypotheses with extensive empirical research, not least on the growth of Pentecostal movements in the Global South.[71] The title of the latest offering by Steve Bruce, an ardent and able defender of the standard account of secularization, is in itself telling: *Secularization: In Defence of an Unfashionable Theory*.[72] Nevertheless, the empirically grounded research of sociologists such as Bruce and David Voas[73] points to overwhelming data establishing that Christianity in Britain has seen remarkable decline, whatever the indicators. However, it remains far from obvious how these changes should be theorized and understood. In a world where religion seems to be thriving, Europe is increasingly looking like the exception rather than the lead that others will follow, as assumed by classical secularization theory. In Britain, Martin and Grace Davie have been the strongest proponents of such an 'exceptionalist' view, arguing that in the context of the secularization debate, 'religious' and 'modern' no longer appear as polar opposites.[74] Shmuel Eisenstadt's 'multiple modernities' thesis has been widely cited as a plausible explanation. He argues that there is no one process of modernity, but rather that different conditions in various parts of the world have created different trajectories for different modernities.[75] Hence, modernization as such cannot sufficiently account for the demise of Christianity in Britain.

A second contentious topic within this field of study is the question of what precisely has replaced traditional religion. Even Bruce is forced to admit that the space once occupied by religion has not been superseded by a 'scientific worldview', but rather by a 'jumble'.[76] Davie's influential theory, captured by the phrase 'believing without belonging', is that religion in Britain has undergone a deinstitutionalization. While people might no longer attend church services, 'aspects of religious belief demonstrate considerable persistence in contemporary Britain'.[77] A further thesis is philosopher Charles Taylor's *The Secular Age*, in which he explores the new conditions of belief. Taylor recasts the notion of secularization altogether. Secularization should not be viewed in terms of the decline of religion as such, but rather as a process occurring over centuries, which gradually 'takes us from a society in which it was virtually impossible not to believe in God, to one in which faith, even for the staunchest believer, is one human possibility among others'.[78] Thus, the nature of the world in which we live renders attempts to impose monopolizing world views implausible. Secularization is thus linked with pluralization, the growth of competing and coexisting modes of understanding the world. Like Davie, Taylor has argued that the pluralization of world views in the West has led to the privatization of religion.

Interestingly, Karl Mannheim's analysis in *Utopia and Ideology* of an epistemological turn from medieval 'object-orientation' to modern subjectivity suggests something akin to this position. Although Mannheim refers to the decline in religious practice and rituals, the real issue is that a unitary world view, such as the religious one, is subtly undermined in the new epistemological climate.[79] However, while Mannheim's historical analysis centres on an epistemological turn among the intellectual elites, Taylor's story investigates complex social processes of shifting notions of the self, which makes unbelief a possibility.[80] From these perspectives, Christianity is not inevitably relegated to the European past, but rather remains as one possible episteme amongst others – a list which would also include secular humanism itself.[81]

Thirdly, a number of historical accounts demand a revaluation of the dating of the demise of Christianity in Britain. Timothy Larsen's *Crisis of Doubt* challenges the depiction of nineteenth-century Britain as the age of crisis of faith.[82] By recounting the biographies of a number of intellectual reconverts from secularism back to faith, Larsen narrates an alternative historiography, 'reminding us of the intellectual vitality of Christianity and religion in the nineteenth century they serve as a necessary corrective to the distorted picture in which doubt is triumphant over all'.[83] Unfortunately, no equivalent overview has been conducted on secularization and the faith of intellectuals in the early twentieth century. However, available statistics on the religious practices and beliefs of the British population reveal a continued strong position for the church until the 1960s.⁸⁴ In *The Death of Christian Britain*, Callum Brown intends to 're-brand Britain 1800–1963 as a highly religious nation',⁸⁵ arguing that secularization needs to be ascribed to a much later date than commonly fixed in our history books. Interpreting available data, Brown concludes 'that people's lives in the 1950s were very acutely affected by genuflection to religious symbols, authority and activities'.⁸⁶

In terms of the church's status in public affairs, Matthew Grimley has credibly established a similar revisionist argument in *Citizenship, Community, and the Church of England*. He contends that the church 'remained an important strain in English political thought until after the Second World War',⁸⁷ and the real decline of its position was not set in motion until the 1960s.⁸⁸ Furthermore, Phillip Coupland has argued that the cosmopolitanism of the 'New Christendom' movement was a real force in European internationalism in the 1940s and 1950s as the churches maintained strong links with the political elite and establishment. He concludes that the 'neglect [of this influence] by historians is puzzling'.⁸⁹

Secularization, Modernism and Christianity

In the context of traditional accounts of secularization, the Moot could naturally be dismissed as an anomaly: as a final and misplaced attempt to resist the forces of secularization in a battle already lost. Yet, even though in the Moot members' own analysis secularization was challenging the rudiments of Western societies, they still considered the re-Christianization of society a difficult but *possible* task. Certainly, Mannheim was optimistic that their historical situation presented a unique opportunity for Christianity to revitalize society and provided a rallying point in the struggle against fascism.⁹⁰ The Moot's idea of a 'New Christendom' – suggesting a reconfigured medieval Christian social order – was from their historical viewpoint conceivable.

More importantly, the alternative historiography of Christianity in Britain outlined above suggests that Griffin's dismissal of Christianity as outmoded is premature. It is precisely because Christianity still occupied a central role in the national discourse at the height of Modernism that cannot be ignored. To neglect this historical context would be to underestimate Christianity's resilience as a sociocultural force, and the extent to which the Modernists were forced to contend with it. This is not to deny that the processes of modernization had radically altered how large parts of the population came to engage and relate to religious practices, beliefs and institutions in Western European societies. Nonetheless, how we apprehend these changes affects the way we understand both Modernism and the Moot. Standard accounts of the nineteenth century as the century of doubt and the twentieth century as predominantly secular can no longer be assumed.

In a number of disciplines, history has already been revisited and rewritten in light of these perspectives. This shift is also reflected in Modernist studies, where recent accounts are making the religious, the spiritual and the transcendent more visible. For instance, plenty of research has addressed the occult and spiritualism in Modernist art and literature. Published in 1993, Leon Surette's study on Ezra Pound, T. S. Eliot and W. B. Yeats sets out to readdress the neglect of occultism within Modernist studies. Surette attributes this oversight to a postmodernist tendency to read Modernism as 'positivist', which oversees 'literary modernism's more "romantic" and mystical tendencies'.[91] Since then, a number of further studies have appeared. One could point to Roger Luckhurst's chapter, where he questions 'ideas of a simple rupture and crisis of faith', since 'forms of modernism appeared in cultures that remained saturated with religious ideas' and 'the occult revival ... suggest[s] that far from being anti- or counter-modern', they were aspects of experiments in modern subjectivity.[92] In his account of the religious experience of Modernist writers, Pericles Lewis argues that the Modernists in fact rebelled against their forefathers' crisis of faith in the nineteenth century, and did not 'embrace a world emptied of the sacred', but rather experimented with fresh religions and spiritual expressions.[93] Thus, he holds, '[i]f God died in the nineteenth century, he had an active afterlife in the twentieth'.[94] Lewis therefore calls on 'scholars of Modernism ... to re-evaluate the nature of this change'.[95]

The idea of Modernism as a search for replacement religions also features prominently in Griffin's conception. Clearly, Griffin does not subscribe to a unidirectional secularization theory that assumes a steady emptying of the sacred from Western societies since the Enlightenment. On the contrary, Griffin records the religious undertones of Modernism as an antidote to the dreariness and *anomie* of modern materialism. For instance, he notes that the sacralization of politics by the fascist regimes that bestowed on these projects a quasi-religious aura has been widely narrated in the scholarship on political religion.[96] The mythical past provided a fabric for metaphysical discourses that gave impetus to these utopian visions. Accordingly, the fascist regimes are understood as secular replacement religions, supposedly filling the gap left behind by Christianity.

Thus far, Christianity has been largely excluded from this renewed recognition of the sacred, transcendent and spiritual in Modernist studies. For Lewis, the Modernist search for spiritual renewal was a search for replacement religions and alternative spiritualties that often, but not always, excluded orthodox Christianity.[97] As noted above, while Griffin emphasizes the centrality of transcendence, Christianity is glaringly absent in his work. Christianity is construed as an element of the fallen *nomos* – that which no longer can provide overarching meaning – and is thereby overlooked as a potential source for Modernist revitalist movements.[98]

It is obvious that the benefit of using a concept such as 'Programmatic Modernism' as an analytical device is that it clarifies and focuses certain features of the subject of research. However, in the process of accentuating some facets, a framework can also obscure or neglect others. In the case of Griffin's Modernism, however, it is not merely that Christianity falls outside the scope of the subject matter of his investigation; rather, there are assumptions within his 'ideal type' that render Christianity invisible.

It is suggestive, for instance, that Griffin rejects Frank Kermode's claim that the Modernists' apocalyptic outlook derives from a *Christian* millenarianism. Instead, Griffin suggests 'looking beyond the parameter of Christian history' to the universal practice of rite of passage as a more fruitful interpretation of the root of the modern sense of apocalypse.[99] In Griffin's 'maximalist' definition of Modernism, the 'primordial' human condition as chaos is assumed as ontological. Borrowing from Peter Berger's terminology, Griffin turns to the post-structuralist portrayal of the human predicament as a constant struggle to overcome the forces of chaos by constructing 'sacred canopies' that bring order and meaning to their existence. Periodically, the pillars of these 'sacred canopies' crumble, laying bare reality. Exposure to this ontological nakedness in turn propels the construction of new canopies to restore the sense of order. Griffin speaks of this process of 'palingenesis', meaning rebirth, as a rite of passage which brings a new stability, new vitality and new beginnings. This revitalizing process 'enables human beings to nourish themselves with metaphysical energy unavailable in "normal" phases of reality, and thus refuel society with transcendence on their symbolic return to it'.[100] Accordingly, Griffin holds that the human inclination towards the apocalyptic can be traced to the primordial need to create order out of chaos and to conquer 'our primal terror of the void',[101] rather than the Christian millenarianism assumed by Kermode.

In the end, it is unclear how Griffin's overall thesis profits from this 'primordial interpretation',[102] and it is of little consequence for how his framework will be applied to the Moot. Nevertheless, it does reveal his underlying secular assumptions that tend to disguise the role Christianity played in forming the Modernist revitalization movements. This is something this study sets out to challenge, by presenting the Moot as a Modernist revitalization movement drawing upon Christian traditions as a source of renewal.

In fact, via John Milbank's work, the extent to which Christianity has implicitly informed Griffin's thesis becomes apparent. In his genealogy of 'the secular', Milbank describes the metaphysical assumption that not only is evident here in Griffin's theory, but also underpins the whole of the secular episteme, as an 'ontology of violence', meaning 'a reading of the world which assumes the priority of force'.[103] The gist of Milbank's thesis can be summarized in the opening sentence of his *magnum opus, Theology and Social Theory*: 'Once, there was no "secular."' Milbank forcefully contends that '[the] secular as a domain had to be instituted or *imagined*, both in theory and in practice'.[104] What is challenged here is the prevailing discourse that once the process of disenchantment has emptied society of the sacred, the secular is the neutral space that we are left with.[105] Milbank's contention is, rather, that 'the secular' is as much a construct – a 'sacred canopy' – as 'the religious', with its own metaphysical presuppositions. More important for the sake of the argument developed here is Milbank's tracing of the formation of 'the secular' over centuries to its theological roots. With its starting point in Duns Scotus' nominalist theology, a process of 'bracketing' between God and the world opened up the space in which the secular was steadily constructed, until its conclusion in Nietzsche's death of God declaration.[106] The ensuing nihilism logically leads to the Nietzschean will-to-power to conquer and overcome the void or chaos. It is striking that in Griffin's universalizing of this primordial chaos, he refers to 'a deep kinship with much older philosophical traditions, such as Buddhism, Hinduism, and Stoicism',[107] which is also assumed in the Nietzschean 'will-to-power'. Milbank's thesis is that this discourse that dominates the social sciences and is found in Griffin cannot – as illustrated by Nietzsche's 'Antichrist' – be understood autonomously from Christian theology for it was posed as its direct antithesis. As Milbank writes, 'since ... it is bound to recognize in Christianity a precise opposite to nihilism ... Christianity has to be dealt with dialectically, and is thereby accorded a pivotal role'.[108] Thus, this secular reasoning is steeped in theology and ultimately evolved as an alternative to Christianity and its 'ontology of peace'. The irony, then, is that in his attempt to establish non-Christian sources of Modernism, Griffin has appealed to an episteme that is inescapably intertwined with Christianity.

This line of reasoning is central to Erik Tonning's recent study, in which he argues that Modernism cannot be understood apart from its theological roots. Tracing the 'formative and continuing impact of Christianity upon the cultural movement known as Modernism', Tonning contends that any given account of

Modernism 'that neglects or minimizes that impact is inevitably flawed'.[109] In *Modernism and Christianity*, Tonning demonstrates how this inevitable impact of Christianity is manifested in various case studies of Modernist personalities, whether expressing itself as a hostile rejection or as a source of Modernist renewal. Tonning utilizes the 'Griffinite Modernism' for his own thesis since the emphasis on renewal and transcendence provides a conceptual starting point to conceive of Christian Modernisms. However, in contrast to Griffin, Tonning's contention is that Modernism emerges through a process of 'formative tension' with Christianity. Even when construed as part of the fallen *nomos*:

> the 'sense of a beginning' described by Griffin necessarily involved some definite stance on the past, present, and future of Christianity in Western culture. The very idea of epochal transformation, in fact, involves a specific imaginative construction of the Old Era in contradistinction from the New.[110]

As 'Modernism did not emerge in a cultural vacuum', Tonning challenges Griffin's denial of the Christian roots of the Modernist version of the apocalyptic. He further contends that 'the Christian tradition was still a force to be reckoned with by all, and any imagined "apocalyptic" transition into a New Era at this time would be profoundly coloured by, indeed articulated through, the vocabulary and images drawn from Christian history'.[111]

One benefit of Tonning's thesis is that it allows for reconciling the perceived anomaly of Modernists' conversion to traditional forms of Christianity. For example, the standard secular discourse of Modernism struggles to accommodate T. S. Eliot's conversion to Anglo-Catholicism in 1927. Thus, Tonning's work opens up the possibility of integrating Christian versions of Modernism into mainstream accounts of the movement. In such accounts, Christianity *per se* does not constitute that which needs to be overcome, but rather, in renewed or perhaps more radical form, is in fact a potential fuel to revitalize modernity. Tonning's thesis thereby legitimizes a Modernist interpretation of the Moot.

Continuing in Tonning's line of investigation, this volume ventures beyond the artistic loci of his research into the sociopolitical. While Tonning convincingly establishes that Christianity cannot be neglected in the aesthetic modes of Modernism, the Moot demonstrates that Christianity needs to be considered as a case of a political equivalent. As such, this case study of the Moot pushes the boundaries in two respects. While carving out a space for Christianity as a potential source of regeneration in Griffin's Political Modernism, it also acts as an extension of Tonning's work into the sociopolitical sphere. Thereby, it challenges the secular assumptions of Griffin's thought and fuels the recent refiguring of the relation between Modernism and Christianity as heralded by Tonning.

Notes on Sources and Methodology

Owing to Eric Fenn's meticulous minute-taking, the Moot meetings were recorded almost verbatim and are thus a remarkable resource for historians. In total, minutes from nineteen meetings have been located. Complete with extensive annotations, Keith Clements published these in 2010 as *The Moot Papers*. These minutes, together with the surviving position papers by members and guests, and the abundance of correspondences permit a detailed archival reconstruction of the Moot.[112] The methodological assumption of the study is, as such, that the extensive cache of archival material collected for this research on the Moot allows for a solid empirical investigation and is essential in procuring historical accuracy. For example, as will be showcased in Chapter 5, bringing together the available material allows for more nuanced understandings of both Eliot's and Mannheim's positions in and engagement with the Moot than in the existing literature.

The limits of the archival approach are apparent. It is quite conceivable that further archival material will be uncovered, which either puts a different spin on or complements the historiography. For instance, the minutes of the last four to five meetings, if they at all exist, have yet to be discovered. Moreover, the unearthing of further correspondence between members might challenge existing readings of their disposition within the Moot. Many of the Moot members were keen writers publishing an abundance of books and articles before, during and after the Moot. These publications supplement the archival material in significant ways by furthering both the mapping of the individual members' various outlooks and how they appropriate and engaged with the Moot discussions. This in turn creates a set of hermeneutical considerations. What weight in the argument should be given to the published versus unpublished material? Furthermore, minutes from meetings, correspondences and publications are different genres written for different audiences. They are the products of different social and institutional settings and therefore have to be analysed accordingly. Minutes are the product of the note-taker, and although in the case of the Moot they appear as close to verbatim, there is inevitably a process of editing and redaction involved. The tension between Polanyi and Mannheim at the 21st meeting, or the 'ding-dong' battle as Philip Mairet called it, is not apparent from the minutes.[113] In addition, the Moot papers and minutes are all marked 'strictly confidential'. This confidentiality suggests a context which allows the intellectual and often public figure to be less guarded in their exploration of ideas than for instance in a published article or radio broadcast. Correspondence gives rise to a different set of interpretative issues. What weight should be attributed to an informal letter to a friend possibly venting in a moment of frustration, or to the more formal letter that expresses exaggerated praise? Thus, while the comprehensive archival methodology strengthens the historiography, the historian will always fall short of completeness. As Richard Evans notes, 'historians have always known, that we can only see the past "through a glass, darkly"'.[114]

Notes

1   J. H. Oldham, 'Lessons of the Crisis', in *The Times* (London: 5 October 1938).
2   Roger Griffin, *Modernism and Fascism: The Sense of a Beginning under Mussolini and Hitler* (Basingstoke: Palgrave, 2007).
3   J. H. Oldham, ed. *The Churches Survey Their Task: The Report of the Conference at Oxford, July 1937, on Church, Community, and State* (London: George Allen & Unwin, 1937), 22.
4   J. H. Oldham, 'Letter to Delegates', 6 October 1937, WCC/42.0062/1.1.
5   See Oldham, *The Churches Survey Their Task*.
6   T. S. Eliot, 'Letter to J. H. Oldham', 9 August 1943, OLD/9/5/6.
7   This point has been made by Keith Clements in his biography of Oldham (Keith Clements, *Faith on the Frontier: A Life of J. H. Oldham* (Edinburgh: T&T Clark, 1999), 373).
8   Cf. T. S. Eliot, 'Letter to Herbert Read', 3 April 1943, HF/8/33.
9   In interviews with Keith Clements, several Moot members recalled the experience of having to speak into Oldham's hearing aid (Clements, *Faith on the Frontier*, 373).
10 At least Adolf Löwe considered Vickers to have been a 'member' although he only attended two meetings (see Jeanne Vickers, *Rethinking the Future: The Correspondence between Geoffrey Vickers and Adolph Lowe* (London: Transaction Publishers, 1991), 193).
11 For a list of members and visitors, see the appendix. Also, see Keith Clements' brief biographical notes on the Moot members (Keith Clements, *The Moot Papers: Faith, Freedom and Society 1938–1944* (London: T&T Clark, 2010), 24ff).
12 Oldham claimed that the Moot convened twenty-six to twenty-seven times, but in fact there are only records from a total of twenty-four meetings. See minutes from St Julian's Group (OLD/13/3/47).

13 See, for example, 'Economic Reconstruction and Social Reconstruction' by the think tank Political and Economic Planning (see Oldham's 'Letter to Moot Members', 12 April 1940, IOE/MOO/23); H. Richard Niebuhr, 'Kingdom of God and Eschatology (Social Gospel and Barthianism)', [1941], IOE/MOO/60; OLD/14/6/40; Paul Tillich, 'Notes on Post-War Reconstruction in Europe', [1943], OLD/13/7/10.

14 It is likely that the confidentiality of the meetings and proceedings was based on the same rationale as the 'Chatham House Rule' or the Royal Institute of International Affairs, namely, to facilitate free and honest discussion on controversial issues without fear of falling into disrepute. Oldham was well aware of the procedures at the Chatham House (see Clements, *Moot Papers*, 162 (3rd meeting, 6–9 January 1939)). The complete minutes of nineteen meetings were published by Keith Clements in *The Moot Papers* (2010). When referring to the minutes, I will throughout the book reference the pagination in Clements' volume.

15 There are many examples of these: William Temple sent comments on Murry's 'Towards a Theory of a Christian Society (see ibid., 78)'; H. A. Hodges' 'Towards a Plan for New Summa' was commented on by C. S. Lewis ([1938], LM/SEC3); W. E. Hocking, idealist professor at Harvard University, was one of the many intellectuals to respond to Oldham's 'The Re-birth of the West'; and Mannheim's 'Planning for Freedom' was sent to the research department of the ecumenical movement in Geneva (cf. Hans Schönfeld, 'Letter to J. H. Oldham', [1939], OLD/9/2/1).

16 Cf. J. H. Oldham, 'Letter to Moot Members', 13 June 1944 (MPP/15/3).

17 See Oldham's comments in 'Minutes from the 1st meeting of the St Julian Group', 19–22 December 1947, OLD/13/3/47.

18 For a brief sketch of how 'Modernism' has developed and applied over the last few centuries, see Christopher Wilk, 'Introduction: What Was Modernism', in *Modernism: Designing a New World: 1914–1939*, ed. Christopher Wilk (London: V&A Publications, 2006).

19 Maurice Beebe, 'Introduction: What Modernism Was', *Journal of Modern Literature* 3, no. 5 (1974), 1073.

20 Astradur Eysteinsson, *The Concept of Modernism* (Ithaca, NY: Cornell University Press, 1990), 8.

21 Peter Gay, *Modernism: The Lure of Heresy from Baudelaire to Beckett and Beyond* (London: Vintage Books, 2009), 3.

22 Eysteinsson, *The Concept of Modernism*, 9.

23 Ibid., 12.

24 Leon Surette, *The Birth of Modernism: Ezra Pound, T.S. Eliot, W.B. Yeats, and the Occult* (Montreal: McGill-Queen's University Press, 1993), 4.

25 Malcolm Bradbury and James McFarlane, 'The Name and Nature of Modernism', in *Modernism: 1890–1930*, ed. Malcolm Bradbury and James McFarlane (Harmondsworth: Penguin Books, 1976), 27.

26 Eysteinsson, *The Concept of Modernism*, 16.
27 Raymond Williams, *The Politics of Modernism: Against the New Conformists* (London: Verso Press, 1989), 34.
28 Frank Kermode, *Sense of an Ending: Studies in the Theory of Fiction* (New York: Oxford University Press, 2000), 98.
29 Wilk, 'Introduction: What Was Modernism', 14.
30 Sara Blair, 'Modernism and the Politics of Culture', in *Cambridge Companion to Modernism*, ed. Michael Levenson (Cambridge: Cambridge University Press, 2011), 157.
31 Alan Munton, 'Modernist Politics: Socialism, Anarchism, Fascism', in *The Oxford Handbook of Modernisms*, ed. Peter Brooker, et al. (Oxford: Oxford University Press, 2010), 500.
32 As cited in Beebe, 'What Modernism Was', 1074.
33 See Munton, 'Modernist Politics: Socialism, Anarchism, Fascism'.
34 Dominic Manganiello, *Joyce's Politics* (London: Routledge & Kegan Paul, 1980), 113–14.
35 Georg Lukács, *The Meaning of Contemporary Realism* (London: Merlin Press, 1972 [1963]), 20.
36 Manganiello, *Joyce's Politics*, 219.
37 Richard Overy, *The Morbid Age: Britain and the Crisis of Civilization, 1919–1939* (London: Penguin Books, 2010), 3.
38 T. S. Eliot, *After Strange Gods: A Primer on Modern Heresy* (London: Faber & Faber, 1934), 28. Eliot's views on tradition in literature can be found articulated in T. S. Eliot, 'Tradition and the Individual Talent', *Egoist* VI (1919), and in a wider sociocultural sense in T. S. Eliot, *The Idea of a Christian Society* (London: Faber & Faber, 1939).
39 Virginia Woolf, 'Why Art Today Follows Politics', in *Virginia Woolf: Selected Essays*, ed. David Bradshaw (Oxford: Oxford University Press, 2008), 215.
40 See Samuel Hynes, *The Auden Generation: Literature and Politics in England in the 1930's* (London: Faber & Faber, 1979); Valentine Cunningham, *British Writers of the Thirties* (Oxford: Oxford University Press, 1988), 27f.
41 Wyndham Lewis later retracted his support for Hitler in 1939.
42 Cf. Michael North, *The Political Aesthetic of Yeats, Eliot, and Pound* (Cambridge: Cambridge University Press, 1991); Leon Surette, *Dreams of a Totalitarian Utopia: Literary Modernism and Politics* (Montreal: McGill-Queen's University Press, 2011).
43 Kermode, *Sense of an Ending*, 9.
44 Ibid., 93.
45 Griffin, *Modernism and Fascism*, 51.
46 Ibid., 53.
47 Ibid., 54.

48 Ibid., 62.
49 Ibid., 62.
50 Ibid., 68.
51 Ibid., 116–17.
52 Ibid., 55.
53 Cf. Leon Surette, *A Light from Eleusis: A Study of Ezra Pound's Cantos* (Oxford; New York: Clarendon Press; Oxford University Press, 1979).
54 Griffin, *Modernism and Fascism*, 31.
55 Ibid., 4.
56 This idea can also been found in Richard Allen Landes, *Heaven on Earth the Varieties of the Millennial Experience* (Oxford: Oxford University Press, 2011), ch. 11; David Redles, 'National Socialist Millennialism', in *The Oxford Handbook on Millennialism*, ed. Catherine Wessinger (Oxford: Oxford University Press, 2011).; James M. Rhodes, *The Hitler Movement: A Modern Millennarian Revolution* (Stanford, CA: The Hoover Institution, 1980).
57 Griffin, *Modernism and Fascism*, 33, author's emphasis.
58 Ibid., 1.
59 See Barry Spurr, '*Anglo-Catholic in Religion*' *T.S. Eliot and Christianity* (Cambridge: Lutterworth Press, 2010); Margret Schuhard, 'T. S. Eliot and Adolf Lowe in Dialogue', *Arbeiten aus Anglistik und Amerikanistik* 31, no. 1 (2006), 3–24; Wolfgang Wicht, 'Eliot and Karl Mannheim: Cultural Reconstruction Vs. The Destruction of Culture', *Zeitschrift für Anglistik und Amerikanistik* 36 (1988), 197–204; Stefan Collini, 'The European Modernist as Anglican Moralist: The Later Criticism of T. S. Eliot', in *Enlightenment, Passion, Modernity: Historical Essays in European Thought and Culture*, ed. Mark S. Micale and Robert L. Dietle (Stanford, CA: Stanford University Press, 2000); David Kettler and Volker Meja, *Karl Mannheim and the Crisis of Liberalism* (New Brunswick and London: Transaction, 1995); Yoshiyuki Kudomi, 'Karl Mannheim in Britain: An Interim Research Report', *Hitotsuabashi Journal of Social Studies* 28, no. 2 (1996), 43–56; Sigrid Ziffus, 'Karl Mannheim Und Der Moot-Kreis: Ein Wenig Beachteter Aspekt Seines Wirkens Im Englischen Exil', in *Exil, Wissenschaft, Identität*, ed. Ilja Srubar (Frankfurt am Main: Suhrkamp, 1988); Colin Loader, *The Intellectual Development of Karl Mannheim* (Cambridge: Cambridge University Press, 1985); Phil Mullins, 'Michael Polanyi and J. H. Oldham: In Praise of Friendship', *Appraisal* 1, no. 4 (1997), 179–89; Éva Gábor, 'Michael Polanyi in the Moot', *Polanyiana* 1-2, no. 2 (1992), 120–6; Keith Clements, 'John Baillie and the Moot', in *Christ, Church and Society: Essays on John Baillie and Donald Baillie*, ed. David Fergusson (Edinburgh: T&T Clark, 1993).
60 Clements, *Faith on the Frontier*. See also the introduction to *The Moot Papers*.
61 Roger Kojecky, *T. S. Eliot's Social Criticism* (New York: Farrar, Straus and Giroux, 1972).

62 Matthew Grimley, 'Civil Society and the Clerisy: Christian Élites and National Culture, C. 1930–1950', in *Civil Society in British History: Ideas, Identities, Institutions*, ed. Jose Harris (Oxford: Oxford University Press, 2003).
63 Clements, *Moot Papers*, 265 (7th meeting, 9–12 February 1940). Mannheim's proclamation seems to reflect the cyclical theory of history of Oswald Spengler's *The Decline of the West*. Spengler's volume caught the imagination of his generation as it captures the pessimism of the interwar era (Oswald Spengler, *The Decline of the West* (London: Allen & Unwin, 1961 [1926])).
64 J. H. Oldham, 'Letter to the Times', 3 October 1937.
65 Stephen Schloesser, *Jazz Age Catholicism: Mystic Modernism in Postwar Paris, 1919–1933* (Toronto: University of Toronto Press, 2005), 142, 151.
66 Clements, *Moot Papers*, 115 (2nd meeting, 23–26 September 1938).
67 For example, Peter Berger and Thomas Luckmann, *The Social Construction of Reality – A Treatise in the Sociology of Knowledge* (London: Penguin Books, 1971); Peter L. Berger, *The Sacred Canopy* (Garden City, NY: Anchor Books, 1967); Bryan Wilson, *Religion in Sociological Perspective* (Oxford: Oxford University Press, 1982).
68 Peter L. Berger, 'The Desecularization of the World: A Global Overview', in *The Desecularization of the World: Resurgent Religion and World Politics*, ed. Peter Berger (Grand Rapids, MI: Eerdmans, 1999), 2.
69 Cf. David Martin, 'Towards Eliminating the Concept of Secularization', in *Penguin Survey of the Social Sciences*, ed. Julius Gould (Harmondsworth: Penguin, 1965).
70 David Martin, *A General Theory of Secularization* (Oxford: Blackwell, 1978).
71 Cf. David Martin, *Pentecostalism: The World Their Parish* (Oxford: Blackwell, 2002).
72 Steve Bruce, *Secularization: In Defence of an Unfashionable Theory* (Oxford: Oxford University Press, 2011). Bruce departs slightly from the classical secularization theory in that he qualifies that secularization is only an inevitable and irreversible outcome of the uniquely European processes of modernization (Steve Bruce, *God Is Dead-Secularisation in the West* (Oxford: Blackwell Publishing, 2002), 38).
73 David Voas and Alasdair Crockett, 'Religion in Britain: Neither Believing nor Belonging', *Sociology* 39, no. 1 (2005), 11–28.
74 For example, Grace Davie, *Europe: The Exceptional Case: Parameters of Faith in the Modern World* (London: Darton, Longman and Todd, 2002); David Martin, 'Secularisation and the Future of Christianity', *Journal of Contemporary Religion* 20, no. 2 (2005), 145–50.
75 Shmuel Eisenstadt, 'Multiple Modernities', *Daedalus* 129 (2000), 1–30.
76 Interview 18 August 2010.
77 Grace Davie, *Religion in Britain since 1945: Believing without Belonging* (Oxford: Blackwell, 1994), 4–5.
78 Charles Taylor, *A Secular Age* (Cambridge: Harvard University Press, 2007), 3.

79 Karl Mannheim, *Ideology and Utopia* (New York: Harvest Books, 1968 [1936]), 36. Mannheim believed that the impasse resulting for the pluralization of world view would eventually be overcome by democratic consensus. My thanks to Joseph Sverker for pointing out this correlation.

80 Taylor, *A Secular Age*, 31.

81 In a recent article, Peter Berger argues that not only do secular and religious discourses coexist in the modern world but that the fault lines are drawn within the individual so it can 'alternate between secular and religious definitions of reality' (Peter L. Berger, 'Further Thoughts on Religion and Modernity', *Sociology* 49 (2012), 315).

82 A classic account of the 'crisis of faith' discourse of the nineteenth century can be seen in Owen Chadwick, *The Secularization of the European Mind in the Nineteenth Century* (Cambridge: Cambridge University Press, 1975).

83 Timothy Larsen, *Crisis of Doubt: Honest Faith in Nineteenth-Century England* (Oxford; New York: Oxford University Press, 2006), 17.

84 Church membership in Britain fell from a high of 19.3 per cent in 1910 to 17.6 per cent in 1950. Membership declined during the World Wars but in both cases recovered in the post-war eras. The trend is similar in terms of baptism, church weddings, and funerals. Although the decline in church attendance was far more radical from a possible high in the 1851 census of 59 per cent of the population, Brown argues that this was caused by less-frequent attendance rather than a decline in religious affiliation (statistics as compiled by Callum G. Brown, *The Death of Christian Britain*, 2nd ed. (London: Routledge, 2009), 161–4).

85 Ibid., 9.

86 Ibid., 7.

87 Matthew Grimley, *Citizenship, Community, and the Church of England: Liberal Anglican Theories of the State between the Wars* (Oxford: Clarendon Press, 2004), 5.

88 Ibid., 13.

89 See Philip M. Coupland, *Britannia, Europa and Christendom: British Christians and European Integration* (New York: Palgrave MacMillan, 2006), 4.

90 For example, Clements, *Moot Papers*, 96.

91 Surette, *Birth of Modernism*, 5–6.

92 Roger Luckhurst, 'Religion, Psychical Research, Spiritualism, and the Occult', in *Oxford Handbook of Modernisms*, ed. Peter Brooker et al. (Oxford: Oxford University Press, 2010).

93 Pericles Lewis, *Religious Experience and the Modernist Novel* (Cambridge: Cambridge University Press, 2010), 19.

94 Ibid., 25.

95 Pericles Lewis, 'Modernism and Religion', in *The Cambridge Companion to Modernism*, ed. Michael Levenson (Cambridge: Cambridge University Press, 2011), 181.

96 For example, Emilio Gentile, *Politics as Religion*, trans. George Staunton (Princeton, NJ: Princeton University Press, 2006).
97 Lewis, *Religious Experience*, 31.
98 See Griffin's ideal type definition, Griffin, *Modernism and Fascism*, 116–17.
99 Ibid., 102.
100 Ibid., 102–4.
101 Ibid., 340.
102 David Roberts charges the primordial layer of Griffin's model for being reductionist. He argues that fascism cannot be reduced to the primordial cry for order out of chaos (David D. Roberts, 'Fascism, Modernism and the Quest for an Alternative Modernity', *Patterns of Prejudice* 43, no. 1 (2009): 94).
103 John Milbank, *Theology and Social Theory: Beyond Secular Reason*, 2nd ed. (Oxford: Blackwell, 2006), 4.
104 Ibid., 9.
105 Charles Taylor also challenges this 'subtraction' narrative, which assumes disenchantment as a process of casting of the religious out of which a purified human being emerges (Taylor, *A Secular Age*, 22).
106 See Simon Oliver, 'Introducing Radical Orthodoxy: From Participation to Late Modernity', in *Radical Orthodoxy Reader*, ed. Simon Oliver and John Milbank (London: Routledge, 2009), 22).
107 Griffin, *Modernism and Fascism*, 340–1.
108 Milbank, *Theology and Social Theory*, 288–9.
109 Erik Tonning, *Modernism and Christianity* (Basingstoke: Palgrave Macmillan, 2014), 1.
110 Ibid., 4.
111 Erik Tonning, 'Introduction', in *Modernism, Christianity, and Apocalypse*, ed. Erik Tonning, Matthew Feldman, and David Addyman (Leiden: Brill, 2014), 5.
112 I have discussed the available archival in detail in Jonas Kurlberg, 'Resisting Totalitarianism: The Moot and a New Christendom', *Religion Compass* 7, no. 12 (2013), 517–31.
113 See Kojecky, *T. S. Eliot's Social Criticism*, 155.
114 Richard J. Evans, *In Defence of History* (London: Granta Publications, 2000 [1997]), 104.

2

The Moot and Civilizational Crisis

Introduction

Frank Kermode suggests that every era breeds its own prophets of doom and every generation deems its own particular 'crisis' as the most preeminent and disastrous.[1] Nevertheless, while the apocalyptic 'sense of an ending' can be traced in all periods of European history, modernity, on Kermode's reading, is an epoch of 'eternal transition and perpetual crisis' when 'transition itself becomes an age'.[2] In a comparable analysis, social theorist Zygmunt Bauman claims that modernity is susceptible to a permanent condition of 'ambivalence'. That is, modernity is marked by the presupposition that reality is ultimately chaotic, and thus demands ordering. Ambivalence arises out of the consciousness that such ordering is at once necessary to overcome a reality that is chaotic, and yet also futile since it is a mere social construction without ontological basis. Thus, chaos as the negation of order constantly looms, fuelling the state of ambiguity: 'Order and chaos are *modern* twins.'[3]

The Moot gathered during a time when such ambivalence was particularly patent. In his compelling survey of the interwar years, Richard Overy captures the ubiquitous sense of civilizational crisis in every class of British society from the elites to the masses. He suggests that 'the prospect of imminent crisis … became a habitual way of looking at the world'.[4] As discussed in the introduction, this consciousness of decadence is a central tenet of the artistic expressions in the first half of the last century identified as 'Modernist'. The discourse of decadence is also vital to understanding the particular manifestations of the political and cultural movements that Roger Griffin has construed as 'programmatic Modernist'. Since these political movements sought to provide a remedy for the ills of modernity, there is naturally a direct connection between the analysis of the situation and the solution prescribed. Accordingly, the Moot's response makes little sense without considering this discourse of interwar decadence.

Any endeavour to comprehend the rationale of the group necessarily involves investigating the Moot's analysis of the conditions that they sought to address. The narrative of decadence figures as a constant backdrop in their search for renewal, whether implicitly or explicitly.

There were only a few occasions on which 'the crisis' featured as an expressed item on the Moot agenda. Nevertheless, that their civilization was heading towards cataclysmic destruction was a powerful presumption that guided much of their deliberations. Traces of this conception of decadence are scattered throughout the Moot material and in publications by the group's members. This chapter will piece together the Moot's interpretations of the perceived civilizational crisis prevalent in the 1930s and continuing into the 1940s. While the Moot members emphasized different aspects of the conditions of modernity, there was a surprising level of agreement in their analyses. The chapter will also establish how the Moot ultimately attributed the malaise of modern society to spiritual causes and to the rejection of the Christian world view.

Christianity and crisis

While there is much merit to Overy's above-mentioned study *The Morbid Age*, it overlooks the extent to which the interwar discourse of crisis was narrated in spiritual and religious terms. The religious impact on the decadence narrative is limited to discussing a few cases in passing, such as Arnold Toynbee's theory that the rise and fall of civilization was intimately bound with religious vitality, and his appeal 'to embrace Christianity as the key to humanity's survival (Overy's words)'.[5]

In contrast to Overy, Griffin explicitly recognizes the Modernist crisis as one of transcendence. As touched upon in the introduction, the understanding of Modernism as a reaction against the perceived spiritual bankruptcy of modernity has gained currency in Modernist studies. For instance, Pericles Lewis challenges the secularist reading of Modernism by contending that the Modernist writers 'did regard the challenges of modernity as essentially spiritual'.[6] However one interprets secularization, it is clear that by the turn of the century, the privileged status of Christianity in Western societies could no longer be taken for granted. For Griffin, this implies a transcendental crisis since the predominant guiding *nomos* could no longer provide society with overarching meaning.[7] It is also for this reason, as Tonning argues, impossible to uncouple this discourse of spiritual decadence from Christianity.[8]

There is a strong case to be made that Christian actors directly influenced the narration of spiritual decadence. There is, indeed, a wide range of publications from Christian quarters advancing the view that Western societies were facing a crisis due to spiritual and religious negligence, and only Christianity could provide a lasting solution. Despite the eroding influence of Christianity at the time, one cannot ignore the Church of England and other Christian voices which featured prominently in the national public debate. The Christian contribution to the crisis narrative therefore demands greater attention.

For instance, in the wake of the Munich Agreement, the SCM published a series called 'Crisis Booklets' between November 1938 and January 1939 in '[an] attempt to help Christians to clear their minds as to the nature of the present situation'. The 'Crisis Booklets' include contributions by Moot members Eric Fenn and Walter Moberly, as well as Nathaniel Micklem, the Principal of Mansfield College, Oxford, who had some interaction with the Moot.[9] The editor, Hugh Martin, introduced the series by deploring 'modern Europe with all its incredible barbarianism': 'a bad dream' he hoped to wake up from. Ultimately, the crisis was a crisis of foundations, foundations which, according to Martin, could only be secured on a religious basis.[10] In the first booklet, Micklem – while not denying political, economic and social causes – essentially attributed the crisis to underlying theological causes. He wrote: 'we apprehend neither crisis nor the hope till we see that fundamentally the issue is religious.'[11]

While mainly operating in North America, theologian Reinhold Niebuhr had a large following in Britain not least amongst influential churchmen and Christian elites.[12] In *Reflections at the End of an Era,* Niebuhr announced: 'the liberal culture of modernity is quite unable to give guidance and direction to a confused generation which faces the disintegration of a social system and the task of building a new one'. This new order must at once encompass 'conservative religious conviction' with a 'radical political orientation'.[13] Another example can be found in William Temple's article for the *CNL*, suggesting that 'the troubles and anxieties of this time' were 'the consequence, according to God's law, of our neglect of His command and defiance of His will'.[14]

Messages concerning the spiritual nature of the crisis were further reinforced in the popular mind through major media outlets. In a letter to *The Times* on 21 December 1940, at a time when Nazi victory appeared inevitable, the heads of the largest churches in the UK issued a joint statement. It declared that the true cause of the 'present evils in the world' was a deeper spiritual crisis 'due to nations and peoples' failure to carry out the laws of God'.[15]

Another illustration can be found in the tireless efforts of Frank Buchman. Through broadcasting, public speeches and publications, he reached millions both in Britain and abroad with the message that only spiritual regeneration could offer a remedy for the destructive patterns of Western civilization. For example, in his typical polemical fashion, he declared in a broadcast for the BBC on 27 November 1938 that the nations were 'fighting a greater war than ever … not nation against nation, but Chaos against God'.[16] The Buchman-inspired Oxford Group Movement, which launched the Moral Re-armament Movement, gained substantial support amongst all strata of society. A letter to *The Times* on 1 September 1938 in support of the movement, signed by thirty-three members of parliament across party lines, bears witness to the momentum the movement gained in the late 1930s.[17] Ten days later, another group of prominent public figures, including former prime minister Stanley Baldwin, declared their endorsement.[18] Baldwin had, from the early 1930s, repeatedly and publicly pronounced that the threat of Stalinism, Hitlerism and Mussolini's fascism was not primarily political, but spiritual. Christianity, as the source of freedom and liberty, was ultimately incompatible with totalitarianism, and thus, 'if freedom has to be abolished and room has to be made for the slave state, Christianity must go because slavery and Christianity cannot live together'.[19]

A number of prominent Christians furthered the religious crisis discourse by insisting on Christianity as the sole answer to the civilizational crisis at hand. A few examples will suffice to illustrate the point. With the threat of war looming in the latter half of the 1930s, Rev. P. T. R. Kirk, the general director of the Industrial Christian Fellowship (ICF), summoned the church to take greater social responsibility, advancing a Christian alternative to the solutions offered by communism and fascism to 'our social and economic and political troubles'.[20] Kirk's work at the ICF meant that he had a significant hearing amongst the industrial workers. Another case can be found in Sir Richard Livingstone's chapter 'The Crisis of Civilisation', published in the volume *The Deeper Causes of War*, edited by Sydney E. Hooper, with contributions by Ernest Barker, William Beveridge and others. Livingstone identified liberal intellectuals' destruction of the Christian foundation of Western civilization as the cause of the modern crisis: '[t]o attack Christianity was ultimately to attack the spiritual life of Europe; to weaken it was to weaken that life'.[21] On this reading, liberal intellectuals were so set on deconstructing Christianity that they failed to construct an alternative in its place.[22]

The works of two historians are also worth mentioning. Firstly, Arnold Toynbee's theories on the rise and fall of civilization, discussed above, were widely read. A condensed version of Toynbee's *The Study of History* sold 300,000 copies between 1934 and 1938 – a remarkable feat for an historical work. Secondly, Lionel Curtis, who held a leading position at the Royal Institute of International

Affairs (Chatham House), argued that Western civilization stood before its greatest challenge since the disintegration of the Roman Empire into the Dark Ages. In his thousand-page volume *Civitas Dei: The Commonwealth of God* published in 1938, Curtis searched through history for solutions to address the modern crisis. In a résumé, Curtis declared that 'no time … appears so fraught with disaster to the human race as a whole as the present'. He suggested the nativity myth is the gem of the future fulfilment of the 'Kingdom of God upon earth'; a 'Divine Commonwealth, a human society based on the laws of God, on the one abiding reality, the infinite duty of men to God, of one to another'.[23]

Several of the Moot members contributed directly to this discourse of crisis in the 1930s. In an open letter addressed to the nation after the Munich Agreement published in *The Times* on 3 October 1938, Oldham stated that, '[t]he basal truth is that the spiritual foundations of western civilization have been undermined'.[24] Even before his conversion to Anglo-Catholicism in 1927, Eliot captured something of the spiritual barrenness felt in modern Europe after the Great War in *The Waste Land*. After his conversion, Eliot attributed this spiritual crisis more directly to Christianity or the rejection thereof. For instance, in his pamphlet *Thoughts After Lambeth*, Eliot expected the imminent breakdown of a society that had sought 'to form a civilized but non-Christian mentality', while predicting that this 'experiment will fail'.[25] The following year, in 1932, Eliot sought to convince the readers of BBC's *The Listener* that 'all our problems turn out ultimately to be religious'. Even the most pressing issue of the early 1930s – the collapse of the market – was in essence religious, since the economy 'depends … on moral questions, as morals depend on religion'.[26] Referring to this particular article, Eliot wrote at a later date for *The Christian Register* that 'we have become so accustomed to gloomy predictions of the future of civilization that we take them as a matter of fact, or as a pleasant opiate'. In Eliot's eyes, Western society had already reached the 'beginning of the Dark Ages'.[27]

By 1938, the self-confessed communist John Middleton Murry had committed himself to the Anglican Church. As the editor of the left-wing *Adelphi*, he felt compelled to offer an 'Apologia' to his readers for these personal developments. Fearing that the world was on the cusp of 'a terrible lapse into barbarianism which is beyond my power to imagine', he proposed the church as the antidote.[28] In the preface to *Europe in Travail* (1940), this message is even more explicit. The 'disease' of Europe is of a spiritual kind, declared Murry, and thus its remedy, a 'spiritual revolution' entailing a 're-discovery of Christianity'.[29]

As a leading Catholic historian, Christopher Dawson's analysis of the modern state gained some traction. He problematized the rise of the modern state and its tendency to encroach on all spheres of life including the religious. As such, the modern state, whether fascist, communist or even democratic, developed towards *ersatz* religions standing in direct competition with Christianity.[30] Referring to Dawson's analysis, Oldham wrote in a summary of the instrumental 1937 Oxford Conference that it was 'very near to the heart of the matter'.[31] The issue of the rise of the totalitarian state, its implied challenge to the church and the consequent crisis in Western Society was a central concern at the Oxford Conference led by Oldham. In the introduction to the report on the conference, Oldham suggested that its 'theme' had been the 'life and death struggle between Christian faith and the secular and pagan tendencies of our time'.[32] A booklet offering a summary of the conference states that the gathering in Oxford was an attempt 'to look without illusion at the chaos and disintegration of the world, the injustices of the social order and the menace and horror of war'.[33]

Not only did the conference gather the leading Christian thinkers of the time and result in a number of widely read publications, but it also enjoyed extensive coverage in the British media. The BBC published several articles in *The Listener* in the months leading up to the conference and produced a broadcasting series discussing the outcomes. Talks were given by Walter Moberly, Arnold Toynbee, T. E. Jessop, H. G. Wood, Lord Lothian and T. S. Eliot.[34] Furthermore, amongst the broadsheets, *The Times* reported daily from the conference, while *The Manchester Guardian* sent a correspondent to cover the event. Thus, the conference bolstered perceptions of the spiritual causes of the discourse of civilizational crisis.

These examples, from a spectrum of public figures and intellectuals, amply illustrate the extent to which the 1930s decadence discourse was shaped by Christian voices filtering through to the wider population through their influential publications and media outlets. Any historiography that features the economic and political factors while ignoring this spiritual dimension of the perceived civilizational crisis is therefore reductionist.

The Moot and crisis

The breakdown of the spiritual foundation

It is hardly surprising, then, that the accent of the Moot members' analysis was upon the spiritual roots of the peril around them. They understood themselves to be living in a secular society where the church had been marginalized and the social influence of Christianity was diminishing. This historical development was one of the central issues discussed during a session on 'The Nature of the Crisis' at the 1st meeting, 1–4 April 1938.[35] Moberly observed that the Church had become separated from the life of the community and had therefore lost its relevance in the everyday lives of the population.[36] Hodges, on the other hand, complained that 'Christianity had been superseded by a civilization determined to be humanist. We were seeing the outcome of this – possibly a necessary outcome in the unchristian and disunited state of human society.'[37] At a later meeting, Oldham attributed the declining influence of the church to its inability to engage with changing times. The church's 'weakness was first due to the loss of hold on the new divine order, second, the loss of touch with social reality, and third, to the fact that Christians, by pitting these two against one another neutralized their effort'.[38] Hodges commented during the discussion concerning his paper 'Christian Thinking To-day' at the 12th meeting that their historical situation was unprecedented:

> There used to be heresies and false religions as chief opponents of the Church: now we lived in a civilisation where the meaning had been gradually drained out of the word "God", until there was nothing left although at the same time every grade of "God-belief" was alive in society.[39]

Hodges blamed modern science for this trend of secularization. In a context where science 'has become the standard by which all claims to knowledge and truth' are judged, he argued that it is, 'inevitable that religion should not be at the hub of things'.[40] Since the church had failed to address the new epistemological climate, its message had become unintelligible for modern man and thereby the church had lost its voice in 'determinative decisions'.[41] Despite fearing that readers had reached a 'saturation point in diagnoses of the present situation', Alec Vidler still published *Secular Despair and Christian Faith* in 1941.[42] In the book, Vidler concluded that under the veneer of material success 'there was fundamental chaos – moral and spiritual chaos: we have arrived at the wasteland [a reference to Eliot?]'.[43]

Laissez-faire liberalism, loss of shared values and cultural crisis

The Moot thus understood the church to be in a state of decadence and Christianity to be threatened by the destructive forces of paganism, resulting in disintegration and chaos. The consequences of this spiritual crisis were grave and numerous. Without the possibility of an appeal to metaphysical authority, liberal societies had lost the rationale that permitted a shared value base. The 'neutrality' of liberal secular society had failed to provide a common world view, and without a shared 'idea' – a social philosophy – to live by, the individual was increasingly lost and the nation without direction. Lamenting the 'crisis of valuation', Mannheim emphasized that the 'abandonment of Christian and then of humanitarian valuations by modern man is the final cause of our crisis'.[44] He was sympathetic to the dominant position within the Moot that 'unless we restore spiritual unity our civilization is bound to crash'.[45] A problem within modern society was, according to Mannheim, that traditional values had not been adjusted to modern conditions, for the readjustment process of valuation itself had broken down.[46] Mannheim suggested that the breakdown of a homogeneous world view had led to a state of confusion: '[w]e do not even agree to whether this great variety of opinions is good or bad, whether the greater conformity of the past or the modern emphasis on choice is to be preferred'.[47]

Eliot echoed this sentiment, suggesting that the loss of common values under liberalism had resulted in the loss of guiding principles to determine what constitutes 'the good life'. 'For the modern British', wrote Eliot, 'do not even know what to eat and drink: their minds are too lazy.'[48] Eliot famously denounced modern society as 'wormeaten with Liberalism' in his controversial 1934 volume *After Strange Gods*.[49] The theme of modern disintegration was further expounded upon in his Moot-influenced *The Idea of a Christian Society*:

> By destroying traditional social habits of the people, by dissolving their natural collective consciousness into individual constituents, by licensing the opinions of the most foolish, by substituting instruction for education, by encouraging cleverness rather than wisdom, the upstart rather than the qualified, by fostering a notion of getting on to which the alternative is a hopeless apathy, Liberalism can prepare the way for that which is its own negation: the artificial, mechanised or brutalised control which is a desperate remedy for its chaos.[50]

The problem with liberalism, Eliot reasoned, was its wilful deconstruction of long-lasting traditions, resulting in social disintegration and anarchy. Sharing these ideas, Oldham suggested that '[t]he real crisis of our time is … not primarily moral but a cultural crisis'.[51]

Others proposed that the effect of the loss of the common culture once held under Christendom was further exposed in wartime. Vidler wrote that the British government spoke the language of utopianism, yet 'they have no political or social philosophy at all that is worthy of the name' other than the pragmatism of *laissez faire* that addresses issues as they arise.[52] Similarly, Murry regretted that the democratic countries have no shared 'faith' and that the English have 'no policy in which we can, as a nation, *believe*'.[53]

Nature of man, individualism and the breakdown of community

The Moot members perceived the disintegration of liberal society to be fuelled by modern assumptions about human nature. The radical individualism implied by the Enlightenment had led to the breakdown of community, the egotistic exploitation of the world and fellow humans, and to conflict and strife. The idea that changing notions of the purposes and ends of human existence were a cause of the modern malaise had been a favoured theme of Oldham's since the early 1930s.[54] Oldham, whose strength lay in popularizing ideas rather than fashioning original ones, drew upon a number of continental thinkers to reason about modern notions of personhood.

He was deeply persuaded by Jacques Maritain's analysis of the modern condition as determined by an anthropocentric anthropology that places the individual at the centre of the universe and by which man consequently 'has been thrown into disorder and become a monster'.[55] Oldham agreed that the liberal doctrine of the intrinsic value of the human individual had religious roots, yet as this Christian foundation had been neglected and rejected through the Enlightenment, man had become separated from his true nature.[56] Thus, in contrast to a Christian anthropology of human beings as dependent on nature, fellow men and God, modern man was embracing an independent egotistic individualism free from all constraints.[57] Oldham spoke of this shift in a paper presented in an early Moot meeting: 'May not the deepest cause of the present evils in the world be that man has sought the meaning and end of his existence in himself and thereby denied and perverted his true nature as a being created by God and for God?'[58]

Another significant source of influence on Oldham's thinking was Martin Buber's distinction between *I-Thou* and *I-It* encounters. In the modern world, with its expansion of scientism, industrialization and statism, human subjects are increasingly reduced to instrumental objects (*It*),[59] and true community was no longer a possibility. Buber's line of reasoning is similar to that of Eberhard Grisebach's, another of Oldham's favoured thinkers. Using Grisebach's critique of the liberal individualistic 'monologism' imbued in bourgeois Enlightenment, Oldham argued that under modernity, the individual – as the centre of the universe – extends himself or herself to exploit the world.[60] While cooperation is an essential factor in industrialized society, the rationale of this cooperation is chiefly for the sake of personal gain. Oldham explained Grisebach's concept in his manifesto 'The Christian Witness in the Present Crisis':

> In the monological approach to reality there is always a latent titanism; the possibilities of the expansion of the self are infinite. The ego-centric self seeks fulfilment in exploiting these, and this is the root cause of our present distresses.[61]

Elsewhere, Oldham cites W. E. Hocking's phrase 'commotive' as a critique of liberalism for failing to apprehend this cooperative function, which enables 'men to move and act together'.[62] While liberalism omitted this basic human communal urge, the totalitarian regimes readily manipulated its mass psychology. With the rise of a radical individualism, the communal aspect of human interaction was severely undermined.

Alec Vidler similarly expressed regret for the loss of communal aspects of society, a process the church itself was partly responsible for by assuming the doctrine of individualism. 'The individualism of modern Christianity had proved false', claimed Vidler, 'and we must return to the concepts of people and Church: of "man in community."'[63] A critique of the breakdown of community in liberal societies can also be found in John Baillie's volume *What Is Christian Civilization?* where he argued that the modern notion of progress, although Christian in origin, had disrupted community life. The Enlightenment is here blamed for this process, since in urbanized societies it is difficult to cultivate neighbourly relations. Baillie's critique illustrates why the Moot attributed such significance to community. For Oldham, communal aspects of human existence concerned the created order, and Baillie argued that a close-knit community life was a prerequisite for a vibrant practice of Christianity.[64]

Capitalism and industrialized societies

According to the Moot, the failings of modern societies were further related to structural problems concerning capitalism and industrialization. A recurrent idea amongst its members was that while promising freedom and liberty, liberal societies had, because of their scientific world view and industrialization, resulted in a world of domination and exploitation. Hodges complained that industrialized society assumed a logic of exploitation, 'making competition the normal relation between individuals and groups'.[65] In Vidler's opinion, an irony within liberal society was that while it emphasized morality as an individual response, under the conditions of industrialization, the individual was shackled by collective processes. Subjected to impersonal forces of the 'machine age':

we may well wonder whether he is anything more than the plaything of collective forces which he is powerless either to understand, to control, or even to resist … The monotonous pressure of mass production, mass propaganda, mass entertainment, flatten out individual personality, which seems reduced to the status of a cog in a vast machine.[66]

Oldham, in a similar Weberian analysis, held that industrialized society is under the dominion of impersonal forces. While technological advancement has brought a greater control over the elements of nature, the individual has become entrapped in systems of bureaucracy that limit the possibility of autonomous decision-making.[67] Elsewhere, Oldham stated that the individual was caught in machinery and that 'industrial society is failing to provide … essential human satisfaction'.[68]

In a paper titled 'Freedom and Vocation' circulated for the 13th meeting, Dawson provided a slightly different angle on the same topic. He maintained that in a pre-industrial society, private property meant the possibility of freedom in vocation. However, in the industrial age where profit-making had become the rationale for all work, this freedom had been lost. This development, together with the rise of the bureaucratic state, had enslaved man.[69] In his *Beyond Politics*, Dawson concluded that it was not that modern man was more capable of cruelty than in previous generations, but that society itself had come under the dominion of inhuman mechanisms, rendering it inhumane.[70]

Murry identified mass unemployment as the greatest social ill of the machine age. Unemployment was deemed to correlate to industrialization, for the machine inevitably reduced the demand for labour. Moreover, argued Murry, the political will to find new and creative sources of employment for the labourers freed up by the coming of industrialization was lacking in democratic societies due to the primacy of individualism over the collective.[71] Others also expounded upon the injustices and inequalities of the capitalistic system. Mannheim was convinced that the social and economic injustices caused by capitalism would eventually cause social disruption.[72] Discussing the use of the concepts 'freedom' and 'democracy', Eliot contended that the totalitarian regimes could justifiably accuse the 'democratic countries' of being dominated by capitalistic, monopolistic oligarchies.[73]

Threat of totalitarianism

The long-term processes of secularization and industrialization had over centuries finally reached a point of crisis. Historical realities had shattered the myth of progress, thereby undermining the whole Enlightenment project.[74] As far as the Moot was concerned, Western civilization stood at the crossroads between paganism – epitomized by the totalitarian regimes on the continent – and a revitalized Christianity.[75] Emilio Gentile, in *Politics as Religion*, correctly groups Oldham with several other Moot-associated Christian thinkers who saw the totalitarianism of communism and fascism as a direct threat to Christianity and Christian values.[76] In Dawson's analysis, found in several volumes published in the 1930s, the primary issue was not secularization, but quite the reverse: namely, the 'desecularisation' of the state. The state tended towards occupying the space previously held by the church. The result was a new totalitarian state: 'The State was now the priest and king instead of the policeman.'[77] As the privatization of religion in liberal society had served, in Dawson's judgement, to weaken the church's social and political stature, the church did not have the capacity to counterbalance the rising omnipotent totalitarian state.[78] In his lengthiest Moot paper, Mannheim suggested that the demise of Christianity as an integrative force and the consequent failure of competing value systems to fill the space had left Western society in a position of weakness readily exposed by 'the spiritual and political challenge coming from the totalitarian state'.[79] Thus, the Moot members saw the rise of these pagan semi-religions as a consequence of the inherent weaknesses of modern society.[80] The new movements provided the masses with a compelling moral vision – which the *laissez faire* of liberalism had failed to do – and were able to fill the spiritual vacuum through the sacralization of class, race or nation.

The fear of the potency of totalitarianism was amplified for the Moot by the idea that industrialized societies in themselves held a propensity towards totalitarianism. As industrialized societies require a greater level of co-ordination, and thus centralization, they produce conditions favourable for totalitarianism.[81] Thus, as Oldham wrote, '[whether] we like it or not, social life is being increasingly planned both as a whole and in its various parts. Where there is a plan, the individual has either to conform or to refuse his cooperation and suffer the consequences.'[82] Technological advances had necessitated large organizations for production and marketing. In such a society, even people's thoughts and words were to a great extent 'determined by some central authority representing the community as a whole or a relatively small number of persons who control the agencies of information and education'.[83] Furthermore, Oldham suggested that techniques of propaganda made it possible to shape the minds of the masses:

> The totalitarian state has at its disposal modern techniques which enable the holders to enslave not only men's bodies but their souls. The positions of control in modern society whet the appetite for power in the ambitious; and even

where power is not concentrated to one centre, there are strong forces making for the growth of a homogenous mass mind and the destructions of initiative, responsibility and community.[84]

In this light, the Moot could be seen, on the one hand, as a reaction against the decadence of modernity and, on the other, as consciously attempting to provide an alternative to the inhumanity of the pagan totalitarian regimes. Communism and fascism continuously figure in the Moot discourses as the evil Other while still arousing an element of admiration for their efficiency, and therefore in part to be emulated.[85]

War and crisis

The outbreak of the war in September 1939 was seen by the Moot members as the logical outcome of industrialized Western societies. Mannheim claimed that the war was 'an organic consequence of the antagonisms operating in a late capitalist society'.[86] Restating a common Marxist critique, Murry commented a year before the final outbreak of the war that the capitalistic order encouraged armed conflict since its economic system thrived on rearmament.[87] The only way to avoid war was 'a revolutionary readaptation [sic] of society'.[88]

However, the rationale for war was also accounted for in spiritual terms. Vidler claimed that the war was God's passive judgement on Europe.[89] Dawson argued that, historically, wars were temporal struggles fought by armies over political powers. What made modern wars different was that they were total wars involving the whole of society. Therefore, they required moral and spiritual judgement:

> The fact is that the problem of modern war cannot be solved by a simple division of things that are of God's and the things that are of Caesar's. In the old days war could be regarded as Caesar's proper business, but today it is everybody's business and it touches the things of God as well as those of man.[90]

The mood of the Moot during the early years of the war was understandably pessimistic. At the height of the 'Blitz', Karl Mannheim wrote dramatically to the Moot members: 'Intellectually we can see that the world is on the edge of an abyss.'[91] This sentiment was expressed in a paper for the 10th meeting held from 10 to 13 January 1941. It is hardly coincidental that the culmination of the crisis language of the Moot was reached at this point in time. Those gathered agreed that forces of disintegration were bringing British society close to the brink of a total collapse. Various members expressed their impressions of a general pessimism verging on nihilism amongst their compatriots. The gloomy conclusion of Hodges' sketch of European history is striking:

> We were at the end of the first great experiment of European Man. We might see another reconstruction on a lower level, but it would be impermanent. We had not yet reached the end of the process of disintegration. Nihilism had reached the point to which the whole process was leading. We thought there was something to be saved: it was possible that nothing could be saved. Philosophy might end in scepticism and religion in some unpredictable impasse. The rise of Science had seemed to offer hope in providing a new type of knowledge: but the power of this natural world had destroyed the concept of another world and had ended in the Machine. Perhaps this was the Dark Night of which all mysticism spoke. A religious interpretation was then the only hope of recovery. There was no evidence in Christianity that civilisation was bound to continue. The Mediaeval System incorporated Christianity (cf. Bowman: *The Meaning of the Secular*). We might have to lose ourselves in nature. The church might have to die that it might rise again – but really die. We had then a short-term hope but a long-term despair. It would certainly need a strong moral effort to maintain the moral person and to be both a Christian and a reasonable person, and to retain sanity amid all this.[92]

This citation highlights several tensions that the Moot grappled with. Had the disintegration of liberal society reached the point of no return? What of the old order could be salvaged? Should efforts be put towards the struggle against the immediate threat of totalitarianism or should defeat be admitted in the short term for the benefit of long-term transformations? Adolf Löwe expressed this dilemma already at the 1st meeting where he argued that there were two separate issues: understanding historical trends leading to the current crisis and the immediate threat of the totalitarian regimes, of which he had first-hand experience. 'The question was whether the world could be saved from immediate catastrophe and what were the responsibilities of individuals and communities in the world as it is.'[93] This question continued to surface throughout the Moot's deliberations, and no real resolution was reached.

As the tide of the war turned in favour of the Allied forces, there was possibly a change in the Moot's articulation of the crisis discourse. In quite an astounding debate at the 17th meeting in June 1943, Hodges charged the Moot with ignoring socialism as the 'central issue of political life'.[94] The paper led to a lively debate, and while the majority of those present agreed with Hodges' contention, Mannheim held that the paper was 'twenty years too late'.[95] In a follow-up paper, Hodges reiterated Marx's historical materialism and suggested that capitalism was the fundamental cause of the modern 'illness': 'the dictatorship, the terrorism, the militarism, the totalitarianism, are after all no more than scenes in the melodrama of capitalism'.[96] While the one does not exclude the other, the fact of the Moot's general consensus on Hodges' diagnosis indicates a certain shift from an emphasis on spiritual and cultural causes of the interwar crisis to the economic emphasis that came to dominate the post-war reconstruction debates.

Conclusion

No doubt the 'apocalyptic' cycle of decadence and renewal is a pattern that can be observed at various stages of human history.[97] What makes the Moot's 'sense of an ending' particularly 'Modernist' is that it is tied up with the historically unique conditions of nineteenth- and early twentieth-century Western modernity. The analysis of modern society in terms of 'decadence' chimes with Griffin's model in *Modernism and Fascism*, and the Moot, like so many contemporary groups, feared that modern society was approaching an apocalyptic calamity. The group's analysis of the malaise of modern society reflects the gloom of the 1930s: the nineteenth-century ideology of Progress seemed suspect to them; the economic crisis revealed the weaknesses of capitalism; liberalism, unable to provide a coherent world view, had resulted in social fragmentation and nihilism; industrialization had caused inhumane living and working conditions for large segments of the society; and secularization had left their civilization hollow and empty. The Modernist framing thus highlights the extent to which their whole project is underpinned by a critique of modernity. In short, the Moot can be viewed as a response to the interwar decadence discourse.

Notes

1 Kermode, *Sense of an Ending*, 94.
2 Ibid., 101.
3 Zygmunt Bauman, *Modernity and Ambivalence* (Cambridge: Polity Press, 1991), 4.
4 Overy, *The Morbid Age*, 3.
5 Ibid., 43.
6 Lewis, *Religious Experience*, 25.
7 Griffin, *Modernism and Fascism*, 110.
8 Tonning, *Modernism and Christianity*, 4.

9   Nathaniel Micklem wrote a comment on Oldham's Moot Paper 'A Fraternity of the Spirit' (Nathaniel Micklem, 'Letter from Principal Micklem', [1941], IOE/MOO/46).
10 Nathaniel Micklem, *The Crisis and the Christian*, ed. Hugh Martin, Crisis Booklet (London: SCM Press, 1938), 9.
11 Ibid., 18.
12 Niebuhr's political theology had significant influence on the Moot, and he attended the 5th and 14th meetings.
13 Reinhold Niebuhr, *Reflections on the End of an Era* (New York: Charles Scribner's Sons, 1936), ix.
14 John Middleton Murry, 'Towards a Christian Society', *Adelphi* 15, no. 1 (1938), 9–13.
15 The letter was signed by Cosmo Lang, Archbishop of Canterbury; William Temple, Archbishop of York; Walter H. Armstrong, Moderator Free Church Federal Council; and Cardinal Hinsley, Archbishop of Westminster (Cosmo Lang et al., 'Foundations of Peace', *The Times* (1940), 5).
16 Frank N. D. Buchman, *Remaking the World: The Speeches of Frank N. D. Buchman* (London: Blandford Press, 1947), 85.
17 'The Rule of Law', *The Times*, 1 September 1938.
18 Baldwin of Bewdley et al., 'Moral Rearmament', *The Times*, 10 October 1938.
19 Stanley Baldwin, *The Times*, 17 August 1934, as cited in Philip Williamson, 'Christian Conservatives and the Totalitarian Challenge, 1933–40', *English Historical Review* 115, no. 462 (2000), 617.
20 P. T. R. Kirk, *The Church and Social Evils* (London: Industrial Christian Fellowship, 1937), 15.
21 Richard Livingstone, 'The Crisis of Civilisation', in *The Deeper Causes of the War*, ed. Sydney E. Hooper (London: George Allen and Unwin, 1940), 99.
22 Ibid., 100–1.
23 Lionel Curtis, *Civitas Dei: The Commonwealth of God* (Edinburgh: R & R Clark, 1938), 822.
24 Oldham, 'Lessons of the Crisis'. The fact that T. S. Eliot included the letter in full as an appendix to *The Idea of a Christian Society* suggests his concurrence with Oldham.
25 T. S. Eliot, *Thoughts after Lambeth* (London: Faber & Faber, 1931), 32.
26 T. S. Eliot, 'Christianity and Communism', *The Listener* 7, no. 166 (1932), 382.
27 T. S. Eliot, 'The Modern Dilemma', *The Christian Register* 102, no. 41 (1933), 675.
28 John Middleton Murry, 'Apologia', *Adelphi* 14, no. 6 (1938), 169.
29 John Middleton Murry, *Europe in Travail*, ed. Alec R. Vidler, Christian News-Letter Books (London: The Sheldon Press, 1940), vii.
30 Christopher Dawson, *Religion and the Modern State* (London: Sheed and Ward, 1935), 45–58.

31 J. H. Oldham, 'The Situation Disclosed by the Oxford Conference and the Demands on the Churches', 22 October 1937, COE/LP/BELL/3/34–43.
32 Oldham, *The Churches Survey Their Task: The Report of the Conference at Oxford, July 1937, on Church, Community, and State*, 10.
33 Ibid., 63.
34 Cf. Eliot, *Lambeth*.
35 Clements, *Moot Papers*, 39–50 (1st meeting, 1–4 April 1938). See also Karl Mannheim, 'Towards a New Social Philosophy: A Challenge to Christian Thinkers by a Sociologist', [1941], BA/5/22.
36 Clements, *Moot Papers*, 39–40 (1st meeting, 1–4 April 1938).
37 Ibid., 48 (1st meeting, 1–4 April 1938).
38 Ibid., 107 (2nd meeting, 23–26 September 1938).
39 Ibid., 413 (12th meeting, 1–3 August 1941).
40 H. A. Hodges, 'Christian Thinking Today', [1941], IOE/MOO/63; MPP/15/6; OLD/14/2/5.
41 Ibid.
42 Alec R. Vidler, *Secular Despair and Christian Faith* (London: SCM Press, 1941), 5.
43 Ibid., 14.
44 Karl Mannheim, 'The Crisis in Valuation', 3 March 1942, IOE/MOO/77; OLD/14/3/40.
45 Ibid.
46 Ibid.
47 Ibid.
48 T. S. Eliot, 'Notes on Social Philosophy', [1940], IOE/MOO/123; OLD/14/6/24.
49 Eliot, *After Strange Gods*, 13.
50 Eliot, *Idea*, 16.
51 J. H. Oldham, 'The Christian Witness in the Present Crisis', 6 October 1943, OLD/9/5/19.
52 Alec R. Vidler, *God's Judgment on Europe* (London: Longmans, Green and Co., 1940), 25.
53 John Middleton Murry, 'Democracy and the Totalitarian Ideal', *Adelphi* 15, no. 4 (1939), 152.
54 Cf. J. H. Oldham, *The Question of the Church in the World of to-Day* (London: Edinburgh House Press, 1936). See also T. S. Eliot, 'Towards a Christian Britain', in *The Church Looks Ahead*, ed. J. H. Oldham (London: Faber & Faber, 1941); J. H. Oldham, *Real Life Is Meeting*, Christian News-Letter Books No. 14 (London: Sheldon Press, 1942).
55 Jacques Maritain, *True Humanism* (London: The Centenary Press, 1938), 22.
56 Mannheim affirmed a similar idea that the Reformation by its implicit individualization provided a theological backdrop to the liberal *weltanschauung*

constructed over the centuries to come (cf. Karl Mannheim, 'Towards a New Social Philosophy: A Challenge to Christian Thinkers by a Sociologist', [1941], BA/5/22).
57 J. H. Oldham, 'The Way Out', *Christian News-Letter*, no. 45 (1940). This article was circulated prior to the 10th meeting held on 10–13 January 1941.
58 J. H Oldham, 'The Problems and Tasks of the Council on the Christian Faith and the Common Life', [1938], OLD/13/8/73.
59 Martin Buber, *I and Thou* (Edinburgh: T&T Clark, 1937), 47. Incidentally, the English translator of *I and Thou*, Ronald Gregor Smith, instances Oldham as an example of Buber's extensive influence on the British Isles (ibid., viii). Oldham had promoted Buber's ideas at the 1937 Oxford Conference and further sought to popularize these ideas by publishing a summary of Buber's argument in supplement to the *CNL* (J. H. Oldham, 'All Real Life Is Meeting', *Christian News-Letter*, no. 112 (1941)), which later became a chapter of his *Real Life is Meeting*.
60 See J. H. Oldham, *The Resurrection of Christendom* (London: Sheldon Press, 1940), 126–8.
61 Oldham, 'The Christian Witness in the Present Crisis'.
62 J. H. Oldham, 'Fraternity of the Spirit', 7 March 1941, IOE/MOO/40. Hocking wrote that 'the blind spot of the Liberal conception of politics is just in this absence of perception of the commotive function as an essential for large groups (William Ernest Hocking, *The Lasting Elements of Individualism* (New Haven, CT: Yale University Press, 1937), 109)'.
63 Clements, *Moot Papers*, 271 (7th meeting, 9–12 February 1940).
64 John Baillie, *What Is Christian Civilization?* (London: Oxford University Press, 1945), 29.
65 H. A. Hodges, 'Christian Thinking Today', [1941], IOE/MOO/63; MPP/15/6; OLD/14/2/5.
66 Vidler, *God's Judgment*, 53–4.
67 J. H. Oldham, 'A Reborn Christendom', August 1939, IOE/MOO/2. Max Weber's fatalism regarding the 'iron cage' of rationalization under capitalism can be traced to both Oldham's and Vidler's arguments here (see Max Weber, *The Protestant Ethic and the Spirit of Capitalism*, trans. Talcott Parsons (London: George Allen & Unwin, 1930), 181).
68 J. H. Oldham, 'The Christian Witness in the Present Crisis', [1943], OLD/9/5/19.
69 Christopher Dawson, 'Freedom and Vocation', [1941], OLD/14/4/37.
70 Christopher Dawson, *Beyond Politics* (London: Sheed & Ward, 1939), 5f.
71 Murry, *Europe in Travail*.
72 Karl Mannheim, 'Planning for Freedom', [1938] LM/SEC7; OLD/14/3/67.
73 Eliot, *Idea*, 15.
74 Cf. Vidler, *God's Judgment*, 18–9; Christopher Dawson, *The Judgement of the Nations* (London: Sheed & Ward, 1943), 47; Karl Mannheim, *Diagnosis of Our Time: Wartime Essays of a Sociologist* (London: Kegan Paul, 1943), 121–2.

75 Cf. Eliot, *Idea*, 13; Oldham, *The Resurrection*, 50.
76 Gentile, *Politics as Religion*, 74f.
77 Clements, *Moot Papers*, 52 (1st meeting, 1–4 April 1938). Oldham expressed similar ideas in Oldham, *The Question*.
78 Clements, *Moot Papers*, 46–7 (1st meeting, 1–4 April 1938).
79 Karl Mannheim, 'Towards a New Social Philosophy: A Challenge to Christian Thinkers by a Sociologist. Part II: Christian Values in the Changing Environment', [1941], IOE/MOO/75; OLD/14/3/94.
80 See also John Middleton Murry, *Adam and Eve: An Essay Towards a New and Better Society* (London: Andrew Dakers, 1944), 10f.
81 Cf. Karl Mannheim, 'Planning for Freedom', [1938], LM/SEC7; OLD/14/3/67; John Middleton Murry, 'Towards a Christian Theory of Society', [1938], OLD/14/5/37; J. H. Oldham, 'A Reborn Christendom', August 1939, IOE/MOO/2.
82 J. H. Oldham, 'A Reborn Christendom', August 1939, IOE/MOO/2.
83 Ibid.
84 J. H. Oldham, 'Fraternity of the Spirit', 7 March 1941, IOE/MOO/40.
85 Cf. Eliot, *Idea*, 9. The Moot member's responses to totalitarianism and liberal democracy will be explored in further detail in Chapter 4.
86 Clements, *Moot Papers*, 300 (8th meeting, 19–22 April 1940).
87 Ibid., 53–4 (1st meeting, 1–4 April 1938).
88 Ibid., 54 (1st meeting, 1–4 April 1938).
89 Vidler, *God's Judgment*, 72.
90 Christopher Dawson, 'Sword of the Spirit', December 1940, IOE/MOO/37; OLD/14/4/1.
91 Karl Mannheim, 'Topics for the Next Meeting of the Moot', [1941], IOE/MOO/32; LD/215; OLD/14/3/86.
92 Clements, *Moot Papers*, 360 (10th meeting, 10–13 January 1941).
93 Ibid., 43 (1st meeting, 1–4 April 1938).
94 H. A. Hodges, 'Politics and the Moot', 9 June 1943, OLD/14/1/43.
95 Clements, *Moot Papers*, 585 (17th meeting, 18–21 June 1943).
96 H. A. Hodges, 'Comments on the Moot's Fifteen Points', 29 July 1943, OLD/14/1/53.
97 See Landes, *Heaven on Earth*.

3

The Rebirth of Christendom

Introduction

In one of his morale-boosting introductory speeches, Oldham reiterated the basis for the Moot's collaboration: 'We were concerned with the historical situation of the Church of Christ in the world and whether the Church, at present insignificant, might be reborn as a vitalizing force of human society.'[1] Having positioned the Moot firmly within the decadence discourse of the 1930s in the previous chapter, the present discussion serves to further substantiate the suggestion that the Moot may be fruitfully analysed as an example of 'Programmatic Modernism'. Taking its cue from the 'apocalyptic' decadence-and-renewal pattern so characteristic of Modernism, this chapter investigates the Moot's intellectual work on a remedy for the ills of their age.

Both Frank Kermode and Roger Griffin develop their 'apocalyptic' interpretations of the Modernist renewal impulses drawing upon insights from anthropologists. Notable here is Anthony Wallace, whose term 'revitalization movements' describes the recurring phenomenon of 'cultural-system innovation' that appears in periods of societal disorientation.[2] All human societies go through periods of dissonance when 'the mazeway' (Wallace's term for 'the image' that individuals project in order to make sense of the world) can no longer provide meaningful interpretations of a society's practices. Revitalization movements emerge as responses to societal crisis that reformulate the mazeway, allowing society to re-emerge in a new form.[3] This 'revitalization' perspective makes sense of the dynamics of the Modernist expressions arising out of the disorientation caused by the conditions of late-nineteenth- to early-twentieth-century Western *modernity*.

The Moot can, I propose, be most comprehensively understood through this framework, that is, as a Modernist revitalization movement attempting to create a new synthesis or blueprint to overcome the interwar disorientation, which could point forward to a new epoch within Western societies. Oldham's words above – suggesting that the Church could act as a 'revitalizing force' – point towards the argument that will be developed. What defined the Moot's programme was the conviction that Christian tradition was the fundamental source of revitalization for a decadent modernity. Exemplifying what Griffin calls a Modernist appropriation of the 'mythic past', the Moot turned to medieval Christendom as a source of renewal and model of a *future* Christian society. In the Moot's thinking, these visions of a renewed Christian social order were synthesized with the realities of modern life. This can be seen in their engagement with Mannheim's technocratic political theory of 'Planning for Freedom', which was an attempt to resolve the problem of freedom versus authority in modern society. If their vision of a New Christendom involved an appropriation of the 'mythic past', the incorporation of Mannheim's 'Planning for Freedom' evidences a Modernist impulse to 'make it new'.

New beginnings through a New Christendom

Looking ahead

Despite their acute sense of despair at a civilization falling apart, there was nonetheless a determined optimism within the Moot. Members were confident that the crisis in the late 1930s presented an opportunity for a Christian revival through galvanizing believers and forming alliances with sympathetic humanists to defeat the dark powers of totalitarianism.[4] In a pamphlet explaining the rationale behind the 1937 Oxford Conference, Oldham spoke of the opportunities that lay ahead in the wake of what he saw as one of 'the great turning-points in human history', and as the 'old order ... passing into something new'.[5] Baillie suggested that there was a new generation of men and women for whom scientific claims proved less of a hurdle to Christian faith than in previous decades.[6] According to Eliot, the future of Western civilization was open-ended. England was still 'Christian' in some senses, yet it had also 'become positively something else', and thus he argued that 'the choice before us is between the formation of a new Christian culture, and the acceptance of a pagan one'.[7] In this state of uncertainty, the future was there to be possessed, shaped and moulded. Driven by this belief, the Moot set out to fashion ideas that would shape the nation for generations to come.

Although it was a concern for the continuous impact of Christianity on society that had brought the group together, it would be a mistake to assume that they simply envisioned a return to past ideals. The world had changed, and a Christian challenge to the burgeoning paganism of modern society had to engage with the present and future as much as it looked to the past. Oldham's letter published in *The Times*, October 1938, aptly expresses this:[8]

> May our salvation lie in an attempt to recover our Christian heritage, not in the sense of going back to the past but of discovering in the central affirmations and insights of the Christian faith new spiritual energies to regenerate and vitalise our sick society.[9]

This sentiment is also evident in a paper presented at the 2nd Moot meeting by Murry, who wrote that '[a] modern theory of a Christian society must be a theory of a *modern* Christian society'.[10] At the same meeting, Mannheim spoke of the need to 'revitalise the traditional elements and re-adapt them to new social needs'.[11] This to some extent required a breaking up of the old to allow the new and healthy to re-emerge. Hector Hetherington expressed his agreement more strongly, stating that 'there had been an ossification of tradition which needed an explosion to blow it up and make room for new life'.[12] Even Eliot, who is routinely branded a 'conservative', believed that a stable society needed a living tradition, which balanced continuity of the past with a dynamic creativity in the present.[13]

New Christendom language in Christian social thought

The central line of investigation of the Moot was the search for a common idea, a new social philosophy, around which the like-minded could rally. The slogan of a 'New Christendom' became a focal point of this collective social thinking. In a letter addressed to the Moot dated 23 August 1939, Oldham directly related their work on a 'common body of convictions' with the birth of a 'New Christendom'.[14]

This concept had already been entertained in Christian social thought for decades. For example, it was a central idea in the Christendom Group, which in the early 1920s published the collaborative volume *The Return of Christendom*.[15] Almost thirty years later, in the final editorial of the group's journal, *Christendom*, Maurice Reckitt reiterated the central theme of their agenda: 'Let us repeat for the thousandth time that if we "go back to the Middle Ages" it is precisely because … it is from there that we can hope to go forward.'[16] Furthermore, according to Philip Coupland, the British churches played an instrumental role in the European post-war reconstruction and Christendom language was a defining theme in these efforts. Coupland concludes that '[if] medieval Christendom was the lost golden age of Christian reconstruction discourse, Christendom reborn was its utopia'.[17] For Coupland, the reconstructionist Peace Aims Group, chaired by William Temple, was the central vehicle for this drive.[18] Temple had for some time been an advocate for the reestablishment of international Christian order. In an article titled 'The Restoration of Christendom', published in 1936, he proposed that an international 'common aspiration to cooperate with the righteous purpose of God ... would be a priceless blessing to the world'.[19] In a further historiography on the North American Christian 'realists', Mark Edwards discusses how Oldham's associates H. P. Van Dusen and Reinhold Niebuhr, amongst others, mobilized the vision of a global 'New Christendom' as a counter-totalitarian measure.[20] Finally, narrating the influence of the ecumenical movement on the UN Universal Declaration of Human Rights, John Nurser suggests that Oldham was 'a principal witness for the claim that a revisionist concept of "Christendom" ... was the driving vision for the ecumenical movement in the generation before 1960'.[21]

Maritain's neo-Thomism, medieval modernism and the Moot

Christendom language was evidently widely floated in theological and ecclesial circles during this period. However, the medieval influences on the Moot's strategizing most evidently made inroads through the French Neo-Scholastic thinker Jacques Maritain. Maritain is particularly interesting for conceptual reasons. Returning to Griffin's framework of Political Modernism, the medieval inspiration via Maritain is perhaps the clearest example of how the Moot sought to reappropriate the 'mythic past' into a present-day vision of a regenerated society.[22]

That Modernism draws upon ancient sources is widely accepted amongst critics. In *The Tradition of Return*, Jeffrey Perl, like Griffin, conceives of Modernism as a 'return' to the past for creative impulses aimed at rebirth: a second, modern renaissance that would complete the first. Perl assumes that the Modernist return was a return to classicism. Perl's model draws attention to what Erik Tonning has described as the 'formative tensions' between Modernism and Christianity.[23] Within Perl's scheme, Christianity represents an awkward middle stage, which Modernists nevertheless had to contend with.[24]

However, *contra* Perl, a return to classicism is just one of the several possible 'returns' within Modernism. An alternative Modernist 'return' is to the Middle Ages. Indeed, in *Saving Civilization*, Lucy McDiarmid speaks of the Middle

Ages as representing a mythical 'golden time', idealized by poets Yeats, Eliot and Auden as a lost civilization of 'Edenic qualities of unity and perfection'.[25] This medieval vein of Modernism originates, according to Paul Robichaud, in the dialogue on Thomas Aquinas between Stephen Dedalus and his companion, Lunch, in James Joyce's *A Portrait of the Artist as a Young Man* (1916).[26] Another example of the Modernist fascination with the medieval can be found in Ezra Pound's engagement with Dante in *Draft of XXX Cantos*.[27]

Within the visual arts, the arts and crafts movement, inspired by nineteenth-century medievalist John Ruskin and William Morris, aspired to revive the spiritual integration and harmony of the Middle Ages. Michael Saler suggests that there is a story to be told about the neglected network of functionalist 'medieval Modernists', which contrasts the formalistic Modernism typified by the Bloomsbury circle.[28] The central figures in this discourse are Frank Pick, William Rothenstein, Herbert Read and Eric Gill. Saler writes that these 'medieval' Modernists 'sought unifying mythic and spiritual values that would remedy the perceived excesses of bourgeois liberalism, rationalism, industrialism, urbanism, and secularism – of modernity'.[29] Embracing the 'programmatic' mode of Modernism (my interpretation) – the drive towards the creation of a new age – the medieval Modernists' art could be mobilized as a political, moral and even religious force against the degenerative, de-spiritualized aspects of industrialized Britain. Saler also argues that the 'medieval Modernists' in England, rather than seeking a break with their Protestant heritage, embraced its ethos not least for its 'practicality'.

What is interesting is that Jacques Maritain's Neo-Scholasticism had a defining influence on the aesthetic theorizing of the Eric Gill circle and its associate David Jones. When the community press of Gill's experimental guild at Ditchling translated and published Maritain's classic *Art et Scolastique* in 1923, Gill wrote in the foreword that the book offered an antidote – or a 'cooling medicine' – to triumphant industrialism. David Jones' biographer René Hague suggests that *Art et Scolastique* became a 'textbook' for the Gill circle.[30] Maritain argued that the satisfaction of labour was lost in the 'beastlabour or machinelabour' of industrialized societies.[31] The significance of Maritain's book, argued Gill, was its attempt to recover notions of art as not merely the activity of the elites but as found in all modes of *making*.[32]

It would be tempting to think of *Art et Scolastique* as reactionary. However, as Joseph Frank notes, Maritain's Neo-Scholasticism draws upon Aquinas as a justification for *modern* experimental art.[33] Maritain's medieval Modernism was highly influential among the Parisian intellectual elite during the 1920s and '30s.

Maritain is, as such, a central case study in Stephen Schloesser's framing of the interwar *renouveau catholique* as a Modernist religio-cultural movement. Given the anti-Modernism of Pope Pius IX's 1864 *Syllabus of Errors*, which explicitly rejects the possibility of a synthesis between Catholicism and modernity, such a narration appears contradictory. However, in keeping with my definition here, Schloesser legitimizes this conceptualization on the understanding that Modernism constitutes 'a rage against modernity'. He suggests that through its very *antimoderne* stance 'Catholicism can also be located within a panoply of postwar avant-gardists'.[34] As a case in point for Schloesser's study, he records Maritain's adaptation of a Thomist 'hylomorphism', an Aristotelian term describing objects as consisting of the combination of accidental 'matter' and eternal 'form', which brings order and unity to the object. Equipped with the theory of hylomorphism, Maritain could join the Modernist artists' antipathy towards nineteenth-century naturalism in favour of the celebration of eternal form, innovatively depicted in changing, historically situated matter, whilst simultaneously affirming the ever-adjusting incarnations of Catholic tradition. Schloesser writes that 'Maritain could now repudiate representational art of every kind and simultaneously reconcile the most abstract of modern art with the most ancient of Catholic texts'.[35] Maritain, in Schloesser's words, had 'reconfigured the language of overtly anti-Modernist Thomism into a Catholic ultramodernism', thereby spawning the Catholic renewal in French avant-garde circles.[36]

This neo-Thomism of Maritain invokes formalistic, aesthetic modes of Modernism. However, there is arguably a parallel between the Thomist hylomorphism in *Art et Scolastique* and the integral humanism in his political theorizing of *True Humanism*. In *Antimoderne* (1922), Maritain suggested that the return to the Middle Ages was a return to a deeper spiritual reality. 'We hope to see,' wrote Maritain, 'the spiritual principles and the eternal norms which medieval civilization has given us returned/reproduced in a new world, informing a new matter.'[37] The eternal and permanent can be reapplied in new ways into a new cultural context. This is a central assumption in *True Humanism*, where Maritain sought to *analogously* apply a Neo-Scholastic theory of a Christian anthropology to the conditions under modernity.[38] Both in his art theory and political thought, the hylomorphic elements of continuity and change are present. In the arts, hylomorphism speaks of permanent form endlessly transforming accidental matter; in politics, eternal principles are constantly readjusted to evolving societies. The transition to 'the new age of Christian culture' presupposes a hylomorphic transformation, suggested Maritain, of both social structures (matter) and the arousal of the inner 'spiritual realities' (form).[39] Thus, Maritain's 'Catholic ultramodernism' gathers several threads that are significant to the theoretical discussion on the Moot. Maritain's 'Modernism' in *True Humanism* brings together the political (programmatic), medievalism and Christianity.

The influence of Jacques Maritain's *True Humanism* on the Moot

While the Eric Gill circle used Maritain's theory of art as a source of inspiration for their vision of a renewal of medieval guilds, and craftsmanship as an antidote to the dehumanization of industrialization, the Moot was drawn to his theocentric humanism and vision of a secular Christian society. In the early years of the Moot, Maritain became something of a sage for the group. His vision of a 'New Christendom' was one of the few ideas that they unanimously endorsed. The concluding comment from the minutes of the 3rd meeting, during which Maritain's *True Humanism* was studied in detail, states: 'The discussion revealed no fundamental criticism of Maritain; all were disposed to accept his central position as the basis for the work of the Moot.'[40]

Although the Moot had an ecumenical outlook, it is intriguing how a French Catholic thinker came to exert such influence on a predominantly Protestant and English group. Yet Maritain's *True Humanism* had come to be regarded as one of the seminal works on Christian sociopolitical engagement of the day and enjoyed influence beyond Catholic circles.[41] Even Baillie, a reformed Church of Scotland minister, had to admit that Maritain's thesis was compelling. Baillie could embrace *True Humanism* since he felt that Martian's use of Aquinas was opportunistic.[42] As Vidler noted, there was significant overlap between Maritain and Protestant theologians such as Reinhold Niebuhr and Emil Brunner and with no decisive conflict with Protestant theology.[43] In addition, there were several connections between Maritain and members that predate the Moot. Eliot had long been an admirer of Maritain, having met him as early as June 1926 – before Eliot's conversion – to discuss theology.[44] In a letter to Jeanette McPherrin dated 8 April 1935, Eliot wrote: '[Maritain] is one of the most charming and even saintly men that I know'.[45] Mannheim also had some personal contact with Maritain having disclosed to the Moot that he had met him in Paris.[46]

Ultimately, Maritain's grand vision resonated with the Moot members. In his comments on *True Humanism,* Vidler wrote: 'I have been immensely struck by the coherent way in which Maritain's book seems to gather up and follow on what was said and felt at the last meeting of the Moot.'[47] Baillie listed a number of these correlating ideas in his summary paper. Firstly, Maritain's diagnosis of modern society mirrored that of the Moot's. Secondly, a Christian conception of man occupied a central position in their respective visions of a future society. Thirdly, they acknowledged the necessity of exploring questions concerning the relation between the sacred *civitas Dei* and the secular *civitas terrena* and between the precepts of the Gospel and politics. Fourthly, Maritain's emphasis on the activism of laypersons in the political sphere had long been a central affirmation of Oldham's. And finally, they shared the view that the survival of Western civilization depended on charting a middle path between the *laissez faire* of liberalism and totalitarianism.[48]

The Moot's interaction with Maritain continued beyond the 3rd meeting. Maritain commented upon Moot papers by Hodges and Mannheim,[49] and half a dozen of the members had the opportunity to meet Maritain in person during a dinner 'at Eliot's club' on 10 May 1939.[50] The unknown author of notes from the meeting concluded that although the discussion was stimulating, the main benefit of the gathering was 'to help the members of the Moot who were there to feel again more deeply their common commitment'.[51] That Maritain left an imprint on the Moot can be further substantiated in the number of references to him in the publications of individual Moot members.[52] In short, an analysis of Maritain is therefore an entry point into understanding the central lines of exploration in the Moot and legitimates the conceptual framing of the Moot as a manifestation of Modernism.

Lessons from medieval Christendom

As with Maritain, the Moot did not envision a wholesale return to the medieval order but rather drew upon some of its terminology and infused it with new meaning. The Christendom of the Middle Ages was for Maritain and the Moot a historical realization of a Christian society from which they could draw lessons. So, for instance, Murry's attitude towards medievalism was ambivalent; on the one hand, he professed that '[w]e generally idealize the medieval Church'[53] but, on the other, when envisaging the nature of a future Christian society, he suggested that '[m]edieval Christendom can, at best, give us only a clue'.[54] Vidler similarly warned against idealizing the medieval world yet said it was 'the most magnificent attempt' at a Christian social order.⁵⁵ Even in Maritain's words, medieval Christendom was an imperfect society which nevertheless was a 'liveable' society, more effectively channelling the 'world of grace' than the present order.⁵⁶ Maintaining his allegiance to Aquinas, Maritain held that the fundamental principles of medieval Christendom could only analogously be reapplied to modern society, for 'the Christendom of the Middle Ages was only one of its possible forms of realisation'.⁵⁷

There were also the critical voices, such as Hodges, who dismissed Thomism as an outdated mode of reasoning, which had little to offer modern man. In fact, '[t]he attempt to return to the past was dangerous … because the intervening history of thought had been a misguided attempt to deal with the real problems'.⁵⁸ While Hodges' was a minority voice, the scholastic influence on the Moot should not be exaggerated.

From an anthropocentric to a theocentric humanism

As man's rebellion against God was, for the Moot, understood to be the germ of the modern crisis, Maritain's 'theocentric humanism' provided an attractive alternative anthropology as the basis for their social vision. In an extensive historical analysis, Maritain outlined the progression from the Reformation to the modern world, which had resulted in an anthropocentric humanism. This anthropocentric humanism had come to reject God in the search for autonomy, but in the process had cut 'man' off from the first cause of all good, the source of grace. In neglecting the supernatural ontology of human nature, humanism had become nothing but an inhuman humanism.⁵⁹ However, this humanistic liberalism had by the twentieth century reached its natural end. Through Darwin's survival of the fittest and Freud's psychology of the subconscious, the rationalistic conception of man suffered severe blows. Man could no longer be understood as a purely rational being, but rather as a creature ruled by survival and sexual instincts.⁶⁰ Furthermore, the implied liberalism of the anthropocentric humanism, argued Maritain, 'was palpably a purely negative energy' and could not sustain a positive culture.⁶¹ The anti-liberal revolutionary movements in the twentieth century, in turn, had emerged as a direct response to the dualism, division and disintegration of liberalism. Nevertheless, since these secular totalitarian movements lacked the natural inner spiritual propensity for societal unity, they were left to resort to 'rousing heroism, faith and an almost religious devotion' artificially through compulsion, propaganda and manipulation. Thus, by a singular process of dialectic the christian [sic] absolutism which followed on the medieval world has been rejected by anti-christian liberalism, and the latter having itself been overthrown by the very fact of its success the space is open for a new absolutism, this time a materialistic one and more inimical to Christianity than ever.[62]

At this point in history, suggested Maritain, only Christianity 'seems able to defend … the freedom of the individual and … those positive liberties which correspond on the social and political to that spiritual freedom'. Quoting Charles Péguy, Maritain declared 'Christendom will come back in the hour of distress.'[63] The circle was about to be fully drawn.

In response to the anthropocentric humanism of the Enlightenment and the materialism of contemporary totalitarian regimes, Maritain called for a return to a Thomist 'integral humanism, the humanism of the incarnation'. This integral humanism *rehabilitates* man from the secular/sacred divide haunting him since the Reformation, by recovering man's true nature as temporal and yet spiritual and therefore dependent on God.[64] Maritain's alternative social philosophy was founded upon a return to a theocentric humanism, by which he primarily denoted a humanism which holds that man's true destiny and fulfilment is ultimately found *in* God. Imbued with divine love, the individual – 'the new man who is from God' – is able to act sacrificially and as a responsible agent in the *earthly city*, bringing about 'a veritable socio-temporal realisation of the Gospels'.[65] This is what Maritain called Christian heroism. The symbol of his new man is, thus, not the *übermensch* but the saint. Maritain wrote:

> What I wish to put forward is that this attitude of the saint, which is truly one of no contempt for things, but rather the raising up, the transfiguration of things in a love which is higher than they, this standpoint taken as generalised, as become common, as become a commonplace of christian [sic] psychology, corresponds to the *rehabilitation of the creature in God* which I see as characterising a new age of Christendom and a new humanism … [T]he type of theocentric humanism is the saint: nor, indeed, can it be realised unless undertaken by saints.[66]

The 'saint' as a political figure is thus the instigator of the New Christendom, and for Maritain, as for the Moot, a renewal of the temporal world could only materialize through a spiritual revitalization of man.[67] The integral humanism proposed here, the reintegration of the sacred and secular dualism, suggests a sociopolitical counterpart to the reconciliation of Modernist art and scholasticism in Maritain's previous work. As discussed above, Schlosser terms this conception of art and Catholicism a 'Catholic ultramodernism'. It is therefore not too great a leap to term *True Humanism* a work of 'Catholic Political Modernism'.

This idea of spiritually renewed and socially conscious Christian leaders was broadly accepted by the Moot members. A Christian anthropology, focused upon the true ends of man's nature and destiny, was central to their attempt to forge a social movement. This stems from the claim of a casual relation between anthropology and culture. Such themes are particularly central to the arguments presented in a number of Oldham's memorandums aimed at forging a manifesto for the 'New Christendom'. Clearly borrowing from Maritain, Oldham wrote in a document circulated for the 3rd meeting that the task of the Church in contemporary society was firstly 'to seek to replace an anthropocentric humanism by one that finds its centre in God'.[68] In another of Oldham's manifestos titled 'A Reborn Christendom', his reliance on Maritain verges on plagiarism:

> If it is God's purpose out of the strife and sufferings of our time to bring to birth a society in which the true ends of man's life are more fully achieved, the human response to that purpose must be that of Christian heroism. A vitally Christian renewal will be the work of sainthood. The only way in which a new social order can be born is that multitudes of individual men and women should find a new specific vocation in the dedication of themselves to the service of God in the sphere of citizenship. If there is to be a New Christendom, the Christian cause must have its storm-troops – its adventurers of the spirit, pioneers and martyrs. A community of free and responsible persons makes larger demands than any other on the character and loyalty of its members.[69]

In this booklet, Oldham argued for the need for a new political faith, based on a Christian view of man's end, to permeate public life. Clearly then, the Moot's call for a New Christendom was intimately bound up with a Christian anthropology, and in particular an understanding of humans as created in the image of God as free and responsible agents.[70] Indeed, reflecting on the basic premise for the Moot's desired popular movement, Oldham advanced the idea of '[a] society in which men live together in freedom and responsibility'.[71] This affirmation was fundamental to Oldham's social criticism.

Another publication elaborating this outlook is *God's Judgement on Europe* (1940), where Vidler argued that the reconstruction of Christendom would depend upon a Christian understanding of man. Such an anthropology would acknowledge man as 'fallen' and emphasize both the temporal and eternal nature of human beings and that human fulfilment lay in their destiny as responsible agents in communion with God.[72] Furthermore, it implied a realism that would safeguard against the utopianism assumed by the competing secular ideologies and world views of the time.[73] Apart from his obvious reliance upon Maritain, it is clear here that Vidler was influenced by Reinhold Niebuhr, who during the Gifford lectures in 1939 – in reaction to liberal theology and modern conceptions of the nature of man – had emphasized human finitude and man's 'inclination to abuse his freedom, to overestimate his power and significance'.

A secular Christian order, pluralism and minimal unity

Thus, it is through the rediscovery of a Thomist conception of human nature that the Moot signalled a Modernist 'return' to the mythical past for sources of renewal. This idea of an integral humanism had direct implications on political and social theory, for it suggests a greater level of harmony between sacred and secular that shaped the political sphere in the Middle Ages. In the context of the perceived disintegration of liberal society, the social, cultural and religious unity of Christendom was naturally an attractive model. However, although wishing to recreate the principle of unity of the temporal and sacred spheres, Maritain rejected medieval Christendom's 'consecrational conception of the temporal order' and the *sacrum imperium*. Instead, he called for a 'secular Christian order' contextually appropriate for the modern age.[74] In such an order, the temporal and sacred spheres unite, not through ecclesial consecration of the state, but through the organic proliferation of a Christian ethos throughout society by the activism of a Christian lay movement and fraternity. The relative autonomy of the secular sphere, that is, the separation between church and state, was a further necessary consequence in a society where Christians found themselves in a minority and where adherence to Christian dogma could not be expected to be a prerequisite for political leadership.[75] As Eliot wrote in *The Idea of a Christian Society,* a book heavily influenced by Maritain's *True Humanism,* '[i]t is not primarily the Christianity of the statesman that matters, but their being confined ... to a Christian framework'.[76]

It was, however, this issue – the relation between Church and State – that had caused contention during the 2nd meeting of the Moot in the discussion of Murry's thesis 'Towards a Christian Society'. *Contra* Maritain, Murry held that for the Church to retain its influence in modern society, a fusion with the State was vital. To insist on the autonomy of the Church, Murry contended, would, in a centralized society where the State was increasingly ubiquitous, merely serve to further marginalize the Church.[77] Apart from Löwe and Mannheim, the comments on Murry's paper evidence a negative reaction to this particular argument fearing a latent theocracy. In reply to Dawson's protest that the secular and spiritual unity of medieval Christendom had failed, Murry maintained that 'it will have to be tried again'.[78] In this regard, he perhaps had a more medieval outlook than others in the Moot.[79]

The secular Christian society that Maritain called for was a third way between the disintegration of liberal humanism and the absolutism of totalitarianism. He spoke of a 'minimal unity' allowing for pluralism and yet attaining a measure of societal unity through a shared orientation towards common action based on Christian principles.[80] To such an end, and once more citing Aquinas, Maritain's ideal conception of 'New Christendom' was both *communal* and *personalist*:[81] communal in that the individual does not, in the temporal order, rise above the common good, but personalist in its reference to spiritual freedom and transcendent aspirations.[82] Ultimately, unity in the Christian order was to be a unity of 'friendship' created through the 'bearers of this christian [sic] conception'.[83]

This idea of a pluralistic Christian society was explicitly embraced by several Moot members. During a discussion of 'Minorities in a Planned Society' at the 13th meeting, Eleanora Iredale, in one of her rare interventions, aptly noted the issue at stake in this balancing of unity and pluralism that Maritain spoke of: '[It] was the willingness to believe in the majority, and to trust and allow the full contribution of any vital minority. We must do both or fall into Totalitarianism'.[84] Another treatise steeped in this thinking is *What is Christian Civilization?* (1945), where Baillie suggested an 'open Christian civilization', which differs from the medieval conception in its toleration and lack of compulsion.[85] Baillie believed that he had come close to the pluralism Eliot had envisioned in *Idea* and Maritain's notion of a 'minimal unity'. The theme of the pluralistic society is also central to *Notes*, where Eliot argued that a stratification through classes maintains a pluralism that is essential for the vitality of a society.[86]

New 'monasticism'

A final idea that Maritain shared with the Moot concerned the mechanism for the inauguration of the 'New Christendom'. Maritain argued that for a 'New Christendom' to be realized, it required a new type of political formation. Maritain's proposal consisted in a network of cells made up of lay Christian visionaries amounting to a 'third party',

> which will be purely secular and so differ from the religious orders ... and which will be founded on the principle of respect for human personality and the

spiritual force of evangelical love, so differing from a secular and atheistic order like, for example, the Communist Party of to-day.[87]

Despite Maritain's exclusive focus on the temporal here, the idea of the 'third party' still evokes the role of the religious orders in the Middle Ages. The members of the new political formation were expected to put into practice the precepts of the gospel with a fervour that escaped ordinary members of society and thereby act as the vanguard of a Christian society.

The formation of a new type of lay Order was one of the most repeated items on the Moot agenda. A more extensive discussion of the proposed Order will appear in the 6th chapter of this thesis, and therefore just a few comments will suffice here. The Order appeared in the Moot under various guises – cells, party, Fraternity of the Spirit, clerisy, Community of Christians – but the essential idea remained the same. The Order was to be a Christian elite consisting of a network of intellectuals who were spiritually alert and yet actively seeking the diffusion of Christian principles into all levels of society.[88] They would be united by an adherence to a shared social philosophy while at the same time assuming a measure of plurality as opinions on the practical application of the philosophy might vary.[89]

Natural law and shared value basis

The vision of a secular Christian order inevitably led to discussions concerning the question of how and to what extent Christian precepts can be translated into a political reality. In a society where the majority no longer professed to the Christian faith, discussions of natural law became central.

Indeed, Hodges raised this issue at an early meeting, pointing to the example of Rome's adaption of 'the theory of natural law' as a historical precedent.[90] The concept of natural law predates Christianity and in ancient Greek thought denotes an underlying universal system of law deriving from human nature and intelligible through reason. Aristotle, as a classic exponent of natural law, differentiated between particular local law based on local customs and tradition and a higher universally applicable law.[91] In Thomist thought, 'eternal law', meaning God's ordering, is assumed to be imprinted on creation itself. Natural law is the engagement with eternal law through human reasoning. It is, as Aquinas writes, 'nothing else but the rational creature's participation of the eternal law'.[92] In distinction to this natural law that is available to all humans through reason (and therefore an appropriate basis for political argumentation),[93] Aquinas held that there were additional precepts derived by revelation alone. This 'divine law' could not be legislated for but was still applicable to the Christian individual.[94]

While conspicuously absent from *True Humanism*,[95] discussions on natural law as a common basis for sociopolitical action, Vidler suggested, 'run through the Moot discussions like a recurring decimal'.[96] It is another instance of the Moot's use of concepts strongly associated with medieval Christendom and adjusting them to modern conditions. In a liberal society fragmented by competing world views and ideologies, the appeal of natural law for the Moot was that it provided a means to speak of shared values to which Christians and non-Christians could subscribe. Deliberations over reviving the concept of natural law were, however, fraught with tension.

One challenge in these discussions was that while the Moot agreed that the universality implied by natural law was desirable for the sake of social stability, such 'law' was nevertheless historically contingent and thus inherently unstable. This can, for example, be seen in Vidler's Moot paper 'Two Approaches to "Natural Law"', where he asserted that any norms are 'inextricably interwoven with relative and changing conditions' and 'every formulation more or less reflects the particular interests of the period of people who are responsible for it'.[97] The difficulty of establishing guiding norms was further exacerbated in an 'age of relativism' such as theirs.[98] Eliot alike agreed to the contingency of the principles of scholastic natural law. He suggested that for Aquinas, who lived in a homogenous society, the argument for a common human nature was more sustainable. In the modern era, however, with a greater awareness of other cultures, it was harder to sustain such claims.[99] The Moot was then largely sceptical of a return to the absoluteness of scholastic natural law.[100]

A solution to this dilemma was offered via Mannheim's functionalism. Mannheim insisted that while it was no longer possible to appeal to natural law on ontological grounds, there was nevertheless a rationale in suggesting that certain values were essential for society to operate.[101] The advantage of this functionalism, according to Mannheim, was that it acknowledged the historicity of guiding principles and values while also overcoming the problem of the 'sic volo' attitude prevalent in a relativistic society. Mannheim also claimed that there was an affinity between Thomism and this functionalism as both 'lined credo with ratio'.[102] Thus, a feature of this 'modern' version of natural law was that it was open to adjustment according to changing historical conditions.[103]

Yet, some Moot members still wished to defend an element of permanency. Having critiqued the Catholic tradition for neglecting the historical contingency of natural law, Moberly nevertheless insisted on some essential human nature as a rationale for evaluating different forms of society.[104] Arguing against Mannheim's thesis of the adjustability of values, Baillie maintained that the effect of relativism had been exaggerated and conversely the majority of the population, whether Christian or not, still subscribed to certain eternal standards. Furthermore, 'the Christian had certain eternal values to which circumstances must be adjusted'.[105] However, others including Eliot were satisfied with Mannheim's position since a *reinterpretation* of Christian values in itself implied 'an element of the permanent'.[106]

There was also an aversion against the abstraction of scholastic natural law. Oldham therefore warned against allowing discussions on natural law to dominate their time, for in his words, 'there are more urgent things to do'.[107] His adaption of the concept of the 'middle axiom' was an attempt to provide foundational ideas that would guide the course of action taken by those engaged in the foreseen movement. These 'convictions', wrote Oldham, 'can have historical importance only in so far as they are not arbitrary judgements brought to bear on the situation from a detached position about it, but an answer demanded by the structure and tendencies of our present historical existence viewed in the light of Christian faith'.[108]

Another debate concerned the extent to which natural law, *per se*, demands a Christian conception of life. Discussions on natural law can be found in the social philosophies submitted by a number of members for the 9th meeting in July 1940. Building on Aquinas' and Rousseau's ideas of the 'responsible freedom' of the individual, Murry assumed a social philosophy that could be determined by 'natural reason' without reference to Christianity.[109] However, Murry found little support for this purely rational conception amongst other Moot members, who preferred a greater priority to specifically Christian values. Hodges accepted Murry's claim that on a macro level any society must be built upon the premise that there is a common good; however, the content of that common good would differ depending on the underlying social philosophy that a society endorses. The Christian social ideal was ultimately not the product of human dialectics but revelation as manifested in the incarnation.[110] On a similar line of reasoning, Oldham agreed that anthropological and historical insights can be illuminating, but opposed any 'barren arguments about Natural Law as having an authority other than revelation'.[111] Vidler was sympathetic to Karl Barth's objection to natural law as a basis for Christian social thought.[112] Barth had argued that natural law was an unsatisfactory starting point for Christian social engagement since there was nothing inherently Christian about it, even the Nazi's appeal to natural law, argued Barth.[113] Vidler was not, however, willing to reject the conception of natural law altogether as Barth did. Instead, he proposed a 'second approach to Natural Law', which 'starts from the Christian Faith and asks what light does this throw on the conditions of man's earthly existence'.[114]

As such, these Moot members predominantly believed that their venture of creating a blueprint for a future Christian society hinged on the premise of establishing shared *Christian* values. They were confident that despite the very Christian premise of their conception of natural law, it would nevertheless be greeted with approval from non-Christians. In an age where multiple social philosophies competed for loyalties, Hodges held that it was possible through the art of persuasion and argument to convince members of society of the coherence of the Christian point of view. Nevertheless, in a 'mixed society' between Christians and non-Christians, it would be 'necessary to appeal to something less than the full Christian principle'.[115] Oldham was more assertive, claiming that if Christian principles were true, they would inevitably arouse support even from those without a faith commitment.[116] Vidler was also confident that a specifically Christian declaration of social thought would 'enlist more support outside the Churches than within them'.[117] Eliot wished to a greater extent to maintain the classic differentiation between nature and revelation as he held this distinction to be essential in a 'mixed society' where social unity and values must be derived from sources other than purely religious ones. Nevertheless, what was required was a supranational authority which could deliver a universal account of natural law. Ultimately, Eliot believed that this could only materialize through 'a re-union of Christendom'.[118]

Taking these discussions into consideration, reaching a consensus on principles proved complicated. They were sceptical of a Catholic understanding of natural law and yet they were unwilling to discard it altogether. As Eliot suggested, natural law was a matter of wisdom rather than logical deduction. While agreeing to the difficulties of rationally defending the concept of natural law, it could not be done away with: 'You could not defend Natural Law, but it would turn up again and again.'[119]

Despite these reservations, a few attempts at producing a more concrete set of values and principles were made. Even though Oldham was sceptical of the merit of outlining 'Christian values' in the abstract,[120] he nevertheless outlined the core attributes that he argued were consistent with Christianity and particularly pertinent for political action in modern society. These 'middle axioms' include religious and political tolerance, social justice, pluralism through decentralization, reverence of nature, the family as a unit for loving relations and, finally, the universality and autonomy of the church.[121] Another example is Baillie's list. Commissioned by Oldham to outline fundamental Christian values, Baillie suggested three 'master values' from which further values could be deduced, namely, knowledge as the prerequisite for communion, communion, and service to God and fellow human beings.[122]

Building on Mannheim, Hodges pursued a different line of reasoning in an attempt to resolve the tensions outlined above. Mannheim had argued that the future planned society could not emerge without guiding purposes or principles. In any given society, these purposes are embodied in certain 'archetypes', which in turn, through paradigmatic experiences, continue consciously or subconsciously to shape the ethics of a community. Thus, inspired by Mannheim's premise that archetypes as a 'pattern of interpretation … deeply rooted in the mind' were the 'most important integrating force',[123] Hodges set out to investigate a Christian approach, showing how archetypes and symbols shape the church in a more dynamic way than any principles or values spoken of in the abstract. As an example, Hodges presented the crucifixion of Christ as 'a principle of action and suffering which ought increasingly to inform our mind and life'.[124] Such Christian archetypes had governed Western societies for centuries, but in the modern era, they lost their power and had been superseded by secular variants. Hence, Hodges suggested a re-Christianization through an intellectual reflection on 'what Christianity has to offer our archetypes',[125] and a practical task of rediscovering them 'by living them out'.[126] The theologian could increase the theological knowledge of the people that they might become tools for a Christian interpretation. Hodges came to write a number of lengthy papers on these themes in the final years of the Moot. The discussion of these reveals no fundamental objections (although Eliot found it tedious).[127]

Summary

There were, then, a number of aspects that the Moot drew from medieval Christendom. Via Maritain's Neo-Scholasticism, the Moot sought to build their programme on a theocentric anthropology as an antidote to the individualism of the Enlightenment. The Moot, further, wished to revive the social unity of the medieval world, but through fraternity rather than coercion. The vehicle of societal renewal was to emulate the vitalism brought by the religious orders through a modern-day layperson movement exerting influence and challenging social and political structures. Finally, natural law – a central concept in medieval political thought, however fraught – came to figure as a recurring theme in the Moot's discussion as a possible basis on which to maintain a Christian impact on society while enlisting support by non-Christians. Ultimately, the Moot offered no definite alternative as to how a modern-day version of natural law might be tailored.

Over the years, the Moot discourse shifted away from the 'New Christendom' language. Nevertheless, the group's agenda remained the same: to catalyse a movement employing strategies for the creation of a new Christian social order. Oldham's search for a common 'idea' around which Christians could rally culminated in a statement titled 'The Christian Witness in the Present Crisis'.[128] His confidence in the statement was such that he thought it radical enough to cause a Copernican Revolution in Christian social thought.[129] The document – widely commented upon by Moot members and others – can be understood as a synthesis of the ideas entertained in the Moot over the years. To increase its impact, an edited version by the Archbishop of Canterbury, William Temple – a supporter of the Moot – was published in the *Christian News-Letter* on 29 December 1943.[130] In letters to close collaborators in the ecumenical movement, Oldham deemed the document highly significant and acknowledged the inspiration of Maritain and a few other thinkers upon it.[131] Oldham wrote that human dignity derives from 'being created by God and for God' and that this transcendent nature is the essence of 'true humanism'. Evidently, the influence of Maritain's integral humanism was lasting.[132]

Planning for Freedom

The premise of 'Planning for Freedom'

If 'New Christendom' via Maritain encapsulates the Moot's attempt at designing a social philosophy, Mannheim's 'Planning for Freedom' was its most promising political theory. Mannheim's thesis was offered in his Moot paper 'Planning for Freedom', discussed at the 4th meeting in April 1939, but it is suggestive that it had already been circulated prior to the 3rd meeting. Oldham had clearly intended for 'Planning for Freedom' to have been discussed alongside with 'True Humanism'. The ideas of the paper came to influence the discussion in the Moot for years to come.

Mannheim's thesis rested upon his diagnosis that industrialized societies require centralized planning in order to function. Centralization and planning were, according to Mannheim, not merely an option in complex modern society, but a given reality. The real question was whether societal planning would lead to repressive totalitarian regimes or promote liberty under the guidance of a coordinated intellectual elite subject to democratic controls. Given this analysis, Mannheim insisted on a necessary shift from a *laissez faire* liberal society to a planned democratic society, which would both recognize the need for central coordination in modern society and resist totalitarian tendencies through safeguarding spheres of freedom and cultivating a strong civil society. He argued that 'since planning and coordination are characteristic of the age', these changes and trends needed to be studied and monitored by a new kind of body consisting of 'the practical men, politicians, economists, sociologists, educationalists and religious thinkers: i.e. people who are able to understand the human aspect of the transformation of society'.[133] The task of this coordinating elite was to create a 'new social system' or 'Summa' by prudently interpreting the social changes taking place while having the imaginative foresight to anticipate the consequences of these and the courage to look beyond the constraints of existing modes of thinking. Concluding the paper, Mannheim emphasized the importance of ongoing research and interdisciplinary collaboration between intellectuals. He identified seven topics that had to be addressed:

I. Economics
II. Political Organization
III. Social Organization
IV. Churches
V. Education
VI. Public Opinion and Propaganda
VII. Social Work.

In each of these areas, Mannheim proceeded to outline the possible implications of his 'Planning for Freedom'. A few examples here will suffice to give a flavour of his thinking. In economics, Mannheim argued for measures to be taken in order to eliminate trade cycles and factors that contribute to instability. In terms of political organization, greater executive powers had to be entrusted to the government for the sake of efficiency. To tackle the dehumanizing drifts of modern society due to industrialization and urbanization, Mannheim suggested a 'new type of social worker who is able to give the help which was once given by the family and the neighbourhood'. This social worker was to offer the confused modern urbanite the kind of guidance previously provided by the traditional organic community.[134]

'Planning for Freedom' and Christianity

'Planning for Freedom' was essentially Mannheim's petition to the Moot to grab hold of all available means to create structures to enable a peaceful transition from a *laissez faire* to a planned society. As Mannheim wrote: '[i]t is just as important to plan the transition as to plan the goal'.[135] Part of the ongoing task of the envisioned coordinating group was to work out a viable social philosophy or a new 'Summa' that would provide society with the ultimate ends and aims. It was on this premise that he was eagerly engaged in discussions regarding the role of Christianity in the coming epoch.

As a secular Jew and sociologist, Mannheim held a functionalist view of religion.[136] He had first-hand experience of the power of political religion as an integrating force and a moral motivator in Nazi Germany. Mannheim argued, in a Moot paper on social philosophy, that wartimes such as theirs heightened the spiritual dimension of human existence:

> In times of prosperity and peace it looked as if man could live on Hollywood and ice-cream soda alone. But now that mankind is engaged in a life and death struggle for civilisation even the engineer realises that society is rooted in deeper layers of the human soul than he ever thought.[137]

The idea of 'Planning for Freedom' was originally presented in his major volume *Man and Society*, originally appearing in German in 1935 and an extended version in English in 1940.[138] Here, Mannheim maintained that the epochal transition that Western society was enduring required the 'remaking of man', and this entailed a psychological transformation. Religion was largely ignored. However, through his participation in the Moot, Mannheim came to appreciate a greater role for religious experience and Christianity in his planned vision. Evidence of this can be seen in a correspondence with Dawson. In *The Judgement of the Nations* (1943), Dawson critiqued Mannheim's vision of 'Planning for Freedom' as seeking to create a society on a purely rational basis.[139] In a private letter to Dawson, whilst agreeing that this would be a fair assessment of *Man and Society*, Mannheim complained that Dawson had not taken into consideration his contributions in the Moot. '[A]s you will remember my [Moot paper] "Towards a New Social Philosophy,"' wrote Mannheim, 'made it clear that planning without a religious background would be detrimental.'[140] Already in his paper 'Planning for Freedom', Mannheim had proposed that the dehumanizing tendencies of modern bureaucracy 'can be corrected in a spirit of Christianity'.[141] Hence, a spiritual revival was an essential factor for the fulfilment of his otherwise more empirical and instrumental programme of 'Planning for Freedom'.

Therein lay the appeal of Maritain's ideal of the saint: it added a vitalism to Mannheim's otherwise technical and bureaucratic scheme. Interestingly, in a letter to the Moot dated 16 April 1939, Maritain commented that his own ideas and Mannheim's 'Planning for Freedom' were largely compatible.[142]

The reception of 'Planning for Freedom'

There can be little doubt that Mannheim held a dominant position in the Moot's discussions, and his 'Planning for Freedom' was seriously entertained as a worthwhile line of investigation. However, there are questions over how the other members received his ideas. Due to his commitment to the Moot and the importance of the group to his work in the final period of his life, Mannheim's role has been studied in some detail in the existing literature. An extreme position is that of Yoshiyuki Kudomi, who deduces that 'The Moot was Mannheim'.[143] Sigrid Ziffus's article 'Karl Mannheim und der Moot-Kreis' also portrays Mannheim's status in the Moot in a positive light, yet she fails to discuss the tensions between Mannheim and other members.[144] According to Colin Loader, who devotes the final chapter of *Karl Mannheim and His Intellectual Development* to the Moot period, Mannheim 'received as much from that group as he contributed to it'.[145] In the end, Mannheim seems to have overestimated the popularity of his ideas, concludes Loader.[146] David Kettler *et al.* arrive at a similar verdict arguing that Mannheim's lack of opportunity as a Jewish émigré in British academia explains his investment in the Moot. Still, even in the Moot, Mannheim found his influence limited: 'He was on a mission amongst missionaries. Yet the experiment was not wholly successful.'[147]

Given Mannheim's personal gain and intellectual development during his time in the Moot, it is somewhat surprising that Mannheim scholars have limited exposure to the Moot material.[148] It is true that most of Mannheim's Moot papers were published in *Diagnosis of Our Time* (1943) and much of his thinking during the Moot period has been reproduced in his posthumous *Freedom, Power and Democratic Planning* (1950); however, the archival material warrants further investigation. A closer examination of these primary sources gives a more accurate understanding of the reception of Mannheim's ideas amongst the Moot members and of his standing in the group.

Comments submitted by Moot members on Mannheim's original article were positive (e.g. Oldham, Vidler) or at worst guarded (Eliot, Moberly).[149] Fred Clarke's assessment was the most positive. He enthusiastically proclaimed that 'Mannheim's programme seems to merit reading again and again', commending it as a possible resolution to the failures of the democratic societies.[150] Only Dawson's reaction was outright dismissive, stating that he was 'inclined to differ from Mannheim regarding the optimism of his views concerning the prospect of planning'.[151]

Over time, several Moot members incorporated Mannheim's vision into their position papers for the Moot and in their publications. Perhaps his most ardent disciple was Clarke. Clarke built on Mannheim's ideas in his Moot paper on British education, and these were later included in his influential *Education and Social Change*.[152] In 1948, Clarke hyperbolically declared that he 'merely happened to be the mouthpiece' of Mannheim.[153] His *Freedom in the Educative Society* – a book 'about freedom and the strains and demands that "planning for freedom" in contemporary Britain must impose upon the agencies that educate' – is dedicated 'In Memoriam K. M.'.[154] Furthermore, in his capacity as director, Clarke was instrumental in appointing Mannheim as professor at the Institute of Education in late 1945.[155] Other members influenced by Mannheim include Löwe, who expounded on the theme of education and planning in his 'Notes on University Reform'.[156] Hodges, who professed to be a 'follower',[157] wrote a synthesis between his own work on Christian archetypes and Mannheim's social-planning scheme during the autumn of 1943.[158] Another Mannheim-influenced work was Walter Moberly's *Plato's Conception of Education and Its Meaning Today*, which accepts the necessity of planning.[159] Furthermore, the central tenets of Mannheim's theory can be found in Hector Hetherington's BBC broadcast talk 'The Prolegomena to Planning', where he argued that the 'absolute protection' of liberal values and of the individual against 'direct action of the state' was essential in a planned modern society.[160]

The support from Oldham, who obviously set the agenda for the Moot, explains the continuous space given to Mannheim within the Moot. In a pamphlet titled *Church, Community and State* (1935), Oldham had already grappled with the question of liberty in relation to authority and state intervention. It suggests that the 'central problem of modern life' is the demand for centralization whilst at the same time safeguarding 'freedom of thought and expression'.[161] On the basis of this publication, Oldham's attraction to Mannheim's idea of 'Planning for Freedom' becomes apparent. For Oldham, 'Planning for Freedom' was one of the essential 'commitments' of the envisioned popular movement.[162] Oldham's support of Mannheim can also be seen in his ringing endorsements in the *Christian News-Letter* and in the volume *Real Life is Meeting*.[163]

Mannheim's favourable position within the Moot can be further illustrated by Moberly's comment during a discussion at the 7th meeting in February 1940.

Debating V. A. Demant's petition for a return to an organic medieval society, Moberly stated that such a conception was incompatible with 'the view generally accepted by the Moot in Mannheim's paper "Planning for Freedom"'.[164]

However, on careful reading of the Moot material and publications by members, voices of apprehension can also be heard. Vidler, who in his autobiography stated that no thought had greater impact on the Moot than Mannheim's vision of 'Planning for Freedom',[165] also expressed fears of a Huxleyan nightmare: 'I anticipate that our mass-industrialized society is bound to become totalitarian, but I do not regard this as the way into a great new epoch, Mannheim's Brave New World.'[166] Yet, in an editorial for *Theology*, Vidler spoke of the reality of centralization in modern industrialized society, and that in such a society, '[f]reedom can now be preserved only if it is the deliberate aim of those who have the power to plan'. He implored Christians and 'men of good will' to unite under 'the banner of "Planning for Freedom"'.[167] Murry seemingly held a similar ambivalence. When 'Planning for Freedom' was initially discussed during the 3rd meeting, he grudgingly consented to Mannheim's scheme.[168] By the 8th meeting, however, Murry announced his loss of confidence, declaring: 'I lack faith in his prognosis.'[169] Eric Fenn, who never vented his misgivings publicly, confessed in a private letter to Oldham that intellectually he accepted Mannheim's prognosis, but spiritually and emotionally he rejected it. He wrote, 'I recognise the gathering tendency towards a vast increase of central control; but it doesn't hearten me at all. On the contrary, it fills me with profound despair.'[170]

Dawson's, Polanyi's and Eliot's critique of Mannheim was more public and vocal. Dawson rejected the 'purely rational' scientism of Mannheim's social planning, fearing that it would constitute a greater threat to liberty than the totalitarian powers.[171] The direct confrontation (or the 'ding-dong battle' as Philip Mairet called it) between Mannheim and newcomer Michael Polanyi during the 20th meeting on central planning has been widely recounted, not least by Roger Kojecky.[172] Eliot, for his part, was personally sympathetic towards Mannheim, yet he remained highly sceptical of his ideas. As I will argue in the 5th chapter, Eliot's aversion to Mannheim boils down to differences in their definitions of culture, conflicts over the nature of elites and a trust in divine providence that led him to reject man-made blueprints.

Thus, bringing together the available material allows for a more nuanced understanding of Mannheim's position in the Moot and is illustrative of the difficulties that the Moot faced in constructing a programme. A general agreement could be found on the level of 'principles'. However, such abstractions were not a sufficient basis for collective action. In turn, in the case of concretization, such as Mannheim's 'Planning for Freedom', there was simply not a strong enough consensus for it to become central to their programme.

Conclusion: 'Programmatic Modernism', prospects and tensions

The argument presented in this chapter is that the Moot exhibits the core characteristic of Programmatic Modernism as per Griffin's definition. That is, in the face of a perceived societal crisis, the Moot sought to produce an 'idea' that could catalyse a sociopolitical revitalization movement, dragging modern society out of decades of decay and decline into a new era. Whilst tensions and disagreement arose due to the group's diverse composition, nonetheless, with Oldham firmly in control, the dominant voices drove the group in search of a programme that would fuel a Christian sociopolitical movement. As with other Modernist movements in this period, the Moot turned to its Western heritage to find the means to create a new future, and this entailed a 'return' to the Middle Ages. This did not represent a desire for a wholesale adaptation of the medieval order. Rather, as evident in their engagement with Maritain, this return to Christendom entailed a salvaging of the positive aspects of the medieval world, borrowing from its core features whilst infusing them with new meaning and reinterpreting them for the modern era. Maritain used the Thomist term 'analogy' to explain how the Christian order of the Middle Ages could inspire a new conception of a Christian society in the twentieth century. Analogy also aptly describes how the Moot engaged with medieval Christendom. Theologically speaking, the Moot sought a middle path between the immanence of Protestant liberal theology, which marginalized God's providence, and the neo-orthodoxy, which emphasized divine sovereignty at the expense of human freedom. Herein lay the attraction of Maritain's integralist neo-Thomism, which overcame the dualism of the sacred and the temporal, and between human freedom and divine grace. Borrowing from this 'scholastic' conception of a theocentric humanism, the Moot adopted this to its vision of a modern world.

Whilst the slogan of 'New Christendom' encapsulates the Moot's return to past ideals, Mannheim's idea of 'Planning for Freedom' provided the group with a potential modern political theory. The relation of 'Modernist' movements to Western modernity was always ambivalent. Fascist regimes exemplify a contradiction in the sense that they were driven by an anti-rationalism undermining the spirit of the Enlightenment. At the same time, they freely made use of the fruits of the rationality that had produced technological advancement and scientific gain.[173] For instance, in his lucid exposition *Modernity and the Holocaust*, Zygmunt Bauman suggests that the Holocaust is not an aberration of modernity, but in fact 'demonstrates what the rationalizing, engineering tendencies of modernity are capable of if not checked'.[174] The Moot was not anti-rationalistic nor did it suggest anything that is comparable to the horrors of the Holocaust, yet to an extent it reflected a similar ambivalence towards modernity. Members rejected the individualism, progressivism and materialism of the Enlightenment, appealed to the metaphysical as the basic premise of their social philosophizing and embraced religion as a cohesive force in society. Yet, the religious foundations of their social philosophizing demanded a pragmatic readjustment to the object of their project: modern society. As Mannheim wrote, '[i]t is not the idea of Christian action which changes with the changing structure of society but the strategic points where it should concentrate its attack'.[175] Mannheim more than any other member was willing to embrace modern inventions as a means to their ends. Social techniques and propaganda were merely neutral tools that could be mobilized for different purposes.[176] Mannheim's work was the most apparent example of the Moot's merging of the irrational with the rational, the premodern with the modern, of the Modernist 'making it new'.

Given that Wallace argues that Christianity itself originates as a revitalization movement, there is nothing inherently contradictory about interpreting the Moot in this way.[177] Griffin's idea of Programmatic or Political Modernism itself patently assumes Christian and not least Pauline concepts. The lament of the corruption of the present age, the expectations of the imminent advent of apocalyptic times, the eschatological vision of the in-breaking of a new *aeon*, the Pauline phrases 'new creation' and 'the old has gone, the *new* is here'[178] and the new community constructing an alternative sacred canopy are all themes rooted in the Christian metanarrative.

However, Griffin assumes that by the first half of the twentieth century secularization had rendered Christianity obsolete in modern societies. Christianity is understood to be part of that which no longer could sustain 'the mazeway', and thus by definition cannot be conceived to be part of the solution. An alternative reading is offered by Tonning, who suggests that the rise of political religions as a response to modern decadence was symptomatic of the interwar, widespread speculation that political resolutions alone were not adequate to address a crisis that was ultimately seen to be spiritual. In this context, there is no reason why a renewal of Christianity could not be located *vis-à-vis* other political *'isms'*. 'Christianity could now plausibly be understood,' writes Tonning, 'as providing an independent critique and historical analysis of *all* political "isms"; as a bulwark against impending chaos; and as a vital source of values – offering its own regeneration cure.'[179] Bringing together Griffin's 'Programmatic Modernism', the 'medieval Modernism' as narrated by Saler and the 'Catholic Modernism' of Schloesser, the conceptual justification for construing the Moot as a Christian Programmatic Modernist venture has been firmly established. As the Moot exemplifies then, a revitalized Christianity can sit quite comfortably in Griffin's Political Modernist framework.

Notes

1 Clements, *Moot Papers*, 107 (3rd meeting, 6–9 January 1939).
2 Anthony W. C. Wallace, 'Revitalization Movements', *American Anthropologist* 58, no. 2 (1956), 264.
3 Ibid., 268–70.
4 Cf. Clements, *Moot Papers*, 317 (9th meeting, 12–15 July 1941).
5 Oldham, *The Question*, 7.
6 Clements, *Moot Papers*, 415 (12th meeting, 1–3 August 1941).
7 Eliot, *Idea*, 13.
8 Cf. Clements, *Moot Papers*, 107 (2nd meeting, 23–26 September 1938). Keith Clements suggests in his biography of J. H. Oldham that the message of the letter for *The Times* explains the rationale of the Moot (Clements, *Faith on the Frontier*, 364).
9 Oldham, 'Lessons of the Crisis'.
10 John Middleton Murry, 'Towards a Christian Theory of Society', [1938], OLD 14/5/37.
11 Clements, *Moot Papers*, 96 (2nd meeting, 23–26 September 1938).
12 Ibid., 359 (10th meeting, 10–13 January 1941). Hector Hetherington was the principal of Glasgow University and joined the Moot in 1941.
13 Eliot, *After Strange Gods*, 19. See also *The Idea*, where Eliot writes that 'neither Liberalism and Conservatism… is enough to guide us (Eliot, *Idea*, 17)'.
14 J. H. Oldham, 'Letter to the Moot Members', 23 August 1939, IOE/MOO/1; LM/SEC12.
15 Charles Gore et al., *The Return of Christendom* (London: George Allen and Unwin, 1922). The links between the Moot and the Christendom Group will be discussed in Chapter 6.

16　Maurice Reckitt, 'Editorial: Valedictory', *Christendom* XVI, no. 80 (1950), 251.
17　Coupland, *Britannia*, 10.
18　Ibid., 18.
19　William Temple, 'The Restoration of Christendom', *Christendom* 1 (1936), 26. The *Christendom* journal was published by the ecumenical movement Faith and Order and is not to be confused with the British *Christendom* journal published by the Christendom Group.
20　M. T. Edwards, *The Right of the Protestant Left: God's Totalitarianism* (New York: Palgrave Macmillan, 2012), 4%. Both Van Dusen and Niebuhr were active in the ecumenical movement and thereby in regular contact with Oldham. Niebuhr was actively participating in the Moot through papers, correspondence and even attending meetings. Even Van Dusen had insight into the Moot as Oldham occasionally sent him Moot papers (e.g. J. H. Oldham, 'Letter to H. P. Van Dusen', 18 November 1943, OLD/9/5/38).
21　John S. Nurser, *For All the Peoples and All Nations: The Ecumenical Church and Human Rights* (Washington, DC: Georgetown University Press, 2005), 16.
22　Cf. Griffin, *Modernism and Fascism*, 117.
23　Tonning, *Modernism and Christianity*, 4–5.
24　Jeffrey M. Perl, *The Tradition of Return: The Implicit History of Modern Literature* (Princeton, NJ: Princeton University Press, 1984), 12.
25　Lucy McDiarmid, *Saving Civilization: Yeats, Eliot, and Auden between the Wars* (Cambridge: Cambridge University Press, 1984), 35.
26　Paul Robichaud, *Making the Past Present: David Jones, the Middle Ages, & Modernism* (Washington, DC: The Catholic University of America Press, 2006), 139.
27　See section XIV–XV were Pound uses *The Divine Comedy* to expound his vision of hell (Ezra Pound, *The Cantos of Ezra Pound* (London: Faber & Faber, 1964)).
28　As made apparent in the Introduction, it is questionable whether a strong distinction between formalism and functionalism can be made. Even the 'formalists' of the Bloomsbury type understood the political implications of art.
29　Michael Saler, *The Avant-Garde of Interwar England: Medieval Modernism and the London Underground* (Oxford: Oxford University Press, 1999), 10.
30　René Hague, *David Jones* (Cardiff: University of Wales Press, 1975), 27.
31　Maritain wrote that: 'Artistic labour is properly human labour as opposed to (Jacques Maritain, *The Philosophy of Art*, trans. John O'Connor (Ditchling: S. Dominic's Press, 1923), 9).'
32　Ibid., i–iii.
33　Joseph Frank, *Responses to Modernity: Essays in the Politics of Culture* (Bronx: Fordham University Press, 2012), 28.
34　Schloesser, *Jazz Age Catholicism*, 16.
35　Ibid., 149.

36 Ibid., 163, citation from p. 172.
37 As cited in ibid., 164.
38 See, Maritain, *True Humanism*, 133.
39 Ibid., 82.
40 Clements, *Moot Papers*, 145 (3rd meeting, 6–9 January 1939).
41 See Donald MacKinnon, 'Surveys: Christian Social Thought', *Theology* 38, no. 227 (1939), 378. MacKinnon participated in the final years of the Moot and its successor the St Julians Group.
42 John Baillie, 'Paper on Maritain's *True Humanism*', [1939], LM/SEC1; OLD/14/7/18.
43 Alec Vidler, 'Comments on M. Maritain's *True Humanism*', [1939], LM/SEC1; OLD/14/6/89.
44 T. S. Eliot, 'Letter to His Mother', 24 June 1926, in *The Letters of T.S. Eliot Volume 3*, ed. T. S. Eliot, Valerie Eliot, and John Haffenden (London: Faber & Faber, 2012).
45 T. S. Eliot, 'Letter to Jeanette McPherrin', 8 April 1935, MS Valerie Eliot.
46 Clements, *Moot Papers*, 208 (4th meeting, 14–17 April 1939).
47 Alec Vidler, 'Comments on M. Maritain's *True Humanism*', [1939], LM/SEC1; OLD/14/6/89. The focus of the discussion in the 2nd meeting was Murry's 'Towards a Christian Theory of Society' and the role of Christianity within industrialized societies.
48 John Baillie, 'Paper on Maritain's *True Humanism*', [1939], LM/SEC1; OLD/14/7/18.
49 Jacques Maritain, 'Copy of Letter from M. Jacques Maritain', 16 April 1939, LM/SEC10.
50 T. S. Eliot, 'Letter to Jacques Maritain', 19 April 1939, NWE/II/1/41.
51 Anon., 'Notes from a Dinner with Maritain', [May 1939], OLD/13/7/misc.
52 E.g. Eliot, *Idea*; Baillie, *What Is Christian Civilization?*; Oldham, *The Resurrection*; Vidler, *God's Judgment*.
53 John Middleton Murry, 'Comments on Maritain's *True Humanism*', [1938], 14/5/22; LM/SEC1; OLD/14/5/22.
54 John Middleton Murry, 'Paper Read at the Moot, 23–26 Sept 1938', [1938], OLD 14/5/1.
55 Vidler, *God's Judgment*, 57.
56 Maritain, *True Humanism*, 105.
57 Ibid., 131. Maritain defines Christendom as denoting 'a certain *temporal* regime whose formations… bear the stamp of the christian [sic] conception of life (ibid., 121, author's emphasis)'.
58 Clements, *Moot Papers*, 49 (1st meeting, 1–4 April 1938). In his first of many papers for the Moot, H. A. Hodges rejected the metaphysical argumentation of Thomism as a legitimate basis of apologetics in the modern world. Thus, Hodges argued, if modern man was to accept theism, a new Summa was required (H. A. Hodges, 'Towards a Plan for a New Summa', [1939], LM/SEC8; OLD/14/2/25).

59 Maritain, *True Humanism*, 19.
60 Ibid., 21. Christopher Dawson whose historical account of humanism mirrors that what Maritain wrote in 1931 that modern '[m]an was stripped of his glory and freedom and left as a naked human animal shivering in an inhumane universe (Christopher Dawson, *Christianity and the New Age* (London: Sheed & Ward, 1931), 18)'.
61 Maritain, *True Humanism*, 152.
62 Ibid., 153. While the Moot members were generally sympathetic to this analysis in one of the few negative criticisms against Maritain, historian Dawson found the historical overview of humanism inadequate (Christopher Dawson, 'Comments on M. Maritain's *True Humanism*', [1939], LM/SEC1; OLD/14/4/31).
63 Maritain, *True Humanism*, 155.
64 Ibid., 65.
65 Ibid., 86.
66 Ibid., 66.
67 Ibid., 115.
68 J. H Oldham, 'The Problems and Tasks of the Council on the Christian Faith and the Common Life', [1938] OLD/13/8/73. The CCFCL was a more formal organization than the Moot that Oldham founded to reflect on Christian responses to social issues of the time. See Chapter 6 for further details.
69 J. H. Oldham, 'A Reborn Christendom', August 1939, IOE/MOO/2; LM/SEC11.
70 Ibid.
71 Clements, *Moot Papers*, 316 (9th meeting, 12–15 July 1940).
72 Vidler, *God's Judgment*, 78–9.
73 Reinhold Niebuhr, *The Nature and Destiny of Man: A Christian Interpretation: Vol I* (Louisville: Westminster John Knox Press, 1996), 92.
74 Maritain, *True Humanism*, 156f.
75 It is interesting to note that Maritain and the Moot failed to address perhaps the defining feature of the Medieval order, namely, that citizenship was defined by baptism, and not by juridical law as in the post-Reformation era. The real political power that the church could yield was the threat of excommunication and by implication exclusion from participation in society.
76 Eliot, *Idea*, 27.
77 John Middleton Murry, 'Towards a Christian Theory of Society', [1938], OA/14/5/37.
78 John Middleton Murry, 'Paper Read at the Moot, Sept. 23–26, 1938', [1938], OLD/14/5/1. It is therefore curious that Murry does not raise any points of disagreement when commenting on Maritain's *True Humanism* a few months later (John Middleton Murry, 'Comments on M. Maritain's *True Humanism*', [1938], LM/SEC1; OLD/14/5/22).
79 There is a realist's acceptance of the statism of modern industrialized society in his paper 'Towards a Theory of a Christian Society'. However, in a memorandum,

circulated in early 1940, attacking the centralization implicit in Mannheim's 'Planning for Freedom', Murry stated that, 'I see no solution except through a painful process of disintegration of our centralised industrial society', and suggested the alternative of decentralized was 'self-supportive Christian communities', an idea he sought to embody in his experimental farming community at Lodge Farm (John Middleton Murry, 'Memoradnum by J. Middleton Murry', [1940], IOE/MOO/129). Murry's apparent affinity for Guild Socialism sheds further light on his romanticizing of the Middle Ages.
80 Maritain, *True Humanism*, 166–7.
81 Maritain here cites Thomas Aquinas, *Summa Theologiae* I-II, 64, 2 and I–II, 21, 4.
82 Maritain, *True Humanism*, 127–9.
83 Ibid., 168.
84 Clements, *Moot Papers*, 453 (13th meeting, 19–22 December 1941).
85 Baillie, *What Is Christian Civilization?*, 34.
86 T. S. Eliot, *Notes Towards the Definition of Culture*, 2nd ed. (London: Faber & Faber, 1962 [1948]), 25.
87 Maritain, *True Humanism*, 266.
88 Clements, *Moot Papers*, 208 (4th meeting, 14–17 April 1939).
89 Ibid., 189 (4th meeting, 14–17 April 1939).
90 Cf. H. A. Hodges' comments at the 2nd meeting (ibid., 102 (2nd meeting, 23–26 September 1938)).
91 Aristotle, *Rhetorics,* 1373b2–8.
92 Aquinas, *Summa Theologiae*, I.II 91.2.
93 Ibid., I.II 91.3.
94 Ibid., I.II 91.4, 5.
95 In his summary of *True Humanism*, Baillie suggested that Maritain rejected the Thomist natural law in favour of the principle of the lesser evil (John Baillie, 'Paper on Maritain's *True Humanism*', [1939], LM/SEC1; OLD/14/7/18). However, in Maritain's 1944 *The Rights of Man*, he takes a classical Thomist natural law theory as his point of departure in defence of human rights (Jacques Maritain, *The Rights of Man and Natural Law* (London: The Centenary Press, 1944), 34–7). This publication was never discussed in the Moot.
96 Alec Vidler, 'Two Approaches to Natural Law', [1942], IOE/MOO/78. The discussion on natural law intensified during 9th and 12–14th meetings.
97 Alec Vidler, 'Two Approaches to "Natural Law"', [1942], OLD/14/6/83; IOE/MOO/78. A version of this paper was published in *Theology* (Alec Vidler, 'Inquiries Concerning Natural Law', *Theology* 44, no. 260 (1942), 65–73). Vidler expressed the same sentiment in his 'Notes on Social Philosophy' circulated prior to the 9th meeting (Alec Vidler, 'Notes on Social Philosophy', [1940], IOE/MOO/126, OLD/14/94/6).

98   Ibid.
99   Clements, *Moot Papers*, 428 (12th meeting, 1–3 August 1941). Similar cases were also argued by Hodges and Mannheim at the 9th meeting (ibid., 327 (9th meeting, 12–15 July 1941).
100 Vidler admitted that Thomas Aquinas was not unaware of the contingency of natural law, but in a modern age the relativity of such norms was all the more apparent (Alec Vidler, 'Two Approaches to Natural Law', [1942], IOE/MOO/78; OLD/14/6/83).
101 Clements, *Moot Papers*, 326–8 (9th meeting, 12–15 July 1941). See also Mannheim's 'The Crisis in Valuation', where he argued that values are the 'traffic lights' in society. Karl Mannheim, 'The Crisis in Valuation', [1942], IOE/MOO/77; OLD/14/3/40.
102 Clements, *Moot Papers*, 333–4 (9th meeting, 12–15 July 1941).
103 Karl Mannheim, 'The Crisis in Valuation', [1942], IOE/MOO/77; OLD/14/3/40.
104 Clements, *Moot Papers*, 329–30 (9th meeting, 12–15 July 1941).
105 Ibid., 426 (12th meeting, 1–3 August 1941).
106 Ibid. 451.
107 Ibid. 335 (9th meeting, 12–15 July 1941).
108 J. H. Oldham, 'The Christian Witness in the Present Crisis', 6 October 1943, OLD/9/5/19.
109 John Middleton Murry, 'Notes on Social Philosophy', [1940], IOE/MOO/127; OLD/14/5/35.
110 H. A. Hodges, 'Notes on Social Philosophy', [1940], IOE/MOO/125; OLD/14/2/53.
111 Clements, *Moot Papers*, 335–6 (9th meeting, 12–15 July 1941). Oldham's focus on revelation betrays his neo-orthodox leaning. However, he is closer to Emil Brunner than Karl Barth. In contrast to Barth, Brunner argued that just as the sculpture communicates something about the artist, so creation in itself leaves traces of the creator. However, this revelation in nature is not sufficient for salvation (Emil Brunner and Karl Barth, *Natural Theology*, trans. Peter Fraenkel (London: The Centenary Press, 1946), 26).
112 Alec Vidler, 'Two Approaches to Natural Law', [1942], IOE/MOO/78; OLD/14/6/83).
113 Karl Barth, *A Letter to Great Britain from Switzerland* (London: The Sheldon Press, 1941), 16–17. The booklet was published by Christian News-Letter Books, which was edited by Vidler and Oldham.
114 Alec Vidler, 'Two Approaches to Natural Law', [1942], IOE/MOO/78; OLD/14/6/83.
115 H. A. Hodges, 'Notes on Social Philosophy', [1940], IOE/MOO/125; OLD/14/2/53.
116 Clements, *Moot Papers*, 335–6 (9th meeting, 12–15 July 1941).
117 Alec Vidler, 'Two Approaches to Natural Law', [1942], IOE/MOO/78; OLD/14/6/83. Vidler's estimation might have been an exaggeration, but 'Christian

values and principles' held some currency in the public debate. Unbeliever William Beveridge, for instance, wrote that the proposition suggested by leaders of the churches in a letter to *The Times* on 21 December 1940 'deserves our support' as he affirmed the social function of religion (William Beveridge, *The Pillars of Security: And Other War-Time Essays and Addresses* (London: George Allen & Unwin, 1943), 40).

118   T. S. Eliot, 'Notes on Social Philosophy', [1940], IOE/MOO/123; OLD/14/6/24.
119   Clements, *Moot Papers*, 332.
120   See W. A. Visser 'T Hooft and J. H. Oldham, *The Church and Its Function in Society* (London: George Allen & Allen, 1937), 209ff.
121   J. H. Oldham, 'A Reborn Christendom', August 1939, IOE/MOO/2; LM/SEC11. A similar list of principles was included in Oldham's later 'The Christian Witness in the Present Crisis' (J. H. Oldham, 'The Christian Witness in the Present Crisis', 6 October 1943, OLD/9/5/19).
122   John Baillie, 'Approach to Deduction of Values', 28 August 1942, IOE/MOO/86; OLD/14/7/8.
123   Mannheim's comments during the 12th meeting (Clements, *Moot Papers*, 419 (12th meeting, 1–3 August 1941)).
124   H. A. Hodges, 'Christian Archetypes and Symbols', 22 August 1942, BA/5/9; OLD 14/1/23.
125   H. A. Hodges, 'More About Archetypes and Symbols', 28 August 1942, BA/5/11; OLD 14/1/38.
126   Ibid.
127   H. A. Hodges, 'Archetypes and Paradigms in a Future Society', 6 September 1943, BA/5/29 (page 4 missing); OLD/14/1/57; H. A. Hodges: 'Christian Archetypes, Paradigms and Symbols in the Future', 22 October 1943 BA/5/28; OLD/9/5/33; Hodges, 'The Collective Commonwealth and the Christian', 22 January 1944, OLD 14/1/71; 'Ethics and the Christian in the Collective Commonwealth', 24 April 1944, OLD 14/1/80; H. A. Hodges, 'Paradigms and Archetypes in the Collective Commonwealth', 27 February 1945, BA/5/45; MPP/15/7; H. A. Hodges, 'What is an Archetype?' 27 August 1945, MPP/15/7; H. A. Hodges, 'Christian Archetypes and Paradigms', November 1945, MPP/15/7. See T. S. Eliot, 'Letter to Mary Trevelyan', 29 May 1944, HLE/bMS AM/1691.2/29.
128   J. H. Oldham, 'The Christian Witness in the Present Crisis', [1943], OLD/9/5/19.
129   Clements, *Moot Papers*, 639 (18th meeting, 29 October–1 November 1943).
130   William Temple, 'What Christians Stand for in the Secular World', *Christian News-Letter Supplement*, no. 198 (1943). Although Oldham had deliberately excluded Temple from the Moot due to fears that he would be too domineering, there were few persons who had a greater standing in Britain at the time.
131   J. H. Oldham, 'Letter to H. P. Van Dusen', 18 November 1943, OLD/9/5/38, J. H. Oldham, 'Letter to W.A. Visser' t'Hooft', 30 December 1943, OLD/9/5/41.

132 Another piece of evidence of Maritain's lasting influence on Oldham is BBC broadcast titled 'Christian Humanism' in which Oldham contrast a 'man-centred' versus a 'God-centred humanism' (J. H. Oldham, 'Christian Humanism', in *Humanism: Three B.B.C. Talks* (London: Watts & Co., 1944), 19).
133 Karl Mannheim, 'Planning for Freedom', [1938], LM/SEC7; OLD/14/3/67.
134 Ibid.
135 Ibid.
136 Cf. Karl Mannheim, 'Planning for Freedom', [1938], LM/SEC7; OLD/14/3/67. Emile Durkheim, as one of the pioneering sociologists, sought to investigate religion primarily through its function in society rather than its normative truth claims. In his eminent *Elementary Forms of Religious Life*, Durkheim concluded that 'religion is something eminently social' and the glue of society enforcing social unity (Emile Durkheim, *The Elementary Forms of the Religious Life*, trans. Joseph Ward Swain (London: George Allen & Unwin, 1964 [1915]), 10, 43).
137 Karl Mannheim, 'Towards a New Social Philosophy Part II. Christian values in the Changing Environment', [1941], IOE/MOO/75; OLD/14/3/94.
138 Karl Mannheim, *Man and Society: In an Age of Reconstruction* (London: Kegan Paul, 1940). The original German thesis was published already in 1935.
139 Dawson, *Judgement*, 83.
140 Karl Mannheim, 'Letter to Christopher Dawson', 26 January 1943, CDP/15/42.
141 Karl Mannheim, 'Planning for Freedom', [1938], LM/SEC7; OLD/14/3/67.
142 Jacques Maritain, 'Copy of a Letter from Jacques Maritain', 14 April 1939, OL/SEC10.
143 Kudomi, 'Karl Mannheim in Britain', 51.
144 Ziffus, 'Karl Mannheim Und Der Moot-Kreis'.
145 Loader, *The Intellectual Development*,156.
146 Ibid., 177.
147 David Kettler, Volker Meja, and Nico Stehr, *Karl Mannheim* (Chichester: Ellis Horwood Tavistock, 1984), 134.
148 Ibid.; Kettler and Meja, *Mannheim and the Crisis*; Loader, *The Intellectual Development*; H. E. S Woldring, *Karl Mannheim: The Development of His Thought* (Assen: Van Gorcum, 1986).
149 J. H. Oldham, 'Comments on Mannheim's Paper', [1939], LM/SEC3; Alec Vidler, 'By Alec Vidler', [1939], LM/SEC3; T. S. Eliot, 'Comments on Papers by Mannheim and Hodges', [1939], LM/SEC3; Walter Moberly, 'Short Notes on Mannheim and Hodges' Papers', [1939], LM/SEC3.
150 Fred Clarke, 'Comments on Paper by Mannheim', [1939], LM/SEC3; OLD/13/7/46.
151 Christopher Dawson, 'Letter from Christopher Dawson', [1939], OLD/9/3/18.
152 Fred Clarke, 'Some Notes on English Educational Institutions in the light of the necessities of "Planning for Freedom" in the coming Collectivized Regime', 21

August 1939, IOE/MOO/7; OLD/14/7/31; Fred Clarke, *Education and Social Change: An English Interpretation*, Christian News-Letter Books (London: The Sheldon Press, 1940).
153   Fred Clarke, 'Karl Mannheim at the Institute: The Beginnings', [1948], IOE/FC/1/35. The paper was first published in the appendix of F. W. Mitchell, *Sir Fred Clarke: Master Teacher 1880–1952* (London: Longmans, 1967).
154   Fred Clarke, *Freedom in the Educative Society* (London: University of London Press, 1948), 9.
155   See Fred Clarke, 'Karl Mannheim at the Institute: The Beginnings', [1948], IOE/FC/1/35.
156   Adolf Löwe, 'Some Notes on University Reform', [1940], IOE/MOO/18; OLD/14/4/66.
157   Clements, *Moot Papers*, 398 (11th meeting, 4–7 April).
158   H. A. Hodges, 'Archetypes and Paradigms in a Future Society', 6 September 1943, BA/5/29; OLD/14/1/57.
159   Walter Moberly, *Plato's Conception of Education and Its Meaning for to-Day* (Oxford: Oxford University Press, 1944).
160   H. J. W. Hetherington, 'The Prolegomena to Planning: The essential freedom', 28 August 1942, IOE/MOO/85; OLD/14/9/32.
161   J. H. Oldham, 'The Roots of Our Troubles', in *The Church Looks Ahead*, ed. J. H. [and others] Oldham (London: Faber & Faber, 1941), 25.
162   J. H. Oldham, 'Fraternity of the Spirit', 7 March 1941, IOE/MOO/40.
163   J. H. Oldham, 'Freedom and Planning', *Christian News-Letter* 104, Supplement (1941); J. H. Oldham, 'Diagnosis of Our Time', *Christian News-Letter*, no. 174 (1943); Oldham, *Real Life*.
164   Clements, *Moot Papers*, 274 (7th meeting, 9–12 February 1940).
165   Alec R. Vidler, *Scenes from a Clerical Life* (London: Collins, 1977), 119.
166   Clements, *Moot Papers*, 313 (8th meeting, 19–22 April 1940).
167   Alec Vidler, 'Editorial: Planning for What', *Theology* 44, no. 266 (1942), 67–8.
168   Clements, *Moot Papers*, 165 (3rd meeting, 6–9 January 1939).
169   John Middleton Murry, 'Memorandum by J. Middleton Murry', [1940], IOE/MOO/127.
170   Erik Fenn. 'Letter J. H. Oldham', 8 April 1940, BBC/JHO/1B.
171   Dawson, *Judgement*, 83, 85. The relevant section of this publication was circulated in Moot early 1941 (Christopher Dawson, 'Planning and Culture', [1941], IOE/MOO/128).
172   Kojecky, *T. S. Eliot's Social Criticism*, 155.
173   See the discussion in Griffin, *Modernism and Fascism*, 15–21. Similarly, Jeffrey Herf points to the paradox in 'reactionary Modernism' (here referring to Nazism), which 'rejected reason but embraced technology' (Jeffrey Herf, *Reactionary Modernism: Technology, Culture, and Politics in Weimar and the Third Reich* (Cambridge: Cambridge University Press, 1986), 224).

174 Zygmunt Bauman, *Modernity and the Holocaust* (Cambridge: Polity Press, 1989), 114.
175 Karl Mannheim, 'Planning for Freedom', [1938], LM/SEC7; OLD/14/3/67.
176 Ibid.
177 Wallace, 'Revitalization Movements', 267. For an example of how the term 'revitalization movement' has been applied to biblical studies, see Kenneth D. Tollefson, 'Titus: Epistle of Religious Revitalization', *Biblical Theology Bulletin: A Journal of Bible and Theology* 30, no. 4 (2000), 145–57.
178 2 Cor. 5:17.
179 Tonning, *Modernism and Christianity*, 58, *author's emphasis*.

4

'Why We Hate the Gestapo': Liberalism, Totalitarianism and the Third Way

Introduction

> The immense danger in which we stand is that the fact that what the nation is fighting is something utterly inhuman and evil may make us forget that anti-Christ is not only incarnated in the Nazi leaders, but is an active and present force among ourselves and in our own hearts. Only the strongest spiritual effort can save us from becoming assimilated into what we oppose.[1]

The forces set in motion during the interwar decades were for the Moot, here via Oldham, not merely engulfing the foreign enemy but deeply intertwined with the processes of modernity, and they were therefore a threat to Britain from within. The period was defined by a political turmoil resulting in the rise of totalitarian regimes across Europe. On the one hand, the dominant political system of their age – liberal democracy – seemed ineffectual in addressing pressing issues, whereas, on the other hand, the emerging alternatives were creating structures that were gravely impeding on human liberty. It comes as no surprise that this issue occupied a central place in the discussions of the sociopolitically minded Moot. In fact, the explicitly stated motivation for the Moot was to combat totalitarianism, especially in its modern forms of fascism and communism. In a letter to his friend, Louis Wirth, in August 1938, Mannheim expressed his hopes that the Moot would form the nucleus of a democratic renaissance to combat fascism.[2] At the 14th meeting, Oldham reminded the Moot that its aim was not a Christian society *per se*, but to combat totalitarianism by offering an alternative,

---

During the 9th meeting Oldham discussed the content of a 'statement of purpose and convictions' for a national movement. The opening section should, Oldham suggested, be titled 'why we hate the Gestapo'. No further detail is given; see Clements, *Moot Papers*, 337 (9th meeting, 14–17 July 1940).

a Third Way.³ Similarly, in a postscript for the 17th meeting, Hodges identified 'freedom and totalitarianism' as their principal lines of investigation.⁴

Given the centrality of totalitarianism in the Moot discourse, it is noteworthy that little direct attention has been given to the theme in the secondary literature to date. The closest we get to any substantive reflection is Michael Lackey's brief notes in his review of Keith Clements' publication *The Moot Papers*. Here, Lackey objects that Clements' editing and annotating 'misrepresent' and ignore the more worrying implications of the Moot's deliberations of a Christian totalitarianism and the legitimization of 'the use of coercion or force in the re-Christianization of society'.⁵ Lackey develops this argument in the more recent volume *The Modernist God State*, where he summons the Moot as exemplifying an 'in-depth Christianization'. Lackey borrows the concept from Michel Foucault, arguing that as modernity saw a greater separation between church and state, Christian leaders during the first half of the twentieth century adopted new strategies coercing Western societies into a subconscious Christianization.⁶ There are further studies on the emerging transatlantic ecumenical networks that implicate the Moot. In Graeme Smith's analysis of the 1937 Oxford conference, Oldham, as the prime mover, is represented as steering the conference towards the mirror image of what it sought to overcome, namely, a 'Christian Totalitarianism'.⁷ Another example is Mark T. Edwards' study on 'God's Totalitarianism' – equated with the North American Protestant left and the transatlantic ecumenical alliance – which pulls Oldham and the Moot indirectly into its investigative orbit.⁸ These perspectives, either directly or by implication, suggest that although the Moot understood itself as constituting a counter-totalitarian force, in fact it was little more than a Christian equivalent, or a competing totalizing hegemony. A thorough study of totalitarianism and the Moot will thus examine these claims.

In addition to addressing the positions taken within the secondary literature, 'totalitarianism and the Moot' is a highly relevant topic for my theoretical framing of the Moot as politically 'Modernist'. Scholars have extensively studied the affinity between Modernist writers and radical politics. In an age of societal turmoil, Raymond Williams suggests that Modernists' options were either a withdrawal from society into a 'sacred realm' of art or towards 'revolutionary doctrine' and the usage of 'art as the liberating vanguard'.⁹ Those opting for the latter either joined the socialist revolution or sympathized with fascism.¹⁰ Frank Kermode suggests that the affinity between Modernist art and literature and fascism is not incidental, as both accentuate order.¹¹ For Kermode, Eliot's 'persistent nostalgia for closed, immobile hierarchical societies' epitomizes

Modernist authoritarianism.[12] Michael North sees a corresponding antipathy towards liberal democracy in the 'aesthetic Modernism' and the reactionary 'political aesthetics' of Yeats, Eliot and Pound.[13] Another example can be found in Charles Ferrall's *Modernist Writing and Reactionary Politics*, where he notes that the 'reactionary Modernists' 'combined a radical aesthetic modernity with an almost outright rejection of even the emancipatory aspects of bourgeois modernity'.[14] The attraction of right-wing ideology, Ferrall explains, was due to a shared hostility towards modernity.[15] Similarly, in a more recent contribution, Leon Surette suggests that the political views of Pound, Wyndham Lewis and Eliot can be understood in the light of their distaste for mass society and capitalism. In this context, Surette writes, 'the only alternative to rule by a secret oligarchy was either monarchy or tyranny'.[16] The association of Eliot with the far-right circles in these writings is naturally of particular interest for my topic and will be commented upon below.[17]

There has also been a substantial scholarly interest in left-wing politics amongst Modernist writers in the interwar period. Communism offered an alternative solution to the interwar decadence for those to whom fascism appeared abhorrent. In Valentine Cunningham's narration of the 'thirties generation' (including C. Day Lewis, W. H. Auden, Stephen Spender, Christopher Caudwell and others), the pull towards the left is ascribed to communism's promise of comradeship and community in the face of modernity's individualism and disintegration.[18] Samuel Hynes' *The Auden Generation* revolves around a generation of young writers and their pull towards political engagement on the political left. In a time of societal crisis and the formulations of rivalling creeds, these authors, suggests Hynes, struggled to come to terms with the political role of the artist.[19]

Moving away from individual Modernist writers to so-called Political Modernist movements, we even here find a strong affinity to totalitarianism. For Griffin, fascism can 'be seen as a form of *political modernism* seeking to establish an alternative modernity within a new temporality'.[20] Given my Modernist reading, this suggested correlation further calls for a comparative investigation of the Moot *vis-à-vis* the radical political ideologies of their era. All in all, a discussion about the Moot's relation to totalitarianism is pivotal to understanding their agenda. It provides, further, an opportunity to put the Moot on the political map and examine how they sought to engage with such issues in a decade of much political controversy. This chapter, then, seeks to establish how the Moot can be positioned in the context of collapsing political structures and the emergence of new ones.

The Church, Community and State conference, and Christian totalitarianism

Throughout the 1930s, the Moot members sought to be engaged extensively with the changing political climate and the rise of the totalitarian state. It is possible to detect two emphases in these investigations. In *Man and Society in an Age of Reconstruction,* originally published in German in 1935, Mannheim demonstrated the causal relation between industrial liberal societies and their propensity to totalitarianism. Arguments about the correlation between centralization, planning and totalitarianism were central to his sociological approach. They will be discussed in further detail below.

Dawson represents the other strand, emphasizing ideological and quasi-religious features of totalitarian regimes. The most expansive treatise on the modern state *vis-à-vis* the church can be found in *Religion and the Modern State* published in 1935. Here, Dawson argued that modern states – whether communist, fascist or *liberal democratic* – were subject to the same processes, leading to 'the mechanization of human life and the complete subordination of the individual to the state and the economic process'.[21] For Christians, the trend towards the totalitarian state was problematic, according to Dawson, for such political systems claim for themselves the totality of the person and profess human ends in mere political and economic terms rather than spiritual.[22] As such, the totalitarian state had come to occupy the spiritual sphere previously occupied by the church.[23] His writings had a profound impact upon the 1937 Oxford Conference as well as Oldham and Eliot, and thereupon the Moot.[24]

Dawson was not alone in portraying the totalitarian regimes in spiritual terms. More recently, Emilio Gentile has theorized the quasi-religious nature of the modern state, making a strong argument that modernity yielded a sacralization of politics in its drive to seize the role played by traditional religion in previous centuries. The totalitarian regimes of the 1930s constitute prime examples of what he calls 'political religions'.[25] His contention that totalitarian regimes can be understood in religious terms rests partly upon evidence that commentators during this period understood these political regimes as such.[26] Gentile cites several figures related to the Moot, including Oldham, Maritain, Niebuhr and Dawson, in support of his argument. He concludes that for these Christian thinkers, the political religions were threatening precisely because of their inherent anti-Christian essence and the fact that the totalitarian 'state that wished to control all aspects of human life' would unavoidably lead to a conflictual relation to the church.[27]

These issues, as Gentile observes, were central to the Oldham-led 1937 Oxford conference on 'Church, Community and State'. Witnessing the increasing omnipotence of the modern state, Oldham – along with other leaders in the ecumenical networks – felt a pressing need to address the issue from a Christian perspective. Gathering 400 delegates from various parts of the world, the conference unanimously declared that totalitarianism was a threat to Christianity and civilization. The 'Longer Report on the Church and State' clearly reflects the 'sacralization of politics' that Gentile identifies. The report speaks of the 'birth-pangs of new forms of human behaviour and community life' in the wake of the disintegration of modern society as a result of industrialization, urbanization, the 'mechanisation of life' and secularization.[28] In a bid to replace the unifying qualities of traditional religion and to fill the spiritual vacuum, '[m]en are following social and political symbols with religious fervour'[29] and the increasingly powerful modern state 'is given religious meaning'.[30] A statement from the conference contains a robust warning that any 'deification of nation, race, or class, or of political or cultural ideals, is idolatry, and can only lead to increasing division and disaster'.[31]

For the Moot, the 1937 conference was particularly significant. Not only did a number of founding members attend (Moberly, Farmer, Fenn, Baillie, Eliot, Iredale and Oldham),[32] but also the group was formed as a practical response to its conclusions and can thus be seen as carrying forth its central line of investigation. That is also why Graeme Smith's analysis of the conference has a bearing on an analysis of the Moot's stance on totalitarianism. Smith's main thesis is that as a consequence of an 'inculturation' – a missiological term used to denote the process of assimilation of cultural practices and beliefs with the Christian faith – the conference resulted in the endorsement of 'elements of contemporary totalitarian regime[s]'.[33] Smith claims that Oldham did not reject the 'structure' of the totalitarian state as such but merely the heretical religious claims made by the secular totalitarian ideologies at the time. In fact, Smith argues that for Oldham, 'the churches, but only the churches, should be totalitarian in structure'.[34]

Smith's argument is problematic on a number of accounts. Firstly, while the report under the section 'Church and the Community' chaired by Moberly does speak of the 'true totalitarianism of Christ',[35] this does not entail a vision of a Christian state but is rather a claim concerning the ultimate sovereignty of God and the call to the individual to obey him. This call to voluntary submission is not a submission to the church or any other human institution, but to God himself. Conversely, in scholarly terms, the modern political phenomenon of state-party totalitarianism implies the coercive submission to a state apparatus. Secondly, in Oldham's understanding, the invasion of political (state) into spiritual (church) is a central tenet of totalitarianism. Yet nowhere do we find the argument for the reverse, namely, that the church should subsume the function of the state. Oldham argued for a close relationship between church and state, but nevertheless with a clear demarcation affording a level of freedom for each institution to act in its own sphere of influence. It is only thus that the church could act as a bulwark against an encroaching, omnipotent state.[36] It is therefore unclear in what sense Oldham adhered to a Christian totalitarianism in 'structure'. Thirdly, as seen in Dawson's analysis of totalitarianism, the sacralization of politics threatened the distinction between church and state. Such a deification of the immanent entities of state, race, nation and class was in Christian terms understood as idolatry. Thus, Christian totalitarianism would from this point of view have been a contradiction in terms. Finally, being supportive of authoritarian measures in times of crisis, as Oldham clearly was,[37] does not inherently suggest support for totalitarian forms of governance. Historically, democratically elected governments have taken authoritarian measures in times of crisis, such as Churchill's wartime government. Furthermore, as Hannah Arendt points out, a regime can be authoritarian without being totalitarian.[38]

It is, then, debatable whether the conference advanced a Christian version of totalitarianism. Smith's arguments are conceptually weak and largely unsupported, and to speak of a 'Christian totalitarianism' is to confuse the discussion. A more fruitful interpretive lens for Oldham and this ecumenical gathering than that offered by Smith's 'missiological' lens is that of Political Modernism that I advance in this book. As we shall see, it allows for a clearer appreciation of the overlap and divergences between the totalitarian regimes and the ecumenical movement's sociopolitical pronouncements.

The Moot on liberalism and democracy

A good starting point for this comparative perspective is to investigate how the Moot and its members engaged with the 'defunct' sociopolitical paradigm of their day. Like many of their contemporaries, the Moot members were dismayed at the political inadequacy of an ineffectual liberal democracy and the philosophical assumptions of its guiding principles. Scepticism towards liberal democracy and liberalism was not limited to radicals, whether on the extreme left or right. It was a widely shared assumption amongst British intelligentsia that liberalism could not remain the dominant paradigm if Western civilization was to survive.[39] W. H. Auden's oft-cited statement regarding his age's predicament, written at the end of the 1930s, might well have been uttered at the Moot:

> The most obvious social fact of the last forty years is the failure of liberal capitalist democracy, based on the premises that every individual is born free and equal, each an absolute entity independent of all others; and that a formal political equality, the right to vote, the right to a fair trial, the right of free speech, is enough to guarantee his freedom of action in his relation with his fellow men. The results are only too familiar to us all. By denying the social nature of personality, and by ignoring the social power of money, it has created the most impersonal, the most mechanical and the most unequal civilisation the world has ever seen, a civilisation in which the only emotion common to all classes is a feeling of individual isolation from everyone else, a civilisation torn apart by the opposing emotions born of economic injustice, the just envy of the poor and the selfish terror of the rich.[40]

Throughout the Moot's conversations, Nazism and other totalitarian regimes were repeatedly singled out as an enemy to overcome. However, its members shared with these regimes and many of their contemporaries an assumption that 'liberalism' had run its course, impelling them to design viable alternatives.

Liberal democracy and discontentment

Certainly, the archival material bears witness to an ambivalence towards liberal democracy. The recorded minutes from the 4th, 9th and 14th meetings are particularly revealing in terms of the Moot's discussion on the nature of democracy.[41] The Moot understood liberal democracy to be in a state of crisis and there was a lingering scepticism of democratic parliamentarianism. This suspicion can arguably be understood in the light of a tradition of anti-parliamentarianism within the British intelligentsia during the first decades of the twentieth century. Tom Villis, who reconstructs this narrative through analysing the networks that emerged around two right-wing journals, *Eye-Witness/New Witness* and *New Age,* writes that in these circles parliament was understood as 'a sham show put on to mislead the people while real power was manipulated behind the scenes'.[42] True power in democratic societies was in the hands of a powerful capitalistic oligarchy. A residue of this antipathy towards liberal democracy was evident in some quarters of the Moot. The suspicion of democracy being an oligarchic front is evident in Eliot's writings from the interwar period. In a commentary for the *Criterion* in 1937, he suggested that democracy is a term 'used by people whose activities are really directed towards one kind of oligarchy or another'.[43] In *The Idea*, Eliot claimed that 'the defenders of the totalitarian system' rightly accuse the democratic nations, that is, Britain and the United States, of being run by 'financial oligarchy' rather than true democratic governments.[44] This viewpoint was endorsed by Mannheim, who at the 4th meeting argued that democracy had become a term largely synonymous with oligarchy.[45] At the same meeting, Oldham critiqued 'English society in its current pluto-democratic form'.[46] In an article originally appearing in German in 1933, Mannheim drew similar conclusions on the tendencies towards oligarchy in democratic political systems. Furthermore, citing Carl Schmitt, Mannheim pointed in this article to the dysfunctionality of parliamentarianism in its struggle to reach consensus for decision-making.[47] Dawson echoed this sentiment predicting a collapse of English parliamentarianism due to its proneness to indecision in times of crisis. It was subject to an electorate with 'a floating mass of opinion that has no absolute convictions'.[48] Liberal democracy, Dawson continued, lacked the vitalism to arouse the interest of the population, crippled leadership through its high levels of bureaucracy and had no social philosophy that could give the people a vision in which to believe.[49]

Thus, like many of their contemporaries, the Moot's misgivings about liberal democracy were furthered by their disdain for the perceived herd mentality of mass society.[50] For Mannheim, modern democracy had become a mere manipulation of the masses.[51] In his definition, democracy did not mean 'everybody deciding about everything',[52] to which Baillie concurred that 'we did not mean by "democracy" government by mass'.[53] The Moot's apprehension towards liberal democracy, then, was due to the perception that it was a mere masquerade shoring up elite interests, and that it was liable to instability, manipulation and injustice.

Definitions of democracy

As seen in the minutes of the 4th meeting, there was some hesitancy as to whether democracy, as a term, was worth defending. Eliot had elsewhere expressed scepticism of its usage: 'If anybody ever attacked democracy, I might discover what the word meant'.[54] At the Moot, Eliot requested that Mannheim defined democracy, warning that 'there was a danger of a sentimental and unexamined attachment to the term'.[55] For his part, Oldham felt that the term was too emotionally charged and therefore not worth retaining.[56]

Indeed, the definition of and meaning given to democracy was far from uniform. For the most part its definition was assumed, but an interesting discussion arose at the 14th meeting in March 1942. Mannheim here defined democracy as 'the co-operative of production and control rather than mere voting power'.[57] In response, Moberly insisted that democracy in its modern-day incarnation necessarily entailed representative government. Vidler, in turn, maintained that the key element of democracy was universal suffrage.[58] In the context of this discussion, Oldham proceeded to define democratic society according to the following characteristics: a society which enables human encounters and settles differences through discussion, distribution of power, checks and balances, and the council of the wisest (an elite).[59] An apparent omission is universal suffrage. At a later meeting Mannheim appears to be endorsing a more 'liberal' conception of democracy as 'the idea of government of the people by the people' and expressed the hope that the transformation of British society into a planned democracy could be undertaken by 'parliamentarian methods' rather than through violent revolution.[60]

The renewal of democracy

Despite these perceived weaknesses and ambiguities, the prevalent stance favoured a purging of its shortcomings rather than abandonment altogether. Prior to the war, Moberly expressed what many Britons felt at that time, namely, that 'democracy' and 'freedom' defined that which differentiated British society from the totalitarian and a unifying cause: '[if] there were war tomorrow we should feel that we were fighting for some kind of individual freedom and some kind of decency'.[61] During a meeting in July 1940, at one of the bleakest points of the war, a discussion unfolded over what practical resistance could be offered by the Moot. Clarke suggested that a regeneration of British democracy was the key to any such resistance, to which Oldham concurred that '[w]e want faith for democracy'.[62] Others suggested any such renewal was dependent upon maintaining freedom of expression, a liberty that was under threat due to wartime censorship.[63]

Discussions on democracy can be found elsewhere in the writings of the Moot members. In an article for the *Adelphi* just before the outbreak of the war, Murry contrasted democratic systems' moral superiority with repressive fascist totalitarianism. While admitting to the weakness of indecision in democratic systems, their 'core rightness' was still worth defending, not least since, 'they are incapable of the hideous persecution of Jews which is now raging in Germany'.[64]

In the following issue of the *Adelphi*, Murry identified a Christian ideal of the individual's worth as the 'vital principle of democracy'.[65] Democracy is a central focus in two of Murry's books published in the early years of the war. In *A Defence of Democracy* Murry declared his 'belief in democracy' as the 'noblest form of society'.[66] Yet he rejected democracy's 'natural bias' towards capitalistic competition, which whet the 'appetites of the animal man'.[67] His solution to this weakness was 'a new social discipline', by which citizens voluntarily accepted social responsibility,[68] and a restructuring of society into a federation of small communities.[69] Such a sentiment was shared by Dawson. While he repeatedly lambasted the weaknesses of liberal democracy, Dawson nevertheless defended British parliamentarianism, declaring it non-totalitarian by nature. Its survival, however, depended on the renewal of 'the life of the nation' and a 'democratic organisation of culture'.[70] Clearly the idea of democracy suggested for the Moot members a resistance to totalitarianism.

Mannheim's militant democracy

Mannheim's views on democracy demand closer attention. Citing private letters to Löwe and Tillich, Colin Loader describes how Mannheim renewed his faith in democracy upon experiencing parliamentarianism in England as an émigré.[71] In his Moot paper 'Planning for Freedom', Mannheim acknowledged that despite its weaknesses, there was much to celebrate in the advances made by democracy, and 'unbridled criticism of the form of freedom and democracy which has existed in past decades must therefore cease'.[72] For Mannheim, democracy entailed consensus-building around central societal issues, democratic control of the use of new social control techniques, the pursuit of the greatest possible individual freedom and a commitment to social justice.[73] Furthermore, Mannheim felt it necessary to address the 'neutrality' of liberal democracy through a conscious defence of its central values. 'Our democracy is like a sleeping beauty, sleeping and sleepy', he lamented at the 14th meeting.[74] By way of solution, Mannheim proposed a 'militant democracy', which entailed an enforced basic conformity. In his earliest Moot paper, he maintained that on the issue of basic values 'we could be as militant as the totalitarian states … for it is surely a misinterpretation of democracy to believe that one must tolerate the intolerant'.[75] In his position paper 'Problem of Youth in Modern Society', Mannheim stipulated that the vigorous defence of core values ought be balanced with the provision of the greatest possible individual freedom.[76] Beyond this, Mannheim sought to maintain liberalism's spirit of plurality, leaving the 'more complicated values open to creed, individual choice or free experimentation'.[77] On the surface, Mannheim's militant democracy comes troublingly close to Benito Mussolini's definition of fascist corporatism 'as an organised, centralised authoritarian democracy'.[78] However, in contradistinction to Mussolini's authoritarianism – which is 'definitely and absolutely opposed to the doctrines of liberalism'[79] – Mannheim wished to maintain the primacy of freedom. The following quotation from Mannheim's 'Towards a New Social Philosophy' summarizes his conception of militant democracy:

> [We] can learn from Liberalism that the highest forms of spiritual life flourish best in Freedom. To put it quite briefly, we must establish a set of basic virtues such as decency, mutual help, honesty and social justice, which can be brought home through education and social influence, whereas the higher forms of thought, art, literature, etc., remain as free as they were in the philosophy of Liberalism. It must be one of our main concerns to establish the list of those primary virtues without which no civilization can exist, and which make for that basic conformity which gives stability and soundness to social life.[80]

Despite advocating for this militant defence of core values, Mannheim ascribed no absolutism to values as such. The core values governing Western societies ought to be agreed upon through ongoing democratic processes of collective deliberation and consensus-building. At a later meeting (14th meeting, March 1942), Mannheim argued that this relativistic notion of values defined 'the essential difference between us and the totalitarians'.[81]

Liberal values

It is important to note that the widespread antipathy towards liberalism within the group does not necessarily equate to a rejection of liberal values. Mannheim, for example, wrote in *Man and Society* that 'from the wreckage of Liberalism nothing can be saved but its values'.[82] For the Moot, liberalism conveyed quite the opposite, namely, a neutrality towards values and an extreme form of individualism, which undermines the possibility of a common *Weltanschauung*. Under conditions of pluralism, all talk of values becomes obscure, for values demand some form of collective agreement. Neither did the Moot's critique of totalitarian regimes as political religions that threaten Christianity and the church imply that the encroachment of individual liberty by totalitarianism was simply a subordinate concern. The Moot, by and large, equated 'liberal values' and the possibility of maintaining them with Christianity itself.[83] Thus, the threat that totalitarian regimes posed to Christianity was also a threat to these values. In fact, 'liberal values' were repeatedly defended throughout the Moot papers.

A good instance is offered by the discussion of V. A. Demant's critique of H. G. Wells' *The Rights of Man* during the 7th meeting of the Moot. Wells wrote his declaration at the outbreak of the war in order to encourage the British government to give the people 'War Aims': something worth fighting for.[84] Demant's critique does not reject the values proposed in the declaration of rights *per se*, but rather questions whether modern society possesses the cultural conditions for such rights to function in any meaningful way. Rather than safeguarding individuals' rights through a supranational policing agency, as Wells suggested, Demant favoured a more decentralized, organic and pluralistic society, one where religion serves to foster a certain mentality that is able to resist the mechanization of society.[85] The Moot agreed with Demant's assertion that the effectiveness of a declaration of universal rights is dependent on a certain type of society, yet there was disagreement over the nature of such a society.[86]

A further example of the Moot's fundamental defence of liberal values can be illustrated by George Vickers' interjection at the following meeting, where he challenged members to take equality as the starting point for their social philosophy: '[t]he richness and uniqueness of individual diversities is perhaps the central liberal value which we want to carry over into the new age'.[87] The staunchest defence of parliamentarianism and fundamental liberal principles found in the Moot material was offered by Hector Hetherington in his paper circulated for the meeting in September 1942. He suggested that at the end of the liberal era and at the cusp of the planned society of tomorrow, it was possible to safeguard some of the liberties hitherto enjoyed. This by the absolute protection of the individual against 'direct action of the state' and by maintaining the freedom of worship; freedom of assembly, speech and press; freedom to education; freedom to choose vocation; and finally, through a responsible government which could be dismissed by a parliament.[88] In a similar vein, Mannheim's 'militant democracy' was a defence of 'core values'. While elsewhere admitting to the 'difficulties in defining basic virtues',[89] in 'Diagnosis of Our Time', Mannheim nevertheless listed 'brotherly love, mutual help, decency, social justice, freedom, respect for the person'.[90] These values derived, according to Mannheim, from the humanistic and Christian traditions. A final example can be found in the draft of Oldham's penultimate declaration, 'The Christian Witness in the Present Crisis'. The declaration includes a statement on 'essential rights' for all citizens of industrial societies. These rights include (1) 'economic security', (2) 'status' denoting a sense of belonging, (3) 'function' meaning job satisfaction and (4) 'freedom'. However, Oldham noted his hesitancy over including the last of these, for the term 'freedom' created 'a host of problems, without any contribution to their problem'.[91]

On the nature of freedom

It is thus important to note that the Moot did not support what they took to be liberalism's conception of freedom. As Graeme Smith rightly points out, Oldham rejected the Enlightenment conception of the autonomous individual.[92] Freedom in this liberal sense was taken to refer to the unbounded individual able to exercise his or her will. However, drawing upon Eberhard Grisebach, Oldham held that this humanistic freedom is fictive, for in meeting with the otherness of another person, we come up against the will of the other, which inevitably limits ours.[93] Oldham further discarded the humanistic conception of liberty as it 'is fundamentally individualistic and cannot create community'.[94]

In contrast to liberalism's negative notion of freedom as freedom from all constraints, Oldham held a positive understanding of freedom. That is, for Oldham, freedom is a freedom to fulfil one's human nature and towards human flourishing. It assumes relationality, responsibility and therefore a code of morality. This particular affirmation of freedom is rooted in a doctrine of creation, holding that humans are created with the freedom to live in responsible relationship with God, creation and fellow human beings. Thus, Oldham saw liberty as safeguarded by the worth bestowed upon humans in their status as sons and daughters of God, but it is a freedom that is directed towards building human relationships and community. This was a repeated theme in Oldham's writings as an ideological point of resistance to totalitarianism.[95] In his memorandum 'A Reborn Christendom', Oldham argued that only a new anthropology of man as free and responsible before God held the power to resist the totalitarian spirit engulfing their world.[96] Hodges endorsed a similar line of argument, suggesting that unlimited freedom had to be measured by responsibility. Hodges noted that not all 'individuals or groups' possess the maturity to handle such freedom. Therefore, he posited restraint on unbridled freedom to mitigate abuses and for further state education of citizens 'towards freedom'.[97]

Dawson's notion of human freedom, however, diverged from the above. He held that a distinction between 'spiritual freedom' and 'political and economic liberty' must be drawn.⁹⁸ In the face of the threat of totalitarianism, Dawson argued that since there is nothing inherently Christian about parliamentary democracy and economic liberalism, it is merely 'spiritual freedom that the church is called to defend'.⁹⁹ This implied that spiritual freedom could be retained even under conditions of political and economic repression. For this reason, Dawson's opposition to totalitarianism was on religious grounds.

None of the Moot members used the term freedom more keenly than Mannheim. While his understanding of freedom is less pronounced than that of Oldham and Dawson, he associated freedom with Enlightenment conceptions concerning individual choice, freedom to experiment, freedom of opinion and conscience, and self-determination.¹⁰⁰ As with Oldham, Mannheim emphasized that individual liberties needed to be balanced with social responsibility.¹⁰¹ However, whereas Oldham held that freedom itself is found in communion between persons, Mannheim's approach was more functional. That is, a democratic society required individuals to take responsibility and conform to the collective. However, rather than being an aspect of freedom itself, this was, according to Mannheim, a necessary delimitation of freedom.

Summary

If one takes a contemporary view of the Moot members, for instance via Joseph A. Schumpeter's classic definition of democracy – 'that institutional arrangement for arriving at political decisions ... by making the people itself decide issues through the election of individuals who are to assemble in order to carry out its will'¹⁰² – the Moot was largely undemocratic. Yet, despite the belief that liberal democracy – not least with universal suffrage – had some inherent weaknesses, for the Moot, when associated with open deliberation, consensus-building and the protection of individual liberties, democracy was worth fighting for.

Furthermore, the critique of liberalism does not assume a rejection of liberal values. Summarizing Mannheim's thought, Oldham wrote in an article for the *CNL* that the survival of democracy in the fight against totalitarianism depended on a conformity to 'essential values'. This 'implies a definite break with the liberal conception of the tolerance of all ideas as having equal authority'.¹⁰³ Oldham and the Moot, *contra* Smith,¹⁰⁴ did not reject modernity for its values of individual freedom and rights of man, but because the *laissez faire* of liberal practice undermined the possibility of maintaining such corporate values, thereby making society vulnerable to competing alternatives such as totalitarianism.

Engaging with the political alternatives

Right-wing allegiances

Given that fascism and communism were also responses to the perceived collapse of liberalism, a reasonable line of enquiry is how the Moot engaged with these dominant alternatives. The radical ideas associated with the totalitarian political movements of this age were after all endorsed in some Christian quarters and to some extent even by individual Moot members. Paul Jackson has collated a valuable survey of the clergy and Christian intellectuals who were sympathetic to British fascism during the interwar period. He suggests that a theme amongst this group of Christians was the romanticizing of medieval Christendom, an ideal that provided this movement with a counter-narrative to degenerate liberal modern values.[105] As we have seen, this theme was also clearly present in the Moot discourse. Another volume addressing similar themes is Tom Villis' *British Catholics and Fascism*, which focuses upon British Catholics' often-ambiguous stance towards fascism. Although the Moot was overwhelmingly Protestant, Villis' narrative is relevant given his discussion of Christopher Dawson.

In many ways, Dawson epitomizes Villis' portrayal of Catholic attraction to fascism at the time. On the one hand, Dawson held much in common with interwar fascist movements: ideals of hierarchy and authority; an antipathy towards liberalism, capitalism and communism; and the critique of an overweening materialism in the modern age. On the other hand, he felt an antipathy towards the violence and totalitarianism of fascism. Villis concludes that '[w]hile Dawson did not sympathise with fascism, he *empathised* with it'.[106] To be sure, attending only three meetings and commenting on a handful of position papers, Dawson's participation in the Moot was limited. In correspondence with his friend George Every, Dawson expressed his own concern with the Moot, rejecting its ideas of politics and religion.[107] Yet, his influence as a historian is nevertheless evidenced in several members' thinking. As noted above, both Oldham and Eliot drew extensively on Dawson's critique of liberal society and its supposed inclination towards totalitarianism. There was also an affinity between Sword of the Spirit movement, which Dawson endorsed, and the proposed Order the Moot.[108]

Eliot is another Moot member who has been scrutinized for his right-wing tendencies. Much has been made of young Eliot's attraction to radical right-wing ideas, not least to Charles Maurras' Action Française. Whether Maurras' movement should be labelled 'fascist', 'proto-fascist' or simply 'right-wing populist' is contentious. Nevertheless, the political group advocated hierarchy, order, nationalism, the restoration of the monarchy (authoritarian rule) and paramilitarism: all recognizable far-right traits.[109] Maurras was, in addition, an unapologetic anti-Semite. What is striking about Eliot's relation to Action Française and Maurras is that he never appears to totally sever the link. Leon Surette argues that Eliot, who continued his endorsement of Maurras into the 1950s, should be understood as 'reactionary' rather than 'fascist'.[110] An ambivalence towards Maurras is clearly discernible in Eliot's editorial for the *CNL* in August 1940. Discussing the reactionary elements of French Catholicism, Eliot described Maurras as a 'man of powerful but narrow mind' whose ideas on the Catholic hierarchy had been misunderstood.[111] Eliot's apparent refusal to publicly repudiate his allegiance with Action Française can be compared with another Moot associate, Jacques Maritain. In the years after the Great War, as the columnist for the *Revue Universelle* – the mouthpiece for the Catholic wing of the movement – Maritain became one of the central philosophers of Action Française.[112] After the papal condemnation in 1926, he publicly renounced the movement, and during the 1940s, Maritain established himself as a human rights advocate.[113] One commentator notes that this past association with the patently anti-Semitic Maurras 'proved a great source of embarrassment to [Jacques and Raïssa Maritain] later'.[114]

Eliot's own anti-Semitic remarks in poetry and prose have also been fiercely debated. Allegations have in recent decades been refuelled by Anthony Julius' thesis *T. S. Eliot, Anti-Semitism, and Literary Form*.[115] In response, several scholars have rallied to Eliot's defence. Ronald Schuchard, for example, has argued that Eliot's derogative descriptions of Jews should be understood in the light of religion and not race.[116] Eliot himself refuted the charge of anti-Semitism in several personal correspondences. For example, in May 1940, J. V. Healy questioned Eliot over his controversial sentence 'make any large number of free-thinking of Jews undesirable' in *After Strange Gods*. Eliot replied that Jew could be replaced with any other free-thinking person.[117] Furthermore, Eliot did condemn the violent persecution of Jews under the Vichy government, calling 'French ecclesiastical authorities' to 'protest against such injustices'.[118]

While it is true that Eliot's sociopolitical outlook was 'right-wing' or 'conservative', that he was sceptical towards liberal democracy, that he gave his friend Ezra Pound a platform to publish in *The Criterion* and so forth, it is clear that Eliot distanced himself from fascism. In a brief letter for the *NEW*, Eliot pointed out that many Christians opposed communism purely on the basis of the repression of the church in Bolshevik Russia, but have failed to respond to the 'puerile' and 'anathema' of Oswald Mosley's fascism.[119] Another example can be seen in a BBC broadcast in 1937, 'The Church's Message to the World', where Eliot denounced the ideologies of both fascism and communism as 'incompatible with Christianity'.[120] Furthermore, in *The Idea*, he labels fascism 'pagan', which in Eliot's terms is a strong condemnation.[121]

Eliot was not primarily interested in political theory or structures, not because these were unimportant to him, but because the cultural and religious ideals of a society mattered more. Religion is what makes culture flourish, and culture is the stuff of politics. In other words, religion is a prerequisite for politics. Eliot was one of the few writers to have abstained from taking sides in the questionnaire that the *Left Review* sent to writers to gauge their stances on the Spanish Civil War in 1937. Eliot claimed that it was the duty of 'at least a few men of letters' to 'remain isolated'.[122] Thus, while this neutrality could be interpreted as a refusal to condemn fascism, Eliot's motivation was to maintain a critical distance from day-to-day politics.

Furthermore, Eliot's sociopolitical view differed in several fundamental ways from the fascist movements across Europe. Firstly, he never condoned the oppression or violence of the fascist regimes. Secondly, while Eliot was a monarchist, this cannot be equated with an endorsement of the charismatic leadership of the totalitarian regimes. In fact, Eliot viewed the monarchy as one of several centres of power that provided checks and balances on power.[123] Thirdly, Surette's claim that Eliot was attracted to Muarras' ideas of centralization and totalitarianism is mistaken.[124] This is patent in his rejection of Mannheim's drive towards a planned society.[125] Finally, as Stefan Collini suggests, Eliot's later social criticism bears greater resemblance to the Anglican radical socialism, such as the Christendom Group, than the reactionary Action Française.[126]

Admiration for totalitarian regimes

It is difficult to gauge the extent to which Eliot's right-wing tendencies influenced the direction of discussions at the Moot. Concern over the injustices of capitalism, scepticism of liberal democracy and calls for order were widespread at the time and not merely prevalent among 'the radicals'. Furthermore, the success of Hitler's ascent to power and the efficiency with which he implemented his political agenda were widely admired, and this admiration, however fervently Nazism was rejected, was clearly evident in numerous pages of the Moot meeting minutes. For example, during the 1st meeting, H. H. Farmer, a theologian at Westminster College, Cambridge, suggested that there were lessons to be drawn from the success of the Nazi party's route from a 'position of minority to dominance'. Farmer attributed this success firstly to the Nazi social philosophy and its ability to provide a transcendent vision yet address immediate issues, and secondly to the sense of community that they had created and their educational efforts to see their ideas widely spread.[127]

Mannheim had no qualms about adopting aspects of 'all existing social experiments' from capitalism to communism and fascism.[128] While presenting a programme of practical steps for implementing his 'Planning for Freedom', Mannheim suggested 'the development of a new technique of penetration into society and the soul of man. This would need to be a carefully considered technique of propaganda.'[129] The invention of social techniques – including weapons, education, mass media, modern psychology and sociology – was a central feature of the rise of totalitarianism in Mannheim's diagnosis. Fearing the herd mentality of the masses, he felt that propaganda and the use of social techniques were legitimate as long as they were used to galvanize basic democratic values, that is, values which themselves were the result of a consensus-building and public deliberation.[130] Another example of Mannheim's admiration for Nazi techniques of propaganda is his suggestion during the 11th meeting to emulate Hitler's youth movement. Education was the main channel by which Britain could be re-Christianized, and Mannheim wished to set up a youth movement, reminiscent of the 'Hitlerjugend', that would form the moral character and democratic personality of future generations.[131]

It is clear enough that Oldham's inappropriate wish to create a manifesto analogous to *Mein Kampf* does not represent an endorsement of the Führer's politics, but is rather further evidence of a fascination with his success. Oldham's esteem for Hitler's capacity to move the masses was by no means unique. Examples of such admiration for the efficiency of the totalitarian regimes abounded amongst intellectuals at the time. During the war, Fredrick Hayek, a champion of liberalism, wrote despairingly that 'there is scarcely a leaf out of Hitler's book [*Mein Kampf*] which somebody or other in this country has not recommended us to take and use for our own purposes'.[132] An example can be found in an unpublished essay dated 11 May 1939 by Catholic poet David Jones who praised Hitler for seeking to resolutely address 'capitalist exploitation and money power'. Jones appears to have justified the brutality of the regimes to achieve their goals, as such acts are:

> the price paid for daring to deal arbitrarily, physically and directly with some of those very problems ... [Fascism and Nazism] represent, for all their alarming characteristics, an heroic attempt to cope with certain admitted corruptions in our civilization.[133]

In the context of the sociopolitical upheaval of the 1930s, fascism and communism appeared to some as viable solutions for the underlying problems of capitalistic, democratic and liberal societies. Surrette argues that with this background in mind, we can be more forgiving of the intellectuals who in some sense gravitated towards far-right ideas.[134]

If the British intelligentsia expressed admiration for Hitler's and Mussolini's regimes, this is true to an even greater extent for Stalin's USSR. The willingness of the reformist social democratic left to turn a blind eye to the repression in the Soviet is staggering. A prime example can be found in leading socialist figures Beatrice and Sydney Webb's immense two-volume study, *Soviet Communism: A New Civilisation?*[135] Despite claims of scientific rigour, it reads as a carefully crafted work of propaganda, concluding that the Soviet was the purest form of democracy in history. The Webbs justified the 'purges' within the Communist Party as a healthy process for maintaining its vitality,[136] uncritically ignored the violent repression in operation through the Gulags, denied Stalin's dictatorship[137] and, more notoriously, dismissed the systematic starvation of millions of Ukrainians as exaggerated propaganda by 'persons hostile to Soviet Communism'.[138] It seems as though a significant portion of the British intellectual elite was willing to overlook the violence of the totalitarian regimes on the basis that the ends justify the means.[139]

In light of the comments of these respected intellectuals, the Moot members' recognition of the totalitarian regimes' success in animating the masses appears less remarkable. No justification (not even in the qualified form offered by Jones' essay) of the violence of these regimes can be found in the Moot material, and over time, as the war raged on and the level of repression became more apparent, the language of admiration diminished.

Manipulating and coercing the masses

Some thought must, however, be given to the arguments found in the Moot material concerning the use of social techniques and manipulation to procure influence. In a critical reading of the Moot, Michael Lackey – in his review of Clements' *The Moot Papers*, but particularly in his monograph *Modernist God State* – draws attention to its discussions on shaping the population at a subconscious level and the coercion this implies. Lackey explores the Moot as an example of a conspiratorial 'in-depth Christianization' – a concept borrowed from Michel Foucault – referring to strategies adopted by Christian leaders to maintain the social influence of Christianity in the wake of the formal breakdown between church and state in modern states. Lackey uses this concept 'to clarify not only how but also the degree to which Christianity exerted, at the level of the subconscious, an overwhelming power to shape everyday people's political views and to determine their behaviour in the early to mid-twentieth century'.[140]

While Lackey rightly exposes the more sinister aspects present in the Moot's discussion (which will become apparent in my argument as it unfolds), his theory-driven gaze causes him to overstate his case. This applies to claims of the conspiratorial secrecy of the Moot. Oldham himself did use the language of 'conspiracy' in relation to his Christianizing movement, but it was to be an 'open conspiracy' that would capture the imagination of ordinary people who in turn would transform society from within.[141] Furthermore, while the discussions were kept behind closed doors, most of the ideas uttered in the Moot were subsequently expressed in publications by individuals. It is telling that in building his case, Lackey cites freely from Mannheim's and Eliot's publications rather than their confidential Moot papers. Even the citations from Oldham's memorandum 'A Reborn Christendom'[142] – a Moot paper marked 'strictly confidential' – were published virtually word for word in *The Resurrection of Christendom* (1940).

For Lackey, the rationale for the Moot's justification of the use of coercive means can be traced to their adherence to original sin and natural law. On this reading, original sin signifies a legitimization of violence, and the essentialism of natural law purports to be inherently coercive.[143] It might well be that natural law from a post-structuralist perspective constitutes a universalizing exclusivity that insinuates coercion. For the Moot, however, it provided a common ground that could enable cooperation and resistance against totalitarian forces between citizens who held very different sets of beliefs. Even then, when applied to the Moot, such designations are simplistic and do not sufficiently consider the deep suspicion Moot members harboured towards abstract universal principles and absolutes, including natural law itself. I have provided a detailed survey of the Moot's views on natural law in Chapter 3 and do not wish to repeat these here; however, at an epistemological level, the Moot sought a balance between the perceived moral relativism of liberalism and the absolutism of totalitarianism and even scholasticism.[144]

It is true that most of the Moot members' social criticism was informed by the doctrine of original sin, not least via Reinhold Niebuhr's Christian realism. Christian realism denotes a balancing of Christian ideals with the innate fallenness of the world suggested by the doctrine of original sin. Niebuhr argued that Christian *agape* (charitable love) needs to be countered with a biblical demand for justice in a world corrupted by sin.[145] In political terms, Niebuhr's realism legitimizes state coercion as a necessary counterforce to evil and for the sake of justice. An instance of Niebuhr's influence on the Moot can be seen in Vidler's assertion that 'justice, equality, and law' could only be maintained by the 'minimum of coercion through propaganda'.[146] Nevertheless, to assume the necessity of some level of state coercion is hardly controversial in political theory. Niebuhr's realism, at least in his own view, also countervails absolutism, as original sin posits human finitude and therefore humility.

In Eliot's case, there does appear to be a direct correlation between original sin and his justification of applying a social pressure for the sake of conformity beyond the jurisdiction of the state. In an article for the *CNL* on 'Education in a Christian Society (1940)', he wrote of a societal responsibility to 'exercise some unconscious pressure on its members to want to do the right thing' via education. Such measures of 'inculcating the right values (i.e. Christian values)' are by Eliot deemed necessary in a world ridden by sin.[147] Based on the arguments in this article, Lackey places strong emphasis on the role of original sin in shaping Eliot's views: 'given the consequences of sin Christian political leaders have the moral responsibility to subtly coercing the people into adopting the right values … (Lackey's words)'.[148] Yet, the premise of Eliot's argument does not stem from original sin alone, but from his observations concerning the shortcomings of liberal society. Eliot argues that without a few guiding principles, liberalism was creating an 'atomised society', dangerously vulnerable to oppressive countermeasures leading to totalitarianism. This sentiment is reflected in other writings of Eliot from this period. In *The Idea*, he critiques liberalism for its negation of any positive social vision, resulting in 'the artificial, mechanised or brutalised control which is a desperate remedy for its chaos'.[149] On the basis of the perceived social disintegration of liberalism, Eliot calls on his readers to consider the alternatives. It is in this context that he envisions a society governed by a Christian spirit or 'a way of life' that consciously and unconsciously informs social, political and economic structures.[150] But Eliot is deliberately vague about the means by which such a society could be brought into being. In *The Idea*, he suggests a defining role for an informal Christian elite that exerts influence in various spheres of society. Through his interaction with Mannheim at the Moot, Eliot came to deepen his aversion towards strategic projects of cultural remodelling further.[151] He developed a disposition of eschatological waiting and a 'dark age attitude': 'retiring with a few of the best books, to till the soil and milk the cow'.[152] Eliot's calls for subtle coercion are subtle indeed.

It is, further, suggestive that Mannheim, who discarded original sin as deterministic, was the Moot member who most vocally favoured using insights from modern psychology and the sciences to influence the valuation of the population.[153] As observed above, there is an element of 'coercion' in his notion of a 'militant democracy'. Mannheim contended that propaganda was a legitimate tool to reintegrate disruptive elements in society. In times of upheaval, there was a risk that these disruptive movements could attain too much influence on the masses, turning them into 'terrorist groups'. In the endeavour to counter these groups, Mannheim proposed that:

> Propaganda is not evil in of itself and it is the most successful way of dealing with instincts and desires which are not wholly embodied in the groups in which we live: it is the simplest, as well as the most superficial, form of re-integration.[154]

However, in contradistinction to the totalitarian state where propaganda permeates the society through the state apparatus, Mannheim intended to limit its use to 'capture disorganised groups and individuals' for the sake of integration.[155] Mannheim justified the use of propaganda as a necessary temporary emergency measure, utilized in order to pull the individual out of a dangerous 'dependence on mass emotion' and into a long-term educational formation with the democratically informed and responsible person as the *telos*.[156] It remains somewhat unclear, though, just what Mannheim meant by 'propaganda'. It certainly did not denote the distortion of 'truth',[157] but rather using all means available to influence the human person through *ratio* as well as appealing to the irrational, or emotional, through archetypes, symbols and symbolic actions.[158]

Mannheim's mindset, then, saw fit to use social techniques to 'mould' the anonymous masses. This elitism is entirely consistent with Zygmunt Bauman's metaphor of the *modern* intellectual as a 'legislator', who makes 'authoritative statements which arbitrate in controversies of opinions[...] legitimized by superior (objective) knowledge to which intellectuals have a better access than the non-intellectual part of society'.[159] Indeed, Bauman advances Mannheim's work on ideology as archetypal of this 'legislator' role: 'Mannheim's intellectuals stand above the politicians, as their analysts, judges, critics'.[160] Mannheim's rationale for sanctioning the use of social techniques was bound to his elitism, that is, he believed the masses were not educated enough to make informed moral and ethical judgements. It might well be that even as a secular Jew, Mannheim's thinking is implicitly imbued with Christian thought-structures, but his reasoning for justifying the use of propaganda arguably derives to a greater extent from the logic of the Enlightenment than from Christian doctrine.

Finally, while discussions on 'influencing the masses' through propaganda do exist in the Moot papers, the appeals to rational persuasion in the group's scheme should not be ignored. Time and again Moot members affirmed the demand for a programme that would attract both Christians and others. Oldham suggested that in a secular society where 'professing Christians' were in a minority, a Christian social philosophy 'must gain assent on grounds which appeal to natural reason',[161] and that the task of the Christianization of society was to be carried out by 'persuasion rather than control'.[162] Another such example can be found in an article for the *CNL*, in which Hodges deliberates over how Christians ought to seek to influence the social order as minority voices in a 'mixed society'. Hodges was convinced that enough common ground existed with those of no faith to build a 'healthy society'. The Christian needed to use the art of persuasion to convince non-Christians that certain virtues were beneficial to all.[163]

Christian totalitarianism?

Given that the Moot sought to overcome the weaknesses of liberal democracy, was it at risk of becoming a Christian counterpart to the totalitarian regime? Certainly the Moot entertained the possibility of a Christian totalitarianism. Such suggestions were seriously considered during a tense debate at the 1st gathering of the Moot, where Löwe (also a secular Jew and a refugee from Nazi Germany) tabled the idea that the only alternative to pagan totalitarianism was a 'Christian dictatorship'.[164] A new integration between the state and its milieu was bound to occur, and at least a benevolent totalitarianism based on Christian values was preferable to the pagan alternatives, he argued. Baillie appeared to agree that if the 'police state' was to be taken as a given in modern society, then theocracy was one option to be explored. Moberly aptly drew a distinction between dictatorship and totalitarian forms of society. The former was from a theological perspective conceivable, but the 'all-embracing community' of the totalitarian state was an intrinsic threat to the church.[165] Others reacted more negatively. Dawson, while admitting that the Kingdom of God is ultimately totalitarian, argued that an eschatological view had to be taken in terms of its realization.[166] Judging from Murry's comments later on in the discussion, what Dawson was alluding to was that a Christian totalitarianism implied an over-realized eschatology, that is, something which cannot or should not be aimed at in this *aeon*.[167] Eliot inferred that 'the best thing a Christian totalitarian state could do would be to abdicate'. His view was that 'Christianity had existed in [...] natural community life', and that the totalitarian state was inimical to such conditions.[168] Even Oldham strongly repudiated the idea of Christian totalitarianism, concluding the discussion with the unqualified statement that a 'Christian totalitarian state appalled him'.[169] Thus, Graeme Smith's claim that Oldham advocated a form of Christian totalitarianism would have been belied by Oldham himself.

For the subsequent meeting, Murry submitted 'Towards a Theory of a Christian Society', in which, in line with Löwe, he accepted the inevitability of central control in the 'Machine Age'. He argued that under such conditions, the church's only hope was to be incorporated into the state, or else it would risk further marginalization.[170] However, the amalgamation of 'state' and 'church' had been deemed a defining trait of totalitarianism at the Oxford conference. Therefore, it is no wonder that the paper triggered a lively debate in the dozen or so pre-circulated critiques and during the meeting itself. The majority of respondents were apprehensive of Murry's thesis. Notably, Eliot expressed his fears that a fusion of state and church would result in compromises to Christian dogma, and the implied nationalization of the church would undermine its ability to keep the state accountable.[171] Nevertheless, while Löwe raised concerns about the implications of nationalism in Murry's idea, he enthusiastically accepted Murry's suggested union of state and church as giving 'shape to the vague notion of a "Christian Totalitarianism" which I put forward at our last meeting'.[172] It should be noted that Löwe's use of totalitarianism is fairly vague, for in the same letter in which he praised Murry's 'Christian totalitarianism', he also issued a warning against big states as liable to abuses of power and 'the attempt to suppress all individuality and personal liberty'.[173]

Clarifying the semantics: Totalitarianism and centralization

We have seen that while some members rejected the notion of a Christian totalitarian order, others held that there is nothing inherently contradictory between Christianity and totalitarian forms of governance. It should be noted that terms such as 'democracy', 'freedom' and 'totalitarianism' are shrouded in ambiguity and thus the discussion in the Moot demands conceptual clarification. It is important to recognize that for the Moot, totalitarianism did for the most part have negative connotations associated with repression and total domination. Nevertheless, their usage of the term differs in significant ways from post-war definitions. Hans Maier identifies the major tenets of totalitarianism as found in the scholarly literature as, 'the unleashing of political power, its liberation from legal moral norms, its perversion in "sheer" tyrannical power'.[174] A seminal volume addressing this topic is Hannah Arendt's *The Origins of Totalitarianism*, which was written during the immediate aftermath of the war as Europe was reckoning with the monstrosity of Nazi crimes and continuing brutality of the Soviet regime. It is true that Dawson already in the 1930s anticipated Arendt's claim regarding the 'total domination' wielded over 'each single individual in each and every sphere of life' in the totalitarian regimes.[175] However, the Moot's equation of totalitarianism with processes of centralization pales in comparison with Arendt's account of the tyrannical and violent surge for utter dominance, a dominance achieved through the 'total terror of the camp'.[176] The objective here is not to validate one definition of totalitarianism over another, but simply to point out the disparity between the Moot's use of the term and how it has been theorized after the logic and workings of the Nazi and Soviet regimes were fully exposed. Totalitarianism is for these reasons a more emotively loaded and intellectually substantial term after the war than before.[177]

For the Moot, totalitarianism was not confined to the enemy out there, but was a tendency seen in all modern societies, including the British. Thus, as Vidler stated at the 4th meeting: 'whether or not there was war, the situation in England was moving towards Totalitarianism'.[178] In *Beyond Politics* (1939), Dawson stressed that the challenge facing democratic societies was 'to make themselves strong enough to exist in face of the new powers, without abandoning the principles of personal liberty and tolerance on which they are based'.[179] Citing Dawson, Eliot argued that out of the chaos of liberalism a totalitarian democracy would emerge, a reference that should be understood in the light of growing state control and centralization.[180] Even in late 1943, when the Allied forces were enjoying considerable success, Mannheim predicted that Anglo-American societies would still be susceptible to fascism after the war unless democratic institutions and power relations were deliberately planned for. The state of chaos in the allied nations meant, in his estimation, that there was only a 5 per cent chance of escaping totalitarianism.[181]

The underlying reasoning behind this analysis was that totalitarianism was seen by the Moot to be intrinsic to modern liberal society. The new totalitarian movements of the twentieth century provided the masses with a compelling moral vision, a social philosophy, which the *laissez faire* of liberalism had failed to do. They were able to fill the spiritual vacuum created by secularization through the sacralization of class, race or nation.[182] In addition to the argument that totalitarian regimes offered the masses compelling transcendent visions, Mannheim and Murry especially emphasized more structural causes. They held that since industrialized societies required a greater level of co-ordination and central control, they produced conditions favourable to totalitarian control: centralization implies power in the hands of a few.[183] Furthermore, Murry suggested that the totalitarian regimes were a response to 'the social disintegration caused by advanced industrialism'.[184] The threat of totalitarianism, then, did not merely come in the form of an external enemy or a political ideology and structure, but from the logic of modernity.

This interpretation of a totalitarian propensity in modern liberal society particularly makes sense in the light of the strong affinity drawn between totalitarianism and centralization. To begin with, Dawson's observation regarding the sacralization of politics can be seen as an aspect of increased centralization. In an article for *The Criterion* in October 1935, Dawson suggested that 'the state is not merely becoming more centralised, but that society and culture are *politicised*'.[185] Dawson here used 'state control' and 'totalitarianism' interchangeably. He therefore maintained that states under democratic control can be seen as another facet of totalitarianism.[186] Another example can be found in *God's Judgment of Europe*, where Vidler simply defines totalitarianism as 'a society in which all the technical resources of the machine age are used for the collective pursuit of the ends of the society'.[187] It is interesting that when Frank Pakenham, William Beveridge's assistant, made a guest appearance at the 17th meeting to discuss the Beveridge Report, he felt compelled to qualify that 'the social service State was not necessarily totalitarian'.[188] The 1942 Beveridge Report laid the foundation for the British welfare model after the war, and this caveat almost seems odd from a post-war perspective. Yet, in light of the widespread view that centralization was nothing but totalitarianism in disguise, such qualifications are less startling. A prime example of this stance can be seen in Frederick A. Hayek's widely read *The Road to Serfdom*, published shortly after the Beveridge Report was made public. For Hayek, there was no 'middle path' between liberalism and totalitarianism,[189] but rather all planning that restricted choice and competition lead to a slippery slope towards totalitarianism.[190] Mannheim, as Hayek's colleague at the London School of Economics, came under direct attack. Hayek particularly rejected Mannheim's idea that planning could be subjected to democratic control as such a structure 'will tend towards [...] plebiscitarian dictatorship'. A planning elite might be democratically elected, but would invariably enforce its will on the people.[191]

In the light of this conceptual clarification, Löwe's proposal for a Christian totalitarianism together with his advocacy for personal liberty appears less contradictory. Löwe held that unless further industrialization itself was to be opposed, the trend towards centralization had to be accepted. By associating centralization with totalitarianism, the question was not whether totalitarianism could be rejected, but what type of 'totalitarianism' was to be preferred. While in Arendt's – and most contemporary scholars' – understandings there is nothing democratic about the totalitarian regimes systematically disposing of millions of people, for Löwe it is fully consistent to speak of a democratic totalitarianism.

Nevertheless, there remains an ambiguity around Löwe's disposition. As Britain was increasing its war efforts, Mannheim, at the 7th meeting in February 1940, observed that Britain was approaching a 'benevolent despotism', and in this context elitism was justified if it could secure the cooperation of 'the masses'. Murry was uneasy with this argument as he felt it resembled the logic of Dostoyevsky's Grand Inquisitor: 'the burden of freedom was intolerable, therefore let the enlightened Despot remove it'. Löwe, however, responded that if the Grand Inquisitor had truly been governed by a Christian spirit, then matters would have been different – implying that a Christian authoritarian rule is a viable possibility.[192]

'Planning for Freedom': Centralization or totalitarianism?

The discussion illustrates how the Moot struggled with a central tension between faith, freedom and authority. The perceived failure of liberalism and *laissez faire* capitalism pointed towards the need for greater centralized control; however, totalitarian regimes on the continent illustrated the dangers of such control. By and large, totalitarianism was for the Moot members something oppressive to be resisted, while some degree of central planning was to be accepted.[193] The debate revolved around the question of whether a route between *laissez faire* liberalism and authoritarianism could be established.

The increased centralization in industrialized societies was then largely taken as given. However, the question was whether this trend should be resisted or simply accepted.[194] Most members took the latter view and consequently had to consider the question of how far centralization ought to be extended: at what point would centralization evolve into something oppressive? As illustrated in Murry's 1939 *Europe in Travail*, totalitarianism and centralization were seen to be a matter of degree. Murry described a movement towards totalitarianism in Britain in terms of encroachments on personal liberty, first and foremost in financial terms, but then also with regard to freedom of speech and centralization. He accepted a partial 'totalitarianism', which would safeguard 'the good in totalitarianism while rejecting the evil'.[195]

At the heart of the debate over centralization is the problem of power and freedom. This issue was addressed in the manifesto 'The Christian Witness in the Present Crisis', compiled by Oldham in 1943. In modern society, the power possessed by irresponsible economic interest demands to be checked by a stronger, more centralized and bureaucratic state, which in turn risks unleashing forces of 'tyranny'. Therefore, the statement suggests, as a countermeasure to the dominant state, power ought to be distributed into 'multiple, subsidiary centres' coupled with a continuous deliberate debate over 'the organisation of freedom'.[196] Elsewhere, Oldham argued that safeguards against the excesses of power in a centralized society could further be tempered with a Christian anthropology. The notion that human beings are created to live in a fellowship characterized by responsibility and mutuality implies that power cannot be exercised *over* another person. In this view, exertion of power limits the individual's possibility of exercising the freedom of responsibility bestowed upon them. Under such an idea of personhood, authoritarian rule and dictatorship cannot persist; 'it must perish in the end by its inherent untruth'.[197] Another call for checks on power can be found in a position paper by Hodges for the 20th meeting in June 1944. Hodges, who was positively inclined towards Mannheim's planned society, held that liberalism had to be replaced by collectivism. He proposed that the risks of power abuses under centralized administration could be balanced with the checks offered by parliamentary control.[198]

This tension can further be found in the deliberations over Mannheim's work. His programme for a 'democratically planned society' became central to the Moot's discussion of a possible 'third way' between liberalism and totalitarianism.[199] As late as the 14th meeting in March 1942, Oldham introduced the weekend by arguing that Mannheim's work still 'offered the most promising' alternative to totalitarianism and was worth pursing 'until we became sure that it was a dead end'.[200]

Emphasizing the inevitability of centralization and planning in industrialized societies, Mannheim maintained that totalitarian tendencies could be countered by a mass co-ordination aimed at maintaining liberties.[201] His proposal involved a meticulously planned society, differentiated from totalitarian societies in that it consciously sought to safeguard freedom through the protection of certain spheres from state interference, educational reforms, encouraging local autonomy and by a religious revitalization.[202] In his analysis, modern society provided unprecedented possibilities for social control. Unless a deliberate effort was made to harness this power for good, it would, by default, be utilized by darker forces. Thus, urging the Moot to 'adopt this or face chaos or totalitarianism', he saw his planned but democratic society as the only viable alternative to the crisis they faced.[203] In his early position paper, he foresaw two possible scenarios for Western societies:

> We are living in an age of transition from *laissez faire* controlled by a few numerically limited élites, to a form of planned society, which will either be ruled by a minority dictatorship or by a new form of government, which in spite of its increased power, will be democratically controlled.[204]

Mannheim envisioned that planning could be democratically controlled in the sense that planners would be accountable to parliament.[205] These ideas had already been developed in Mannheim's *Man and Society*. While the English translation – which had been revised to account for the British context – was published in 1940, the German original version dates back to 1935. As such, Mannheim entered the Moot with a comprehensive model for addressing the major issues of the age. It is quite clear from his earliest Moot paper that Mannheim felt that the group could potentially be the nucleus, which 'could devote itself to these tasks'.[206] The transition from a *laissez faire* liberal society to a democratically planned society was to be overseen by an elite that could fashion a social philosophy that would act as a guide.

For all his desire to protect freedom, advance a democratic culture and a limited pluralism, there is – to draw upon Zygmunt Bauman's metaphor – a 'gardening' mentality in Mannheim's talk of moulding the masses, using social control techniques and in his extensive sociocultural planning. Mannheim's vision finds an echo in aspects of Bauman's metaphor of the 'gardening state', which refers to an inclination of modern states to overcome the ambivalence of modernity by ordering society through rationalization, technology and science.[207] As such, while Mannheim's sociological analysis emerged as a central focus in the combat against totalitarianism, he did not win over the sceptics in the Moot network. For several members of the Moot there was a lingering suspicion that it contained some of the very elements of what they sought to overcome.

The first openly expressed objections to Mannheim's planning were posed at the 8th meeting, as concerns about the dangers of power corruption were vented. In fact, several of the participants viewed 'Planning for Freedom' as 'semi-totalitarian'. The ambivalence that many members held can be seen in Vidler's reasoning. In *God's Judgment of Europe*, he appears to endorse Mannheim's planning vision, arguing that there is scope for experimenting with using the totalitarian techniques for the planning and ordering of a society which will provide full scope for personal freedom and responsibility – a society which will carry forward the best elements in the English tradition into a collectivist order – a totalitarian democracy.[208]

In essence, Vidler here condones the use of all tools available to foster the free and responsible individual in a democracy. In an editorial for the journal *Theology* in 1942, his sanctioning of Mannheim's vision was even stronger, declaring that under the conditions of modernity, 'the banner of "Planning for Freedom" should enlist the support of all non-Christian men of good will as well [as Christians]'.[209] Despite this recommendation, at the Moot, Vidler had expressed fears that a planned society would turn into a Huxleyian nightmare: 'I anticipate that our mass-industrialised society is bound to become totalitarian, but I do not regard this as the way into a great new epoch, Mannheim's Brave New World.'[210] In his 1977 autobiography, Vidler noted that it was only in the absence of alternatives that he had been willing to press ahead with Mannheim's ideas.[211]

As for Murry, he grudgingly consented to Mannheim's scheme when first aired at the Moot.[212] Yet, a year later Murry had a change of heart. In a memorandum, he argued for greater decentralization and local autonomy, thus on this basis rejecting Mannheim's vision of a planned society.[213] In the six talks he gave for the BBC during the winter of 1939–1940 – which were published as *Europe in Travail* (1940) – Murry accepted that in wartime a greater measure of totalitarian control is preferable to anarchy. However, for the long term, he posited that the future of the nation depended on a return to the land, on decentralization and a renewal of democracy, which entailed a greater level of self-governance for local communities.[214]

A discussion at the 18th Moot meeting in the autumn of 1943 gives further insight into the apprehension felt by many of the Moot members towards 'Planning for Freedom'. The discussion was dominated by Lex Miller, who questioned whether 'democratic planning' was a realistic possibility as it demands a strong civil society, which in turn cannot be planned.[215] Even Hodges, who had throughout been supportive of Mannheim, concurred that democratic planning was a 'phantasy' for this reason.[216] Mannheim, in turn, retorted that such a sentiment was defeatist, surrendering to fascism. Nevertheless, Hodges insisted that without a strong civil society, the only option was to 'organise spiritual recovery under totalitarian regime', and Miller stated that Mannheim's ideas inevitably presumed an authoritarian regime. Mannheim was forced to admit that the chance of the survival of democracy in the face of totalitarian regimes was less than 5 per cent, but yet maintained that there was a real difference between democratic planning and 'veiled totalitarianism'.[217]

The fiercest resistance to Mannheim's planning scheme came from the Moot's most 'right-wing' members: Dawson and Eliot. In a response to Oldham's endorsement of Mannheim's 'Planning for Freedom' in the *CNL*,[218] Dawson issued a warning against 'scientists on the one hand, and the more intransigent Christians on the other … who inevitably tend to adopt totalitarian methods, without ideological bias, in a purely utilitarian or technical spirit'.[219] While not rejecting cultural planning outright, Dawson rejected the 'purely rational' scientism of Mannheim's social and cultural planning. A political 'remoulding of human nature' would constitute a greater threat to liberty than the totalitarian powers.[220] To his friend George Every, Dawson wrote that Oldham had not comprehended the risk of a 'Philistine dictatorship' in Mannheim's planning.[221]

Another of Mannheim's opponents within the Moot was Eliot, who for his part was personally sympathetic towards Mannheim, while remaining highly sceptical of his ideas. As a self-confessed monarchist, he was no stranger to authoritarian forms of governance, but his aversion to industrialization meant that he favoured more organic social models to centralization. Eliot clearly had an inclination towards social order and hierarchy, but his ideals of culture – defined as a society's 'way of life' – were such that he consistently rejected another totalitarian ideal, namely, statism. He simply held that if a culture were to flourish, it had to develop organically. The tensions between Mannheim and Eliot will be discussed in greater detail in the next chapter.

Finally, there is the open confrontation – or 'ding-dong' battle as Mairet called it – between Mannheim and newcomer Michael Polanyi during the 20th meeting.[222] Even before his inclusion into the Moot, Polanyi had in a private correspondence made clear his antipathy towards Mannheim's 'Planning for Freedom'.[223] While Mannheim was positive about the invitation to Polanyi to join the group,[224] Kettler and Meja have suggested that his arrival coincided with Mannheim's declining influence and commitment. It signified an infusion of more liberal elements into the Moot discourse and the marginalization of Mannheim's ideas regarding planning.[225]

A turn towards socialism?

Having in some detail sought to position the Moot within the major sociopolitical currents of their day, I wish to conclude this chapter by considering the predominant political disposition of the Moot. It is tempting to assume that a group that endorsed Christianity as the basis for their sociopolitical outlook was conservative or even reactionary. However, the economic turmoil of the interwar period had impelled a quest for alternative economic systems leading to a surge in leftist sympathies. The Moot was no different. On the radical left, Murry, during the early 1930s, had made his sympathies with communism clear. In *The Necessity of Communism* (1932), Murry conceived of communism as a secular religion, suggesting that Karl Marx belonged to the same tradition as the Old Testament prophets and Jesus Christ. He understood communism to be a modern-day fulfilment of a godless Christianity.[226] By the late 1930s, Murry's religious outlook took a sharp turn. While he remained committed to socialist ideals, he renounced his earlier atheism and returned to the Anglican Church. Murry kept many of his ideas to himself during his time in the Moot, something that Hodges attributed to a fear of causing unnecessary divisions.[227] However, several other Moot members also identified with socialist politics. In his autobiography, Vidler described his 'conversion' to socialism during his student years at Selwyn College, Cambridge. His first post after ordination was at a slum parish in Tyneside, Newcastle, where he campaigned for Labour candidate Sir Charles Trevelyan.[228] While Mannheim's political allegiances are not easily categorized, during his years at the University of Budapest (1912–1919), he had been active in socialist circles, including that of Oscar Jászi's Society for Social Science. In the late 1920s and early 30s, Mannheim, together with his friend Löwe, connected with Tillich's Christian Socialists at Frankfurt.[229]

Tillich was one of several intellectuals with left-wing leanings who came to influence the Moot. The most developed argument in defence of socialism can be found in his *The Socialist Decision* originally published in German in 1933.[230] Another influential voice on the Moot was that of Archbishop William Temple. Temple is credited with coining the term 'welfare state' in the late 1920s,[231] and his name is strongly linked with Christian Socialism. Another example is Reinhold Niebuhr, who, moved by the plight of the conditions of the working class, was involved with leftist movements in the 1920s and 1930s.[232]

Yet socialism had been curiously absent from the agenda in the early years of the Moot. As the war turned decisively in favour of the Allies, the Moot's attention turned to post-war reconstruction. Murry's overlooked socialism was somewhat vindicated in a paper by Hodges, circulated for the 17th meeting.[233] It is possible that Hodges was prompted by the discussion of the Beveridge Report at the previous meeting as well as Tillich's circulated paper on socialism and power.[234] Hodges argued that the Moot had ignored the primary political force of their age, namely, socialism. This was a mistake, suggested Hodges, for if one was to appeal to the masses, one had to start with the interests of the people. And these interests in the modern world were primarily economic. Citing Temple, Maritain and Sir Richard Acland, the co-founder of the socialistic Common Wealth Party, Hodges linked socialism with the ablest of Christian social thinkers of the time. As the finest achievement of the political sciences, Hodges held that socialism warranted consideration in the Moot. It is rather striking that Hodges rejected the idea that Christianity *per se* could or ought to be the premise of modern politics.[235] Hodges' paper became the centre of attention for much of the meeting, and it evidently resonated with the rest of the members. An exception was Mannheim, who dismissed socialism as dated since he deemed class war obsolete.[236]

The discussion in June 1943 continued along these lines. Hector Hetherington, the principal of Glasgow University, felt that class struggle could not be ignored.[237] Lex Miller, a Presbyterian minister with a history of engagement in social justice issues,[238] also held that Hodges had raised a significant issue. He queried whether Mannheim's gradualism could achieve the level of social and economic overhaul required to avoid class war and revolution.[239] As a visitor at the meeting, Reinhold Niebuhr suggested that although issues of social justice remained, Marxism as practised in Soviet Russia was a spent force.[240] Niebuhr held that the democratic state *could* check domineering economic interests, *vis-à-vis* Murry, who had given up on the modern state, and yet, *contra* Mannheim, class struggle was still a reality.[241] Niebuhr's fear of socialism was its socialization of capital, which potentially created a dangerous concentration of power – a contention that Oldham endorsed. Concluding his remarks, Niebuhr asserted, 'Monopoly must be broken in order to free the markets, but absolute planning would be absolute totalitarianism.'[242] Hodges concluded the discussion by claiming that it had achieved the purpose for writing the paper: the 'Moot had discussed politics as politics without mentioning Christianity'.[243]

The meeting ended with a unanimous consent to a statement, 'Fifteen points of Agreement', compiled by Hetherington and Hodges over the weekend. In a postscript to the meeting, Hodges explained that the 15 points were 'read out at dictation speed, amended in discussion, and finally agreed to in their amended form by everyone present'.[244] The statement sets out by affirming that '[a]ll power ought to be socially responsible', and that the concentration of power afforded to wealthy capitalists in modern society is undesirable and irresponsible. Since the 'present controllers of industry' would resist any changes to these conditions, a measure of 'compulsion' would be necessary. The statement, nevertheless, affirms the right to private property as instrumental in the defence of freedom. Still, the use of force in order to implement necessary changes could lead to 'dictatorship', and therefore, 'normal political action' rather than revolution was deemed to be the preferable channel. Since politics is the sphere of debate and strife between various self-interests, the state must be regarded as an 'association', which here denotes corporation for the common good. The statement ends with a call for Christians to comprehend the political situation and to act with a realism rather than an idealistic 'Christian ethos'.[245] While the word socialism was left out, Hodges understood the statement to be consistent with his definition thereof in 'Politics and the Moot'.

It is therefore surprising that Eliot, who was part of the meeting, would have consented to a statement with such a clear left-wing leaning. While relatively anonymous during this particular weekend, Eliot made his misgivings clear in an ensuing correspondence with Oldham. Eliot's concerns were chiefly over whether the Moot possessed the right qualities to create such a programme,[246] but more so, he rejected the implied Marxist disposition of giving priority to structural change over personal moral change.[247] While distancing himself from mere conservativism, Eliot complained that Hodges' 'exhortations' tended to 'smack of the progressive fallacy', namely, seeking changes without reflecting on the possible outcomes.[248]

As at other times when the Moot appeared to reach a point of agreement, the follow-up exchanges petered out. Eliot was not alone in observing that the Moot did not possess the right propensities to set a political programme in motion. Even Hodges admitted that the Moot did not have the connections to effectively influence the political elite;[249] Gilbert Shaw similarly held that the Moot lacked the leadership skills required.[250]

The debate sparked by Hodges' paper witnesses to the continued prominence of the themes discussed in this chapter: the crisis and injustices of capitalism, the debate over appropriate distribution of power – and especially the power balance between economic interest and the state – and thereby, a fear that centralization would lead to tyranny and totalitarianism. The debate further muddles the simple correlation between Christianity and politics, a correlation that the Moot continuously struggled to define. And, finally, as Eliot's private correspondence with Oldham shows, their exchange demonstrates the Moot's inability to agree on anything definite. It is difficult to see how this could amount to a 'Christian totalitarianism', unless the term is applied so liberally as to elide Stalinism, Nazism and Anglo-American parliamentarianism.

Conclusion

This chapter has surveyed the Moot material in order to investigate its engagement with the central political ideas of its age. As the 1930s were drawing to a close, a particular focus in the Moot was placed upon the various incarnations of totalitarianism that threatened to engulf the whole of Europe and beyond. Moot members argued that the underlying forces of modernity had unleashed this leviathan, initiating an ever-increasing state apparatus at the expense of individual dignity and liberty. The undeniable default position of the Moot was that of opposition to this phenomenon. They were united in their resolve to oppose the dehumanizing propensities of totalitarianism through a re-Christianization of modern society. Armed with a Christian understanding of the nature of man – that is, the belief in humans as created free but bestowed with responsibilities – they sought to address what they perceived to be the socially disintegrative radical individualism of liberalism, on the one hand, and the oppressive collectivism of totalitarian regimes, on the other.

This is not to deny that there was an attraction to the methods and successes of totalitarianism, German Nazism in particular, which even fuelled talk of the possibility of a Christian totalitarianism within the Moot. Neither is it to deny their misgivings about the viability of liberal democracy and their elitism. There were also justifications made for a limited use of coercion for the sake of political order, and the legitimatization of the use of tools of manipulation by some Moot members, not least in Mannheim's insistence that a defence of democratic values warranted the use of propaganda. This does open up for questions as to whether the Moot risked becoming a mirror image of what they sought to overcome. A number of caveats should therefore be made in order to do the Moot justice.

Firstly, the group never arrived at a corporate programme and failed to provide a robust alternative to totalitarianism upon which all could agree. Although there were plenty of shared ideas, such as a New Christendom and the prerequisite of a guiding elite, the group was and remained both politically and religiously conflicted. Within the Moot, an array of political opinions were held, from Dawson and Eliot's hierarchical societies, to Murry's 'spiritual' communism, Polanyi's liberalism, Vidler's socialism and Mannheim's strong emphasis on central planning. Such plurality challenges any historiography seeking to present a unified whole.

Secondly, it is tempting to assume that due to many of the Moot members' scepticism towards liberalism, capitalism and liberal democracy, they embraced broadly 'right-wing' politics and values or even totalitarian forms of society.

However, as with large segments of British intelligentsia in the 1930s, the Moot was preoccupied with addressing the weaknesses of these principles, alongside their political and economic structures, rather than simply imagining their abandonment altogether.

Thirdly, any conclusion is complicated by a number of conceptual varieties. Concepts such as democracy and totalitarianism remain contested, and the Moot members themselves used these terms in divergent ways. This adds to the complexity of determining the Moot's stance on totalitarianism. At some points in the Moot discourse, totalitarianism is more or less equated with centralization and the bureaucratization of modern societies, and it is thus accepted as given fact. This appears to be the sense in which Löwe understood the term when he envisioned a Christian totalitarianism. At other points, the term is used to describe attempts by totalitarian regimes to control the human soul and their suppression of basic human (and Christian) liberties. Certainly, totalitarianism became a more emotively loaded term carrying an implicit value judgement during and immediately after the Second World War. An awareness of how the Moot used the concept is therefore significant.

Fourthly, facing the question of power in an age of totalitarian regimes, the Moot sought to navigate between the Scylla of unlimited freedom and the Charybdis of tyrannical authority. These discussions should be seen in the light of the wartime situation that the Moot faced in the short term, while being also driven in the longer term by a movement of ever-increasing centralization and bureaucracy under the processes of modernization. Mannheim's third way between *laissez faire* liberalism and totalitarian repression became the focal point in the Moot's debate. If the democratic society were to survive, it required a deliberate effort, a plan for freedom. A highly centralized state inevitably raises questions of authority and power. At what stage does state interference turn into something oppressive? Where is the line between non-totalitarianism and totalitarianism? Is Mannheim's centralizing 'Planning for Freedom' merely a softer totalitarianism in disguise? Dawson, indeed, suspected that Mannheim's scheme implied an unwanted form of dictatorship. Other members were also apprehensive. Yet it is worth pointing out that these questions continue to haunt the welfare states today as implied, for example, in Michel Foucault's term 'governmentality'.[251] If totalitarianism in theory is defined as the total domination of the individual by the state, such a condition has never been realized in practice. Therefore, totalitarianism, when ascribed to a political movement, will always be a matter of degree. An outcome of this chapter has been to problematize simplistic categorizations.

Finally, from a postmodern or post-structuralist perspective, the Moot may well constitute another totalizing hegemony. Yet such a broad abstract category unhelpfully confuses real totalitarianism with ascribed 'totalization'. This conceptual differentiation lies behind Mark Edwards' notion of 'God's totalitarianism', where he investigates the transatlantic ecumenical network's vision of a New Christendom. For Edwards, the Protestant left with which he couples the Moot cannot simply be equated with 'technocratic nightmares of the Third Reich or Supreme Soviet', but nevertheless, their alternative 'would have proven little better than the real thing'.[252] It seems simply bizarre to liken the enterprise of 'New Christendom' to the regimes that created the Gulag and Auschwitz, as Edwards does. As Slavoj Žižek suggests, the label of totalitarianism is in academia too readily applied as 'an ideological notion that sustained the complex operation of "taming the radicals"'. That is, totalitarianism as a concept is applied to anyone who challenges the hegemony of liberal democracy, even when it is evidently corrupt.[253] In conclusion, Matthew Grimley's observation rather better accounts for the Moot's endeavour: 'At a time when communism and Nazism were offering an attractively all-embracing moral unity, British critics of those ideologies had to come up with an alternative which evoked the same moral unity, and which was totalizing without being totalitarian.'[254]

Notes

1   J. H. Oldham, 'Letter to the Moot Members', 6 September 1939, LM/SEC12; OLD/9/2/34.
2   Karl Mannheim, 'Letter to Louis Wirth', 13 August 1938, LWP/VII/11.
3   Clements, *Moot Papers*, 518 (14th meeting, 27–30 March 1942). Oldham's use of the term 'Third Way' differs from far-right designations, which emphasize the opposition to communism and capitalism.
4   H. A. Hodges, 'Comment on the Moot's Fifteen Points', 29 July 1943, OLD/14/1/53. See also Vidler, *Scenes from a Clerical Life*, 117.
5   Michael Lackey, 'The Moot Papers: Faith, Freedom and Society 1938–1947', *Modernism/Modernity* 17, no. 4 (2010), 959.
6   Michael Lackey, *The Modernist God State: A Literary Study of the Nazi's Christian Reich* (New York: Continuum, 2012), ch. 3.
7   Graeme Smith, 'Christian Totalitarianism: Joseph Oldham and Oxford 1937', *Political Theology* 3, no. 1 (2001), 32–46; Graeme Smith, *Oxford 1937: The Universal Christian Council for Life and Work Conference* (Frankfurt am Main: Peter Lang).

8 M. T. Edwards, '"God's Totalitarianism": Ecumenical Protestant Discourse During the Good War, 1941–45', *Totalitarian Movements and Political Religions* 10, no. 3–4 (2009), 285–302; Edwards, *The Right of the Protestant Left: God's Totalitarianism*.
9 Williams, *The Politics of Modernism*, 34.
10 Ibid., 55.
11 Kermode, *Sense of an Ending*, 111.
12 Ibid., 112.
13 North, *The Political Aesthetic*, 2–3.
14 Charles Ferrall, *Modernist Writing and Reactionary Politics* (Cambridge: Cambridge University Press, 2001), 2. Ferrall includes T. S. Eliot, W. B. Yeats, Ezra Pound, Wyndham Lewis and D. H. Lawrence in this discourse of 'reactionary Modernists'.
15 Ibid., 2.
16 Surette, *Dreams of a Totalitarian Utopia*, 9.
17 Ironically, a reference in the leftist *Daily Worker* in 1949 prompted the FBI open a file on Eliot (Claire A. Culleton and Karen Leick, 'Silence, Acquiescence, and Dread', in *Modernism on File: Writers, Artists, and the FBI, 1920–1950*, ed. Claire A. Culleton and Karen Leick (New York: Palgrave Macmillan, 2008), 2. My thanks to Matthew Feldman for this reference.
18 Cunningham, *British Writers of the Thirties*, 211–40.
19 Hynes, *The Auden Generation*, 12.
20 Griffin, *Modernism and Fascism*, 180–1.
21 Dawson, *Religion and the Modern State*, xv. See also Dawson, *Christianity and the New Age*, 16–17.
22 Dawson, *Religion and the Modern State*, xv–xvi.
23 Ibid., 58.
24 See Oldham, *The Churches Survey Their Task*, 9; Eliot, *Idea*, 15; and discussion at the 1st meeting (Clements, *Moot Papers*, 51–2, (1st meeting, 1–4 April 1938)) and the paper 'The Sword of the Spirit' (Christopher Dawson, 'The Sword of the Spirit', December 1940, IOE/MOO/37; OLD/14/4/1).
25 Gentile, *Politics as Religion*, xiv–xv, xvii–xviii.
26 Ibid., 70.
27 Ibid., 71.
28 Oldham, *The Churches Survey Their Task*, 242.
29 Ibid., 244.
30 Ibid., 246.
31 Ibid., 58.
32 See Appendix F in ibid.
33 Smith, *Oxford 1937*, 205.
34 Ibid., 132.
35 Oldham, *The Churches Survey Their Task*, 81.

36 See ibid., 41.
37 J. H. Oldham, *Church, Community and State: A World Issue* (London: SCM Press, 1935), 14.
38 See Hannah Arendt and Jerome Kohn, 'On the Nature of Totalitarianism: An Essay in Understanding', in *Essays in Understanding: 1930–1954* (New York: Harcourt Brace, 1994).
39 There were naturally exceptions. E. M. Forster defends liberal democracy as 'the less hateful' alternative (E. M. Forster, 'What I Believe', in *Two Cheers for Democracy*, ed. E. M. Forster (London: Edward Arnold, 1972 [1938]), 66–7).
40 W. H. Auden, 'The Public V. The Late Mr. William Butler Yeats', in *The English Auden: Poems, Essays and Dramatic Writings 1927–1939*, ed. Edward Mendelson (London: Faber & Faber, 1977), 392–3.
41 Furthermore, Murry's paper 'The General Problem of Democracy' (9 September 1946, MPP/15/7; OLD/14/5/16) was discussed at the 24th and last meeting of the Moot, 10–13 January 1947. No minutes from this meeting have survived.
42 Tom Villis, *Reaction and the Avant-Garde: The Revolt against Liberal Democracy in Early Twentieth-Century Britain* (London: Tauris Academic Studies, 2006), 74–5.
43 T. S. Eliot, 'A Commentary', *The Criterion* XVII, no. 66 (1937), 83.
44 Eliot, *Idea*, 15.
45 Clements, *Moot Papers*, 194 (4th meeting, 14–17 April 1939).
46 Ibid., 194 (4th meeting, 14–17 April 1939).
47 Karl Mannheim, 'The Democratization of Culture', in *From Karl Mannheim*, ed. Kurt E. Wolf (New York: Oxford University Press, 1971), 279, 274.
48 Dawson, *Religion and the Modern State*, 27.
49 Ibid., 39–43.
50 Cf. Dawson, *Beyond Politics*, 84. For an exposition on intellectuals attitude towards 'the masses', see John Carey, *The Intellectuals and the Masses: Pride and Prejudice among the Literary Intelligentsia, 1880–1939* (London: Faber & Faber, 1992).
51 Clements, *Moot Papers*, 514 (14th meeting, 27–30 March 1942).
52 Ibid., 194 (4th meeting, 14–17 April 1939).
53 Ibid., 195.
54 Eliot, *Idea*, 15. See also T. S. Eliot, 'On Reading Offciail Reports', *New English Weekly* 15 (1939), 61.
55 Clements, *Moot Papers*, 93 (4th meeting, 14–17 April 1939).
56 Ibid., 195.
57 Ibid., 513 (14th meeting, 27–30 March 1942).
58 Ibid., 514–15.
59 Ibid., 515 (14th meeting, 27–30 March 1942).
60 Ibid., 567 (16th meeting, 8–11 January 1943).

61 Ibid., 193 (4th meeting, 14–17 April 1939).
62 Ibid., 317 (9th meeting, 12–15 July 1941).
63 Ibid., 318.
64 Murry, 'Democracy and the Totalitarian Ideal'.
65 John Middleton Murry, 'The Task of Democracy', *Adelphi* 15, no. 5 (1939), 214.
66 John Middleton Murry, *The Defence of Democracy* (London: Jonathan Cape, 1939), 258.
67 Murry, *Europe in Travail*, 41, 50.
68 Ibid., 45.
69 Ibid., 53.
70 Dawson, *Beyond Politics*, 13–14.
71 Loader, *The Intellectual Development*, 152–3.
72 Karl Mannheim, 'Planning for Freedom', [1938] LM/SEC7; OLD/14/3/67.
73 Ibid.
74 Clements, *Moot Papers*, 391 (11th meeting, 4–7 April 1941).
75 Karl Mannheim, 'Planning for Freedom', [1938] LM/SEC7; OLD/14/3/67.
76 Karl Mannheim, 'Problem of Youth in Modern Society', 3 June 1941, OLD/14/3/1. It is likely that the paper was discussed at the Moot subgroup 6–7 June 1941 (see 'Purposes of the Week-end Meeting, 6–7 June', [1941] OLD/13/4/174).
77 Mannheim, *Diagnosis*.
78 Benito Mussolini, *Fascism: Doctrine and Institutions* (New York: Howard Fertig, 1968 [1935]), 23.
79 Ibid., 23.
80 Published in Mannheim, *Diagnosis*, 110.
81 Clements, *Moot Papers*, 425 (12th meeting, 1–3 August 1941).
82 Mannheim, *Man*, 364. Leon Surette comments that Eliot associated liberalism more with 'worldly prosperity and comfort' than 'individual rights and liberties' (Surette, *Dreams of a Totalitarian Utopia*, 203).
83 Cf. Mannheim, *Diagnosis*, 6; Murry, *Europe in Travail*, 41; Dawson, *Judgement*, 73, 83.
84 H. G. Wells, *The Rights of Man or, What Are We Fighting For?* (Harmondsworth: Penguin, 1940), 23–30.
85 V. A. Demant, 'Christian Faith and the Rights of Man', [1940] IOE/MOO/19; OLD/14/8/6.
86 Clements, *Moot Papers*, 275 (7th meeting, 9–12 February 1940). 275.
87 Ibid., 306–7 (8th meeting, 19–22 April 1940).
88 Hector Hetherington, 'The Prolegomena to Planning: The Essential Freedoms', 28 August 1942, IOE/MOO/85; OLD/14/9/32. There is no record of the paper being discussed at the meeting.
89 Karl Mannheim, 'Planning for Freedom' [1938], LM/SEC7; OLD/14/3/67.

90 Mannheim, *Diagnosis*, 7. The essay was originally presented as a lecture at the Conference of Federal Union at Oxford in January 1941. It appears in the Moot material dated 13 January 1942, which indicates that the paper was circulated in the group (Karl Mannheim, 'Diagnosis of Our Time', 13 January 1942, IOE/MOO/72; KMP/2/R; OLD/14/3/36).

91 J. H. Oldham, 'The Christian Witness in the Present Crisis', 6 October 1943, OLD/9/5/19.

92 Smith, *Oxford 1937*, 130.

93 Fred Clarke et al., *Church, Community, and State in Relation to Education* (London: George Allen & Unwin, 1938), 218–19.

94 Ibid., 218.

95 Cf. Oldham, *The Resurrection*, 12; Oldham, *Real Life*, 16–17.

96 J. H. Oldham, 'A Reborn Christendom', August 1939, IOE/MOO/2; LM/SEC11. See also Oldham, *The Resurrection*, 12; Oldham, *Real Life*, 10.

97 H. A. Hodges, 'Notes on Social Philosophy' [1940], IOE/MOO/125; OLD/14/2/53.

98 Dawson, *Religion and the Modern State*, 50.

99 Ibid., 51.

100 These ideas on the nature of freedom run through the Moot paper 'Towards a New Social Philosophy' circulated for the 12th meeting.

101 Cf. Mannheim, *Diagnosis*, 7–11, 110.

102 Joseph Schumpeter, *Capitalism, Socialism, and Democracy* (London: Routledge, 2003 [1943]), 250.

103 Oldham, 'Freedom and Planning'.

104 Smith, 'Christian Totalitarianism', 40.

105 Paul Jackson, 'Extremes of Faith and Nation: British Fascism and Christianity', *Religion Compass* 4, no. 8 (2010), 512. As historian E. R. Norman points out, apart from some sympathies within the Catholic Church, fascism had little appeal to the British churches (E. R. Norman, *Church and Society in England 1770–1970* (Oxford: Clarendon Press, 1976), 357–61).

106 Tom Villis, *British Catholics & Fascism: Religious Identity and Political Extremism between the Wars* (Basingstoke: Palgrave Macmillan, 2013), 105.

107 See Christina Scott, *A Historian and His World: A Life of Christopher Dawson, 1889–1970* (New Brunswick: Transaction Publishers, 1992), 133.

108 Dawson's article 'The Sword of the Spirit' (December 1940, IOE/MOO/37; OLD/14/4/1) was discussed in the context of the proposed Order at the 10th Meeting, 10–13 January 1941.

109 Ernest Holte sees Action Française as an 'early fascism', which 'anticipates… the characteristic traits of the infinitely cruder and more wholesale methods used in Italy and Germany (Ernest Holts, *Three Faces of Fascism: Action Française, Italian Fascism and National Socialism*, trans. Leila Vennewitz (London: Weidenfeld and Nicolson, 1965), 26).'

110 Surette, *Dreams of a Totalitarian Utopia*, 143, 165.
111 T. S. Eliot, 'Editorial for the CNL, 28th August 1940', *Christian News-Letter*, no. 44 (1940).
112 Cf. Jean-Luc Barré, *Jacques and Raïssa Maritain: Beggars for Heaven*, trans. Bernard E. Doering (Notre Dame, IN: University of Notre Dame, 2005), 158.
113 See Maritain, *The Rights of Man and Natural Law*, and Jacques Maritain, *Christianity and Democracy* (London: The Centenary Press, 1945).
114 Frank, *Responses to Modernity*, 27.
115 See Anthony Julius, *T.S. Eliot, Anti-Semitism, and Literary Form* (Cambridge: Cambridge University Press, 1995).
116 Ronald Schuchard, 'Burbank with a Baedeker, Eliot with a Cigar: American Intellectuals, Anti-Semitism, and the Idea of Culture', *Modernism/Modernity* 10, no. 1 (2003), 16.
117 T. S. Eliot, 'Letter to J. V. Healy', 10 May 1940, UTE/5/12. A similar response is given in T. S. Eliot, 'Letter to Edward Field', 17 March 1947, UTE/4/7.
118 T. S. Eliot, 'Editorial 3rd September', *Christian News-Letter*, no. 97 (1941). I am not here seeking to offer an apologia for Eliot. After all, an anti-Semite is just as unlikely to admit to his anti-Semitism as a racist to his racism. I am rather drawing attention to the allegation of this far-right trait and some of the ambiguity that surrounds it.
119 T. S. Eliot, 'The Church and Society', *New English Weekly* 6, no. 23 (1935), 482.
120 T. S. Eliot, 'The Church's Message to the World', *The Listener* 17, no. 423 (1937): 293–4.
121 Cf. Eliot, *Idea*, 20.
122 Nancy Cunard, *Authors Takes Side on the Spanish Civil War* (Left Review, 1937).
123 T. S. Eliot, 'Editorial 28th August', *Christian News-Letter*, no. 44 (1940).
124 Cf. Surette, *Dreams of a Totalitarian Utopia*, 161.
125 Eliot's interaction with Mannheim will be the focus of Chapter 5 of my thesis.
126 Collini, 'The European Modernist as Anglican Moralist', 228.
127 Clements, *Moot Papers*, 44–5 (1st meeting, 1–4 April 1938).
128 Karl Mannheim, 'Planning for Freedom' [1938], LM/SEC7; OLD/14/3/67.
129 Clements, *Moot Papers*, 191 (4th meeting, 14–17 April 1939).
130 Karl Mannheim, 'Planning for Freedom' [1938], LM/SEC7; OLD/14/3/67.
131 Karl Mannheim: 'Problem of Youth in Modern Society', 3 June 1941, OLD/14/3/1.
132 Fredrick A. Hayek, *The Road to Serfdom* (Abingdon: Routledge, 2001 [1944]), 189.
133 As cited in Thomas Dilworth, 'David Jones and Fascism', *Journal of Modern Literature* 13, no. 1 (1986), 155.
134 Surette, *Dreams of a Totalitarian Utopia*, 11–12.
135 Sidney and Beatrice Webb, *Soviet Communism: A New Civilisation*, 3rd ed. (London: Longman, Green and Co., 1944 [1935]).

136 Ibid., 291–300.
137 Ibid., 334.
138 Ibid., 199.
139 Interestingly, in an article titled 'The Struggle Between Truth and Propaganda' originally published in 1937, Michael Polanyi offers a stinging critique of the Webbs' volumes (Michael Polanyi, *Society, Economics, and Philosophy: Selected Papers* (New Brunswick: Transaction, 1997), 47–60).
140 Lackey, *Modernist God State*, 89–90.
141 Clements, *Moot Papers*, 120–1 (2nd meeting, 23–26 September 1938).
142 J. H. Oldham, 'A Reborn Christendom', August 1939, IOE/MOO/2.
143 Lackey, 'The Moot Papers'.
144 See Chapter 3.
145 Niebuhr himself put forth these views while attending the Moot (Clements, *Moot Papers*, 596 (17th meeting, 18–21 June 1943)).
146 Ibid., 569 (16th meeting, 8–11 January 1943).
147 T. S. Eliot, 'Education in a Christian Society', *Christian News-Letter*, no. 20 (1940).
148 Lackey, *Modernist God State*, 116.
149 Eliot, *Idea*, 21.
150 Ibid., 8–18.
151 See Eliot, *Notes*, 19.
152 T. S. Eliot, 'Man and Society', *The Spectator* (1940).
153 In the Moot, Mannheim commented that the doctrine of original sin lead to 'retrogressive thought' and pessimism concerning 'social and education progress' (Clements, *Moot Papers*, 282 (7th meeting, 9–12 February 1940)).
154 Karl Mannheim, 'Planning for Freedom' [1938], LM/SEC7; OLD/14/3/67.
155 Ibid.
156 Ibid.
157 See Clements, *Moot Papers*, 229 (5th meeting, 23–24 September 1939).
158 Ibid., 339 (9th meeting, 12–15 July 1941).
159 Zygmunt Bauman, *Legislators and Interpreters* (Cambridge: Polity Press, 1989), 4.
160 Ibid., 108–9.
161 Oldham, *The Resurrection*, 24.
162 Clements, *Moot Papers*, 211 (4th meeting, 14–17 April 1939).
163 H. A. Hodges, 'Social Standards in a Mixed Society', *Christian News-Letter*, no. 43 (1940).
164 Clements, *Moot Papers*, 52 (1st meeting, 1–4 April 1938).
165 Ibid., 55.
166 Kojecky has misunderstood Dawson here; see Kojecky, *T. S. Eliot's Social Criticism*, 164. In a letter for the editor of the *CNL* published in 1941, Dawson directly rejected the idea of a Christian totalitarianism (Christopher Dawson, 'What Is the Alternative to Totalitarianism?' *Christian News-Letter*, no. 107 (1941)).

167 Murry says, 'his difficulty with Löwe's view [that of a Christian totalitarian state] was the same as Dawson's, that it implied the Kingdom of God on earth (Clements, *Moot Papers*, 54 (1st meeting, 1–4h April 1938))'.
168 Ibid., 54.
169 Ibid., 57.
170 John Middleton Murry, 'Towards a Christian Theory of Society' [1938], OLD/14/5/37.
171 T. S. Eliot, 'Comments on Middleton Murry's Paper' [1938], OLD/14/6/21. In his paper for the 1941 Malvern Conference, Eliot provided a more extensive critique of Matthew Arnold's idea of a national Church, which Murry here drew upon. Eliot argued that a 'national Christianity' would lead to a 'gradual diminution of Christian belief (T. S. Eliot, 'The Christian Conception of Education', in *Malvern 1941: The Life of the Church the Order of Society* (London: Longmans, 1941), 211)'.
172 Adolf Löwe, 'Comments on Middleton Murry's Paper' [1938], OLD/14/4/43.
173 Ibid.
174 Hans Maier, 'On the Interpretations of Totalitarian Rule 1919–89', in *Totalitarianism and Political Religions, Volume III: Concepts for the Comparison of Dictatorship – Theory and History of Interpretation*, ed. Hans Maier (Abingdom: Routledge, 2007), 11.
175 Hannah Arendt, *The Origins of Totalitarianism*, 2nd ed. (New York: Harcourt, Brace & World, 1958 [1951]), 326.
176 Ibid., 438.
177 For an overview of theoretical perspectives and definitions of totalitarianism, see Richard Shorten, *Modernism and Totalitarianism* (Basingstoke: Palgrave, 2012). Shorten's own thesis is, in contrast to the Moot, that totalitarianism as a phenomenon is better defined through its ideological characteristics, rather than its political structure (p. 1).
178 Clements, *Moot Papers*, 210 (4th meeting, 14–17 April 1939). See also Vidler, *God's Judgment*, 62.
179 Dawson, *Beyond Politics*, 11.
180 Eliot, *Idea*, 15.
181 Clements, *Moot Papers*, 628, 631 (18th meeting, 29 October–1 November 1943).
182 For example, Oldham, *The Churches Survey Their Task*, 9–10; Dawson, *Beyond Politics*, 5–10; Mannheim, *Diagnosis*, 100–1.
183 Cf. John Middleton Murry, 'Towards a Christian Theory of Society' [1938], OLD/14/5/37, Karl Mannheim, 'Planning for Freedom' [1938], LM/SEC7; OLD/14/3/67.
184 Murry, *Europe in Travail*, 19.
185 Christopher Dawson, 'Religion and the Totalitarian State', *The Criterion* 14, no. 54 (1934), 1.

186 Ibid., 3. See also *The Judgement of the Nations*, 77. A draft of this publication was circulated in the Moot (Christopher Dawson, 'Planning and Culture' [1941], IOE/MOO/128).
187 Vidler, *God's Judgment*, 86.
188 Clements, *Moot Papers*, 561 (16th meeting, 8–11 January 1943).
189 Hayek, *The Road*, 43.
190 Ibid., 200.
191 Ibid., 72. Elsewhere, Mannheim is associated with a Hegelian positivism, which implies the possibility of social change through 'conscious control'. Hayek argued that this Hegelianism is the underlying rationale for central planning (Fredrick A. Hayek, *The Counter-Revolution of Science: Studies on the Abuse of Reason* (Glencoe: The Free Press, 1991 [1941]), 88).
192 Clements, *Moot Papers*, 280 (7th meeting, 9–12 February 1940).
193 Murry, Eliot and later Polanyi were the notable exceptions to the acceptance of the inevitability of planning.
194 Cf. Oldham, *The Resurrection*, 18–19; Karl Mannheim, 'Planning for Freedom' [1938], LM/SEC7; OLD/14/3/67.
195 Murry, *Europe in Travail*, 11. Such a 'partial totalitarianism' seems conceptually confused; totalitarianism is at a minimum the desire of total control.
196 J. H. Oldham, 'The Christian Witness in the Present Crisis', 6 October 1943, OLD/9/5/19.
197 Oldham, *Real Life*, 18.
198 H. A. Hodges, 'The Collective Commonwealth and the Christian', 22 January 1944, BA/5/33; MPP/15/6; OLD/14/1/71.
199 Cf. Vidler, *Scenes from a Clerical Life*, 119.
200 Clements, *Moot Papers*, 487 (13th meeting, 19–22 December 1942).
201 Mannheim, *Diagnosis*, 8.
202 Karl Mannheim, 'Planning for Freedom' [1938], LM/SEC7; OLD/14/3/67. See also Mannheim, *Diagnosis*, 101–6.
203 Clements, *Moot Papers*, 397 (11th meeting, 4–7 April).
204 Karl Mannheim, 'Planning for Freedom' [1938], LM/SEC7; OLD/14/3/67.
205 Cf. Clements, *Moot Papers*, 696 (20th meeting, 23–26 June 1944).
206 Karl Mannheim, 'Planning for Freedom', un [1938], LM/SEC7; OLD/14/3/67.
207 Bauman, *Modernity and Ambivalence*, 30–9.
208 Vidler, *God's Judgment*, 88. See also Vidler, *Secular Despair*, 83–4.
209 Vidler, 'Editorial: Planning for What', 67–8.
210 Clements, *Moot Papers*, 313 (8th meeting, 19–22 April 1940).
211 Vidler, *Scenes from a Clerical Life*, 119.
212 Clements, *Moot Papers*, 165 (3rd meeting, 6–9 January 1939).
213 John Middleton Murry, 'Memorandum by J. Middleton Murry', [1940], IOE/MOO/127; Murry, *Europe in Travail*, 53.

214 Ibid., 53. See also Murry, *Adam and Eve*, 23–4.
215 Clements, *Moot Papers*, 629 (18th meeting, 29 October–1 November 1943).
216 Ibid., 630.
217 Ibid., 630–1.
218 Oldham, 'Freedom and Planning'.
219 Christopher Dawson, 'What Is the Alternative to Totalitarianism?'.
220 Dawson, *Judgement*, 83, 85.
221 As cited in Scott, *A Historian and His World*, 133. Dawson did not qualify what he means by 'Philistine dictatorship', but given the context of his consistent objections, it most likely is a reference to Mannheim's vision.
222 See Kojecky, *T. S. Eliot's Social Criticism*, 155.
223 Michael Polanyi, 'Letter to Karl Mannheim', 19 April 1944, MPP/4/11.
224 After Polanyi's first meeting, Mannheim wrote that 'my conscience told me that a meeting will be enrichment to you and to them (Karl Mannheim, "Letter to Michael Polanyi", 29 June 1944, MPP/4/11)'.
225 Kettler and Meja, *Mannheim and the Crisis*, 266.
226 John Middleton Murry, *The Necessity of Communism* (London: Jonathan Cape, 1932), 117–18.
227 H. A. Hodges, 'Comment on the Moot's Fifteen Points', 29 July 1943, OLD/14/1/53.
228 Vidler, *Scenes from a Clerical Life*, 34, 51–2.
229 Kettler and Meja, *Mannheim and the Crisis*, 18, 94.
230 Paul Tillich, *The Socialist Decision* [Die sozialistische Entscheidung], trans. Franklin Sherman (New York: Harper & Row, 1977).
231 Cf. Grimley, *Citizenship*, 1.
232 See P. Merkley, *Reinhold Niebuhr: A Political Account* (Montreal: MQUP, 1975), ProQuest ebrary., 54, 96, 143–5, 148–9.
233 In a postscript written after the meeting, Hodges noted that his own view compared to those of Murry's in his *The Necessity of Communism* (H. A. Hodges, 'Comment on the Moot's Fifteen Points', 29 July 1943, OLD/14/1/53).
234 Paul Tillich, 'The Problem of Power', IOE/MOO/95; OLD/14/6/51.
235 H. A. Hodges, 'Politics and the Moot', 9 June 1943, OLD/14/1/43.
236 Clements, *Moot Papers*, 587 (17th meeting, 18–21 June 1943).
237 Ibid., 588–9 (17th meeting, 18–21 June 1943).
238 Lex Miller appeared as a 'guest' in the minutes of the 17th meeting; however, he became a regular attendee for the remaining Moot weekends.
239 Clements, *Moot Papers*, 591–2 (17th meeting, 18–21 June 1943).
240 Ibid., 590 (17th meeting, 18–21 June 1943).
241 Ibid., 590, 592.
242 Ibid., 593.

243 Ibid., 594.
244 H. A. Hodges, 'Comment on the Moot's Fifteen Points', 29 July 1943, OLD/14/1/53.
245 H. A. Hodges, 'Christianity and Society', 24 June 1943, OLD/13/6/33.
246 T. S. Eliot, 'Letter from T. S. Eliot', 9 August 1943, OLD/9/5/6.
247 T. S. Eliot, 'Letter from T. S. Eliot', 14 August 1943, OLD/9/5/7.
248 T. S. Eliot, 'Letter from T. S. Eliot', 21 August 1943, OLD/9/5/10.
249 H. A. Hodges, 'Comment on the Moot's Fifteen Points', 29 July 1943, OLD/14/1/53.
250 Gilbert Shaw, 'Christianity and Society', 6 September 1943, OLD/14/9/74.
251 See Nikolas Rose, Pat O'Malley and Mariana Valverde, 'Governmentality', *Annual Review of Law and Social Science* 2 (2006), 9.
252 Edwards, 'God's Totalitarianism', 287.
253 Slavoj Žižek, *Did Somebody Say Totalitarianism?: Five Interventions in the (Mis) Use of a Notion* (London: Verso, 2001), 3.
254 Grimley, *Citizenship*, 2–3.

5

Conflicts in Light of Modernism: T. S. Eliot and Karl Mannheim in Dialogue

Introduction

In this volume, I have sought to place the Moot within the wider historical context of the 1930s and '40s by drawing upon Roger Griffin's framework of Programmatic Modernism. Thus far, this lens has been applied to the Moot discourse as a whole. This chapter, however, explores how it can also be applied to engage with the social criticism of individual members. As the most discussed, distinguished and well-known members of the Moot, Karl Mannheim and T. S. Eliot will be used to showcase the benefit of this approach. The aim here is not merely to expound upon the intriguing debate that took place between the two. While the chapter does offer new archival details, their relationship has already been examined in some detail by Stefan Collini,[1] Wolfgang Wicht[2] and Roger Kojecky,[3] amongst others.[4] Rather, a new comparative perspective may be found through viewing this interaction and indeed their whole body of social criticism through the overarching interpretive lens of 'Political Modernism'.

Griffin points to the works of literary critics, who have long observed the pattern of decadence and renewal amongst the Modernist writers, thinkers and artists. The idea that many Modernists held a deep-rooted antagonism towards modernity and that such antipathies sparked a number of counter-reactions and visions of renewal has been widely discussed in Modernist studies. Some such accounts were mentioned in my introductory chapter. Collini's article on Eliot's later social criticism, for example, refers to Peter Gay's assertion of the Weimar Republic Modernists' 'hunger for wholeness' in the face of social disintegration under modernity.[5] Collini concludes that few 'match this profile better than T. S. Eliot'.[6] This Modernist yearning is a significant building block in Griffin's construction, as he draws a parallel between this outlook found amongst individual Modernist writers and that within sociopolitical movements.

Mannheim is certainly not a Modernist in the literary and artistic sense of the term. Nevertheless, once the Political Modernist tag has been expanded to include impulses beyond the confines of 'the arts', there is no reason why individual intellectuals could not be considered through this lens. Decadence-renewal patterns are not limited to the artistic elites of Europe, but can be identified in social thought of the time as well.

In isolation, to point to a pattern of decadence and renewal in political thought in Europe during this era is too generic to be interesting. What makes Griffin's thesis potentially fruitful, however, is his emphasis on the interwar crisis as a crisis of transcendence. That is, the perception that as a consequence of secularization the *nomos* of Christianity governing the Western world was collapsing, fuelling an apocalyptic angst of an imminent end of civilization.[7] It is from this perspective that I wish to approach Mannheim's and Eliot's social criticism.

Mannheim and Eliot lived in an age of transition where new ideas emerged, were tested and reconfigured. In response to a sense of anarchic chaos during the interwar decades, both advanced their own ideal new societies. The Moot became both a testing ground and a battleground for their ideologies. My argument is that as an advocate of centralized planning, Mannheim was driven by the Enlightenment's faith in human agency, whereas Eliot's confidence in divine providence led him to argue for a more passive eschatological preparation for God's intervention.

Eliot and Mannheim at the Moot

As the main forum for their relationship, the conflict between Mannheim and Eliot cannot be understood without an understanding of their respective interaction with the Moot. Ever since Kojecky's extensive treatment of the Moot in *T. S. Eliot's Social Criticism*, it has become commonplace for Eliot scholars to assume that his view of the Moot and Mannheim were essentially positive.[8] David Kettler and Volker Meja are amongst those who put a positive spin on their interaction, suggesting that for Mannheim, who was often a marginalized figure in English intelligentsia, an attentive Eliot became his 'greatest success'.[9] On this reading, Eliot was an influential public figure willing to lend an ear to Mannheim's ideas although his appraisal of these ideas was admittedly not always favourable. Collini's analysis is more critical, highlighting their disparities over definitions of 'culture' and the role and nature of elites. Nevertheless, Collini argues that there was more that united these figures than separated their social outlooks, an analysis Wolfgang Wicht concurs with.[10] Barry Spurr, in his *Anglo-Catholic in Religion*, has further problematized Kojecky's conclusions. On the basis of correspondence between Eliot and Mary Trevelyan, dating from 1943 to 1944, Spurr concludes that Eliot attended the Moot out of a sense of obligation to Oldham, but ultimately held that associations such as the Moot were futile.[11]

While Spurr makes a strong case, some nuancing on Eliot's disposition is required. It appears that Eliot joined the Moot with a positive disposition, but with time grew increasingly frustrated with it. In correspondences to his friends during the early years of the Moot, Eliot spoke highly of Oldham and the 'success' of the first meetings.[12] Nevertheless, despite being one of the most regular members, he maintained a critical distance from the outset, and his nickname for the Moot amongst his friends, the 'argle bargle', is suggestive.[13] Collini proposes that Eliot identified himself as a 'man of letters'. That is, as one observing the comings and goings of society from a critical distance.[14] This mode of engagement fits well with his participation in the Moot. For instance, Eliot also singled out John Middleton Murry as demanding monitoring.[15] Another example of this attitude is evident in a letter to Philip Mairet where Eliot spoke of the increasing influence of Mannheim and Adolf Löwe on the Moot, a situation that 'needs keeping a very critical eye on'.[16]

Indeed, the majority of Eliot's interaction with the Moot was in response to Mannheim's ideas, in terms of both comments at the gatherings and his written contribution. It is apparent that Eliot found Mannheim fascinating. Recalling their relationship in his autobiography, Alec Vidler wrote: 'I was constantly struck by the sympathy that grew between T. S. Eliot and Karl Mannheim and by the way they impressed and influenced each other.'[17] Eliot himself confirmed this friendship in his writings. Yet despite his personal empathy, he came to strongly reject Mannheim's ideas. In a private letter to his close friend Herbert Read, Eliot wrote that he felt compelled to 'warn' people from a wholesale acceptance of Mannheim.[18] Another letter, to Allen Tate, expressed a similar sentiment: 'Karl Mannheim is a very good fellow, but if you read his "Man and Society" you will know that I regard his ideas as dangerous.'[19] In a correspondence regarding 'The Germanisation of Britain' for the *New English Weekly* on 29 March 1945, Eliot wrote that '[no] contemporary thinker has more enriched my mental life in this way more than Dr. Mannheim, to whom I feel I owe a considerable debt'.[20] Nevertheless, this influence was a negative one that had forced Eliot 'to think violently in order to discover the grounds of my disagreement'.[21] Thus,

Eliot found Mannheim a useful dialogue partner, someone he was sympathetic towards but nevertheless strongly disagreed with.

Eliot's mode of engagement with the Moot stands in contrast to that of Mannheim. If Eliot was guarded in his commitment to the Moot, Mannheim embraced it wholeheartedly. If Eliot saw himself on the outskirts of the group looking in, Mannheim sought to occupy its centre. Shortly after his first encounter with the Moot circle, Mannheim, in a letter to his friend Louis Wirth, wrote enthusiastically of having found an influential group of British intellectuals who were willing to engage with him.[22] Mannheim was one of the Moot's most committed members in terms of written contributions and attendance. Furthermore, the minutes of the weekend-long gatherings bear strong imprints of his thought. While Mannheim showed a willingness to engage, he clearly and relentlessly sought to impress on the other members the merits of his suggested cause of action via 'Planning for Freedom'. As Julia Mannheim expressed it in a letter to the Moot members shortly after her husband's death, the Moot had been a 'free and safe place for the mind, soul and spirit'.[23]

Towards the end of the Moot's existence, Mannheim's interaction with the group did decrease. He attended the meetings but submitted no further position papers in the final three years. Nevertheless, the fact that Oldham decided to discontinue the Moot after Mannheim's sudden death on 9 January 1947 bears witness to his significance for the Moot.[24] Eliot, for his part, praised Mannheim in an obituary for *The Times* for having exerted 'remarkable influence' during his time in England, not least on the 'informal discussion among a small group [i.e. the Moot]'. Again, while Eliot acknowledged a degree of influence, he also distanced himself from Mannheim's thought, writing for 'many must be aware of a debt to him, whose points of view are very different from his'.[25]

Common ground

Secularization, eroding canopies and the loss of transcendence

We have seen that Eliot kept a critical distance from Mannheim's ideas. However, as Wolfgang Wicht points out, Eliot and Mannheim's sociopolitical outlooks were 'kindred'.[26] A recurring theme throughout the pages of this volume has been the sense of despair that Moot members felt over the state of Western societies. A Modernist angst of cosmic, apocalyptic chaos also permeates the social criticism of Mannheim and Eliot, respectively, during the 1930s and 1940s. Broadly speaking, their apocalyptic outlook corresponds to Peter Berger's idea of sacred canopies. Berger has argued that all human societies construct a *nomos*, that is, an overarching sense of meaning as 'a shield against terror' in an otherwise chaotic world. From time to time and for various historical reasons, the plausibility structures of such world views crumble, leading to breakdown and chaos.[27]

Arguably, a sacred-canopy-collapse occurred during the late nineteenth century when Christianity, through secularization, lost its dominant position as a social force in Europe. In *The Gay Science*, Friedrich Nietzsche dramatically likened the effects of this 'death of God' to the drinking up of the sea, the wiping away of the horizon and the unchaining of the earth from the sun.[28] Eliot's and Mannheim's sociopolitical outlooks must be ultimately understood from this premise, as responses to the realization of the loss of transcendence in modern societies and its dreadful consequences. These themes are readily identifiable in Mannheim's seminal *Ideology and Utopia*, where he investigated the 'breakdown of the unitary world-view with which the modern era was ushered in.'[29] Mannheim identified a shift with the loss of the Church's 'intellectual monopoly', which had guaranteed the unity of the medieval order, to a fragmented world of competing world views that had rendered society devoid of a common vision.[30] Thus, in a world of constant flux, a new reconstruction was required to shield against 'the perpetually fluid process underlying all things'.[31]

A major theme in *Man and Society* is the failure of liberalism and its *laissez faire* mentality resulting in disintegration and maladjustment.[32] In *Diagnosis of Our Time*, Mannheim's focus had changed somewhat. Here he explored secularization and its detrimental effect on the fundamental 'paradigmatic experiences' that govern every society. An example of a paradigmatic experience would be Jesus' death and resurrection, which had provided Christian Europe with archetypal images that in turn informed social and moral life. A predicament of modernity was its 'despiritualization', robbing Western societies of their powerful Christian archetypes without replacing them:

> Without paradigmatic experiences no consistent conduct, no character formation and no real human coexistence and co-operation are possible. Without them our universe of discourse loses its articulation, conduct falls to pieces, and only disconnected bits of successful behaviour patterns and fragments of adjustment to an ever-changing environment remain.[33]

Mannheim's social thought was profoundly affected by the modern dilemma of the eternal versus the transitory. He celebrated the experimental and spontaneous spirit of the renaissance and liberalism, but lamented its resulting 'neutralisation of values'.[34] During the 12th Moot meeting, Mannheim developed a line of thought akin to what Zygmunt Bauman would later come to speak of as the 'ambivalence of modernity'.[35] The modern psyche – via Bergson, Hegel and Croce, and ultimately Protestantism – cherished change, reasoned Mannheim, yet this mentality laid bare 'an awareness of the abyss ... due to removal of all *eternal scaffolding*'. In turn, modernity was plagued with a sense of 'disintegration and chaos'.[36] In a paper for the Moot in 1941, Mannheim pleaded 'that the world is on the edge of an abyss and only a new social order, a new kind of man can help'.[37] Only a radical reorientation would save modern society from total collapse.

Neither Eliot nor Mannheim believed that a liberal secular society – if by liberal one means neutral – was sustainable. Understood as a disintegrative force, whether in religion or politics, liberalism would 'prepare for that which is its own negation: the artificial, mechanized or brutalized control which is a desperate remedy of its own chaos'.[38] In other words, since liberalism was a negative force, something else would fill the chaotic vacuum that it left behind. Directly borrowing from Christopher Dawson, Eliot anticipated that this reordering in democratic nations would lead to centralized control and a democratic totalitarianism.[39] Nevertheless, claimed Eliot, the Western world was still at a crossroads between 'a new Christian society' and a pagan society.[40] Some years later in a series of broadcasts for Germany in 1946, Eliot starkly spelled out the consequences if Christianity was rejected: 'If Christianity goes, the whole of our culture goes ... You must pass through many centuries of barbarism.'[41] Both Eliot and Mannheim, then, understood the crisis of modernity as a crisis of transcendence. The crumbling structures of Christian Europe and the crisis in liberalism form the backdrop to which their respective social criticism must be understood.

Culture, religion and renewal

Mannheim's alarm over secularization was informed by a definition of religion – inherited from the classical sociologists Saint-Simon, Comte and Durkheim – as an indispensable force of social integration and cultural flourishing.[42] In *Ideology and Utopia*, Mannheim maintained that 'the magical-religious view' has an important meaning-making function 'to make coherent the fragments of the reality of inner psychic as well as objective external experience, and to place them with reference to a certain complex of conduct'.[43]

It is therefore striking that such references to religious structuring of reality are absent in Mannheim's major undertaking on social reconstruction. A central emphasis in *Man and Society* is the remoulding and transformation of 'man'. However, rather than advocating a religious formation, Mannheim drew extensively upon modern psychology as he grappled with how to harness the irrational and subconscious in cultural sublimation.[44] Conversely, in *Diagnosis of our Time* – a book predominantly developed through his interaction at the Moot – religion is viewed as an indispensable social force in the implementation of his democratic, centrally planned society.[45] The appeal of religion, for Mannheim, was that it added life and spirit to his otherwise technocratic ideas of social and cultural planning and potentially holding a society together without compulsion. In a Weber-esque analysis in *Man and Society*, Mannheim feared that the mechanization of modern society could become a 'prison', enslaving the masses.[46] However, during his years with the Moot, he came to appreciate religion as a means to mitigate these dangers of a planned society. Discussing his paper 'Towards a New Social Philosophy', Mannheim admitted that planners themselves could not create a 'unifying purpose'. Thus, '[t]he only alternative to the concentration camp was the spontaneous giving up of deviations, and only a revival of religion could bring this about',[47] implying that only religion could create the organic social integration that the totalitarian regimes could only yield through threats and use of violence.[48] Drawing upon August Comte, Mannheim elaborated on the function of religion in *Freedom, Power and Democratic Planning*, arguing that there was an innate human need for 'a transcendental religious foundation' without which society would become intolerably deprived of purpose.[49]

If Mannheim's outlook derived from classical sociology, Eliot inherited the English tradition of Samuel Coleridge.[50] Thus, whilst Eliot would have reacted against Mannheim's pure utilitarianism, he would nevertheless have agreed on the culture-bearing function of religion. Eliot held that the culture of a society – that is, a people's 'way of life' – is the incarnation of a religion.[51] In other words, religion informs and shapes the institutions, habits and behaviour of a people through and through.[52] An example of how 'religion provides the framework for a culture' can be found in a short letter to the Moot on 'Christian imagination'. Here Eliot related the production of cultural artefacts, such as the arts, to religious experience. Artistic imagination is essentially a religious experience, and according to Eliot, 'capacity' for religious experience is in turn conditioned by social milieu. It follows that in a secular society where culture is deprived of spirituality, imagination 'itself is broken up'.[53] The breakdown of relationship between those in the arts and the religious community is mutually detrimental:

> The tendency then is for the religious sensibility to be stunted, and for the arts to perish slowly – as the religious imagination atrophies, the imagination *tout court* disappears also. The arts, in their decline, pass through the stage of sensationalism; theology and philosophy which cease to be nourished by imagination descend into verbalism.[54]

In short, Eliot asserted that culture could not flourish without religion, for '[n]o culture has appeared or developed except together with a religion'.[55]

Revival of Christianity

There is thus significant overlap between Eliot's and Mannheim's diagnosis of the crisis of modern society. Both held that the crisis of modernity was a result of secularization, for without a religious vision, society had no unifying purpose.

Ultimately, they shared the belief that only the renewal of Christendom could provide gainful foundations for Western societies. None of the major alternative paradigms at hand filled them with much hope. Liberalism was no real alternative for, on their reading, it constituted no positive content and represented mere liberation *from* tradition, a *laissez faire,* with no aim to strive towards; it was a negative, disintegrative force. The totalitarian regimes, as replacement religions, did fill the void previously occupied by Christianity, but at the expense of human dignity and freedom.[56] Thus, as the only viable alternative, both turned to Christianity as the source of societal renewal.

For Eliot, the hope of a Christian society was tied up with his conviction that the claims of Christianity are universally true, but also to his assertion that Christianity has produced 'the highest culture the world has ever known'.[57] Mannheim, however, argued that the 'spirit of Christianity' could correct 'the dehumanisation, which is more or less exacted by the machine'.[58] He repeatedly differentiated between true religion and the false religious expressions seen in the secular religions of the totalitarian regimes.[59] Within this framework, Mannheim claimed that Christianity, as the 'religion of love and universal brotherhood', would in his planned democracy offer an alternative sacred canopy to 'the recent philosophy with the demonic image of man [here referring to fascism]'.[60] In essence, Christianity had the spiritual resources and values that could provide his democratically planned society with religious vitality and transcendent purpose. Furthermore, Mannheim was drawn to the British expression of Christianity with its pluralistic and tolerant spirit. He deemed its tradition flexible enough to be adjusted in an age of transition and as such particularly fruitful as the religious foundation of his planned society.[61]

Clashes on the transformation of culture

Planning versus preparation for the future

Given the significant common ground between Mannheim and Eliot's outlook, why did Mannheim's ideas disturb Eliot? The interaction between Eliot and Mannheim centred on themes of planning, the functions of elites, religion, and the definition, transformation and renewal of culture. In these discussions the point of contention concerned their respective understandings of the mechanism by which the desired cultural and societal renewal should be achieved.

Mannheim's idea of 'Planning for Freedom' was one of the central ideas discussed in the Moot, presented already at the 3rd meeting. It was an attempt to provide a constructive vision of modern society. It sought to address the chaotic *laissez faire* of liberalism, accepted the inevitability of centralization and planning in industrialized mass society, while resisting the stifling totalitarianism of fascism and communism. Mannheim believed that through extensive socio-scientific investigation and experimentation, and in collaboration with a host of intellectuals from other disciplines, sociologists could address the ills of modern society. These elites would be responsible for inculcating the masses with a democratic culture through educating for a new responsible democratic persona. Outlining a detailed course of action, his programme for a democratically planned society was as bold as it was comprehensive, and Mannheim believed that the Moot could form the nucleus that could catalyse his vision into reality.[62]

The vision immediately struck a chord with the Moot members and clearly left Eliot provoked. In a circulated comment, Eliot hailed the paper as a 'masterly outline' and his critique was guarded.[63] However, in a letter to Oldham during this time Eliot professed that '[t]here were so many objections in my mind', but that he was still struggling to articulate these.[64] Eliot further noted that he had been tempted to speak out against 'Mannheim's plan of action' had Oldham himself not tactfully diverted the conversation away from Mannheim's ideas at the final session of the weekend. However, Eliot clearly misjudged Oldham's intentions. Endorsed by Oldham, Mannheim's ideas would figure for years as a central line of investigation in the Moot. It is likely that the seed of Eliot's discontentment with the Moot was sown at this point.

The first public misgiving that Eliot expressed towards Mannheim came in his review of *Man and Society* for *The Spectator* on 6 June 1940. Having approved of Mannheim's social diagnosis, Eliot expressed his fears of a latent totalitarianism in Mannheim's ideas of central planning.[65] 'What is the alternative'? asked Eliot:

It can only be ... that which we may call the "dark age attitude" – waiting, perhaps for many generations, for the storm of the machine age to blow over; retiring with a few of the best books, to a small self-contained community, to till the soil and the cow.[66]

Elsewhere, in his reflections on the 1930 Lambeth Conference, Eliot attached a religious and eschatological dimension to this 'waiting'. Faced with the reality of a society that had endorsed a 'non-Christian mentality', Eliot proposed that, 'we must be very patient in awaiting its collapse; meanwhile redeeming the time: so that the Faith may be preserved alive through the dark ages before us; to renew and rebuild civilization, and save the World from suicide'.[67] While Eliot did paint a vision of the ideal Christian society in *The Idea*, which he hoped would inspire a change in 'social attitude', he did not devise a plan for its realization.[68] His 'dark age attitude' entailed a long-term view of patient waiting.

However, Eliot clearly did not suggest a mere idle passivity. In an editorial for the *CNL*, he emphasized the importance of *preparing* for a 'new world' after the war.[69] Eliot drew a distinction between planning and preparation. The initial step of this preparation consisted of prophetically shaking the nation out of its slumber and awakening it to see the consequences of its wandering into paganism.[70] It was a wake-up call from delusion and a call to repentance.[71] Furthermore, both Eliot and Mannheim held that any society was dependent on the kind of persons inhabiting it. In a BBC broadcast in 1937, Eliot suggested that, 'more important than the intention of a new machine, is the creation of a temper of mind in a people such that they can learn to use a new machine'.[72] Thus, fundamental to the creation of Eliot's envisioned future Christian society was education that would foster the 'type of man' who aspired to the ideals of holiness and wisdom.[73] Eliot himself would have suggested – as he does in a *CNL* article – that central planning is futile in an ever-changing world: we simply do not know what tomorrow will look like.[74] It is, however, possible to instil religious values through education in preparation to meet the future, argued Eliot.

Definitions of culture

The disparity between Eliot's patient waiting and preparation and Mannheim's active planning is related to disputes over the nature of culture, the role of elites and ultimately religious conviction. Firstly, Eliot could afford this 'dark age attitude' because he held a cyclical view of culture. That is, the idea that cultures go through cycles of decay and rebirth. Indeed, in a paper for the Moot,

Eliot contrasted his own cyclical understanding of history with Mannheim's progressivism, which by implication demands greater activism.[75]

The difference in their definitions of culture is further crystallized in Eliot's *Notes*. Here he took issue with Mannheim's proposition that culture originates in the elites and then filters down to mass society.[76] In *Man and Society*, Mannheim had suggested that any 'sociological investigation of the culture in liberal society must begin with the life of those who create culture', that is, the 'intelligentsia'.[77] Such an understanding of culture makes sense in the light of Mannheim's attachment to planning, for if culture springs from the elites, planning is all the more conceivable an outcome of deliberate co-ordination between intellectuals, especially social scientists.

Eliot, on the other hand, had for decades come to understand culture in more dynamic terms. There is, for example, much overlap between the ideas of tradition in Eliot's *After Strange Gods* (1934) and culture in *Notes*. In *After Strange Gods*, tradition is defined as 'all those habitual actions, habits and customs, from the most significant religious rite to our conventional way of greeting a stranger'.[78] In the first chapter of *Notes*, culture is seen as the outcome of multiple processes in different societal segments and classes. Culture, wrote Eliot, includes everyday items and activity such as:

> Derby Day, Henley Regatta Cowes, the twelfth of August, a cup final, the dog races, the pin table, the dart board, Wensleydale cheese, boiled cabbage cut into sections, beetroot in vinegar, nineteenth-century Gothic churches and the music of Elgar.[79]

Cultures, then, are preserved and evolve organically through the often-unconscious actions and habits of a whole people, rather than the outcome of elite interventions and creativity. The implication, as stated in the introduction to *Notes*, is that even if a society possesses all essential 'conditions', culture cannot be generated at will: 'Even if these conditions with which I am concerned, seem to the reader to represent desirable social aims, he must not leap to the conclusion that these aims can be fulfilled solely by deliberate organisation.'[80] Culture cannot be planned; rather, it is the outcome of multiple processes in society that work themselves out separately, merging organically into the total culture of a people.

Is there, then, an apparent paradox between Eliot's emphasis on stability and continuation in his conservative social criticism and the *aufbruch* of his experimental paradigmatic Modernist literature?[81] Arguably, while the *form* might differ, consistent themes are recognizable. For instance, the desolation of a society decaying under materialism expressed in *The Waste Land* finds a parallel in the battle between the material and spiritual world in the dramatization *Murder in the Cathedral* (1935), and also in the juxtaposing of religious versus materialistic world views in *The Idea*. Another identifiable theme is that of suffering and redemption. In the final speech of *Murder in the Cathedral*, the Third Priest breaks out in a doxology in response to Thomas Becket's martyrdom:

> We thank Thee for Thy mercies of blood, for Thy redemption
> by blood. For the blood of Thy martyrs and saints
> Shall enrich the earth, shall create the holy places.[82]

Just as Beckett's sacrifice brings redemption and renewal in Eliot's *Murder in the Cathedral*, so the re-Christianization of modern society goes via a purgatory of 'discipline, inconvenience and discomfort'.[83]

The clerisy debate and the nature of elites

A dominant discussion within the Moot relates to the function of the group itself as an exemplary elite. Mannheim advocated for something between a voluntary organization and a political party: 'a combatant order', similar to the 'nervous system' of a social organism that could be 'co-ordinating its activities' and could 'spiritualize its aims'.[84] He envisioned a group of intellectuals that, through spiritual renewal and mutual support, could offer leadership to the nation or 'revitalize' existing leadership structures.[85] However, Eliot's aversion towards organized corporate action kept him on guard against such developments in the Moot. While Eliot did not in principle reject the idea of an elite, he doubted whether the Moot could establish sufficient common ground to launch such a 'party'. For Eliot, the value of the Moot was its diversity: 'I find in it, not merely agreement achieved and hoped for, but also *significant disagreement*.'[86] Already at the 2nd meeting Eliot had stated his view regarding the benefit of the Moot. The minutes record that, 'T. S. Eliot said that we should not aim at finding a happy formula to which all could agree, but rather at getting below the surface at which everything is unconsciously or potentially Christian.'[87] These comments reflect Eliot's general reluctance to subscribe to easy solutions such as societal blueprints. Programmes were superficial solutions that did not prepare for the kind of society, saturated with Christianity, that Eliot yearned for.

The tension over elites is most clearly presented in the Moot's discussion on Eliot's paper on the clerisy. In *The Idea* Eliot had already drawn upon

Samuel Coleridge's term 'clerisy' to describe an elite that would 'influence and be influenced by each other, and collectively ... form the conscious mind and conscience of the nation'.[88] By the time he wrote 'On the Place and Function of the Clerisy' for the Moot almost six years later, Eliot had considerably altered his definition of the clerisy, downplaying both its educational and spiritual roles. The clerisy is here described as an elite consisting of 'any category of men and women who because of their individual capacities exercise significant power in any particular area'. The clerisy capture ideas and 'alter the sensibility, of their time'.[89] The function of the clerics is thus the transformation of culture, but in contrast to Coleridge, Eliot clearly distanced himself from the idea that the clerisy is the sole agent for cultural transmission, which is rather 'a function of the whole people'. The clerics are agents of alteration in a society, whereas culture is the total way of life of a people and therefore cannot be attributed to one particular class or group.

Eliot's clerisy paper was commented upon by both Mannheim and Michael Polanyi.[90] It is the only instance where Mannheim directly responded to Eliot's writings and thus is relevant for understanding their respective positions. Interestingly, Mannheim's extensive critique of Eliot's paper offers few points of disagreement. In fact, Mannheim argued that Eliot's clerisy comes close to his own use of the term 'intelligentsia', which consists of those who give 'a lead to the change in politically and culturally relevant ideas'.[91] However, Eliot's response was less conciliatory, taking aim at the apparent contradiction in Mannheim's insistence on the spontaneity of the clerisy whilst also claiming that culture can be planned for.[92] Mannheim had suggested that interaction between the clerics would generate new cultural 'patterns'.[93] For Eliot, an implication of such interaction is the unpredictability of the outcome, '[for] I do not see that the "interplay" can be directed or pattern emergent from it be foreseen or planned'.[94] Further, Mannheim had proposed that 'Planning for Freedom' implies that the organizations of elites can be structured by 'unwritten laws' that enable spontaneity and originality.[95] However, Eliot naturally challenged the idea that '"unwritten laws" can be planned'.[96]

The selection of elites, class and the transmission of culture

Mannheim clearly paid heed to Eliot's criticism. Shortly after the clerisy debate, Mannheim published an article for the *CNL* titled 'The Meaning of Popularisation in a Mass Society', in which he argued that the transmission of culture is a task for every class of society. Not only did Mannheim borrow Eliot's ideas, but his use of the phrases 'the whole people' and 'change the sensibility of their time' must be understood as deliberate plagiarism.[97] The article as a whole read as an attempt to reassure Eliot.

As a member of the editorial board of the *CNL*, it is probable that Eliot would have seen Mannheim's article. If so, it did little to alleviate his criticism. Around this time, a combative Eliot wrote the second chapter of *Notes* that was going to 'blow the Moot up'.[98] The chapter in question, which originally appeared as 'The Class and the Elite' in the *New English Weekly* October 1945, further seeks to define the role of the elite in cultural transformation, using Mannheim as a sparring partner.[99] For Eliot, Mannheim exemplified the problematic push amongst his contemporaries towards a classless society, whereby ruling elites selected on the basis of ability replace the functions of dominant classes. As Eliot readily pointed out, even Manheim had to admit to the difficulty of selecting elites in a democratic society. He admitted this in *Man and Society*:

> We have no clear idea of how the selection of élites would work in an open mass society in which only the principle of achievement mattered. It is possible that in such a society, the succession of the elites would take place much too rapidly and social continuity which is essential due to the slow and gradual broadening of the influence of the dominant groups would be lacking in it.[100]

Thus, for Eliot, the problem that Mannheim faced concerned how, in a classless society, culture could be successfully transmitted from one generation to another, as well as how the mechanism of selection for new elites would function. In Eliot's view, a classless society gives rise to cultural degeneration, for on his reading, the vibrancy of culture is dependent upon a stratified society whereby the plurality of the classes reciprocally contributes to the whole. Therefore, while the call for an elite membership based on ability appears to address issues of justice, it assumes the breakdown of classes, thereby breaking up the processes of cultural transmission: 'It posits an atomistic view of society.'[101]

As seen in the clerisy debate, Eliot noted a point of difference between his own view of the elite as that group which creates a more 'conscious', higher level of culture and cultural innovation, versus Mannheim's view of elites as the exclusive culture-generating group of society. The issue that Eliot sought to address was how such elites are created and maintained, along with some wider implications of this. In Eliot's ideal society, a cultural elite would attain its tradition and social cohesion from the 'dominant class'. The members of the elite would be predominantly, but not exclusively, from the 'higher' classes. At a minimum, the elite would be 'coloured' by and 'attached' to the higher classes. There would be a reciprocity between the dominant class and the cultural elite. Classes would be able to nurture able individuals who could assume the responsibility of cultural transmission from generation to generation, thereby maintaining a living tradition which the elite could draw upon. Class, transmitted via the family, would be the best means by which this culture could be transferred to the next generation. Furthermore, by its innovation the elite, in turn, could ensure that the dominant classes did not stagnate.[102] Eliot's critique of Mannheim's classless elite was that '[in] an élite composed of individuals who find their way into it solely for their individual pre-eminence, the differences of background will be so great that they will be united in their common interests, and separated by everything else'.[103] In other words, classless elites would result in social disintegration, for if there were little common group culture and for the sake of the transmission of culture, the elites in a classless society 'will consist solely of individuals whose only common bond will be their professional interest: with no social cohesion, with no social continuity'.[104]

Eliot's ideas on class and the elite are repeatedly linked to the maintenance of 'culture' – defined as 'a way of life' of a people. The implication of Eliot's argument is that although Mannheim's planned society might seek to recover a common purpose, meaning or shared value basis or indeed some reinvigorated 'sacred canopy', it remains an impossible utopia. Without the classes, society cannot maintain a culture or 'a way of life', for the transmission of culture is dependent upon the family (class), and the family lies outside of the scope of the planner.[105] In other words, despite his attempt to reconcile his ideas on culture and elites with Eliot's, in his *CNL* article 'The Meaning of the Popularisation in a Mass Society', Mannheim had still failed to address a crucial problem: 'that of the *transmission of culture*'.[106]

Planning and religious renewal

Another point of contention in the debate over societal transformation concerned whether a religious renewal could be planned. In his lengthy two-part paper 'Towards a New Social Philosophy', Mannheim argued that since there is a social context for even the most transcendent experiences, there are certain conditions in which religion can flourish.[107] Eliot used the paper as his point of departure for his 'notes' on 'Christian Imagination'. Eliot seems to have concurred with Mannheim that religion flourishes under certain conditions. Eliot proposed that imagination – the stuff of great art and thought – is essentially religious and that religious experiences flourish in environments that cultivate such experiences.[108]

It is striking that in these notes Eliot merely hinted at his aversion to Mannheim's proposal regarding the possibility of planning to cultivate conditions conducive for religious experience or imagination.

This omission is all the more puzzling considering Eliot's critical review of *Diagnosis of Our Time*. In 1943, Mannheim published *Diagnosis*, a compilation of articles written during the war that included 'Towards a New Social Philosophy'. The essence of Eliot's rebuff relates to Mannheim's confidence in the sociologist's ability to stage social conditions in which religion, and thus culture, can flourish. In contrast to his previous Moot paper on Christian imagination, Eliot here rejected Mannheim's claim that certain conditions that favour religious revival can be produced by the planners of such a society.[109] For Eliot, it was a question of what comes first: religion or society? As argued in *Notes*, religion is for Eliot that which provides the framework for culture, and not the other way around. This is because religion cannot be reduced to religious experience alone, but also carries dogma. In turn, the particularity of dogma informs the shape a society takes on.

Ultimately, Eliot did not share Mannheim's optimism for the possibility of a fruitful reconstruction. Just as modern society had no architectural tradition which warrants enthusiasm concerning the impending reconstruction of war-torn British cities, so there was no shared value basis or common religious vision on which social construction would yield a constructive cultural renewal.

Humanism versus Christian theism

However, there is another underlying reason for Eliot's continued antipathy towards Mannheim's ideas of a planned society. That is, Mannheim's outlook, informed by the humanism of the Enlightenment, clashed with Eliot's Christian supernaturalism. Both held that social cohesion demands a religious framework without which society cannot flourish. Where they fundamentally differed was on the question of whether such religious frameworks had any ontological basis.

In his review of *Diagnosis*, Eliot refers to Dawson's critique of Mannheim's *Man and Society*. Dawson was concerned that 'the remoulding of human nature', to which Mannheim aspired through planning, 'is a task that far transcends politics'. In fact, such an undertaking would threaten human liberty and therefore, '[the] planning of culture cannot be undertaken in a dictatorial spirit, like a rearmament plan … It must … be undertaken in a really religious spirit'.[110] In his review, Eliot did acknowledge Mannheim's inclusion of religion in more recent writing.¹¹¹ Thus, there is no fundamental disagreement between Mannheim and Dawson on this account. Yet, Eliot recorded a decisive difference: Mannheim was a sociologist 'with no dogmatic faith such as Dawson's'.¹¹² This makes all the difference for Eliot. The comment in *Notes* that 'no religion can fully be "understood" from the outside – even for the sociologist's purpose' must be seen as implicating Mannheim.¹¹³ Eliot mentioned his review of *Diagnosis* in a letter to his friend John Hayward. Here, Eliot confided that he did not esteem Dawson's *The Judgement of the Nations*, but that 'the point of the point is in the concluding remarks about Mannheim'.¹¹⁴

What was subtly hinted at in his review of *Diagnosis* was more plainly stated in a BBC radio broadcast titled 'Towards a Christian Britain' in early 1941. While not directly addressing Mannheim, Eliot expressed here why his Christianity implied an aversion towards planned societies. Having expounded on a threefold duty of worship of God, social action and individual morality as a prerequisite in the formation of a Christian nation, Eliot, in addition, referred to divine providence: 'But we must not forget God, without whom we can do nothing of worth, but with whom we can do everything. It is impossible to make a blue-print of a Christian order, because we cannot fit God into a blue-print.'¹¹⁵ As Eliot wrote in a letter to Fenn who oversaw the broadcast, he wished to emphasize that '"Christianisation" was anything but a superhuman task, too difficult to be carried out by Picture Post without the help of God.'¹¹⁶

Throughout his time with the Moot, Mannheim insisted that his contributions to the group were limited sociological observations that did not concern the truthfulness of religious claims.¹¹⁷ Mannheim saw himself as an agnostic.¹¹⁸ However, in a private conversation at a dinner, Mannheim offended his fellow émigré and Moot member Polanyi by questioning the compatibility of faith commitments and honest scientific enquiry.¹¹⁹ Further, despite his confessed agnosticism towards Christian truth claims, Mannheim's expressed aversion towards the doctrine of original sin became a source of contention in the Moot.¹²⁰ Interestingly, Walter Oakeshott, speaking of the need for the Moot to overcome this 'one doctrinal problem' which 'may prove a real line of division', attributed Mannheim's objection to original sin to his 'humanistic view'.¹²¹

Nevertheless, Mannheim came to appreciate the fundamental necessity for a 'transcendental religious foundation in society', for a 'world without purpose would mean a kind of homelessness hardly tolerable to a thoughtful being'. This was a great dilemma in the modern age, for a scientific world view based on the evolutionary laws of selection and adaptation provided no basis for lived experience: 'It is like admitting in theory that the earth moves round the sun while still experiencing the sun as a rising disk that radiates light day by day.'¹²² A paradox Mannheim sought to overcome is that although religion could no longer simply be considered objectively true, nevertheless, without a reference to the eternal, life descends into nihilism. Mannheim overcame this tension by reference to archetypes and paradigmatic experiences which provided societies with a foundation. Within Christianity, the death and resurrection of Christ is the archetype that informs the beliefs and practices of the community.¹²³ Such archetypes and experiences, rather than dogma and eternal principles, allowed for Mannheim to argue for the possibility of greater flexibility, adjustment and reinterpretation without slipping into relativism. The appeal to Christian archetypes was perhaps one of the most decisive contributions of Mannheim to the Moot.¹²⁴

Religion was for Mannheim real and forceful, but nevertheless a human construction, a historically contingent phenomenon that could be utilized as a tool of social cohesion at the hands of the planner, an attitude consistent with the spirit of the Enlightenment ascribing primacy to human agency in shaping one's own destiny. Eliot accepted sociological perspectives on religion to a point, not least since he understood religion as a cultural force. But in contrast to Mannheim, he held that the transcendent was more than a mere human projection. His affirmation of the supernatural meant that religion, and thereby culture, could not simply be manipulated by modern scientists. Therefore, he held a strong antipathy towards any support of Christianity on functional grounds alone: 'what is *worst of all* is to advocate Christianity, not because it is true, but because it might be beneficial'.¹²⁵

This divergence was most strongly expressed in the interaction that ensued from Eliot's clerisy paper. The emphasis of Polanyi's response to Eliot's clerisy paper was on the clerisy's role in the transmission of tradition; he held that the heritage of European culture 'can continue to live only by a process of *personal transmission*'.¹²⁶ The development of knowledge cannot evolve without this heritage since 'even our freshest thoughts are implanted on a deep stratum of perennial humus: their logic goes back to past centuries'.¹²⁷ Nevertheless, each generation has to test and try the heritage passed on to them. This process cannot be controlled, but it has to be left to each generation, and to divine providence, to determine: 'To this extent the clerisy is at every moment literally in the hands of God.'¹²⁸ While Eliot replied that Polanyi had overemphasized the function of guardians and transmitters of culture – for Eliot this was the function of the classes – Polanyi's theism nevertheless resonated. In response to Polanyi's critique of the clerisy paper, Eliot articulated the essence of his disagreement with Mannheim. In agreement with Polanyi, Eliot wrote:

So, while we can say that there is such a thing as 'culture' (we mean something by the term) we cannot make it a direct object of activity; we can only aim at limited ends which we believe contribute to it. *Culture might be described as that which cannot be planned, except by God.*[129]

The implication of his insistence on God as the ultimate planner is that cultural transformation is not entirely within human control. It is not that Eliot denies human agency; for instance, in a broadcast after the 1937 Oxford Conference, Eliot calls the nation to self-reflection, humility and repentance in preparation 'to receive the grace of God without which human operations are vain'.[130] As we have seen, Eliot embraced a 'dark age attitude' whereby the individual kept the candle burning by whatever he or she could contribute in their sphere of influence. Eliot urged the listeners of the BBC to a virtuous prophetic living in dark times. 'Christian prophets' are those through whom 'God works to convert the habits of feeling and thinking, of desiring and willing, to which we are all more enslaved than we know'.[131]

Some implications

This theistic outlook seriously undermines the attempt to locate Eliot's social criticism within the proto-fascist bracket.[132] To be sure, the younger Eliot's association with proto-fascist Charles Maurras and his Action Française group is well-documented. In fact, Kenneth Asher suggests that Charles Maurras' influence on Eliot's political ideal spanned 'from beginning to end'.[133] As Leon Surette too points out, Eliot never repudiated Maurras. Nevertheless, the degree to which he continued to influence Eliot in the Moot period and beyond is questionable. Surette does not go as far as Asher, but still asserts that 'there is no doubt that Eliot's political views derive in great part from Maurras'.[134] In a recent monograph, *Dreams of a Totalitarian Utopia*, Surette contends that Eliot's views would have correlated to Mussolini's definition of fascism as 'an organised, centralised, authoritarian democracy'.[135] Further, Surette claims that 'Eliot's rejection of fascism was not on grounds of its anti-democratic and totalitarian doctrines … but because he found it inferior to the anti-democratic totalitarian doctrines of Charles Maurras'.[136] However, as an offspring of the Enlightenment, fascism put a strong emphasis on human agency expressed in the totalitarian drive towards total state control. It is true that Eliot to an extent shared with the fascist movements a commitment to a hierarchical society and authoritarian rule.[137] However, it is precisely Eliot's theism, for it implies a waiting upon and living without control, that put him at odds with totalitarianism.[138]

Besides, in contradistinction to the dominant interpretation of Eliot's social criticism, Collini argues that Eliot from the 1930s onwards can be placed with the Anglican social radicalism of the time and within the Whig tradition.[139] There is a correlation between Eliot's conversion in 1927 and his shifting political outlook. From the early 1930s, Eliot regularly attended the meetings of the Christendom (Candos) Group headed by Maurice Reckitt, with V. A. Demant, Philip Mairet and others. Writing his synopsis of the group, Reckitt described its political and cultural outlook as informed by a Christian understanding of man and society.[140] Eliot's fellowship with these intellectuals and regular contributions to the associated journals *Christendom* and *New English Weekly* brought him closer to Anglican social thought at the time. By the time Eliot had joined the Moot, his commitment to hierarchy and order had waivered. At the first Moot meeting, Eliot suggested that Christianity had thrived through 'local circles and small group[s]' within 'natural community life' rather than through the hierarchy of the church.[141] My own argument adds to these voices that argue that Eliot's theism implies a learning to live without control which thereby steers him away from more authoritarian and reactionary ideals. As Erik Tonning suggests, Eliot's 'uncompromising affirmation of Christian supernaturalism' marked a demonstrable shift away from the Right.[142]

It is also, conversely, the implied humanism in Mannheim's 'Planning for Freedom' that was an underlying reason why he never quite managed to convince the Moot members that his scheme was not simply a disguised form of semi-totalitarianism. Eliot made this claim implicitly by referring to Dawson's critique of Mannheim. Dawson used Mannheim to exemplify a trend towards materialistic planning that would result in worse excesses of the repression of freedom than the totalitarian regimes.[143] This was also Polanyi's argument against Mannheim. The logic of materialism is the sovereign state, as articulated in Hobbes' 'Leviathan', for without a religious framework which locates authority in an external morality, the state must be imbued with absolute power; if not, the nation would disintegrate into civil war between competing groups.[144] His confrontation with Mannheim must be understood in the light of this line of thought.[145]

Conclusion

The ongoing exchange between T. S. Eliot and Karl Mannheim is one of the more intriguing subplots of the Moot discourse. There is something incongruous, but arresting, in this battle of ideas between Mannheim, the eminent Hungarian sociologist and secular Jew, and Eliot, famed nationalized American poet and Anglo-Catholic, over the soul of English society amongst a group of British intellectuals.

Their interaction, stretching across nearly a decade, reveals both common ground and deep-rooted differences. In the immediate context of the Moot, Mannheim's ideas of sociopolitical planning were at the heart of their exchange, drawing a strong response from Eliot. Both identified social disintegration under the forces of liberalism as a cause of the civilizational crisis in the West. However, they had different ideas on the mechanisms of cultural renewal. Eliot's rejection of Mannheim concerns the definition of culture and how culture is maintained, nourished and revitalized. These differences led Eliot to repeatedly oppose Mannheim's planned society, for he considered culture to be the product of a whole people, evolving organically from one generation to the next and flourishing through the spontaneous interaction between different social groups and classes. In Eliot's view, such mechanisms for cultural transformation could simply not be planned for, and in fact any top-down attempts at cultural planning would prove to be oppressive.

However, the Programmatic Modernist lens points beyond the immediate issues of definitions of culture, elites and cultural renewal to the rivalling conceptions of the transcendent. I argue that without this perspective we miss fundamental key aspects of their discussion. Eliot and Mannheim lamented the breakdown of transcendence via secularization and its threatening fragmentation, chaos and nihilism. Sharing in this diagnosis, both understood religion as an indispensable social force on which the future cultural reconstruction depended. Considering the alternatives at hand, both deemed a renewed Christianity as preferable to the quasi-religious totalitarian regimes on the continent. This emphasis on Christianity does not, however, imply that Eliot's and Mannheim's ideals for a future society concurred. Mannheim argued that by using insights gained by sociological study, Western societies could be guided through an age of transition from a *laissez faire* liberal society to a democratic planned society. Christianity would provide this society with a common bond, values and transcendent purpose, achieving cohesion without compulsion. Eliot's social criticism in the 1930s and 1940s is dominated by the ideal of the formation of a lived Christian faith more than concrete political structures. He was fixed on something 'beyond politics', to borrow Dawson's phrase. As such, and as David Moody suggests, Eliot's political writing must be approached through 'their governing point of view, their metaphysic'.[146]

It is also in this manner that we must see Eliot's engagement with Mannheim. This is where the kernel of difference in Mannheim's and Eliot's respective social criticism lie. Whereas for Mannheim religion was a means to an end, Eliot held that Christianity, or worship of the Christian God, was the ultimate purpose of human society. It is this determined theism that accounts for Eliot's strong aversion to Mannheim's societal planning. From Mannheim's humanistic stance, the mission to recreate a 'sacred canopy' was firmly within the grasp of the scientific community in collaboration with intellectual elites, whereas for Eliot the renewal of culture was firmly in the hands of God.

The upshot of investigating Eliot and Mannheim through the 'Programmatic Modernism' framework is thus apparent. It brings clarity to their respective social criticism and pinpoints exactly where their differences lie. However, to what extent can these intellectuals be said to embody the Griffinite Modernism? In Griffin's conceptualization, 'Programmatic Modernism' 'expresses itself as a mission to change society, to inaugurate a new epoch, to start time anew', which leads to a 'rhetoric of manifestos and declarations, and encourages the artist/intellectual to collaborate proactively with collective movements for radical change'.[147] Accordingly, Mannheim epitomizes this mode of Modernism, whereas Eliot, arguably the greatest of the Modernist poets, ironically only tentatively fits this description. Both were deeply engaged in a 'mission to change society'; however, Eliot, in contrast to Mannheim, offered a solution to the spiritual barrenness of modernity, but no road map.

Notes

1. Collini, 'The European Modernist as Anglican Moralist'; Stefan Collini, *Absent Minds: Intellectuals in Britain* (Oxford: Oxford University Press, 2006), chapter 13.
2. Wicht, 'Eliot and Karl Mannheim'.
3. Kojecky, *T. S. Eliot's Social Criticism*.
4. Raymond Williams, *Culture and Society 1780–1950* (Hammondsworth: Pelican Books, 1971 [1958]); Loader, *The Intellectual Development*; Kettler and Meja, *Karl Mannheim and the Crisis*.
5. Peter Gay, *Weimar Culture: The Outsider as Insider* (London: Secker & Warburg, 1968). Guy suggests that the 'complex of feelings and responses I have called "the hunger for wholeness" turns out on examination to be a great regression born from a great fear: the fear of modernity (p. 96)'.
6. Collini, 'The European Modernist as Anglican Moralist', 207.
7. For Griffin's 'primordial definition' of Modernism, see Griffin, *Modernism and Fascism*, 116–17.

8   For example, Peter Ackroyd, *T. S. Eliot* (London: Hamish Hamilton, 1984); Kenneth Asher, *T. S. Eliot and Ideology* (Cambridge: Cambridge University Press, 1995).
9   Kettler and Meja, *Mannheim and the Crisis*, 251.
10 Collini, 'The European Modernist as Anglican Moralist'; Williams, *Culture and Society*.
11 Spurr, 'Anglo-Catholic in Religion' *T.S. Eliot and Christianity*, 190–3.
12 T. S. Eliot, 'Letter to John Middleton Murry', 8 February 1938, NWE/II/1/33; T. S. Eliot, 'Letter to John Middleton Murry', 11 April 1938, NWE/II/1/33; T. S. Eliot, 'Letter to George Every', 16 April 1938, *private collection*.
13 Cf. T. S. Eliot. 'Letter to Hayward', 21 November 1939, HB/L/12/209; T. S. Eliot, 'Letter to Virginia Woolf', 12 September 1939, NYE; T. S. Eliot, 'Letter to Jonathan Betjeman', 22 September 1939, *private collection*.
14 Collini, *Absent Minds*, 312.
15 T. S. Eliot, 'Letter to John Hayward', 3 January 1941, HB/L/12/1/18/F271.
16 T. S. Eliot, 'Letter to Philip Mairet', 5 January 1941 (UTE/5.4).
17 Vidler, *Scenes from a Clerical Life*, 119.
18 T. S. Eliot, 'Letter to Herbert Read', 3 April 1943, HF/8/33. I am grateful to David Kettler for sharing this material.
19 T. S. Eliot, 'Letter to Alan Tate', 13 March 1945 as cited in Collini, *Absent Minds*, 319.
20 T. S. Eliot, 'The Germanisation of Britain', *New English Weekly*, 29 March 1945, 192. The correspondence is a response to an article by Montgomery Belgion and reads in this context as an apologia of Mannheim (Montgomery Belgion, 'The Germanization of Britain', *New English Weekly* 26, no. 18 (1945), 138).
21 Eliot, 'The Germanisation of Britain', 192.
22 Karl Mannheim, 'Letter to Louis Wirth', 13 August 1938, LWP/VII/11.
23 Julia Mannheim, 'Letter to the Moot', 19 January 1947, OLD/9/7/41.
24 In the minutes of the 'St Julian's Group', a successor group to the Moot, Oldham noted that Mannheim's death was a decisive factor in ending the Moot (notes from the meeting held at St Julian's 19–22 December 1947, OLD/13/3/47).
25 T. S. Eliot, 'Professor Karl Mannheim', *The Times* (1947), 7.
26 Wicht, 'Eliot and Karl Mannheim', 197.
27 Berger, *The Sacred Canopy*, 26–7.
28 Fredrich Nietzsche, *The Gay Science*, trans. Josefine Nauckhoff (Cambridge: Cambridge University Press, 2001 [1882]), 120.
29 Mannheim, *Ideology and Utopia*, 13, 22.
30 Ibid., 14–15.
31 Ibid., 22.
32 Mannheim, *Man*, 6f.
33 Mannheim, *Diagnosis*, 136.
34 Ibid., 100.
35 See ibid., chapter 2.

36 Clements, *Moot Papers*, 422–3 (12th meeting, 1–3 August 1941), *my emphasis*. The terminology certainly echoes Peter Berger's 'sacred canopy' (Berger, *The Sacred Canopy*, 26–7).
37 Karl Mannheim, 'Topics for the Next Meeting of the Moot' [1941], IOE/MOO/32; LP/215; OLD/14/3/86.
38 Eliot, *Idea*, 16.
39 Ibid., 15. Dawson suspected that the trend towards 'social uniformity and the mechanization of culture' in the wake of liberalism would result in a 'democratic totalitarianism' even in the so-called democratic nations (Dawson, *Beyond Politics*, 3).
40 Eliot, *Idea*, 13.
41 These talks were published in the appendix of Eliot, *Notes*, 122.
42 Mannheim's ideas regarding social integration were particularly influenced by August Comte (see Karl Mannheim, *Freedom, Power and Democratic Planning* (London: Routledge & Kegan Paul, 1951), 285–6).
43 Mannheim, *Ideology and Utopia*, 20–1.
44 Mannheim, *Man*, 199ff.
45 In their preface to Mannheim's posthumous *Freedom, Power and Democratic Planning*, Ernest Bramstedt and Hans Gerth note that through the Moot, Mannheim 'became convinced that sociology and social philosophy cannot afford to remain "religion blind" (Mannheim, *Freedom*, xiv–xv)....'
46 Mannheim, *Man*, 369. Max Weber feared a modern dystopia whereby a secularized society devoid of spirit would enslave individuals' mechanized societies (cf. Weber, *The Protestant Ethic and the Spirit of Capitalism*, 181–2).
47 Clements, *Moot Papers*, 422 (12th meeting, 1–3 August 1941).
48 See also Mannheim, *Diagnosis*, 102–6.
49 Mannheim, *Freedom*, 289.
50 Eliot refers to Coleridge's 'Idea' in his *The Constitution of Church and State* (*Idea*, 67).
51 Eliot, *Notes*, 28.
52 Ibid., 34.
53 T.S. Eliot, 'Letter to Dr. Oldham from T. S. Eliot' [1941], IOE/MOO/68.
54 Ibid. Eliot was not alone in linking secularization and the decline in the arts. Nietzsche, in his *Human, All Too Human*, regrets the detrimental effect of a faithless society on the arts: 'If belief in such heavenly truth declines in general… then that species of art can never flourish again which, like the *Divinia Commedia*, the pictures of Raphael, the frescoes of Michelangelo, the Gothic cathedrals, presupposes not only a cosmic but a *metaphysical* significance in the objects of art (Fredrich Nietzsche, *Human, All Too Human: A Book for Free Spirits*, trans. R. J. Hollingdale (Cambridge: Cambridge University Press, 1996), 102).'

55 Eliot, *Notes*, 28.
56 Cf. Mannheim, *Diagnosis*, 101; Eliot, *Idea*, 18–19.
57 Eliot, *Notes*, 33–4.
58 Karl Mannheim, 'Planning for Freedom' [1938], LM/SEC7; OLD/14/3/67.
59 Karl Mannheim, 'Towards a New Social Philosophy: A Challenge to Christian Thinkers by a Sociologist. Part II: Christian Values in the Changing Environment' [1941], IOE/MOO/75; OLD/14/3/94.
60 Karl Mannheim, 'The Crisis in Valuation' [1942], IOE/MOO/77.
61 Mannheim, *Freedom*, 287–8.
62 Karl Mannheim, 'Planning for Freedom' [1938], OLD/14/3/67; LM/SEC7.
63 T.S. Eliot, 'Comment on Papers by Mannheim and Hodges' [1939], LM/SEC3.
64 Ibid.
65 It should be noted that Eliot's hostility towards planning predates his encounters with Mannheim (Eliot, 'A Commentary', 86).
66 T. S. Eliot, 'Man and Society'.
67 Eliot, *Lambeth*, 32.
68 Eliot, *Idea*, 9, 10.
69 Eliot, 'Editorial for the CNL, 14th August 1940'.
70 Cf. Eliot, *Idea*, 9.
71 Such sentiments are expressed in Eliot, 'The Church's Message to the World', 294; Eliot, 'Towards a Christian Britain', 106.
72 Eliot, 'The Church's Message to the World', 294.
73 Eliot, 'Education in a Christian Society'.
74 Ibid.
75 T. S. Eliot, 'Notes on Mannheim's Paper', 10 January 1941, OLD/14/6/1. Eliot wrote this comment in response to Mannheim's 'Topics for the Next Meeting of the Moot' [1941], OLD/14/3/86.
76 Eliot, *Notes*, 37ff.
77 Mannheim, *Man*, 81.
78 Eliot, *After Strange Gods*, 18.
79 Eliot, *Notes*, 31.
80 Ibid., 19.
81 Eliot himself did acknowledge a disparity between his prose and literature. In *After Strange Gods* he clarified that 'while I maintain the most correct opinions in my criticism, I do nothing but violate them in my verse (Eliot, *After Strange Gods*, 28)'. This inconsistency was due to his insistence that in criticism one could legitimately indulge in ideals, whereas in verse such ring hollow (ibid., 28–9).
82 T. S. Eliot, *Murder in the Cathedral* (London: Faber & Faber, 1965 [1935]), 91.
83 Eliot, *Idea*, 24.
84 Karl Mannheim, 'Planning for Freedom' [1938], OLD/14/3/67; OL/SEC7.

85 Karl Mannheim, 'Topics for the Next Meeting of the Moot' [January 1941], OLD/14/3/86; IOE/MOO/32.
86 T. S. Eliot, 'Notes on Mannheim's Paper', 10 January 1941, OLD/14/6/1.
87 Clements, *Moot Papers*, 113.
88 Eliot, *Idea*, 42.
89 T. S. Eliot, 'On the Place and Function of the Clerisy', 10 November 1944, LP/215; MPP/15/6; OLD/14/6/10).
90 Ibid. The paper was first published in Kojecky, *T. S. Eliot's Social Criticism*. Phil Mullins and Struan Jacobs have published all five texts linked to this debate in full (Phil Mullins and Struan Jacobs, 'T.S. Eliot's Idea of the Clerisy, and Its Discussion by Karl Mannheim and Michael Polanyi in the Context of J.H. Oldham's Moot', *Journal of Classical Sociology* 6, no. 2 (2006), 147–56). Unfortunately, the only surviving minutes from the 21st Moot weekend are some brief handwritten summaries provided by an unknown writer (Anon., 'Minutes, Manuscripts', 21st meeting, 15–18 December 1944, OLD/12/3/27).
91 Karl Mannheim, 'Letter from Karl Mannheim', 20 November 1944, LP/215; MPP/15/6; OLD/9/6/101.
92 T. S. Eliot, 'Comments on Mannheim's by T. S. Eliot', 24 November 1944, LP/215; MPP/15/6; OLD/14/6/14.
93 Karl Mannheim, 'Letter from Karl Mannheim', 20 November 1944, LP/215; MPP/15/6; OLD/9/6/101.
94 T. S. Eliot, 'Comments on Mannheim's by T. S. Eliot', 24 November 1944, LP/215; MPP/15/6; OLD/14/6/14.
95 Karl Mannheim, 'Letter from Karl Mannheim', 20 November 1944, LP/215; MPP/15/6; OLD/9/6/101.
96 T. S. Eliot, 'Comments on Mannheim's by T. S. Eliot', 24 November 1944, LP/215; MPP/15/6; OLD/14/6/14.
97 Karl Mannheim, 'The Meaning of Popularisation in a Mass Society', *Christian News-Letter*, no. 227 (1945), 7.
98 The citation can be found in a private letter to Mary Trevelyan (T. S. Eliot, 'Letter to Mary Trevelyan', 29 January 1945, HLE/bMS AM/1691.2/45).
99 T. S. Eliot, 'The Class and the Élite', *New English Weekly* 11, no. 6 (1945), 499–509.
100 Mannheim, *Man*, 91.
101 Eliot, *Notes*, 37.
102 Ibid., 42. The proposition that culture is transmitted by family and class provoked Lucy McDiarmid to label *Notes* a 'stuffy, reactionary book' (McDiarmid, *Saving Civilization*, 127).
103 Eliot, *Notes*, 42.
104 Ibid., 47.
105 Ibid., 44.

106 Ibid., 40. *Author's emphasis.*
107 The papers were published in Mannheim, *Diagnosis*, ch. 6.
108 T.S. Eliot, 'Letter to Dr. Oldham from T. S. Eliot' [1941], IOE/MOO/68; OLD/9/3/25.
109 T. S. Eliot, 'Planning and Religion', *Theology* XLVI, no. 275 (1943), 104–5.
110 Dawson, *Judgement*, 83.
111 Eliot, 'Planning and Religion', 103. Eliot here directly cites from Dawson's *The Judgement of the Nations*.
112 Ibid., 103.
113 Eliot, *Notes*, 69.
114 T. S. Eliot. 'Letter to Hayward', 2 April 1943, HB/L/12/1/20/F328.
115 Eliot, 'Towards a Christian Britain', 114.
116 T. S. Eliot, 'Letter to Eric Fenn', 7 February 1941, BBC/TSE/SOU1. *Picture Post* was a photojournalistic magazine published between 1938 and 1957. It is probable that Eliot here refers to the magazine's publication of a 'Plan for Britain' in January 1941, which called for an extensive welfare system.
117 Cf. Mannheim, *Diagnosis*, 100n.
118 Engaging with a circle of intellectuals who gathered around theologian Paul Tillich in Frankfurt during the early 1930s, Mannheim declared that, '[a] personal God has never addressed me…. I cannot say that a personal God has spoken, and I remain silent about it (cited in David Kettler and Colin Loader, *Karl Mannheim: Social as Political Education* (New Brunswick: Transaction, 2001), 138'.
119 A private encounter with Michael Polanyi betrays a certain antipathy or incomprehension of religious faith commitments (Michael Polanyi, 'Letter to Karl Mannheim', 19 April 1944, MPP/4/11; Karl Mannheim, 'Letter to Michael Polanyi', 26 April 1944, MPP/4/11).
120 Clements, *Moot Papers*, 282 (7th meeting, 9–12 February 1940).
121 Walter Oakeshott, 'Notes on the "Order"', [1939] IOE/MOO/4; OLD/14/8/63; OL/SEC4.
122 Mannheim, *Freedom*, 289.
123 Karl Mannheim, 'Towards a New Social Philosophy: A Challenge to Christian Thinkers by a Sociologist. Part II: Christian Values in the Changing Environment', [1941], IOE/MOO/75; OLD/14/3/94.
124 Discussion on archetypes became – through Hodges' position paper – a dominant theme from the 15th Moot meeting in September 1942 and onwards (see, for example, H. A. Hodges, 'Christian Archetypes and Symbols', 22 June 1942, BA/5/9; OLD/14/1/23).
125 Eliot, *Idea*, 58. My emphasis.
126 Michael Polanyi, 'Letter from Michael Polanyi', 16 November 1944, MPP/15/6; OLD/9/6/99. *Author's emphasis*. Interestingly, this is the first time Polanyi expressed the kernel of what became his most significant theory, that of 'personal knowledge' (see Gábor, 'Polanyi', 125).

127 Michael Polanyi, 'Letter from Michael Polanyi', 16 November 1944, MPP/15/6; OLD/9/6/99.
128 Ibid.
129 T. S. Eliot, 'Comments by T.S. Eliot on Michael Polanyi's Notes on the Clerisy', 22 November 1944, MPP/15/6; OLD/14/6/13. *My emphasis.*
130 Eliot, 'The Church's Message to the World', 294.
131 Eliot, 'Towards a Christian Britain', 115.
132 Asher, *T. S. Eliot and Ideology*, 2–3.
133 Ibid., 2–3.
134 Ibid., 165.
135 Surette, *Dreams of a Totalitarian Utopia*, 160. Surrette here cites from Mussolini, *Fascism*, 23.
136 Surette, *Dreams of a Totalitarian Utopia*, 161.
137 See for example Eliot's praise of Portugal's Prime Minister António de Olivera Salazar as a benevolent dictator (Eliot, 'Editorial for the CNL, 14th August 1940'). It should be noted that his support for monarchism was softened towards to the end of his life (see preface of second edition of *Notes*).
138 As persuasively shown by Hannah Arendt, authoritarianism cannot be conflated with totalitarianism (Arendt, *The Origins of Totalitarianism*, 460ff.).
139 Collini, 'The European Modernist as Anglican Moralist', 228. In a letter to Mary Trevelyan, Eliot identified himself as a 'Tory (reinforced by a sort of Whig background)', a statement that further confirms Collini's argument (T. S. Eliot, 'Letter to Mary Trevelyan', 2 January 1945, HLE/bMS AM/1691.2/43).
140 Maurice Reckitt, 'The Story of the Candos Group: 1926-66', 13. As cited in Kojecky, *T. S. Eliot's Social Criticism*, 81.
141 Clements, *Moot Papers*, 55 (1st meeting, 1–4 April 1938).
142 Tonning, *Modernism and Christianity*, 65f.
143 Dawson, *Judgement*, 83, 86.
144 Michael Polanyi, 'Science and the Modern Crisis', 14 November 1944, BA/5/39.
145 Ibid. Since there are no surviving minutes from the meeting, it is unclear whether the paper was discussed at the meeting. However, the minutes from the 20th meeting state that Polanyi promised to provide a paper on his views in response to his exchange with Mannheim on 'Planning for Freedom'. It is possible that he circulated 'Science and the Modern Crisis' instead (Clements, *Moot Papers*, 692 (20th meeting, 23–26 June 1944)).
146 A. David Moody, *Thomas Stearn Eliot: Poet*, 2nd ed. (Cambridge: Cambridge University Press, 1994), 319.
147 Griffin, *Modernism and Fascism*, 62.

6

The Moot as a Revitalisation Movement

Introduction

> We must ask what was the right human development of fascism and communism. We must seek rebirth rather than recovery of e.g. medievalism. This required rethinking and refeeling [*sic*] and the prophet had to clear himself of all but fundamentals.¹

The Moot members believed themselves to be living in revolutionary times.² The acute sense of civilizational decadence generated various radical countermeasures to stem the spiral into chaos. The Moot thus aspired to launch a Christian response leading to a radical societal transformation. The group believed that a popular movement based upon a Christian conception of human nature could inspire a more humane vision of society. Discussing the potential of a popular movement, Oldham advocated a 'social revolution' comprising both 'the spiritual acceptance of new values and the change in the structure of society'.³ It required a theological 'Copernican Revolution', which would compel the church to renew its social commitment in the light of contemporary challenges.⁴

The ambitions of the Moot, and Oldham in particular, were astounding. Writing on a proposed Order, Oldham imagined a movement that would have a powerful influence on 'national and international life'.⁵ Mannheim strongly advocated putting his 'Planning for Freedom' model into practice as the only means to 'master, instead of being mastered by the machine'.⁶ Deeply frustrated, Mannheim pleaded with the Moot to take action:

> I am amazed by our lethargy. We are always waiting for means. But are not the means there? e.g. the Christian youth movement which is waiting for a lead, Oldham's access to people in key positions, the C.N.L., the B.B.C., public schools, groups in churches, etc. We are too lazy to move. *Hitler started with six people.* ... We should learn as we move, once we embark on action.⁷

Mannheim's comparison here should be understood as an appreciation of the efficiency of the enemy and a recognition that any response would ultimately need to aim for a similar scale of influence.

These grand ambitions of the Moot appear in hindsight misplaced. However, they are indicative of a desperate historical context in which these intellectuals saw little option but to take drastic action. In fact, they had themselves in their lifetime witnessed the rise of revolutionary movements led initially by small groups capturing the mood and imagination of the masses. If the German NSDAP and the Russian Communist Party could achieve radical social and political change starting from a small number of people, then there was no reason why the Moot could not achieve revitalization of considerable magnitude.

The Moot has routinely been described as a 'think-tank' or 'discussion group' in the secondary literature.[8] Yet it is evident that such designations do not adequately capture the scope of the Moot's ambitions, programme and activities. The argument developed here is that the Moot's aspiration went well beyond that of an ordinary interest group, and a more fitting term for the Moot which better accounts for its dynamics is as what Anthony Wallace has called a 'revitalization movement'. Wallace defines revitalization movements as 'a deliberate, organized, conscious effort by members of a society to construct a more satisfying culture'.[9] Such designation sits comfortably within the Political Modernism framework that has informed my narration. As Griffin argues, Modernist movements of the early twentieth century are *modern* revitalization movements producing 'palingenetic' responses to the decadence of *modern* society.[10]

The Moot's Modernist particularity stands out when analysed in comparison to other groupings in Britain of their time. For instance, the Frank Buchman-led Moral Re-Armament movement (MRA), launched in the same year as the Moot, offers a striking contrast. While both movements sought to address the interwar crisis, the MRA's diagnosis of moral depravity as the root cause of the crisis at hand appeared for the Moot superficial.[11] The Modernist reading underscores the Moot's analysis of the gravity of the modern crisis that could only be countered by an exhaustive overhaul of the culture and institutions of British society.

Another example worth considering is the Christendom Group, spearheaded by Maurice Reckitt. There is much affinity between these two groups. Not only did the Christendom Group share the Moot's misgivings about a liberal modern society, they also turned to the structures of medieval Christendom as a source of fundamental restructuring and renewal.[12] There was also considerable interaction between members. Most notably Philip Mairet attended two meetings, and papers by V. A. Demant and Ruth Kenyon were circulated in the Moot.[13] In turn, several Moot members – including Eliot, Oldham, Hodges and Dawson – contributed to the *Christendom* journal, launched by the Christendom Group in March 1931. However, in contradistinction to the Christendom Group, the Moot deliberately strived towards launching a sociopolitical movement.

In a final example, the Moot can be compared to the politically independent research body Political and Economic Planning (PEP), formed to address the MacDonald government's perceived incompetence to tackle the economic crisis of the 1930s. Its programme, 'A National Plan for Great Britain (1931)', championed national planning as an alternative to fascism and communism as 'the only permanent and general solution of the existing chronic emergency'.[14] There is accordingly an overlap between PEP's ideas of comprehensive planning and Mannheim's programme as 'Planning for Freedom' presented at the Moot. The PEP's method of addressing key issues and topics by forming small consultation and research groups consisting of persons of high competence was emulated by the Moot.[15] Oldham even suggested collaborating with the PEP in possible areas that the Moot could take action.[16] However, in Oldham's eyes the Moot was not simply a research or policy body, he had something more fundamental in mind. He preferred to speak of the Moot as in a process of forming the nucleus of an Order.[17] Oldham agreed with Walter Oakeshott's interference recorded in the minutes of the 2nd meeting: 'the idea that attracted him personally was the formation of an order rather than of a research body'.[18]

Thus, describing the Moot as a revitalization movement draws attention to the way in which the Moot deliberately sought to implement their vision. It is the purpose of this chapter to outline the primary vehicles that the Moot utilized to set in motion a project that was intended to change the course of Western history. In the wake of the 1937 Oxford conference on Church, Community and State, Oldham had begun to plan the architecture for such a movement. Over the next years, he lay the groundwork of an infrastructure of which the Moot was a cornerstone. At the 10th meeting, Oldham himself explicitly referred to four 'elements in the programme now within reach': firstly, 'the council' (CCFCL), which was an organ with official links with the churches and with inroads into Parliament. Secondly, there was 'a body of ideas', which Oldham kept on developing with the Moot. Thirdly, the *CNL* provided a media outlet for the Moot. Finally, there was already a core group 'committed to the recovery of religious meaning and the reshaping of society [i.e. the Moot]'.[19] In addition, Oldham envisioned that a popular movement could be set in motion by co-ordinating and encouraging existing groups and individuals who could be 'animated by a common, consciously shared purpose'.[20] The Moot also set up research groups including one which engaged with the debates over British education. All in all, these practical efforts of the Moot make it plausible to speak of the Moot as part of a wider effort to create a Christian cultural revolution.

Creating a Manifesto

In an 'Age of Faith', wrote E. M. Forster in 1938, 'there are so many militant creeds that, in self-defence, one has to formulate a creed of one's own'.[21] Within the Moot, Oldham set his sights on a 'Christian analogy with *Mein Kampf*.[22] While this undertaking was driven by Oldham, it was a collaborative effort fed by the ideas of the members and the leading Christian thinkers at the time. Chapter 3 of this volume provides greater detail of the content and ideas that were central in these negotiations. The discussion here will focus on the thinking behind and processes involved in the creation of such a manifesto.

Right from the outset Oldham began to work towards a charter for his sociopolitical movement. For the 3rd Moot meeting Oldham had circulated his first attempt.[23] While it was well received, it did not go unchallenged. Mannheim feared that the manifesto was too abstract.[24] Disliking the analogy with 'that diabolical book', *Mein Kampf*, Löwe felt that the statement lacked an offensive impetus and was therefore ineffectual.[25] Murry concurred, for 'anything that was not radical was simply helping the world to go to the devil'.[26] However, most of the discussion concerned the intended target audience and how the statement was to be distributed. To achieve the greatest possible reach, Baillie suggested that the statement ought to be written by Dorothy Sayers.[27] Gilbert Shaw proposed that it should be circulated among those clergy and laity who at present already were involved in 'guerrilla warfare' as there was a real chance of transforming their dispersed efforts into a co-ordinated army.[28] In the end, it was agreed that the statement was to be revised in the light of comments by the Moot members and thereafter sent to '300 key people who would be killed by the next dictator'.[29]

A draft charter titled 'The Rebirth of the West'[30] was to this end widely circulated. At the subsequent meeting, Oldham estimated that 40–50 intellectuals had already consented to it.[31] A document in the Oldham Papers at New College, in fact, lists 66 intellectuals who had subscribed to the general gist of the document. Some of the more intriguing names on the list include Sir Basil Blackwell, the owner of the publishing and bookseller empire; B. S. R. Boase, professor in art history at University of London and later the Vice Chancellor at

Oxford University; Sir Wyndham Deedes, army officer and civil servant; Kurt Hahn, the internationally renowned philosopher of education; H. H. Elvin, a trade unionist; Rt. Revd. Mervyn Heigh, Bishop of Coventry; Rt. Revd. Arthur Karney, Bishop of Southampton; Sir F. W. Ogilvie, the Director General of the BBC 1938–1942; Sir George Schuster, MP for the National Liberals 1938–1945; and Sir Alfred Zimmern, a Zionist and professor of international relations at Oxford University.[32] Another version of the statement, entitled 'A Reborn Christendom', was on the agenda for the 5th meeting on 23–24 September 1939. However, the outbreak of the war overshadowed all other business, and the draft was unfortunately never discussed.[33] While Oldham had envisioned that the manifesto was to be published as a collaborative effort under the auspices of the CCFCL, it was for unknown reasons published by Oldham as *The Resurrection of Christendom* in early 1940.[34]

The quest for a common vision or social philosophy did nevertheless not end with the publication of *The Resurrection of Christendom*. At the meeting on April 1940, Mannheim complained that the Moot had achieved little in terms of practical output. In response, Oldham, Vickers, Iredale and Moberly suggested that no action could be taken until the movement had a social philosophy, 'social gospel' or social purpose.[35] Apparently Oldham's publication was deemed inadequate in this respect. Consequently, before the end of the meeting, Geoffrey Vickers, a lawyer and social theorist, had drafted 'A Bill of Duties', consisting of six duties including equal distribution of resources; public control over national resources; new centres for community building and comradeship; equal opportunities in education; responsible governance of all subjects of the British Empire; and strengthened ties with Britain's main ally, France.[36] The draft was met with enthusiasm, and Vidler stated that '[this] is a crucial moment; you've either got to go all out whether or not the Council [CCFCL] back it, or it must be issued elsewhere'.[37] However, when the conversation turned to the specifics, there was no agreement. Perhaps that is why nothing came of it and the Vickers bill was never discussed again.

Between meetings, Oldham and Iredale had no doubt been inspired by the encouragement of Max Nicholson at the PEP who welcomed the Moot's work on a social philosophy.[38] Oldham was also in conversation with O. S. Franks, Professor of Moral Philosophy at Glasgow University, to convince him to accept the directorship of the CCFCL. It was suggested that his first task would be to pull together the main strands of the Moot's thinking into a manifesto.[39]

The focus of the 9th meeting, which took place on 12–15 July 1940, was given to fundamental questions of a social philosophy. Oldham opened the meeting by suggesting that since a 'party cannot come into existence without an Idea', priority must be given to 'help an Idea to birth'.[40] It was agreed that a new document was to be prepared. Yet, a summary in the minutes reveals the struggle the Moot members faced in arriving at a consensus. Some preferred a programme which began with concrete actions, rather than wasting time on idle intellectual formulations. Furthermore, the Moot struggled with finding the right balance between abstract statements which required little commitment and a detailed programme that might fail to draw a wide consensus.[41] Finally, there was some uncertainty as to how the new statement would differ from Oldham's 'Rebirth of Christendom' (a draft of *The Resurrection of Christendom*).[42] Again the Moot members failed to reach an agreement: 'The difficulty felt was that it was hard to select the right people and no one group would be the right one for all issues.'[43]

In a final push for a programme that could rally support for common action, Oldham wrote 'The Christian Witness in the Present Crisis'. The draft marked a return to a more specifically Christian basis of society and included the main lines of investigation of the Moot. Murry commented that the draft was a 'remarkable synthesis of most of the best thinking that has been done at the Moot'.[44] The focus of the memorandum was on four 'decisions': 'for the transcendent', 'for history', 'for sociality' and 'for the duality of the spheres of law and gospel'.[45] In the agenda sent to the Moot members for the 18th meeting, Oldham reported on the encouraging responses to this widely circulated draft. With hopes running high, Oldham assessed that 'we may be nearer than we suppose to a real common mind and common purpose'.[46] The Moot was to remain 'an informal gathering of friends meeting for the interchange of ideas and experience', but that out of these discussions there might emerge a common mind and thereby 'a force that has the power to change things'.[47]

In the draft sent to the Moot member, Oldham had included extracts from comments which he had received in reply to the memorandum. These extracts suggest an overwhelmingly positive response. However, the conversations at the 18th meeting point towards a different reality. Vidler complained that they constantly discussed principles and ideas, and he 'confessed that Oldham's paper felt stale to him'.[48] Much of the discussion evolved around significance of ideas versus practical actions. Mannheim, who tended to push for action over philosophy and principles, suggested:

> Abstract principles came last; just as Christ made a new world which the theologian then explained ... He agreed that philosophers and theologians had

a role to play, though not the revolutionary role Oldham suggested; they had to understand the need for emerging principles and so explain the common experience of ordinary men.[49]

For Mannheim, then, Oldham's statement was another abstraction that would add little value if no action was taken in conjunction with it. Oldham replied by proposing that the main principles of the memorandum derived directly from their historical reality rather than abstract principles.[50] Satisfied with the statement, Hodges and Shaw felt that the time was ripe to move beyond principles to define a plan of action.[51] Later during the weekend Mannheim declared that he 'had had enough of memoranda'; there were enough people sympathetic with their aims and purposes to set their plans in motion.[52]

Despite the members' apparent apprehension, Oldham's memorandum, 'The Christian Witness in the Present Crisis', was sent to the Archbishop of Canterbury, William Temple, who published an edited version in the *CNL*. In a letter to Temple, Oldham reports on the widespread attention the memorandum had received in national papers such as *The Manchester Guardian, Daily Telegraph, Daily Mail, The Times*, as well as provincial press.[53] Oldham noted that even Eliot, 'who has the most critical mind among my friends', gave 'his whole-hearted assent'.[54] At the subsequent meeting, on 14–17 January 1944, an elated Oldham expressed his confidence that it could become a 'rallying point for future action',[55] but later qualified that 'what happened next depended on the emergence of a group which accepted the challenge', and funding for a staff that could co-ordinate the effort.[56]

Returning to Wallace's revitalization movement, he describes the process of a 'mazeway reformulation' as an initial step in their formation. That is, individuals in any given society hold a 'mazeway', or 'mental image' through which they order their existence, understand their own identity, and learn to orientate, communicate and act within that society.[57] Revitalization movements emerge in order to recreate a new kind of stable image through a reformulation in times when the fundamental assumptions of a society are being challenged or radically disturbed. Often, such a reformulation occurs, suggests Wallace, through hallucinatory visions by a prophetic leader.[58] While the Moot members spoke of a prophetic movement creating a new vision of society, theirs was reached through more rational and sociological approach than the mystical processes described by Wallace. Nevertheless, the Moot were aware that any attempt to recreate a shared vision for society had to touch upon the deeper religious and cultural currents of human existence.

Oldham's councils

The Council on the Christian Faith and the Common Life

A central part of Oldham's venture to renew society was the creation of the Council on the Christian Faith and the Common Life (CCFCL) and later the Christian Frontiers Council (CFC). These were meant to provide the organizational backbone to support but not control the otherwise organic movement.

Already in June 1937, Oldham was working actively towards a 'bold move' that he believed would shape the future of the nation. Oldham strategized for a large-scale endeavour that would influence the clergy, set up a youth organization and work with educationists, industrialists, politicians, civil servants and representatives of the labour movement in a national effort.[59] By January 1938, a committee that was to work with issues of Christianity and 'the national life' was formed under the auspices of the proposed World Council of Churches.[60] A gathering of church leaders at Lambeth Palace on 14 January approved the new body with a board consisting of 24 members. By July 1939, the Anglican representatives were none other than Cosmo Lang (Archbishop of Canterbury), William Temple (at that time the Archbishop of York), Cyric Garbett (Bishop of Winchester) and Clifford Woodward (Bishop of Bristol). The lay representation consisting of persons with different specialisms consisted of W. H. Smith, A.D. Lindsey, Walter Moberly, Walter Oakeshott and Harold Judd amongst others.

There are a number of drafts of policy documents in the Oldham Papers at New College, Edinburgh, enabling a reasonable reconstruction of the rationale, aims, ethos and structure of the CCFCL. Essentially, the dream of a New Christendom would be realized through vitalizing, mobilizing and co-ordinating already-existing Christian organizations and groups and by challenging Christians in positions of influence to bring institutional changes.[61] In Oldham's vision, these thousands of interest groups, organizations and active individuals across the country were to be the 'engine' of the New Christendom, whereas the council would be its 'oil'.[62] The council was to act as a hub linking various agencies together into a co-ordinated effort. Another function of the CCFCL was to encourage the study of modern society and its institutions, offering a prophetic critique in the light of the Christian faith.[63] The CCFCL was also to be responsible for 'implanting in the mind of the nation the idea of a New Christendom'.[64] The creation of the *CNL* in late 1939 can been seen as a step towards this end.

Within this scheme 'to Christianize the nation', the Moot was to provide the intellectual and creative impetus appealing to 'Christian depth and inspiration',[65] while the CCFCL was to be the operational centre and the hub of the movement. The council was an official organ, while the Moot was to retain its informality, providing a space for free, creative and confidential discussion.[66] The relation between the Moot and the council was thus to remain informal. What is interesting is how Oldham used the Moot as a sounding board for the CCFCL. An illustration can be offered in the discussion of a draft of 'The Principles and Policy of the Council on the Christian Faith and the Common Life' at the 3rd meeting.[67] Most of the discussion was given to the ideas of the draft itself. However, several members also addressed more organizational issues, particularly voicing their scepticism of the council's link with the official churches and the strong presence of the clergy on the committee.[68]

The relationship between the CCFCL and the Moot was however ambiguous. There was significant overlap in personnel and in ideas. Already at the first Moot meeting Eliot expressed his own misgivings over the possibility of a functioning relationship between a formal and representative organization such as the CCFCL and an informal group such as the Moot.[69] Further, the demarcation between the CCFCL as the organ concerned with the practical action and the Moot as providing intellectual impetus was never sharply maintained. At a later meeting, Moberly, also a member of the CCFCL board, questioned the boundaries between the council and the Moot, especially since the latter was developing 'an unexpected function as an organising and planning group'. Was the Moot subsuming the role of the council?[70] No direct answer was provided, but Oldham later in the meeting drew a distinction between the Moot as a research branch and the council as a co-ordinate centre.

The CCFCL never developed into the force that Oldham had envisioned. Oldham's biographer Keith Clements argues that the CCFCL has to be 'labelled one of Joe Oldham's brave failures, an adventure that got nowhere'.[71] Right from the outset Oldham had seen the demand for paid staff to make the organization effective.[72] Oldham had identified Leslie Hunter, archdeacon of Northumberland, as its ideal director.[73] However, after a whole year of negotiations, Hunter eventually declined.[74] The failure to secure Hunter was a blow to the council and Oldham. By mid-1939 the council had three employees including Oldham, Eleanora Iredale and Rev. A. C. Craig, but it was apparent that the council still lacked in leadership. A further major issue was the lack of funding. The official churches had pledged £3,500 a year from the start, but in Oldham's estimate a threefold sum was a minimum for the council to operate as intended.[75] There was also a conflict between Oldham and William Paton over the structure of the ecumenical movement in Britain. Paton wished to gather the various ecumenical initiatives under the single umbrella of the British Council of Churches (BCC), while Oldham wished to protect the independence of the CCFCL. According to Eleanor Jackson in her biography, Paton eventually forced Oldham to resign from the CCFCL in July 1941.[76] Oldham himself put his resignation down to the result of lack of resources due to the war situation.[77] Clements calls the conflict between Oldham and Paton 'one of the sadder episodes in British ecumenical history'.[78]

The formation of the Christian Frontiers Council

The CCFCL was in 1942 subsumed into the newly formed BCC, the British branch of the World Council of Churches. This development allowed Oldham to restructure and regroup. The result was the CFC. The council would work 'on the frontier between organised life of the Church and the problems of society' and act as an independent organ but under the auspices of the BCC.[79] A meeting held on 26 February 1942 ratified a resolution drafted by Oldham.[80] The ethos of the CFC was much in line with the CCFCL. In a memorandum, 'The Religious Foundations of the Frontier', authored by Oldham, the CFC is described as an instrument '[to] bring about a fundamental change in the thought, practice and institutional forms of society through the recognition of God and community as the ultimate realities of man's existence'.[81]

The stated aims in the constitution of the CFC are, firstly, 'to provide opportunities for discussing Christian thought and action with non-Christians and in a context other than organised religion'. Second was to conduct research on modern society and how Christian faith might shed light on its institutions and its social units. And third was to bring together people to 'promote the cross fertilisation of thought'.[82] This final aim appears to have been central, for as Moberly wrote in his piece on the CFC for the *CNL*, the council operated in order to 'supplement and assist the work of existing groups and bodies and not to compete with any'.[83] In a paragraph of a draft omitted from the published article, Moberly envisaged a network of independent undercover groups whose tactics 'resembles guerrilla warfare', 'which act independently and on their own responsibility'.[84] This co-ordinated movement comes close to the idea of an Order often discussed at the Moot and previously at the CCFCL.

Both the CCFCL and CFC were intended to encourage lay engagement; however, a difference between the two councils was the absence of official church representation on the committee of the CFC. It is possible that Oldham felt constrained by the clergy on the CCFCL board and imagined that a greater autonomy from the churches for the CFC would release it to pursue pioneering initiatives and be better placed to engage with people who held prejudices against the organized churches.[85] The members of the board of the council, then, consisted of Christians of influence in various spheres of society. For example, as of May 1942, the council included the vice chancellor of Oxford University A. D. Lindsey; Edwin Barker of the YMCA; Conservative MP Henry Brooke; H. C. Dent, the editor of *Times Education Supplement*; W. H. Smith, peer and retailer; H. C. B. Mynors, advisor at the Bank of England; Clifton Robbins at the Ministry of Information; Mary Stocks, the principal of Westfield College; and Barbara Ward, a journalist at *The Economist*.[86]

The procedures of the council are typical of the relational approach valued by Oldham. Those who held shared interests were encouraged to meet together in small groups 'with the object of producing results which will rouse respect through their quality'.[87] During its early years, the CFC facilitated various interest groups discussing economic systems, politics, industry, medicine and healthcare, theological reflection amongst students, and the transition from study to work. The results of these study groups were regularly published in the *CNL*.[88]

The Moot was represented in the committee via Walter Moberly as the council's chairman, T. S. Eliot, Walter Oakeshott and M. Chaning-Pearce.[89] As employed staff Oldham and F. C. Maxwell acted as the officers of the organization. Maxwell did not attend the Moot; however, after his sudden death, the Moot's presence in CFC was strengthened upon Kathleen Bliss joining ranks of the office in November 1943. Thereafter Daniel Jenkins was employed in 1945. Jenkins had by then attended a few of the Moot meetings (18, 19). However, the new council is rarely discussed in the Moot minutes and papers. As the Frontier Council was beginning to gain momentum, the Moot had slowly come to lose its former vitality. It is nevertheless apparent that the members identified the Moot as an element of a wider programme, which included the Frontier Council and the *CNL*.[90]

Both these councils, the CCFCL and the CFC, were formed to channel what Oldham believed to be a growing consensus amongst Christian intellectuals. These ventures of Oldham's can be understood as attempting to organize what Wallace calls the 'elements and subsystems which have already attained currency in the society': a paramount stage of the mazeway reformulation stage of a revitalization movement.[91] The CCFCL and CFC were formed to provide support for a movement deriving out of a common Christian mind.

The Formation of an Order

If the councils were to be the co-ordinating centres in Oldham's revitalization movement, the principal apparatus was to be an 'Order' emerging from within civil society. The envisaged Order was to consist of individuals and groups dedicated to working towards the realization of a Christian society with a commitment to the ideals set out in a manifesto. The Order was seen as a vehicle for renewal of society without the bloodshed of a revolution or compulsion of the totalitarian state. In an early meeting Oldham spoke of an 'open conspiracy' influencing society through a group of people 'committed to the rediscovery of the Church in themselves', rather than through the pressure applied by institutional church lobbying.[92] The conceptualization of a lay Order that could act as the catalyst for a popular Christian movement was one of most regular items on the Moot's agenda. It was also one of the most contested.

Background to the Order

The idea of an informal society influencing the nation was widespread during the 1930s and 1940s. In her feminist manifesto *Three Guineas*, Virginia Woolf spoke of a 'Society of Outsiders', consisting of those working towards 'liberty, equality and peace' by subverting patriarchal society through acts of defiance and non-participation.[93] Another character central in the Bloomsbury group, E. M. Forster, proposed an 'aristocracy' 'of the sensitive, the considerate and the plucky', a secret society without formal membership but united through an intuitive bond by the commitment to the 'true human tradition'.[94] The Moot itself instanced the Round Table Group, one such existing society, as a model. The society was established by South African miner and imperialist Cecil Rhodes and journalist William T. Stead in 1891. By the early twentieth century, a number of 'semisecret' Round Table groups were formed around the British Commonwealth and in the United States that acted with some success as pressure groups in questions of colonial policy and international affairs.[95]

In Christian circles, too, ideas of an Order proliferated. Jacques Maritain imagined 'civic fraternities' that would vitalize society analogously to how religious orders historically have brought renewal to the institutional church.[96] Another significant influence on the Moot was Paul Tillich's thinking on a religious lay Order. Oldham was particularly taken by Tillich's ideas. In a diary entry, Tillich recorded a private conversation with Oldham on 'my theory of mass integration'. 'Oldham is profoundly impressed', reported Tillich, 'and says that he finds my ideas about religious orders a thousand times more important that the whole [1937] Oxford conference'.⁹⁷ In a later entry, Tillich noted that 'the idea of the religious order is encountered everywhere'.⁹⁸ Indeed, one of few practical actions proposed by the 1937 Conference on Church, Community and State was to establish multiple groups and individuals joining together fulfilling Christian responsibilities at home, 'in civic life, in the professions and in industry, in social service and in the political arena'.⁹⁹ Even William Temple was taken by the idea of a network of groups and individuals. Citing T. S. Eliot's idea of 'the Community of Christians', William Temple, writing for the *CNL*, argued for the formation of small local groups dedicated to 'seeking the Christian solution for our problems and doing what might be in their power to act on what they find'. The members of such a movement ought to bear a badge to make themselves visible to others.¹⁰⁰

Moot members advocating for an Order

The idea of the formation of some organ consisting of more or less spontaneous groups seeking to influence society is also strongly present in the writings and activities of the individual Moot members. Dawson was part of an already-existing movement, The Sword of the Spirit, within the Roman Catholic Church in the UK. In his *Beyond Politics*, Dawson explains how such a body would act to overcome the two ills of modern society, namely, the infringement of personal liberty under dictatorship and 'the degeneration of our culture into a mechanized mass civilization which is as hostile to personal freedom and to intellectual integrity as any form of dictatorship'.¹⁰¹ Eliot proposed his own version of an informal society. In his imagined Christian society, a Christian elite would act as its spiritual vanguard. 'The Community of Christians' would be an informal body of clergy and laity of exceptional spirituality and intellectual ability. The members of the elite would 'form the conscious mind and the conscience of the nation'.¹⁰² Inspired by the conference on Church, Community and State, Alec Vidler went from idea to action by forming his own secret society of young Anglicans during the autumn of 1939. Vidler sought to create a network of priests and laity who were disillusioned with the incompetence of the Church of England in addressing the pressing issues of modern society with a 'clear and prophetic witness to the transcendent kingdom of God'.¹⁰³ Some members of the St Deiniol's Koinonia group even formed local 'cells'.¹⁰⁴ As already mentioned, Mannheim early on endorsed the idea of an Order. In his *Ideology and Utopia*, Mannheim had already proposed that the social disintegration of liberal societies could be countered by a new intellectual elite who would 'play the part of watchmen in what otherwise would be a pitch-black night'.[105] In his initial Moot paper on 'Planning for Freedom', the Order is billed as a force that would revitalize society 'and to spread the spirit'. It is worth citing Mannheim at length:

> A combatant order which forms an integral part of the social organism like its nervous system, coordinating its activities and spiritualising its aims, seems to be a necessary innovation in any modern, dynamic society. Thus the analogous institution of the Communist Party in Russia, the National-Socialist Party in Germany, etc. should be studied, as well as the order of Jesuits, which also tried to revitalise society, at once preserving its spiritual tradition and bringing about a rebirth.[106]

The Order was then to have both a political and spiritual dimension. The proposed study of the Russian Communist Party, the National-Socialist Party and the Jesuits shows the extent to which Mannheim was ready to investigate all means possible for the ends of societal renewal. The idea of an Order continued to persist in Mannheim's later writings. In his posthumous *Freedom, Power and Democratic Power*, Mannheim repeated the ideas of a body 'outside the general machinery of the representative system'. The 'Order' would consist of 'highly esteemed' and 'disinterested' intellectuals from a cross section of society whose role would be to give guidance in the democratic decision-making processes. They would act as the 'conscience of the country', seemingly a direct reference to Eliot's 'community of Christians'.[107]

Oldham's vision of an Order

None campaigned harder for the formation of an Order than Oldham who firmly placed this venture at the forefront of the Moot's discussions. Already at the 1st Moot gathering, Oldham proposed that an Order could give a new direction to Christianity in the UK by creating a space for friendship in which real discussions could take place.[108] Those present at this meeting readily consented to work towards the initiation of this endeavour.[109] By the 4th meeting, Oldham had drafted a twelve-point 'constitution' for the Order. The statement envisions the formation of a 'society' consisting of sixty-odd persons from a variety of different occupational backgrounds resolved:

> To foster the growth of a Christian philosophy of man and society,
> To further the examination of the present institutions and activities of society in the light of the Christian understanding of existence,

To assist in bringing about the changes which such examination may show to be necessary.¹¹⁰

Oldham opened the discussion by clarifying the nature of the Moot and how it differed from the Order. The Moot's primary task was 'free, autonomous and anonymous' intellectual enquiry that would provide the CCFCL with intellectual impetus. The Order on the other hand was to include both intellectuals, like themselves, and those working more practically for a New Christendom.¹¹¹ Oldham argued that since the CCFCL did not posit the attributes of a revolutionary movement 'something analogous to the "the Party"' had to come into being.·In order to retain flexibility, Oldham was reluctant to turn the Order into another organization nor did he wish it to be subjected to a constitutional frame. Finally, the mark of membership was a lifetime commitment to the purposes set out by the CCFCL while the practical outcome of its ideals would differ depending on context and individual circumstances.¹¹²

Conflicts and challenges over the Order

Despite an overwhelming support for the formation of an Order, there were both challenges and strong disagreement over its nature and function. The conflict over the nature of the Order was already evident at the 4th meeting in April 1939 when Oldham presented the vision. Mannheim desired swift and decisive political action and for the Order to act as 'bridge to politics'.¹¹³ However, others, including Oldham, suggested that a more long-term view had to be taken which went beyond mere party politics: it was a prophetic movement which distinguished itself from politics in that it operated by 'persuasion rather than control'.¹¹⁴ The Order would not take collective action as such, but its members were to commit to actualize principles in their own respective area of influence.¹¹⁵ Shaw put an even stronger emphasis on the prophetic nature of Order than Oldham. As a 'kind of collectivized Jeremiah', it would reveal to the nation its deep-rooted predicament but at the same time act in symbolic ways to demonstrate a vision for the future.¹¹⁶

In the weeks following the 4th meeting, a number of members wrote responses to Oldham's proposed 'constitution' and to the discussion at the meeting. Adolf Löwe perceptively discerned two points of division in the Moot. Firstly, he pointed to a division between those who preferred a more political focus to the Order and those who were convinced that it ought to take on a 'supra-political', 'prophetic' nature. Secondly, Löwe discerned varying degrees of willingness to make commitments and personal sacrifices. Löwe identified Mannheim and N. F. Hall[117] as those most ready for the radical commitment and sacrifice, whereas Moberly, Vidler and Hodges were labelled as moderates. These cleavages and the difficulty in overcoming them made Löwe uncertain of the feasibility of the Order.[118] Hodges felt that the idea of the Order remained unclear as the Moot had yet to agree on its purposes. In line with Löwe's analysis, Hodges identified two different conceptions: one which saw the Order as a political instrument attracting politicians and the second as a religious society.[119] These two tensions were to plague the discussions of the formation of an Order in the years to come.

Having read the comments, Mannheim firmly refuted Löwe's pessimism that the Moot was not ready for the Order. Writing at the cusp of war, Mannheim, in an emotive plea, implored the Moot to take action 'because we are living in the atmosphere of war or warlike preparation'.[120] Mannheim clarified that he was not in favour of the Order turning into a mere political group. He explained that living in a time of transition, a new type of politics was bound to emerge that went beyond the traditional political divisions. The Order was to become a 'revitalising agency' to 'carry a revolution within the established order of society'.[121] In Mannheim's scheme, the Moot would act as a co-ordinating organ bringing together hundreds of already-existing groups with an appetite for societal change. Thus, backed by this intellectual powerhouse of the Moot and its 'sub-Moots' (research groups), the Order itself would be a spiritual movement consisting of people in key positions committed to 'revive faith, morality, intellectual clarity, and for the concept of a new social order'.[122]

Yet, Mannheim's idea of the Order still gave priority to political and social influence, and other members were wary of such a conception. The problem with a political Order, argued Hodges, was that there are differences in political opinions amongst Christians, leading to obvious difficulties in creating a consensus within a movement. Hodges was more sympathetic of the idea of an Order with a stronger religious outlook.[123] Dawson disclosed his apprehension in private letters to Oldham. Citing Mannheim's idea of the Order as a 'nervous system' influencing society through persons in key positions, Dawson anticipated the danger of political activism trumping religious commitments.[124] Walter Oakeshott, for his part, argued for a movement that would vitalize the church from within, aiming for a transformation that would move the church out of its slumber and into action.[125]

Apart from this tension between the political versus the religious, the deliberations came to focus on the level of commitment demanded of members. Speaking of the function of the Moot at the 2nd meeting, Oakeshott announced his wholehearted support for the idea of an Order, commenting that, '[all] revolutionary movements rested in essence on organization and the devotion of their followers. We might need to show we meant business by cutting off the advantages we now enjoyed in social position and income.'[126] At the 4th Moot meeting, Mannheim also made a case for a greater level of commitment for 'the more it demanded of people the more people would give'.[127] Moberly was, however, concerned that commitments to the Order might clash with other loyalties to employers and family.[128] Eliot argued that commitments could be introduced in stages as the Order developed.[129] Several other Moot members held that individuals should be obliged to submit to the stated purposes of the Order, but that the precise application of these was open-ended. Vidler queried whether membership in the Order would require a commitment to certain dogma.[130] Hodges foresaw an issue in that a high level of commitment to an Order could clash with prior commitments to other authorities, and the Moot members were already divided by their allegiance to various church denominations.[131] Dawson similarly stated that while he was in general agreement with the objectives of the Order, he questioned whether it was achievable and whether his allegiance to his 'people', that is, Catholic authorities, rendered his participation impossible.[132] In a candid letter, John Middleton Murry confessed to his personal inability to commit to an Order since his 'economic insecurity' hindered him from joining something that he thought ought to demand on some level a vow of poverty.[133]

Another question deriving from Oldham's twelve-point constitution was the differentiation between the Moot and the Order at the 4th meeting. In Oldham's mind it was a matter of commitment. The Moot would, like the Order, seek to remain a loosely structured organization; however, in contradistinction to the Order, it would seek open and free discussion without any personal commitment. Mannheim added that the task of the Moot was intellectual, whereas the Order 'should become a kind of nervous system for the whole of society, providing the will to action and penetrating into society'.[134] It was suggested that the Moot remain distinct, but its members would form the nucleus of the Order.[135]

It had been agreed that the 5th Moot meeting, 23–24 September 1939, was to be 'given to the inauguration of the Order'. To this end, eight persons who potentially could be part of the initial core of the Order were invited as guests, including Philip Mairet, editor of the *New English Weekly*; A. C. Goyder, director of the *British International Paper*; R. H. Tawney, historian at the London School of Economics; and theologian Reinhold Niebuhr.[136] However, in the light of the declaration of war, the Order was overshadowed by more pressing issues.

By the 7th meeting in February 1940, Mannheim admitted that the idea of an Order had collapsed due to disagreements over its nature and level of commitment.[137] At the following meeting, Mannheim despondently declared that the Moot had given up on its plans to form an Order.[138]

Renewed attempts at forming an Order

Much work did however take place between meetings and the talk of influencing people in key positions was not idle. Oldham worked tirelessly to influence the political establishment, and as the Conservative Party Archives reveal, his efforts did produce some results. In fact, Oldham's lobbying took him and the Moot right to the top of the Conservative Party and even into the government. A correspondence between Cosmo Lang (then Archbishop of Canterbury) and R. A. Butler, an influential Conservative, is indicative of the stir Oldham had managed to generate around his visions of a popular Christian movement. Writing to Butler on 6 June 1940, the Archbishop conveyed his wish to support Oldham's important endeavour of 'uniting Christian forces against the new paganism' and to discuss ways in which the government could 'help this movement get started'.[139] In reply, Butler noted that he had already discussed 'Oldham's movement' with Lord Halifax, the foreign secretary in Churchill's newly formed cabinet, and reported that 'we are both agreed as to its prime importance'. He promised to work out some ideas together with Halifax on 'the best manner in which the Government can give indirect help'.[140]

In the Moot, the idea of an Order crops up now and again in the minutes of the ensuing meetings, but it is not until the 10th meeting that it is discussed in any greater detail. This weekend took place at Downe House, Cold Ash, during the weekend of 10–13 January 1941 at one of the darkest moments in the war as far as Britain was concerned. Mannheim had during the 9th meeting called for the creation of a 'Vigilance Group', that is, for a nucleus of the Order, consisting of five politicians and five Moot members who would meet weekly to keep a watchful eye on the developments in Parliament and thereby 'trying to prevent the present State becoming Fascist from within'.[141] He developed this line of investigation in a memorandum outlining the future direction of the Moot in early 1941.[142] Mannheim envisioned the creation of an Order consisting of intellectuals, invigorated by a spiritual renewal and mutual support, that would offer leadership to the nation by revitalizing existing elites. It would gather the 'pioneering types who would otherwise remain inefficient in their isolation'.[143] The Order would thereby be comparable to the inner circles of the Nazi and

Russian Communist Party, albeit with a less rigid structure than a political party and remaining more pluralistic than the totalitarian parties.[144]

In opening statements at the 10th meeting, Mannheim continued his plead for a group working to revitalize existing political elites,[145] whereas Oldham held that the Order would be loosely organized and take no corporate action as such. Referring to Dawson's paper 'The Sword of the Spirit',[146] Oldham put a greater emphasis on the Order becoming a spiritual movement, 'a movement, based on Christianity, attracting non-Christians'.[147] There were clearly unsolved issues, but on Mannheim's suggestion the Moot agreed to push ahead without a ready-made constitution.[148] Oldham was charged with the task of making enquiries and bringing together 'a nucleus of people who shared our spiritual convictions'.[149] The meeting ended on a high note.

Between meetings, Oldham sought to amalgamate some of the dominant strands of the discussion to date and as a result produced 'A Fraternity of the Spirit', inspired particularly by Dawson, Mannheim and W. E. Hocking. In an article for the *Dublin Review,* Dawson had posited a prophetic movement as a counter-force to break the domination of totalitarian states engulfing the Western world. Dawson understood totalitarianism to be a spiritual problem which had to be tackled by a spiritual solution consisting of a wielding of the prophetic word of God, that is, 'the Sword of the Spirit'. As such, Dawson dreamt of the mobilization of a 'spiritual crusade' by the Spirit and a mass commitment to prayer, study and action.[150] Oldham used Dawson's article to stress the religious dimension of what the Moot sought to realize and their reliance on the supernatural. Another idea that Oldham referenced was H. E. Hocking's concept of the 'commotive', denoting the innate human propensity towards cooperation.[151] Oldham used Hocking's concept to emphasize the desire for humans to work together as a source of vitality in the new movement. Finally, Oldham incorporated Mannheim's suggestion that a sociopolitical change in Britain would come from an elite consisting of those 'most alive and sensitive to the situation' who would take a lead in a spiritual movement.[152]

Based on these ideas, Oldham argued for a 'Fraternity', united by a religious bond, dedicated to the same aims and purposes, and constituted by those committed to the Christian faith but inclusive of all who shared the vision. Firstly, the movement would be dedicated to act 'in faith in the power of the Holy Spirit', which implied a dedication to spiritual disciplines. A second commitment involved devotion to cultivating a 'free life of the spirit', in face of the stifling compulsion of totalitarianism. A third commitment entailed 'the recognition of man's dependence on nature as God's creation, and on his fellow-men'. Fourthly, members of the Order would commit to a financial system that was set up to serving 'the true values of life'. Finally, the fifth commitment involved resisting state power by mobilization of a strong civil society and a positive utilization of propaganda and education.[153]

The memorandum drew plenty of responses by the members, but rather than uniting the group, it exposed the persisting gulf between them – particularly between those who understood the Order as a sociopolitical elite and others who favoured a stronger religious emphasis. Mannheim feared that an overemphasis on the inward spiritual commitments without addressing the reform of social institutions would lead to a 'kind of escapism',[154] and Murry was unconvinced that a movement which sought to change society could be acting 'beyond politics'.[155] Dawson, however, re-emphasized the need to rediscover the doctrine of the Holy Spirit as the dynamo of Christian action. This would entail 'a waiting on the Holy Spirit, like the disciples at Jerusalem before Pentecost', abiding for the right time for action.[156] With this stress on the religious commitment of the Order, Dawson questioned whether it could in any meaningful way be reconciled with Mannheim's 'political elites'.[157]

Nathaniel Micklem, a theologian and at the time principal of Mansfield College, Oxford, together with Eliot, picked up on Oldham's appeal to Christians and non-Christians by a vague nod towards spirituality.[158] Troubled by Oldham's choice of language, Eliot who wrote that its ambiguity verged 'perilously near to the Spirit of Compromise': 'Either a movement must be definitely religious, and by "definitely" I mean dogmatically Christian – and have social consequences; or else it must be definitely orientated to a social programme.'[159] Vidler held that the 'Fraternity' should simply consist of those living out their Christian convictions as individuals and in local contexts.[160]

The memorandum was further critiqued for being too general to be relevant.[161] Observing that a revolution demands an enemy, Eliot held that the commitments were too general and therefore lacked to the potency to bring real change.[162] Mannheim made the same point.[163] One of the strongest responses came from Geoffrey Vickers who wrote that for all its talk of revolution, the Moot did not possess a revolutionary spirit. Its members were not 'revolutioners', here defined as 'a man with a fanatical but heterodox belief about What Really Matters Most. I.e. the Moot is not strong enough in its convictions'.[164] Vickers had hit the nail on the head.

At the meeting itself, Oldham sought to settle the issue of whether the 'Fraternity' should primarily be religious or political.[165] Much of the ensuing discussion covered old ground. Mannheim eventually took charge and in a statement on the Sunday afternoon session tabled his version of the Order. He argued that the question of Christianity could be laid aside on the grounds that a democratic society is the embodiment of Christian ideals in the first place. Furthermore, his idea of a Third Way demanded a 'party' that would act as a network for cooperation and that would also be saturated with a fraternity derived from a religious spirit. Mannheim proposed three urgent areas that the party ought to prioritize: restructuring of industry, devolution of power and the 're-education of man'.[166]

The responses to Mannheim's programme were approving, if somewhat muted. Murry claimed that it was the 'only way to save democracy as a social order' and suggested that it should be published in the *CNL*, encouraging the readers to consent to the programme 'as a Christian duty'.[167] Oldham consented that he was happy to drop the 'specific Christian label' as the proposal assumed a Christian doctrine of man.[168] Moberly and Hodges also concurred.[169] Vidler was sceptical of whether the plan could realistically be executed, but did not object on principle.[170] What should be noted is that the two strongest voices of dissent towards Mannheim, Dawson and Eliot, were absent from the meeting due to illness.[171] Nevertheless, it seemed as if Mannheim had prevailed in convincing the Moot of his idea of a political elite. It marked a considerable shift from Oldham's 'Fraternity' and earlier ideas of a New Christendom which was conceived of as a more definite Christian movement.

Plans for an Order collapse

Nevertheless, the Order is conspicuously missing from the discussion in the subsequent Moot gatherings, which took on a far more intellectual character. This change is likely to be linked with Oldham's forced resignation from the CCFCL in July 1941.[172] The CCFCL was meant to play a vital part in Oldham's scheme for societal rebirth as a supporting agent of the Order. Thus, losing control of the council was a major blow to these plans. It is telling that the items listed under the heading 'Future Programme' in the minutes from the 12th meeting decisively concerned intellectual enquiry.[173] Henceforth, references to the proposed Order and other types of action are strikingly absent. At the outset of the 14th meeting in March 1942, Oldham acknowledged that it had proved challenging to formulate a common programme but at this point he still held onto the dream that the Moot could prepare to be 'the nucleus of ideas which would govern the next stage in human history'.[174]

Discussions of a possible Order did resurface during the 18th meeting in the autumn of 1943. Oldham had initiated another attempt at creating a manifesto for a broad collaborative effort. This could not merely be another gathering for intellectuals, argued Oldham, but 'must also be a fighting group'.[175] Later during the meeting Oldham spoke of a 'Copernican revolution in theology and practice' that depended on a revolutionary body.[176] However, Erik Fenn pointedly reminded the Moot of its failure to materialize the Order in the past due to disagreements over level of commitment.[177] Undeterred, Oldham introduced Paul Tillich's notion of the 'latent Church' denoting groups outside the institutional church 'in whom the Spiritual Presence's impact is felt'.[178] The discussions rambled on covering similar ground as in previous meetings without reaching a definite agreement.

This review illustrates just how pervasive the idea of an Order remained throughout the Moot's discussions. It bears witness to the extent to which the Moot was committed to act for a far-reaching societal renewal. For a group that identified itself as primarily an intellectual venture, it is noteworthy how central practical action was on their agenda. It also gives evidence of the struggles that such an endeavour entails. These discussions highlight the fault lines that divided the Moot, firstly into those arguing that the religious should be prioritized over the political, and, secondly, into idealists arguing that no forceful movement could come about without a sound social philosophy, versus the utilitarian pragmatists who held that principles take shape in the course of action.

New education, new man

A shared presupposition held in the Moot was that a societal transformation necessarily had to go beyond mere political and economic restructuring to address the deeper cultural backdrop that often unconsciously informs the world view and behaviour of individual citizens. For this reason, education became an important element in the Moot's discussion and its mission to reform society. The following statement, ratified by the Moot (7th meeting), but issued by the CCFCL captures this sentiment:

> That the council take steps to inaugurate an enterprise of the Churches with a view to a more Christian order of society; such initiative being directed in the first instance to the preparation of youth for life in such an order of society, to the basing of education upon the Christian scale of values, to the greater equalisation of educational opportunity and to the making of such provision for

the youth of the nation as may secure to every citizen full development of the faculties bestowed on him by God for the service of the community, the exercise of responsibility and the realisation of fellowship.[179]

In other words, there was a strong belief in the agency of education in character formation that in turn would generate a new society. It was no coincidence that Oldham had recruited two educationists in influential positions, Fred Clarke and Walter Moberly, for the Moot.[180] Further, education became a central area of research for Mannheim during the 1940s, culminating in his appointment as professor at the Institute of Education in 1946.[181] *The Times'* obituary of Karl Mannheim treats the *The Diagnosis of Our Time* as essentially a book on education, which profoundly shaped and was shaped by deliberations at the Moot. The belief in education as a social instrument became a central line of investigation in the Moot's revitalizing endeavour to create a 'new man' and a 'new world'.

The Moot's philosophy of education

A number of themes emerge out of the Moot papers and discussions on education. Firstly, in his Moot paper 'Planning for Freedom', Mannheim had suggested that education was a means to 'coordinating different activities which will neither suppress individuality on the one hand nor subject the growing child to planless influences on the other'.[182] Mannheim's drive towards greater centralized control over education was an idea incorporated into papers by Clarke, Moberly and Löwe.

Second was the Moot's emphasis on the character-forming function of education that runs like a thread throughout these discussions. In Murry's first Moot paper, he discussed Thomas Arnold's idea of educating for a certain character ideal: a responsible individual who disinterestedly serves the interest of the nation.[183] Similarly Mannheim's planned educational system would instil basic values and morals in order that the student might become a responsible participant in society. Without a minimum moral standard, which all citizens are obliged to adhere to, society would disintegrate. Beyond this basic requirement, Mannheim advocated 'for free competition between creeds, doctrines and ideas'.[184] Hodges provided a precise summary of Mannheim's philosophy of education: 'The new system will require a new type of man with a new type of outlook to run it, and education and propaganda will have to be used to produce this new type.'[185] In essence, a 'new society' required a 'new man' trained to act and think according to certain patterns. Education was seen as central in this task. Fred Clarke used a slightly different rhetoric. He had at the Church, Community and State conference defended the traditional telos of English education, namely, the 'freely creative personality'.[186] In his first paper for the Moot, Clarke developed these ideas. Clarke proposed that the emergence of universal primary education in the nineteenth century had only perpetuated class division and the privilege of the upper classes. For while the public schools retained their tradition of 'cultural' education, the state-provided schools tended towards 'vocational training', thereby supplying a modern workforce for the capitalist and the ruling elite.[187] Eliot also rejected the modern emphasis on 'education of the mind alone', but in an article for the *CNL* he suggested that Clarke's education for culture was not Christian enough. Formation of character was not an end in-of-itself but rather a by-product of a deeper spiritual training that would aspire towards 'holiness' and 'wisdom'.[188]

These ideas can be seen repeated in papers on the future of universities by Moberly and Löwe presented at the 7th meeting. Moberly set out his paper by contrasting the humanist ideal of education 'for life itself' as embodied at the Oxbridge colleges with utilitarianism of the modern university. Under the guise of 'neutrality', the modern universities had purposely discarded the humanistic tradition. This neglect might be excusable in times of stability. However, whilst 'living in the end of an era' when social norms can no longer be taken for granted, the policy of 'neutrality' merely served to further the state of confusion. The solution, proposed Moberly, was for the university to enable students to freely explore their own philosophies, but in the Oxbridge spirit, with its bias towards Christianity. The central thesis of this paper was later expanded into Moberly's *Crisis in the University*,[189] one of the most popular books on higher education in Britain since the war.[190] Löwe's basic outlook concurs with that of both Clarke and Moberly. Like Moberly, Löwe praised the 'Ancient Greats' for realizing this ideal, but feared that this tradition was endangered by the increased specialization as evident in the modern universities, resulting in a 'chaos of values'.[191]

Thirdly, for Clarke there was a real tension between the broad cultural education as a guarantee for a flourishing culture and the demand for greater specialization in a technologically advancing society:

> The choice lies between a world which, like Aldous Huxley's 'Brave New World', has surrendered its hold upon real culture in order that it may apply techniques to the more exquisite satisfaction of animal appetites, and a world which adapts its techniques to the enrichment and wider dissemination of a growing contemporary culture.[192]

A transformation of the educational system of England would thereby entail a synthesis between cultural and vocational education. The ideas in the paper were published as *Education and Social Change* in Christian News-Letter Books series in 1940.[193] Also in accordance with Clarke, Moberly suggested that the humanist ideal of 'education for life' held by the elites did need to be supplemented with vocational training for industrialized societies to survive.[194] Löwe suggested that if the ancient universities of England had supplied the ruling class with the 'gentlemen amateur' type, the task of the universities in a new democratically planned society was to educate for the 'enlightened expert'.[195]

Finally, these Moot papers discuss the role of religion in education. Clarke held that the safeguard against the dangers of an instrumentalist approach to education in a planned society was religion: 'Science can cease to be a potential instrument of Satan only when it is seen as a gift of the Spirit.'[196] As we have seen for Moberly, Christianity provided a framework within the universities in which ideas could be explored freely. Ideas on religion and education feature more prominently in a paper by Clarke for the 11th meeting. Buoyed by the potential in shaping the future of religious education in Britain and the possibility of a 'revolutionary' shake up of educational philosophy, Clarke challenged conventional ideas that religious education was synonymous with religious instruction. Rather, '[p]ractical experience would appear to suggest that wherever education achieves real success on any considerable scale there is always within it and behind it a *faith* that must be called religious'.[197] Thus, if there no conscious faith, some unconscious 'adulterine' faith will fill the vacuum. Since religion is 'a way of knowing, a mode of apprehending reality', it cannot become another subject on the curriculum but has to be approached in a similar manner to teaching a 'mother tongue'. This implies an environment that is 'religious'. Much like Eliot's argument in *The Idea*, Clarke argued that religious education demanded not only a 'Christian school' but a Christian society.[198] Clarke's 'notes' were briefly discussed at the 11th meeting. Moberly held that the difficulty of implementing a Christian ethos into the fabric of school communities is that it would presuppose a greater level of Christianity than in society in general and in the lives of the teachers. In response, Oldham suggested that rather than an explicit Christian ideal, a social philosophy based on natural law could be the basis for a wider collaborative effort in changing education.[199]

The Education Group and Butler's 1944 Education Act

Apart from these discussions on educational philosophy, at a more practical level Löwe had at the 7th meeting tabled the suggestion of an experimental college. He argued that the transformation of the university system was likely to be resisted by teachers and therefore recommended an experimental college consisting of '20–40 people living and working together ... [that] might educate the next generation of teachers'. This was greeted with approval, and it was agreed that the possibility of setting it up at Oxford or Cambridge was to be explored.[200] Further, in order to break 'the power of the existing clique', Mannheim suggested as a first step to facilitate the formation of groups of like-minded people within the universities.[201] Oldham was in favour of a new university group consisting of twelve academics.[202]

Little came of these ideas, but an important step in the Moot's drive towards a revitalized Christian society through education was the creation of specialized research groups as discussed already at the 4th meeting. It was agreed that an initial group on education would be formed consisting of Mannheim, Clarke, Löwe, Eliot, Murry and T. F Coade.[203] The evidence on how regularly the group met is incomplete, but there are minutes from four gatherings between 1941 and 1945.[204] Motivated by the assumption that the war situation was an opportunity for a shake-up in English education, the group sought to use their connections with people in powerful positions to influence policy. The part played by some Moot members in the 1944 Education Act is perhaps the most tangible example of the Moot's wider influence on British society.

Much time in the Education Group was given to the question of possible modes of action. The strategy that commanded most attention was to seek the ear of the powerful and influential. More concretely those gathered at the meeting of February 1944 were confident that they could approach the serving Education Minister, R. A. Butler, and the Board of Education with their ideas of educational reform. Such plans were no mere fanciful thinking as several of the members of the group played some part in the developments leading to the 1944 Education Act, a landmark in the history of English education credited to the labours of Butler. Clarke himself was acquainted with Butler and was consulted in the processes, which resulted in the 1944 Act. Frank M. Mitchell, Clarke's biographer, notes but downplays Fred Clarke's role in the development of the Act.[205] However, Hsiao-Yuh Ku's more recent archival study establishes just how significant Clarke was. Clarke's contribution includes his regular correspondence with Butler, his lobbying through publications and public meetings, and the participation in interest groups such as the Moot, both in the years leading up to the Act and its aftermath.[206] Speaking of his Mannheim-influenced book *Education and Social Change* (which began as a Moot paper), Clarke noted that 'I have been given reason to believe that it had some influence on the course of events, helping as it did to guide and crystallize the body of opinion out which came the Education Act of 1944.'²⁰⁷ Clarke was also part of the All Souls Group, led by W. G. S. Adams, which also played a part in the Act. Butler himself attended the group as a guest.²⁰⁸ The importance of Clarke's contribution was further acknowledged by Butler himself, who in a speech after Clarke's death recalled how Clarke 'had advised him and helped him in drawing [the Act] up'.²⁰⁹ Walter Oakeshott, who had participated in the November 1941 education group meeting, was also involved in the early stages of the discussion of the Act.²¹⁰ Further, as the editor who revived the *Times Education Supplement*, H. C. Dent ardently sought to influence public opinion on the educational reform implied by the Act.²¹¹ Interestingly, Gary McCulloch calls Dent the 'most prominent and notable propagandist' of the Act.²¹² A letter in support of the suggested education bill to *The Times* on 15 January 1944, signed by Archbishop William Temple, William Beveridge, Fred Clarke and Sir Richard Livingstone (another participant in the Education Group and soon to become the Vice Chancellor of Oxford University), is further evidence of the group's network and lobbying.²¹³

The discussions in the Moot and the Education Group concur on a number of points with the policies of the 1944 Education Act. For example, the group accepted Mannheim's petition of balancing greater nationalization and planning of education with local autonomy;²¹⁴ most of the group's members valued a social justice and democratization which suggested equal opportunity;²¹⁵ they argued for the defence and promotion of democratic values;²¹⁶ and lobbied for free, compulsory education up to the age of 16.²¹⁷ All these ideas were incorporated in the Act (the final bill agreed on compulsory education to the age of 15 with the possibility of extension to 16). It is naturally impossible to establish a direct causation between the Act in its final form and the work of the Moot's education group. But as Michael Barber proposes, 'Clarke and others played a critical role not only in their ideas and advocacy, but also in the bridge they provided between ministers and officials … and the popular campaign for change'.²¹⁸

It is unclear why the Education Group was discontinued. However, an apparent attempt to revamp it was made as the group met under the auspices of the CFC on 16 July 1945.²¹⁹ The meeting was given to consider some notes by Marjorie Reeves. Reeves advocated for a new group of educationists that would counter any potential apathy in the wake of the success of the 1944 Education Act by addressing the *content* of education over structure and organization.²²⁰ A similar assessment had been expressed by Fred Clarke in a comment on Oldham's draft 'The Christian Witness in Present Crisis'.²²¹ Here Clarke wrote approvingly of the 1944 Act and its 'note of authority' and of a 'new kind of orderliness' which speaks of education as a means of 'social control' but also of the necessity of 'a few broad principles'.[222] As late as September 1946, Oldham asked the Moot members for permission to invite R. A. Butler to the next meeting.[223] Due to insufficient records, it is unclear whether Butler attended the meeting in January 1947. Nonetheless, these examples witness to a desire to build on the 1944 Education Act and to address some of its perceived inadequacies.

Concluding remarks on the Moot and education

For the Moot, education was an antidote to social disintegration under *laissez faire* liberalism. As such, a theme running through their discussion was the idea of education *for life*. That is, they envisioned an education that went beyond a utilitarian vocational training so often characterizing modern schools and universities to an education that sought to instil certain values. There was some unease concerning such 'inculcation' yet it was justified on the grounds it would instil democratic values and contribute to the formation of a mature personality that could handle freedom with responsibility. This is the justification offered by Moberly:

> We had not to teach [sic] other values by the same methods as the Nazis. The justification of any inculcation of values in young children depended on whether it furthered or hindered the child's own choice. If you didn't inculcate some values the odds were the child would be unable to choose. The difference between deliberate moral or religious education and the character formation of Hitlerism was the one produced persons and the other dummies.[224]

The discussion on education, particularly through its Education Group, is the most concrete example of the Moot's wider influence. In their article on 'Oldham's Moot, the Universities and the Adult Citizen', Tom Steele and Richard Taylor demonstrate how the Moot 'was part of the social capital or network that bound together members of the establishment and helped crystallize what Raymond Williams called a "structure of feeling" around the need for social planning, the social sciences, democratic citizenship and equality'.[225] It is, as such, interesting to note the extent to which the outlook of the Education Group was 'liberal'.[226]

The 1944 Education Act was the most significant reform in education since the 1918 Fisher Education Act. However, it was more reformist than revolutionary, resulting in significant but measured changes in British educational system. It was the result of the wide consensus within the political establishment and even 'most of those on the Left recognized that at the time it was as radical an act as could be achieved'.²²⁷ From the Moot's participation it is evident that the group also was part of the 'establishment'. This calls into question the Moot's revolutionary intentions, or at least suggests a definite will to work within the existing political order.

Channels of dissemination

Anthony Wallace's suggestion that 'communication remains one of the primary activities' as of an emerging revitalization movement is hardly surprising.²²⁸ Neither is the Moot's deliberate use of the media channels available to them via the *CNL*, individual publications and, importantly in an era of increasing mass communication, the BBC. The members were conscious of the power of mass media which in not least Mannheim's view was legitimate social techniques to be used to influence the general population.²²⁹ Thus, while they struggled to agree on a joint manifesto, the members made extensive use of various media outlets to participate in the post-war reconstruction conversation.

The Christian News-Letter

While officially under the auspices of the CCFCL, and from February 1942 the CFC, the *CNL* became the principal mouthpiece of the Moot. The Moot played a vital role in shaping the *CNL*'s ethos and content. Oldham outlined plans of a newsletter for the first time during the 5th meeting in September 1939. It was to be formed as a response to the outbreak of the war and the desire for concrete action in light of these historical developments. As a commentary on current issues, it was to cover seven areas of discussion:

1. The religious interpretation of present events.
2. A survey of immediate issues raised.
3. Drawing attention to the lessons of history.
4. Practical problems, for example, evacuation and the 14–10 age group.
5. The making real of the Oecumencial Church.
6. The defence of religious and democratic principles.
7. The formulation of war aims.²³⁰

The *News-Letter* was to be run by the CCFCL, which controlled the appointment of editors but not its content. Oldham explained that the editorial group would consist of Moot members or 'near-members'.²³¹ By the time Oldham presented the idea of the *CNL*, he had secured the cooperation of the leading churchmen in the country and appointed the editorial group including T. S. Eliot, Philip Mairet, W. H. Smith, Alec Vidler and Oldham himself. Nevertheless, prior to launching the project, Oldham wished to attain the full support of the Moot. Oldham not only gained the group's approval but also received extensive feedback as the Moot jointly agreed on a weekly publication, that the target group would be 'all who helped to mould public opinion', that it would have a 'personal touch' and that the style of writing would be accessible.[232] Finally it was agreed that the *CNL* would be 'a means of expressing the ideas current in the Moot'.[233]

The first issue was launched already on 18 October 1939 with Oldham, in his capacity as editor, declaring that the *CNL* would act 'to pool our available resources of Christian understanding and insight' and to 'bring hope and renewal to a decaying civilisation'.[234] Five months later Oldham reminded the readers that 'the central interest of the News-Letter is the coming to birth of a Christian society'.[235] The first issue contained a list of contributors consisting of 48 names, out of which 16 were members or had attended Moot meetings. Some of the more noteworthy collaborators were William Temple, A. D. Lindsey, Reinhold Niebuhr, Dorothy Sayers, Arnold Toynbee and R. H. Tawney.[236] Oldham further explained that the *News-Letter* was a joint effort with a high level of contribution from the collaborators[237] and with the editorial group working on articles together.[238]

The newsletter soon gained a considerable circulation, and by 1 January 1940 it had already 8,114 subscriptions, peaking at 11,592 a year later.[239] A report to the CCFCL in May 1940 discloses that 43 study groups had emerged spontaneously around the country to discuss the *CNL*. It could also boast 900 overseas subscriptions from 37 different countries and the publication of five books in the CNL Books series with over 30,000 copies sold. The report further noted the diversity of the readers, including 'privates in the army, Anglican and Roman Catholic Archbishop, school teachers …, lawyers, doctors, miners, business men, civil servants, nurses, housewives, every variety of person seems to be represented'.[240] In a letter to J. R. Mott, a key leader in the ecumenical movement, Oldham spoke of his own surprise at the success of the *CNL* and how it was even read by members of parliament.[241] That the *CNL* had been well received was not just boastful talk by Oldham. A report by Margaret Godley at the Conservative Research Department (CRD), on 21 August 1940, notes that the *CNL* 'is becoming increasingly well known'.[242] A memorandum from the Central Committee for National Policy proposes the *CNL* as a potential ally as one of several groups sharing their ideas.[243] That the personnel at the

CRD valued the work of the *CNL* is evident by another memorandum titled 'Objects of organisation as discussed with the Prime Minister on 8th January'. It insinuates that the CRD proposed to Winston Churchill, as a party strategy, to collaborate and maintain links with 'the personalities' behind movements such as the *CNL*.[244]

Each issue covered news items in an editorial signed by the editor, and every second issue included a supplement with a more in-depth analysis by some of the leading Christian thinkers of the time. There were for example contributions by Karl Barth, Reinhold Niebuhr and William Temple. The content of the paper offers an absorbing coverage on the war from a distinct Christian standpoint covering an array of topics from moral questioning of bombings of civilian targets, to reports from the churches in countries under Nazi occupation, the Beveridge Report, apologetics, discussions on industry, educational reforms, faith and science, 'Sexual Relationships in War-Time', the ecumenical movement, the genocide of Jews and many more.[245]

Naturally, the strong influence of the Moot on the *CNL* is evident in its general ethos and the representation in the editorial group. Furthermore, throughout its history many topics of the Moot and even its position papers appeared in the bulletin. Oldham's contributions are too considerable to deal with extensively here, but the editorials and supplements are bursting with the central affirmations that he brought to the Moot. The initial supplement of the *News-Letter*, though signed off as a collaborative piece by the editorial group, is nevertheless as Keith Clements suggests 'quintessentially Oldham'.[246] A 'Christian' News-Letter, states the supplement, is distinguished by acknowledging firstly the tension between the in-breaking of a new era through Christ and the reality of a sinful world; secondly, by giving loyalty to the universal church over nation; and thirdly, by a dedication to the renewal of civilization amidst the destruction of war. The piece ended with a call to participation in a forward-looking Christian movement:

> The only force capable of bringing to birth a new society embodying enough of the Christian values to entitle it to be described as a new Christendom is that of alert, adventurous, disciplined men and women, delivered from anxiety of their personal future and from dread of radical social change, and dedicated to the service of a society founded on Christian truth and justice ... Our hope is that the News-Letter may serve as a means of communication between those who are reaching out after this way of life.[247]

Some of Oldham's major pieces of the early years in the *CNL* were published in the CNL books series in 1942 as *Real Life is Meeting*.[248] The volume contains many of the central lines of investigation in the Moot, for instance, the demand of a new movement 'powerful enough to turn in a new direction the tides of history', Christian anthropology (via Jacques Maritain), educational reform instilling a Christian way of life and the inevitability of planning.[249]

While Mannheim was not directly involved in the editorial aspects of the *CNL*, his ideas were introduced through Oldham's summary of 'Planning for Freedom' and in the debates that ensued.[250] A critique was submitted by Christopher Dawson,[251] with Mannheim directly responding by asserting that a planned democratic society 'is a really effective alternative to totalitarianism'.[252] In a further letter, an anonymous reader echoed Mannheim by calling for a progressive government to use propaganda to strengthen the democratic culture of the nation.[253] A few weeks later, 'a life-long student of sociology and public affairs' declared Mannheim's ideas 'to be taken as authoritative'.[254] Then when *Diagnosis of Our Time* was published in 1943, Oldham devoted a supplement to discuss its content.[255] George Every responded with the 'Limits of Planning', which was implicitly directed at Mannheim's claim that religious and cultural renewal could be planned.[256]

It was not only Mannheim's work that was promoted through reviews. Eliot's *Idea* was hailed for its 'unusual originality and power' as 'giving a perceptible direction to Christian thought'.[257] Eliot was a member of the editorial board of the *CNL* until 1946.[258] Up until then, he had played a significant role in shaping the *News-Letter*, not least by standing in for Oldham as a guest editor. To provide a snapshot, his editorials called readers to be prepared to make sacrifices to make way for the new world after war;[259] reflected on the problem of the 'conflicting claims of liberty and order';[260] spoke of Charles Maurras of the *Action Française* as 'a man of powerful and narrow mind';[261] declared that refinement in art and devotion in religion by the few was preferable to the dilution of these among the masses[262]; and discussed the latest in educational policy.[263] Eliot also contributed with a number of supplements. In 'Education in a Christian Society', Eliot argued that the 'education for culture' that Fred Clarke advocated in his Moot-inspired *Education and Social Change* needed to instil 'the atrophied vestiges of wisdom and holiness'.[264] Further, Eliot questioned the prevailing ideas concerning 'equal opportunity' and the notion that formal education ought to be universal.[265] In December 1943, Eliot submitted a paper on 'Power and Responsibility', where he argued that in a healthy society, power is distributed between various groups and spheres of influence that provide checks and balances.[266] Eliot's final contribution to the *CNL* was written under the pseudonym 'Metoikos' in response to an article by John Maud (written under the pseudonym 'Civis'). Maud had argued that it was a Christian responsibility to support the government's 'Full Employment' scheme.[267] Eliot almost quit the board over the article, but was instead convinced by Oldham to write a reply.[268] Eliot strongly repudiated 'Civis' on the basis that to demand the church's unreserved support of the state was to confuse the distinction between church and state and undermine the Christian priority of the eternal over the temporal.[269] Frustrated by the *CNL*'s 'Liberal drift',[270] Eliot eventually quit the editorial board in 1946.[271]

A number of other Moot members made major contributions to the *CNL*. Articles were submitted by the assistant editor Alec Vidler,[272] H. A. Hodges,[273] Walter Moberly,[274] John Baillie,[275] Erik Fenn,[276] Geoffrey Vickers[277] and John Middleton Murry.[278] Most of these articles had originated as Moot papers or had been discussed during the meetings. Finally, Kathleen Bliss, who first joined the Moot in June 1943, took over the editorship from Oldham in May 1945 and continued the work in the same ethos.

Keith Clements argues that Oldham adhered to the wisdom of knowing when to give something up.[279] As the war came to an end, Oldham clearly felt that the time had come to step down from his position at the *CNL*. The last issue was published on 6 July 1949; despite a storm of protests, the *CNL* was discontinued due to economic and personal issues.[280] The paper had been established as part of Oldham's scheme to revitalize the Western world and to propagate for a new Christian society. Although Oldham believed that there was a 'common mind' amongst Christian intellectuals, the *CNL* became too much of an open forum of ideas to be the organ of sociopolitical movement.

The BBC and Moot in collaboration

The Moot's connection with and use of the BBC as an instrument for spreading its ideas bear further witness to the scope of the group's ambition. Through Eric Fenn, who was assistant director at the BBC's department of religion from 1938 to 1944, the Moot developed a close collaboration. It is worth noting that whilst religion is today marginal in the BBC's enormous output, during the Second World War religious broadcasting accounted for 16–17 per cent of its total broadcasting volume.[281] The links with BBC then presented a remarkable opportunity for the Moot to reach a national audience.

It is apparent that Oldham sought to draw the BBC into the Moot's sphere of influence and intentionally drew on his connections for this purpose. In early 1939, Oldham actively lobbied Frederick W. Ogilvie, the Director General of the BBC from 1938 to 1942, sending him several of the Moot papers. In a letter dated

26 January 1939, Oldham invited Ogilvie to meet to discuss a document 'about our plan'.[282] The document that Oldham mentions here is presumably a draft of the Moot's potential manifesto, 'The Rebirth of the West: A New Christendom'.[283] Oldham also unsuccessfully attempted to recruit Ogilvie as a member of the board of the CCFLC.[284] Nevertheless, Ogilvie took a clear interest in Oldham's projects, giving advice on potential staff for the CCFLC and promising to read Hodges' paper 'Some Tasks for Christian Thought'.[285]

It is, however, the correspondence between Oldham and Eric Fenn that most evidently discloses how the Moot used the BBC as a tool to disseminate their ideas on a national scale. It is significant that Fenn and J. W. Welsh, the then director of Religious Broadcasting, turned to Oldham for a Christian response to the news of the outbreak of war. A draft of the talk, 'The Church in War Times', was vetted by T. S. Eliot, Toynbee, Christopher Dawson, Archbishop of Canterbury Cosmo Lang and the then Archbishop of York, William Temple.[286] To maximize its exposure, Fenn and Welsh sought the coveted spot after the 9 p.m. evening news.[287]

Shortly after this broadcast, Fenn and Oldham began to discuss possibilities of collaboration. Referring to an 'enormously enjoyable' Moot meeting during 23–25 September, Fenn promised to reflect on 'ideas as to how we can relate our work here [at the BBC] to what you will be doing'.[288] A few months later, Fenn wrote that 'Welsh and I have a plan in which we should like the cooperation of at least some members of the Moot', while 'naturally keeping the connection between the speakers ... from the Moot dark'.[289] They had in mind a series titled 'A Christian Looks at the World', with talks by Hodges, Löwe and Eliot. The aim of the programme was to provide a Christian point of view on the future of Western civilization, comparing Nazi Germany, Bolshevik Russia and British society.[290] The proposed series was to build on a six-week programme by John Middleton Murry during the winter of 1939–1940 titled 'Europe in Travail', which had as its objective to 'kindle ... the sense of necessity of a new social imagination'.[291]

During these winter months, Oldham and Fenn continued their correspondence, exploring further cooperation between the BBC and the Moot. On 19 December, Oldham wrote of a co-ordinated effort to reach the nation with their vision of societal renewal:

> I should like very much if we could cooperate closely in our plans for the coming year. The situation is so desperate that the need for pooling our too meagre resources seems more evident every day ... What is of the highest moment is

that we should together discover the key ideas in the situation and then use our combined resources to impress them on the public mind in different settings and from different approaches.'[292]

Fenn's reply is affirmative, expressing his readiness to exploit the intellectual wealth of the Moot: 'I naturally have to rely on the Moot and people associated with us in the work of the Moot, because there is no other such body in existence'.[293] Perhaps the best example of how the BBC was used for the Moot's purposes is the series 'A Christian Looks at the World'. On 29 January 1940, Fenn wrote to Oldham requesting time at the upcoming Moot meeting to discuss a production that would become 'very much of an utterance within the experience and conviction of the Moot itself'.[294] It appears that this conversation took place on the Saturday afternoon of the 7th meeting.[295] The plans came to fruition and talks were given by John Middleton Murry, Fred Clarke and Walter Moberly. The ratings during the series range from a high of 3.6 million listeners for Murry's introduction to a low of 1 million. However, in his assessment of the series, Eric Fenn was disappointed with the production, 'because the level of prophetic insight was not high enough', and some talks were too superficial.[296]

A number of further talks ensued in the coming years as a result of the BBC/Moot cooperation. Most noteworthy is a series titled 'The Church Looks Ahead', broadcasted in six parts during February–March 1941. In a two-part talk, Oldham deliberated on the true nature of 'man' as created dependent upon God, fellow human beings and nature.[297] Eliot was asked to present the final talk, 'Towards a Christian Britain'. Eliot was the most prolific contributor to the BBC of all Moot members. Between 1929 and 1963, he was on air around 80 times.[298] From the 1930s and throughout the 1940s, many of these broadcasts addressed topics related to Christianity and society. In 'Towards a Christian Britain', he continued on exploring this theme rhetorically asking 'what can we do to bring about a Christian Britain?'[299] In the end, Eliot appealed to a prophetic living as exemplified in the life of Charles de Foucauld, the French Catholic priest and martyr.[300]

A final example of the Moot/BBC collaboration is Eric Fenn's attempt to produce a broadcast to propagate the content of William Temple's *CNL Supplement* in December 1943 – the Moot's final attempt at a corporate manifesto.[301] Fenn secured talks by William Temple and John Baillie, and approached Oldham for another script;[302] however, there are no further records of this series, and it is possible that it was cut due to the sudden death of William Temple on 26 October 1944.[303]

Apart from these broadcasts, Eric Fenn occasionally used the Moot as a sounding board. During a discussion of possible avenues for societal renewal at the 9th Moot meeting in July 1940, Fenn tabled the suggestion of a 'Broadcast mission' during the coming autumn and asked whether such an idea would be feasible.[304] Moberly felt the idea was 'supremely worth' executing, but feared that the BBC would not allow it to be aired.[305] Others expressed further misgivings. Oldham, for instance, was doubtful 'because we are not yet ready for a frontal attack of this kind. A much greater mobilization of forces was necessary before this could be risked.'[306] Eliot objected to the 'Broadcast Mission' on practical grounds: the amount of work it would demand and the danger of getting the timing wrong were considerable.[307] The proposal was dropped, but the incident exhibits Fenn's wish to engage the Moot strategically in his work at the BBC.

Individual Moot members' publications

The most lasting legacy of the Moot is the publications of individual members that bear the marks of the group's influence. As Alec Vidler noted in his autobiography, if the Moot 'exerted influence, it was by its effects on the thinking and writing and actions of its members'.[308]

A good place to begin is with Eliot's two volumes *The Idea of Christian Society* (1939) and *Notes Towards a Definition of Culture* (1948), both written during the Moot period. *The Idea* was written during the first year of the Moot's existence and is the result of Eliot's developing social criticism of the 1930s. Whilst the gist of the argument can be found in his articles and essays during this period, the Moot at minimum reinforced the influence of Christopher Dawson, Jacques Maritain and John Middleton Murry – who are heavily referenced in the book – upon Eliot's thought.[309] *Notes* is more evidently the result of Eliot's grappling with ideas explored in the Moot. It is a direct response to Mannheim's ideas of democratic planning and a critique of the Moot's adherence to the 'equal opportunities' mantra in education and the classless society it implied. Eliot's criticism of Mannheim was also informed by another Moot-related publication engaging with Mannheim's planned society, namely, Christopher Dawson's *Judgment of the Nations* (1943). In a progressive post-war era, Eliot's social criticism was rendered largely irrelevant and has therefore had limited exposure. For Raymond Williams, the value to Eliot's social criticism is that it forces liberals out of their complacency by 'exposing the limitations of an orthodox "liberalism"'.[310]

From the mid-1930s onwards, Mannheim shifted his focus from the more theoretical work on the sociology of knowledge to the immediate problems of modernity and the crisis of liberalism. The basic premise in *Diagnosis of Our Time* (1943) was already outlined in *Man and Society* (1940), but drafts of most chapters were discussed in the Moot. 'Towards a New Social Philosophy' was written specifically for the group. The paper signifies a greater interest in the role of religion as powerful force for social integration that Mannheim developed as a result of Mannheim's engagement with the Moot. Such reflections on religion were retained in his posthumous *Freedom, Democracy and Planning* (1951).

The influence of the Moot's educationists Fred Clarke and Walter Moberly has already been noted above. Clarke's *Education and Social Change* (1941) contributed to the discussion that resulted in Butler's 1944 Education Act. Moberly's *Crisis in the University* (1949), originating from the Moot paper 'The Universities',[311] has been important in the post-war discussion on higher education. Tracing how the book has been discussed since its publication, Harold Silver claims that '[the] ripples of the book continued long and wide'.[312] Also, Adolf Löwe wrote *The Universities in Transformation* (1940) as a result of the Moot's discussion on education. It was published in the Christian News-Letter Books series.

A number of publications by Moot members were more directly apologias for the Moot's New Christendom paradigm. Of all the members' publications, Oldham's *The Resurrection of Christendom* (1940) most comprehensively lays down a road map towards the Christian society outlined in the Moot. Oldham's second major publication of the Moot era is *Real Life is Meeting* (1941), a compilation of *CNL* articles on some of the central themes in his social criticism based on Martin Buber's personalist philosophy of encounter.[313] Having produced an extensive critique of Maritain's *True Humanism* for the Moot, John Baillie's subsequent volumes *Our Knowledge of God* (1939) and *What is Christian Civilization?* (1945) bear marks of Maritain's influence. The latter book also cites Eliot, Murry, Mannheim, Niebuhr and Oldham and is brimming with ideas discussed at the Moot. In *God's Judgment on Europe* (1940), Alec Vidler offered a critique of modern society. Explicitly drawing upon Eliot's *The Idea of a Christian Society*, Vidler predicted that without Christianity as the foundation of Western civilization, some less-benevolent force would fill the vacuum. In the *Secular Despair and Christian Faith* (1941), Vidler made references to Löwe's *Universities in Transformation*, praised Eliot's Christian society, endorsed Mannheim's planned society and the influence of Niebuhr's Christian realism is apparent.

Murry's output during the early years of the Moot is impressive. *The Price of Leadership* includes a chapter titled 'A Christian Society', which is a version of 'Towards a Theory of a Christian Society', which caused controversy at the Moot for the 2nd meeting in September 1938. The preface of the book also acknowledges Oldham's role in its publication. Another Moot-relevant publication is *Europe in Travail* published in the Christian News-Letter Books series in 1940. It offers a diagnosis of modern society largely corresponding to that of other Moot members. In *Adam and Eve* (1944), Murry continued to argue for a decentralized society which resisted the depersonalization of industrialized societies through a restructuring into autonomous local communities. This argument was, at least in part, developed through Murry's interaction with Mannheim.

All in all, the Moot members were impressively productive during these war times. It is naturally difficult to assess the level of impact these publications have had, but due to the eminence of some of the members, a number of them are still read today.

Revolutionary or reformist?

From the activities outlined in this chapter, it is apparent the Moot was more than a research group or 'think-tank'. While he often referred to the Moot as a group of friends, in reality Oldham saw it as the intellectual powerhouse of a revolutionary movement, which would demand certain commitments of its members.[314] In one of the early editorials for the *CNL*, Oldham wrote that the transition to a New Christendom would require a revolutionary effort: 'a revolution in men's ideas and purposes and scale of values, expressing itself in revolutionary changes in their relations with one another and in the structure of existing society'.[315] A draft of Oldham's manifesto, *The Resurrection of Christendom* – designed to stir up a revolutionary fervour – was circulated amongst the Moot members during the summer of 1939. Discussing whether his declaration entailed something distinctly 'new', Oldham's response was that it depended on whether the ideas were turned into action:

> The effective answer is not the cool judgement of a spectator but the courageous choice of a combatant. If we remain imprisoned in the circle of our present ideas and insist on measuring the possibilities of the future by our limited and narrow understanding of the past, there will be no revolution.[316]

In a later Moot paper, Oldham noted that in contrast to a reformist movement that operates within confines of existing institutions, a truly revolutionary initiative requires radical reorientation that 'aims at making its members new persons with new relations between themselves in order that there may be a new leaven which can work in society'.[317] Oldham here appears to have been rehashing Philip Mairet's sentiment who having attended the 10th meeting was compelled to explain why he understood the Moot to be a revolutionary group:

> It is a feature … of the revolutionary group that it endeavours to make of its own members *new persons* with *new relations* between themselves, as well as to re-coordinate their economic, political or cultural activities in society at large. This *is* revolution. It is seeking to change, deeply, the character of a little bit of society *in order to* effect in a larger portion – or the whole – of society.[318]

In short, the Moot was attempting a total re-imagination of society. That is what made it revolutionary in Mairet's eyes.

The language of revolution resonated with several other members. Murry, a lapsed communist, proclaimed that nothing short of a revolutionary effort would prevent a warmongering capitalist society from another war.[319] At the 2nd meeting of the Moot, several members spoke of the radical nature of what the group sought to accomplish. Walter Oakeshott, on the verge of becoming the Headmaster of one of England's most prestigious educational institutions, St Paul's School, professed his support for a revolutionary movement demanding allegiance, devotion and personal sacrifice.[320] Gilbert Shaw, a respected clergyman working in the poor areas of east London, held that radical changes in their times demanded a progressive 'rebirth' in Christian social thought rather than a reactionary return to medievalism. He argued that the Moot possessed the revolutionary propensities to achieve this.[321] In a letter to the Moot, Shaw commended Mannheim for the achievement of having conceived 'the next stage in human knowledge and living' wherein 'totalitarianism will find its reconciliation' by ridding itself of its oppressive 'misuses', allowing it to be 'sublimated into a new understanding of liberty and corporate living'. The work towards the fulfilment of this vision made the Moot's fundamental intentions revolutionary rather than 'reformist'.[322]

Admittedly, these rally cries for revolution within the Moot were more often than not hyperbolic: no member espoused a violent takeover of political institutions. Other members preferred to use the language of reform rather than revolution. Mannheim was certainly advocating radical change, but he was against violent revolution. This disposition stems partly from observing the British psyche, which he felt was more amenable to transitional change than revolution. He further feared that a violent revolution would lead to dictatorship and oppression.[323] If planned diligently, a reformist movement could gain support from the elites who had the most to lose from the necessary transition into the planned democratic age.[324] Mannheim did occasionally use the phrase 'revolution from above'. One such occasion was at the 7th meeting when the question of a political revolution was raised. Aggravated by the lack of progress in realizing the Moot's ambitions, he exhorted those present to seize the moment: 'We are confronted with either a calamity or a great chance. The chance was still open in this country and lay in manning and influencing the key positions in society. But that (in turn) required an army behind us, and cells.'[325] Challenging the self-confessed paralysis of Murry and Vidler, Mannheim urged the Moot to overcome their inner lethargy and commit to a 'revolution from above' consisting of influencing the mindset of those in power.[326] While this posed challenges, as the elites were likely to cling to their privileges and the Englishman 'was conservative in action in his "gang"', the solution consisted of creating an Order which could 'break the power of existing cliques'. Mannheim pleaded that, '[we] must risk our prestige by going to the "gang" and helping it to become a fighting organisation.'[327] At the 19th meeting in January 1944, when the tide had decisively turned in favour of the Allied forces and the Moot's attention was turning towards domestic post-war reconstruction, Mannheim yet again reiterated the need to remove or drastically influence the ruling elites without revolutionary violence.[328]

The stronger calls for radical change were tempered by a traditionalist Eliot who held that a healthy culture flourishes when it evolves over time through a continuous renewal by the nourishment of the past but nevertheless the incorporation of the new. Eliot did not identify himself as either conservative or liberal, but argued for long-term readjustment.[329] 'Conservatism is too often a conservation of the wrong things; liberalism a relaxation of discipline; revolution a denial of the permanent.'[330]

Giovanni Sartori's concept of pro- and anti-system actors provides a possible means of categorizing the Moot. This framework suggests a distinction between actors who work within the democratic system (pro-system) and those who wish to overthrow it (anti-system).[331] From this perspective the Moot was, as seen in the above citations from Oldham, at least in theory, an anti-system agency seeking to construct new institutions and encourage new modes of action. However, as in the case with Mannheim's 'Planning for Freedom', the Moot often did not in practice reject the democratic institutions (notably parliamentarianism) altogether, but argued for their reform. Again, the Moot's thought on education shows that they were willing to work within the political establishment rather than hold out for a revolutionary toppling of the system. The 'Fifteen Points' endorsed at the 17th meeting is an indication of the Moot's disposition. There is namely an explicit critique of 'the techniques of revolution' as it implies coercion and paves the way for dictatorship. The statement instead affirms a reformist mode of action, through the existing political channels.[332]

This said, there was a split within the Moot between those who wished to give prevalence to political action and those who aspired for a spiritual renewal. That is, for most of the Moot's members something more fundamental than the reordering of political and economic structures was at stake. As I have argued in Chapter 2, the Moot held that Western civilization was deeply spiritually corrupt: something no political revolution alone could amend. Thus, from this perspective the objective of the Moot's 'revolution' was one which alters the religious and cultural foundations of society, and as such, escapes Satori's categorization.

What further can be said about the Moot with some confidence is that despite references to a return to Christianity as the bedrock of Western civilization, the group's outlook was more forward looking than reactionary. The desire of the majority of its members was not to return to pre-industrial society, but to readjust to present realities and look to the future. Oldham's sentiment that '[those] who are open to the changes of the time are likely to be able to give a lead' is fairly representative.[333]

Conclusion: The Moot's failed revolution

In this chapter, I have sought to portray the Moot as a revitalization movement. The benefit of this framing is that it highlights the length to which the Moot went to create the structures for a deep cultural transformation and suggests that the *modus operandi* of the Moot goes beyond that typically associated with a 'think-tank' or discussion group.

In a number of ways, however, the Moot clearly deviates from the characteristics of the movements described by Wallace. My contention is nevertheless that such deviations shed light on the Moot's limited success and explain why their movement failed or was 'abortive' to use Wallace's phrase.[334] Wallace places considerable significance on the role of the prophet spearhead who through revelatory experiences undergoes character transformation which propel them into revolutionary front figures.[335] For one, the Moot clearly lacked such a leader figure. Oldham's strength was to bring people together. He was an organizer, not a charismatic leader type who would stand at the frontlines of a revolution. He gathered the Moot in the hope of collectively producing something like a 'mazeway reformulation', but he overestimated the power of statements or manifestos as forces for social change. Hodges offered an accurate reflection on the impotence of the Moot. Firstly, he identified the lack of leadership and resources:

> I wonder whether the impatience and sense of frustration from several members of the Moot have suffered from may be due to being unable to find such persons or forces as could become the vehicle for our aspirations, while yet refusing to face the possibility and the implications of the possibility that they may not exist at all.[336]

Reflecting on the composition of the Moot, Hodges further concluded that the group suffered 'from the fact that we are so various ....'[337] These differences manifested themselves in the Moot's failure to reach a consensus on a shared social philosophy. On a general level, Oldham was correct in asserting that there was a growing 'common mind'. However, as Hodges argued, the Moot discussions remained at the level of abstract Christian principles since they were not 'clear-sighted enough' to discern what type of action ought to be taken in the given circumstances.[338] Finally, argued Hodges, in contrast to other groups on which the Moot is itself modelled, that is, the 'utilitarians and the Round Table Group', the Moot lacked strong links to the political elite. Instead, 'we speak out of a misty Christian idealism to a bewildered generation of *epigones*'.[339]

Another source of disagreement that the Moot never overcame was the question of whether or not the group was to take corporate action. The meeting of 19–22 April 1940, just weeks after the Nazi invasion of Denmark and Norway, illustrates the obstacles the Moot faced in this regard. Mannheim complained about the inaction of the Moot: 'Will this be another meeting where we exchange stimulating ideas or a meeting as a result of which something will be done?'[340] Oldham in turn responded, '[w]e *want* to launch action', with several other members concurring. Yet, should they take a short-term view and tackle the immediate threat of fascism, or a long-term strategy for cultural transformation? Did they have the necessary resources? Could a social philosophy be formulated and was such a formulation a prerequisite to action? The Moot often found themselves treading in circles such as this.

Yet again, not all members endorsed the call for corporate action. Notably, Eliot resisted such undertakings as he appeared to imply that concrete action was beneath the intellectual: 'I am constantly up against this difficulty; that the people that I find sympathetic are almost always those who are not concerned with any immediate solution of anything.'[341] The benefit of the Moot, submitted Eliot, was the stimulation provided for individual members' thought and for varied 'clinical cases for reciprocal examinations', which lead to self-examination.[342] On the other hand, Murry left the Moot since he was dismayed over the more philosophical turn the Moot had taken. In a letter sent before the 16th meeting, Murry expressed his disappointment at this development. Taking issue with Hodges' papers in particular, he complained that the Moot had become a 'philosophical club' rather than a catalyst for action. He submitted his apologies for not attending the meeting, concluding that, '[p]erhaps it has shot its bolt; perhaps the labour of the mountain has ended in a still-birth. But I no longer feel the urgent and passionate search for truth which I once felt in the Moot.'[343]

In the end, as Hodges clarified, the Moot lacked sufficient 'revolutionary' propensities:

> We, or some of us, talk quite fiercely on occasion, and a casual visitor can even be persuaded to describe us as a revolutionary body. In practice, however, we seem to think in terms of freedom slowly broadening down from precedent to precedent, which is neither drastic nor new.[344]

Similarly, quoting Mannheim, Philip Mairet, in his observations from the one meeting he attended, pointed to the psychological hindrance to carrying out the Moot's revolutionary mission. A revolutionary group must be willing to be open to the scrutiny of other members and to break free from conventions, for 'if a group was going to become a fresh nucleus of *new and innocent* society, that is precisely what it had to do – enter into that psychological problem.'[345] The Moot on this reading did not have the right psyche to launch revolutionary action. The majority of the Moot members were established gentlemen. Several of them simply had too much to lose to make the sacrificial undertakings that their proposed movement demanded. It is telling that Mannheim, the member of the Moot who had the least to lose, was also the most vocal voice for radical action.

Nevertheless, what this chapter highlights is the extent to which the Moot was methodically working towards inaugurating a revitalization movement. Oldham took concrete steps towards setting up the machinery for such a movement. For reasons outlined above, however, the Moot can best be understood as what

Wallace calls an 'abortive' revitalization movement. This failure does not imply that the Moot had no wider influence. The Moot took little corporate action and never agreed on a joint statement. Yet, its influence is perhaps greater than previously acknowledged. The Moot members did have the ear of some of the political elite, their discussions on educational reform did have a measure of influence on the 1944 Education Act, they strategized about and intentionally used mass media, as individuals their volume of publications was impressive and their networking took their ideas right into the Prime Minister's office.

Notes

1. Gilbert Shaw at the 3rd Moot meeting (Clements, *Moot Papers*, 114 (3rd meeting, 6–9 January 1939)).
2. See for example H. A. Hodges' comments (ibid., 663, (19th meeting, 14–17 January 1943)).
3. Ibid., 325 (9th meeting, 12–15 July 1941).
4. Ibid., 638 (18th meeting, 29 October–1 November 1943). Oldham appears to have adopted the idea of a Copernican Revolution from Jacques Maritain (Maritain, *True Humanism*, 247).
5. J. H. Oldham, 'A Fraternity of the Spirit', 7 March 1941, IOE/MOO/40.
6. Clements, *Moot Papers*, 295 (8th meeting, 19–22 April 1940).
7. Ibid., 295.
8. Clements, 'John Baillie and the Moot', 201; William Taylor, 'Education and the Moot', in *In History and Education: Essays Presented to Peter Gordon*, ed. Richard Aldrich (London: Woburn Press, 1996), 159; Grimley, 'Civil Society and the Clerisy'.
9. Wallace, 'Revitalization Movements', 264.
10. Griffin, *Modernism and Fascism*, 104ff.
11. Cf. Clements, *Moot Papers*, 98 (2nd meeting, 23–26 September 1938). For a more thorough critique of the MRA see H. A. Hodges, 'The Meaning of Moral Rearmament', *Theology* 38, no. May (1939), 331. See also Eliot, *Idea*, 83; and Vidler, *God's Judgment*, 14.
12. Cf. Maurice Reckitt, 'The Idea of Christendom in Relation to Modern Society', in *The Return of Christendom*, ed. Charles Gore et al. (London: George Allen and Unwin, 1922), 39.
13. See V. A. Demant, 'Christian Faith and the Rights of Man' [1940] OLD/14/8/6; Ruth Kenyon, 'The Idea of the Natural Law', 27 July 1941, IOE/MOO/64; OLD/14/9/56.
14. As cited in Daniel Ritschel, *The Politics of Planning: The Debate on Economic Planning in Britain in the 1930s*, Oxford Historical Monographs (Oxford: Oxford University Press, 1997), 147.

15 H. A. Hodges mentions that a Theology Group had met, but no archival material appears to have survived (Clements, *The Moot Papers,* 293 (8th meeting, 19–22 April 1940)). The Education Group was more successful (see below for further details).
16 Clements, *Moot Papers*, 476 (13th meeting, 19–22 December 1941).
17 Ibid., 115 (2nd meeting, 23–26 September 1938).
18 Ibid., 114.
19 Ibid., 364–5 (10th meeting, 10–13 January 1941).
20 J. H. Oldham, 'Agenda for the Meeting of the Moot: October 29–31st 1943' [1943], OLD/13/4/171.
21 Forster, 'What I Believe', 65.
22 Clements, *Moot Papers*, 145 (3rd meeting, 6–9 January 1939).
23 J. H. Oldham, 'The Problems and Tasks of the Council on the Christian Faith and the Common Life' [late 1938], OLD/13/8/73.
24 Clements, *Moot Papers*, 149 (3rd meeting, 6–9 January 1939).
25 Ibid., 151.
26 Ibid., 151, 152.
27 Ibid., 148.
28 Ibid., 178.
29 Ibid., 149, 182. The quotation is Mannheim's words.
30 J. H. Oldham, 'The Rebirth of the West' [1939], BBC/JHO/B1. This is one of the several drafts that was eventually published as *The Resurrection of Christendom* (1940).
31 Clements, *Moot Papers*, 213.
32 J. H. Oldham, 'List of persons consulted' [1939], OLD/13/8/misc.
33 Clements, *Moot Papers*, 235 (5th meeting, 23–24 September 1939).
34 See ibid., 146 (3rd meeting, 6–9 January 1939).
35 Ibid., 293 (8th meeting, 19–22 April 1940).
36 Geoffrey Vickers, 'A Bill of Duties for Men in England in April 1940', 21 April 1940, OLD/14/9/76.
37 Clements, *Moot Papers*, 309 (8th meeting, 19–22 April 1940).
38 J. H. Oldham, 'Letter to Moot Members', 8 April 1940, IOE/MOO/21.
39 Clements, *Moot Papers*, 320 (9th meeting, 14–17 July 1940). For unknown reasons, Franks declined the offer as the director of the CCFCL.
40 Ibid., 316.
41 The term 'middle axiom' was regularly used in the Moot as a designation for the balance between the ideals of the gospel and the reality of the concrete situation. See Oldham, *The Churches Survey Their Task*, 209–10.
42 Clements, *Moot Papers*, 337–8 (9th meeting, 14–17 July 1940).
43 Ibid., 323.

44 See the appendix of J. H. Oldham, 'The Christian Witness in the Present Crisis', 6 October 1943, OLD/9/5/19.
45 J. H. Oldham, 'The Christian Witness in the Present Crisis', 6 October 1943, OLD/9/5/19.
46 J. H. Oldham, 'Agenda for the Meeting of the Moot: October 29–31st 1943' [1943], OLD/13/4/171.
47 Ibid.
48 Clements, *Moot Papers*, 622 (18th meeting, 29 October – 1 November 1943).
49 Ibid., 622–3.
50 Ibid., 624.
51 Ibid., 627.
52 Ibid., 645.
53 J. H. Oldham, 'Letter to William Temple', 6 January 1944, LPL/Temple/11/ff.234–5. See Murry, *Adam and Eve*.
54 J. H. Oldham, 'Letter to William Temple', 6 January 1944, LPL/Temple/11/ff.234–5.
55 Clements, *Moot Papers*, 657 (19th meeting, 14–17 January 1944).
56 Ibid., 659.
57 Wallace, 'Revitalization Movements', 266.
58 Ibid., 270.
59 J. H. Oldham, 'Letter to Leslie Hunter', 26 June 1937, OLD/8/6/91.
60 See William Temple, 'Letter to Leslie Hunter', 18 January 1938, OLD/8/9/9.
61 J. H. Oldham, 'Nature and Purpose of Proposed Effort', 24 July 1939, OLD/13/8/27.
62 J. H. Oldham, 'Policy Document', 25 November 1938, OLD/13/8/6.
63 J. H. Oldham, 'The Problems and Tasks of the Council on the Christian Faith and the Common Life' [late 1938], OLD/13/8/73.
64 J. H. Oldham, 'A Reborn Christendom', August 1939, IOE/MOO/2; LM/SEC11.
65 J. H. Oldham, 'The Problems and Tasks of the Council on the Christian Faith and the Common Life' [late 1938], OLD/13/8/73.
66 Ibid.
67 While there is no document in the archives with that title, the references to sections and citations in the minutes match 'The Rebirth of the West (BBC/JHO/1B)', an early draft of Oldham's manifesto, which after a number of revisions appeared as *The Resurrection of Christendom* (1940).
68 Clements, *Moot Papers*, 147 (3rd meeting, 6–9 January 1939).
69 Ibid., 64 (1st meeting, 1–4 April 1938).
70 Ibid., 173 (3rd meeting, 6–9 January 1939).
71 Clements, *Faith on the Frontier*, 359.
72 J. H. Oldham, 'Nature and Purpose of Proposed Effort', 24 July 1939, OLD/13/8/27.
73 J. H. Oldham, 'Letter to Leslie Hunter', 20 January 1938, OLD/8/9/10.
74 See Leslie Hunter, 'Letter to J. H. Oldham', 9 June 1938, OLD/9/1/24.
75 J. H. Oldham, 'Nature and Purpose of Proposed Effort', 24 July 1939, OLD/13/8/27.

76 Eleanor M. Jackson, *Red Tape and the Gospel: A Study of the Significance of the Ecumenical Missionary Struggle of William Paton (1886-1943)* (Birmingham: Phlogiston Publishing, 1980), 273.
77 J. H. Oldham, 'Letter to J. R. Mott', 16 March 1942, OLD/9/4/1.
78 Clements, *Faith on the Frontier*, 410.
79 See J. H. Oldham, 'Letter to W. A. Visser t'Hooft', 19 March 1942, OLD/9/4/3.
80 J. H. Oldham, 'Draft Resolution (CFC)', February 1942, CEA/BCC/7/1/6/1/1. Records of the early years of the CFC are held at the Church of England Archives, Record Centre, Bermondsey.
81 J. H. Oldham, 'The Religious Foundations of the Frontier', July 1942, CEA/BCC/7/1/6/1/1; IOE/MOO/83.
82 J. H. Oldham, 'Draft Resolution (CFC)', February 1942, CEA/BCC/7/1/6/1/1.
83 Walter Moberly, 'The Christian Frontier Council', *Christian News-Letter*, no. 154 (1942).
84 Anon., 'The Christian Frontier', 7 September 1942, CEA/BCC/7/1/6/1/1.
85 See J. H. Oldham, 'Draft Resolution (CFC)', February 1942, CEA/BCC/7/1/6/1/1.
86 See Moberly, 'The Christian Frontier Council'.
87 Ibid.
88 For a more detailed account, see D. E. Jenkins and Majorie Reeves, 'Outside Ecclesiastical Organization: The Christian Frontier Council', in *Christian Thinking and Social Order: Conviction Politics from the 1930s to the Present Day*, ed. Marjorie Reeves (London: Cassell, 1999), 81-5.
89 'Frontier Council', May 1942, CEA/BCC/7/1/6/1/1.
90 Cf. H. A. Hodges, 'Politics and the Moot', 9 June 1943, OLD/14/1/43.
91 Wallace, 'Revitalization Movements', 270.
92 Clements, *Moot Papers*, 120-1 (2nd meeting, 23-26 September 1938).
93 Virginia Woolf, *Three Guineas* (London: Hogarth Press, 1943 [1938]), 193f.
94 Forster, 'What I Believe', 70.
95 Carroll Quigley, *Tragedy and Hope: A History of the World in Our Time* (New York: Macmillan, 1966), 131-3.
96 Maritain, *True Humanism*, 165.
97 Paul Tillich, *My Travel Diary: 1936*, trans. Maria Pelikan (London: SCM Press, 1970), 42.
98 Ibid., 85.
99 Oldham, *The Churches Survey Their Task*, 50.
100 William Temple, 'Begin Now', *Christian News-Letter*, no. 41 (1940). When discussed at the Moot, the members felt that the suggestion of a 'badge was premature (Clements, *Moot Papers*, 326 (9th meeting, 12-15th January 1940)'.
101 Dawson, *Beyond Politics*, 57.
102 Eliot, *Idea*, 42.

103 See a draft of the group's charter (Alec Vidler, 'Memorandum', [1939?], OLD/13/8/41).
104 Vidler, 'Editorial: Planning for What'.
105 Mannheim, *Ideology and Utopia*, 143.
106 Karl Mannheim, 'Planning for Freedom' [1938], LM/SEC7; OLD/14/3/67.
107 Mannheim, *Freedom*, 166. See Eliot, *Idea*, 42.
108 Clements, *Moot Papers*, 63 (1st meeting, 1–4 April 1938).
109 Ibid., 64.
110 J. H. Oldham, 'Suggestions for the Constitution of an Order' [1939], LM/SEC4; OLD 13/8/Misc.
111 Clements, *Moot Papers*, 188–9 (4th meeting, 14–17 April 1939).
112 Ibid., 208–9.
113 Ibid., 212.
114 Ibid., 211.
115 Ibid., 212.
116 Ibid., 211.
117 Noel Hall was the director for the National Institute for Economic and Social Research. He only attended one meeting.
118 Adolf Löwe, 'Letter Regarding the "Order"' [1939], IOE/MOO/3; LM/SEC4; OLD/9/3/1.
119 H. A. Hodges, 'Letter to J. H. Oldham', 17 September 1939, OLD/9/2/39.
120 Karl Mannheim, 'Notes on the Proposed "Order"' [1939], LM/SEC4; OLD/14/3/62).
121 Ibid.
122 Ibid.
123 H. A. Hodges, 'Letter to J. H. Oldham', 17 September 1939, OLD/9/2/39.
124 Christopher Dawson, 'Letter to J. H. Oldham', 25 June 1939, OLD/9/2/9.
125 Walter Oakeshott, 'Notes on the "Order"' [1939] IOE/MOO/4; LM/SEC4; OLD/14/8/63.
126 Clements, *Moot Papers*, 114 (2nd meeting, 23–26 September 1938).
127 Ibid., 210 (4th meeting 14–17 April 1939).
128 Ibid., 215.
129 Ibid., 214.
130 Alec Vidler, 'Notes on the Order' [1939], IOE/MOO/5; LM/SEC4.
131 H. A. Hodges, 'Letter to J. H. Oldham', 17 September 1939, OLD/9/2/39.
132 Christopher Dawson, 'Letter to J. H. Oldham', 5 July 1939, OLD/9/2/14. Dawson asked Oldham not to circulate this letter (Christopher Dawson, 'Letter to J. H. Oldham', 9 July 1939, OLD/9/2/15).
133 John Middleton Murry, 'A Note on the "Order"' [1939], LM/SEC4; OLD/14/5/29.
134 Clements, *Moot Papers*, 213 (4th meeting, 14–17 April 1939).

135 Ibid., 243.
136 Ibid., 218.
137 Ibid., 255 (7th meeting, 9–12 February 1940).
138 Ibid., 293 (8th meeting, 19–22 April 1940).
139 Cosmo Lang, 'Letter to R. A. Butler', 6 June 1940, CRA/CRD/2/28/1.
140 R. A. Butler, 'Letter to Cosmo Lang', 7 June 1940, CRA/CRD/2/28/1.
141 Clements, *Moot Papers*, 322 (9th meeting, 14–17 July 1940).
142 Karl Mannheim, 'Topics for the Next Meeting of the Moot' [1941], IOE/MOO/32; LP/215; OLD/14/3/86.
143 Ibid.
144 Ibid. Eliot responded that he was in favour of an Order but envisioned 'something both more valuable and permanent than a Partei (T.S. Eliot, "Notes on Mannheim's Paper", 10th January, OLD 14/6/1)'.
145 Clements, *Moot Papers*, 362–3 (10th meeting, 10–13 January 1941).
146 Christopher Dawson, 'The Sword of the Spirit', December 1940, IOE/MOO/37; OLD/14/4/1.
147 Clements, *Moot Papers*, 364 (10th meeting, 10–13 January 1941).
148 Ibid., 365.
149 Ibid., 370.
150 Dawson, 'The Sword of the Spirit', December 1940, IOE/MOO/37; OLD/14/4/1. The article was circulated in the Moot prior to the 10th meeting in January 1941 but was never discussed.
151 Cf. Hocking, *The Lasting Elements of Individualism*.
152 J. H. Oldham, 'A Fraternity of the Spirit', 7 March 1941, IOE/MOO/40.
153 Ibid.
154 Karl Mannheim, 'Letter from Karl Mannheim' [1941], IOE/MOO/47; OLD/9/3/14.
155 John Middleton Murry, 'Letter from Middleton Murry' [1941], IOE/MOO/45.
156 The sense of abiding echoes Eliot's 'meanwhile redeeming the time' (a reference to Ephesians 5:15–16) in his pamphlet 'Thoughts After Lambeth' (Eliot, *Lambeth*, 32).
157 Christopher Dawson, 'Some Reflections on Dr Oldham's Note on Commitments', 3 April 1941, OLD/14/4/30.
158 Nathaniel Micklem, 'Letter from Principal Micklem', 11 March 1941, IOE/MOO/46.
159 T. S. Eliot, 'Letter from T. S. Eliot' [1941], IOE/MOO/50; OLD/9/3/23.
160 Alec Vidler, 'Notes on Some Cultural Issues' [1941], IOE/MOO/44; OLD/14/6/85.
161 See John Middleton Murry, 'Letter from Middleton Murry' [1941], IOE/MOO/45; Karl Mannheim, 'Letter from Karl Mannheim' [1941], IOE/MOO/47; OLD/9/3/14.

162 T. S. Eliot, 'Letter from T. S. Eliot' [1941], IOE/MOO/50; OLD/9/3/23.
163 Karl Mannheim, 'Letter from Karl Mannheim' [1941], IOE/MOO/47; OLD/9/3/14.
164 Geoffrey Vickers, 'Letter from Geoffrey Vickers' [1941], IOE/MOO/49; OLD/9/3/34.
165 Clements, *Moot Papers*, 380–2 (11th meeting, 4–7 April 1941).
166 Ibid., 391–6.
167 Ibid., 396, 397.
168 Ibid., 397.
169 Ibid., 397–8.
170 Ibid., 397.
171 Ibid., 379.
172 See Keith Clements' comments in *The Moot Papers*, 404–5.
173 Clements, *Moot Papers*, 437 (12th meeting, 1–3 August 1941).
174 Ibid., 487–8 (14th meeting, 27–30 March 1942).
175 Ibid., 625 (18th meeting, 29 October–1 November 1943).
176 Ibid., 638, 639.
177 Ibid., 640.
178 Cf. Paul Tillich, *Systematic Theology: Volume III* (Chicago: The University of Chicago Press, 1963), 152–5.
179 Clements, *Moot Papers*, 254 (7th meeting, 9–12 February 1940).
180 Fred Clarke was the director of the Institute of Education (1936–1945), and Walter Moberly was the chair of the influential University Grants Committee (1935–1949).
181 The appointment was secured by the Institute's director, Fred Clarke.
182 Karl Mannheim, 'Planning for Freedom' [1938], LM/SEC7; OLD/14/3/67.
183 John Middleton Murry, 'Towards a Christian Theory of Society' [1938], OLD/14/5/37.
184 Karl Mannheim, 'Planning for Freedom' [1938], LM/SEC7; OLD/14/3/67. A more detailed account of Manheim's philosophy of education can be found in his Moot paper 'Sociology of Education Preliminary Remarks', IOE/MOO/11; OLD/14/3/84.
185 H. A. Hodges, 'Christian Archetypes and Symbols', 22 June 1942, BA/5/9; OLD/14/1/23.
186 Fred Clarke, 'The Crisis in Education', in *Church, Community, and State in Relation to Education*, ed. Fred Clarke et al. (London: George Allen & Unwin, 1938), 4.
187 Fred Clarke, 'Some Notes on English Educational Institutions in the Light of the Necessities of "Planning for Freedom" in the Coming Collectivized Regime', 21 August 1939, IOE/MOO/7; OA/14/7/31.

188 Eliot, 'Education in a Christian Society'.
189 Walter Moberly, *The Crisis in the University* (London: SCM Press, 1949).
190 Taylor, 'Education and the Moot', 176. For the reception of this publication, see chapter 6 of Harold Silver, *Higher Education and Opinion Making in Twentieth-Century England* (London: Woburn Press, 2003).
191 Adolf Löwe, 'Some Notes on University Education' [1940], IOE/MOO/18; OLD/14/4/54.
192 Fred Clarke, 'Some Notes on English Educational Institutions in the Light of the Necessities of "Planning for Freedom" in the Coming Collectivized Regime', 21 August 1939, IOE/MOO/7; OLD/14/7/31.
193 Clarke, *Education and Social Change*.
194 Walter Moberly, 'The Universities' [1940], IOE/MOO/16.
195 Adolf Löwe, 'Some Notes on University Education' [1940], IOE/MOO/18; OLD/14/4/54.
196 Ibid.
197 Fred Clarke, 'A Paper on Religious Education in Schools' [1941], IOE/MOO/55; OLD/9/3/8.
198 Ibid.
199 Clements, *Moot Papers*, 399–400 (11th meeting, 4–7 April 1941).
200 Ibid., 257–60 (7th meeting, 9–12 February 1940).
201 Ibid., 260.
202 Ibid., 260.
203 Ibid., 218 (4th meeting, 14–17 April 1939). Thorald Francis Coade was the headmaster of Bryanston School in Dorset.
204 For a more detailed account of the discussions in the Education Group, see my doctoral thesis; Jonas Kurlberg, 'The Rebirth of Christendom: The Moot (1938–1947) as a Modernist Revitalisation Movement' (University of Bergen, 2017).
205 Mitchell, *Sir Fred Clarke*, 113–15.
206 Hsiao-Yuh Ku, 'Education for Liberal Democracy: Fred Clarke and the 1944 Education Act', *History of Education* 42, no. 5 (2013), 578–97. http://dx.doi.org/10.1080/0046760X.2013.823627.
207 Fred Clarke, 'Karl Mannheim at the Institute: The Beginnings' [1948], IOE/FC/1/35.
208 Mitchell, *Sir Fred Clarke*, 111.
209 As cited in Ku, 'Education for Liberal Democracy', 596.
210 John Dancy, *Walter Oakeshott: A Diversity of Gifts* (Norwich: Michael Russell, 1995), 113–19.
211 Michael Barber, *Making of the 1944 Education Act* (London: Continuum, 2000), 6.
212 Gary McCulloch, *Educational Reconstruction: The 1944 Education Act and the Twenty-First Century* (Ilford: Woburn Press, 1994), 45.

213 Cited in Ku, 'Education for Liberal Democracy', 592; W. Cantuar (William Temple), W. H. Beveridge, Fred Clarke and R. W. Livingstone, 'The Need For Adult Education: New Bill Welcomed', *The Times*, 15 January 1944.
214 Karl Mannheim, 'Syllabus: The Diagnosis of Our Time' [1942], IOE/MOO/73; KMP/2/R; OLD/14/3/60. See also 'Minutes from Group on Christian Education', 22–23 November 1941, OLD/13/4/204.
215 Cf. Fred Clarke, 'Notes on Secondary Education in England', 22 February 1942, IOE/MOO/74.
216 See H. C. Dent, 'Reform in Education', 16 May 1942, IOE/MOO/80; OLD/14/9/20. See also 'Minutes from Group on Education', 16–17 May 1942, OLD/13/4/219.
217 Cf. Fred Clarke, 'Notes on Secondary Education in England', 22 February 1942, IOE/MOO/74. See also 'Minutes from Group on Christian Education', 22–23 November 1941, OLD/13/4/204.
218 Barber, *Making of the 1944 Education Act*, 7.
219 'Minutes from Education Group', 16 July 1945, OLD/13/4/228. Present: Kathleen Bliss (chair), H. G. M. Clarke, J. K. Cooper, G. W. Davis, E. Dodds, H. C. Dent, Wilfred Garrett, G. B. Jeffrey, Karl Mannheim, MacKay Muir, M. Parr, Marjorie Reeves, C. G. Vickers, R. Wilson, J. H. Oldham.
220 Marjorie Reeves, 'Paper by Dr. Marjorie Reeves', 3 July 1945, OLD/14/8/67.
221 See J. H. Oldham, 'The Christian Witness in the Present Crisis', 6 October 1943, OLD/9/5/19.
222 Fred Clarke, 'Some Notes on *National Re-Equipment* in Relation to Fundamental Decisions', 31 December 1943, OLD/14/7/58.
223 J. H. Oldham, 'Letter to the Moot Members', 16 September 1946, MPP/15/3.
224 Clements, *Moot Papers*, 425 (12th meeting, 1–3 August 1941).
225 Tom Steele and Richard Kenneth Taylor, 'Oldham's Moot (1938–1947), the Universities and the Adult Citizen', *History of Education* 39, no. 2 (2010), 183–97.
226 This 'liberal' outlook would have been unpalatable for Eliot who only participated in the first of the Education Group meetings. There was a gulf between Eliot's ideas of education, as elucidated in *Notes*, and that reflected in the Education Group and the Moot at large. See Eliot, *Notes*, 107.
227 Barber, *Making of the 1944 Education Act*, 120.
228 Wallace, 'Revitalization Movements', 273.
229 See Karl Mannheim, 'Planning for Freedom' [1938], LM/SEC7; OLD/14/3/67. Mannheim lists mass media as one of the many new methods of social control available to social institutions.
230 Clements, *Moot Papers*, 235 (5th meeting, 23–24 September 1939).
231 Ibid., 235.
232 Ibid., 236–8.
233 Ibid., 240.

234 J. H. Oldham, 'Editorial 18th October 1939', *Christian News-Letter*, no. 0 (1939).
235 J. H. Oldham, 'Editorial 3rd April 1940', *Christian News-Letter*, no. 23 (1940).
236 The full list of collaborators: 'Archbishop of York [William Temple], Rev. M. E. Aubrey, Professor John Baillie, the Master of Balliol [A. D. Lindsey], Conan F. R. Barry, Dr. S. M. Berry, Henry Brooke, the Rev. Henry Carter, Lord David Cecil, J. T. Christie, Professor F. Clarke, Dr. J. Hutchison Cockburn, Canon F. A. Cockin, Dr. A. C. Craig, Christopher Dawson, Sir Wyndham Deedes, the Rev. V. A. Demant, Professor C. H. Dodd, T. S. Eliot, Professor H. H. Farmer, Professor O. S. Franks, the Rev. W. D. L. Greer, Kurt Hahn, Viscount Hambleden, Sir Hector Hetherington, Professor H. A. Hodges, Miss Eleanora Iredale, Professor Karl Mannheim, Principal N. Micklem, the Rev. T. R. Milford, Sir Walter Moberly, J. Middleton Murry, Professor Reinhold Niebuhr, Walter Oakeshott, Dr. William Paton, Miss Margaret Popham, Canon O. C. Quick, Miss Dorothy Sayers, the Rev. Gilbert Shaw, the Bishop of Sheffield [Leslie Hunter], Mrs. Mary Stocks, Professor Norman Sykes, Arnold Toynbee, Professor R. H. Tawney, the rev. A. R. Vidler, President J. S. Whale, the Bishop of Winchester [Cyril Garbet], Sir Alfred Zimmern.'
237 See J. H. Oldham, 'Letter to Collaborators of the CNL', 9 October 1939, OLD/9/2/45.
238 J. H. Oldham, 'Letter to Visser t'Hooft', 5 October 1939, OLD/9/2/43.
239 J. H. Oldham, 'Draft Resolution (CFC)', February 1942, CEA/BCC/7/1/6/1/1.
240 'Report to the Council on C.N.L.', 10 May 1940, OLD/9/2/?.
241 J. H. Oldham, 'Letter to J. R. Mott', 9 November 1940, OLD/9/3/60.
242 Margaret Godley, 'Report on the Work Carried Out by Miss Godley', 21 August 1940, CPA/CRD/2/28/1.
243 Central Committee for National Policy, 'Memorandum', CPA/CRD/2/28/1.
244 'Objects of organisation as discussed with the Prime Minister on 8th January', 8 January [1941], CPA/CRD/2/28/1.
245 For a more detailed survey of the content of the *CNL*, see Marjorie Reeves and Elaine Kaye, 'Tracts for Wartime: *The Christian News-Letter*' in *Christian Thinking and Social Order: Conviction Politics from the 1930s to the Present Day*, ed. Marjorie Reeves (London: Cassell, 1999), 392.
246 Clements, *Faith on the Frontier*, 392.
247 J. H. Oldham, 'What Is a "Christian" News-Letter?', *Christian News-Letter*, no. 0 (1939).
248 Oldham, *Real Life*.
249 J. H. Oldham, 'Planning for Freedom', *Christian News-Letter*, no. 104 (1941).
250 Ibid.
251 Christopher Dawson, 'What Is the Alternative to Totalitarianism', *Christian News-Letter*, no. 107 (1941).

252 Karl Mannheim, 'The Historical Political Task of Britain', *Christian News-Letter*, no. 135 (1942).
253 Anon., 'Letter to the Editor', ibid., no. 143.
254 Anon., 'Letter to the Editor', *Christian News-Letter*, no. 145 (1942).
255 J. H. Oldham, 'Diagnosis of Our Time', *Christian News-Letter*, no. 174 (1943).
256 George Every, 'Planning within Limits', *Christian News-Letter*, no. 160 (1942).
257 J. H. Oldham, 'The Idea of a Christian Society', ibid., no. 18 (1940).
258 T. S. Eliot, 'Letter to Mary Trevelyan', 16 September 1946, HLE/bMS AM/1691.2/62.
259 T. S. Eliot, 'Editorial 14th August', *Christian News-Letter*, no. 42 (1940).
260 T. S. Eliot, 'Editorial 21st August', *Christian News-Letter*, no. 43 (1940).
261 Eliot, 'Editorial 28th August'.
262 T. S. Eliot, 'Editorial 3rd September', *Christian News-Letter*, no. 97 (1941).
263 T. S. Eliot, 'Editorial 8th July', *Christian News-Letter*, no. 141 (1942).
264 T. S. Eliot, 'Education in a Christian Society', *Christian News-Letter*, no. 20 (1940).
265 Ibid.
266 T. S. Eliot, 'Responsibility and Power', *Christian News-Letter*, no. 196 (1943).
267 John Maud, 'Full Employment and the Responsibility of Christians', *Christian News-Letter*, no. 229 (1945).
268 T. S. Eliot, 'Letter to Mary Trevelyan', 13 March 1945, HLE/bMS AM/1691.2/46.
269 T. S. Eliot, 'Full Employment and the Responsibility of Christians', *Christian News-Letter*, no. 230 (1945).
270 T. S. Eliot, 'Letter to Mary Trevelyan', 2 January 1945, HLE/bMS AM/1691.2/43.
271 See T. S. Eliot, 'Letter to Mary Trevelyan', 30 October 1944, HLE/bMS AM/1691.2/37.
272 Alec Vidler, 'The Obedience of a Christian Intellectual', *Christian News-Letter*, no. 272 (1946).
273 H. A. Hodges, 'What Differences Does Christianity Make?', *Christian News-Letter*, no. 27 (1940); Hodges, 'Social Standards in a Mixed Society'; H. A. Hodges, 'The Problem of Archetypes', *Christian News-Letter*, no. 183 (1943); H. A. Hodges, 'Christianity in an Age of Science', *Christian News-Letter*, no. 120 (1942).
274 Moberly, 'The Christian Frontier Council'.
275 John Baillie, 'Does God Defend the Right', *Christian News-Letter*, no. 53 (1940).
276 Erik Fenn, 'Dr. Asmussen Explains', *Christian News-Letter*, no. 254 (1946).
277 Geoffrey Vickers, 'God and Politics', *Christian News-Letter*, no. 260.
278 John Middleton Murry, 'Can Democracy Survive?', *Christian News-Letter*, no. 274; John Middleton Murry, 'The Free Society', *Christian News-Letter*, no. 284 (1947).
279 Clements, *Faith on the Frontier*, 405.
280 *CNL*, 6 July 1949.

281 Hannah Elias, 'The Development of "BBC Religion": Christianity, Democracy and National Identity in Wartime Broadcasting, 1939–1945', paper presented at *Modern Religious Seminars* (University of Oxford, 2014).
282 J. H. Oldham, 'Letter to Frederick W. Ogilvie', 26 January 1939, BBC/JHO/1B.
283 A copy can be found in Oldham's file at the BBC Archives (J. H. Oldham, 'The Rebirth of the West' [1939], BBC/JHO/B1).
284 Ibid.
285 Frederick W. Ogilvie, 'Letter to J. H. Oldham', 20 February 1939, BBC/JHO/1B.
286 J. W. Welsh, 'Memorandum to G. R. Barnett', 12 September 1939, BBC/JHO/1B.
287 Eric Fenn, 'Letter to J. H. Oldham', 12 September 1939, BBC/JHO/1B.
288 Eric Fenn, 'Letter to J. H. Oldham', 28 September 1939, BBC/JHO/1B.
289 Eric Fenn, 'Letter to J. H. Oldham', 14 November 1939, BBC/JHO/1B.
290 Erik Fenn, 'A Christian Looks at the World' [1940], BBC/R51/77.
291 The series was published by the Christian News-Letter Books; Murry, *Europe in Travail*. The citation is taken from page v. of the preface.
292 J. H. Oldham, 'Letter to Eric Fenn', 19 December 1939, BBC/JHO/1B.
293 Eric Fenn, 'Letter to J. H. Oldham', 21 December 1939, BBC/JHO/1B.
294 Eric Fenn, 'Letter to J. H. Oldham', 29 January 1940, BBC/JHO/1B.
295 See Clements, *Moot Papers*, 253 (7th meeting, 9–12 February 1940); J. H. Oldham, 'Letter to Eric Fenn', 1 February 1940, BBC/JHO/1B.
296 See Erik Fenn, 'Notes and Comments on "A Christian Looks at the World"', 16 May 1940, BBC/R51/77.
297 J. H. Oldham, 'Synopsis of Two Talks by J. H. Oldham for 29 January and 5 February 1941' [1941], BBC/JHO/1B.
298 For full list of Eliot's BBC talks, see the appendix of M. Coyle, 'T. S. Eliot on the Air: "Culture" and the Challenges of Mass Communication', in *T. S. Eliot and Our Turning World*, ed. Jewel Spears Brooker (London: Macmillan, 2001), 205–13.
299 Eliot, 'Towards a Christian Britain', 107. The broadcast was also published in the *Listener* (T. S. Eliot, 'Towards a Christian Britain', *The Listener* 25, no. 639 (1941)).
300 Eliot, 'Towards a Christian Britain', 116–17.
301 Eric Fenn, 'Letter to J. H. Oldham', 25 February 1944, BBC/JHO/2.
302 Eric Fenn, 'Letter to J. H. Oldham', 7 September 1944, BBC/JHO/2.
303 It is notable that Mannheim was not considered for these Moot-related broadcasts. However, as 'probably the foremost sociologist of today' – as one internal BBC memo states – Mannheim was a sought-after speaker at the BBC in his own right (Anon., 'Memo to Eleen Sam', 27 November 1942, BBC/KM). Amongst others, he delivered nine talks on ethics in the autumn of 1943 and ten talks in a series called 'What is Sociology?' that ran from January–March 1945, both for the BBC's School Broadcasting, aimed at students in the sixth form (see documents in BBC/KM). Not all at BBC were equally impressed with Mannheim's contributions. Mary Somerville regretted the series altogether, calling it 'a blot on

our departments record (Mary Somerville, "Letter to A. W. Coysh," 26th February 1945, BBC/KM)'.
304 Clements, *Moot Papers*, 323 (9th meeting, 12–15 July 1941).
305 Ibid., 324 (9th meeting, 12–15 July 1941).
306 Ibid., 324 (9th meeting, 12–15 July 1941).
307 Ibid., 325 (9th meeting, 12–15 July 1941).
308 Vidler, *Scenes from a Clerical Life*, 118.
309 An example is Eliot's critique of Murry's use of Matthew Arnold as discussed in the Moot paper 'Towards a Theory of a Christian Society' (John Middleton Murry, 'Towards a Christian Theory of Society' [1938], OLD/14/5/37).
310 Williams, *Culture and Society*, 224, 237.
311 Walter Moberly, 'The Universities' [1940], IOE/MOO/16.
312 Silver, *Higher Education*, 121.
313 Oldham, *Real Life*.
314 Cf. Clements, *Moot Papers*, 115 (3rd meeting, 6–9 January 1939); ibid., 292 (8th meeting, 19–22 April 1940).
315 J. H. Oldham, 'Editorial 3rd January 1940', *Christian News-Letter*, no. 10 (1940).
316 J. H. Oldham, 'A Reborn Christendom', August 1939, IOE/MOO/2; LM/SEC11.
317 J. H. Oldham, 'A Fraternity of the Spirit', 7 March 1941, IOE/MOO/40.
318 Philip Mairet, 'Copy of a Letter from Philip Mairet to Dr. Oldham', 16 January 1941, OLD/9/3/69.
319 Clements, *Moot Papers*, 53–4 (1st meeting, 1–4 April 1938).
320 Ibid., 114 (3rd meeting, 6–9 January 1939).
321 Ibid., 114, 5 (3rd meeting, 6–9 January 1939).
322 Gilbert Shaw, 'Letter from Gilbert Shaw' [1941], IOE/MOO/51; OLD/9/3/36.
323 J. H. Oldham, 'Letter from Karl Mannheim', *Christian News-Letter*, no. 135 (1942).
324 Karl Mannheim, 'Planning for Freedom' [1938], LM/SEC7; OLD/14/3/67.
325 Clements, *Moot Papers*, 265 (7th meeting, 9–12 February 1940).
326 Ibid., 266.
327 Ibid., 267.
328 Ibid., 673 (19th meeting, 14–17 January 1944).
329 See also Eliot, *Idea*, 17.
330 Eliot, 'The Church's Message to the World', 326.
331 Giovanni Sartori, *Parties and Party Systems: A Framework for Analysis* (Cambridge: Cambridge University Press, 1976).
332 H. A. Hodges, 'Christianity and Society', 24 June 1943, OLD/13/6/33.
333 J. H. Oldham, 'A Fraternity of the Spirit', 7 March 1941, IOE/MOO/40.
334 See Wallace, 'Revitalization Movements', 278.
335 Ibid., 270–5.

336 H. A. Hodges, 'Comment on the Moot's Fifteen Points', 29 July 1943, OLD 14/1/53.
337 H. A. Hodges, 'Letter from H. A. Hodges', 6 November 1942, BA/05/26.
338 H. A. Hodges, 'Comments on Middleton Murry's Notes' [1942], OLD/14/2/18.
339 H. A. Hodges, 'Comment on the Moot's Fifteen Points', 29 July 1943, OLD 14/1/53.
340 Clements, *Moot Papers*, 292 (8th meeting, 19–22 April 1940).
341 T. S. Eliot, 'Extract from a letter from T. S. Eliot', 20 December 1942, BA/05/19; OLD/9/4/42.
342 Ibid.
343 John Middleton Murry, 'Letter from J. M. Murry', 14 September 1942, OLD/9/4/13. Murry appears not to have attended any further meetings until the final meeting held on 10–13 January 1947, when he presented a paper titled 'The General Problem of Democracy', 9 September 1946, MPP/15/7.
344 H. A. Hodges, 'Politics and the Moot', 9 June 1943, OLD/14/1/43.
345 Philip Mairet, 'Copy of a Letter from Philip Mairet to Dr. Oldham', 16 January 1941, OLD/9/3/69.

7

Conclusion

This book recounts the history of the Moot. Drawing upon thousands of documents stored in over a dozen archives, I have sought to open a window into the world of an understudied segment of the intellectual life of the British intelligentsia in the late 1930s and '40s. As a case study, it is an exemplification of the vibrant sociopolitical Christian thought that demanded creative solutions at a tumultuous time. The rich material further contributes to our appreciation of the thought of the individual members.

Modernist interpretive framing

A study of the Moot can serve to test, validate or modify current theories on a volatile era of British and European history. In this book, the story of the Moot has been recounted through the investigative lens of Roger Griffin's heuristic framework of 'Political Modernism', exploring the Moot as a Christian manifestation of 'Programmatic Modernism'.

This approach has elucidated the revolutionary propensities of the Moot and situated the group firmly within the context of a turbulent age that demanded radical measures. The 'Programmatic Modernism' lens has shed light on the extent to which the Moot can be read in the context of the widespread interwar discourse of decadence. As argued in the second chapter, the Moot, like many of its contemporaries, observed the sociopolitical turmoil of the interwar decades with dismay, and as pointing to a deeper cultural crisis: a reality attributed to the forces of secularization and its threat to the foundations of Western civilization. Without this underlying 'Modernist' sense of a crisis in transcendence, the rationale and motivation behind the Moot cannot be fully appreciated.

Further, the theoretical framing of the Moot as a Modernist project has highlighted the lengths to which the group went to *deliberately* set in motion a revitalization movement. This designation of the Moot's overall project sheds light on the concrete efforts that were taken by the Moot and its networks to catalyse a Christian sociopolitical movement in Britain and beyond. Such measures include the group's intellectual work towards producing a manifesto that can be seen as an attempted 'mazeway reformulation', a stage that Anthony Wallace sees as a fundamental undertaking of any 'revitalist movement'. Chapter 3 outlines how the Modernist reading of the Moot points to the medievalist source of its 'Programmatic Modernism'. The Moot's adoption of Jacques Maritain's neo-Thomism, in particular, shows how the group found in medieval Christendom a possible historical precedent for a revitalized modern society. This aspiration to inspire a 'New Christendom' exemplifies what Griffin has called an appropriation or 'return' to the 'mythical past' that characterizes Modernist movements. The chapter also discusses Karl Mannheim's programme of 'Planning for Freedom' as a political theory whereby the ideals of the 'New Christendom' could be realized in a modern society.

Having firmly established the Moot as a Modernist experiment, Chapter 4 engaged in comparative analyses of the Moot's vision of society *vis-à-vis* other political revitalization movements of the period. This allowed for a careful charting of the Moot's navigation between a perceived social disintegration in liberal societies and the desire for order and stability whilst resisting the coercion and oppressive aspects of the totalitarian regimes. The Moot itself extensively analysed the totalitarian states, admiring their efficiency, but – with a few exceptions – rejected both fascism and communism for their underlying religious claims, which were seen to pose a direct threat to Christianity, and for their repudiation of liberal values.

The use of the Modernist framework is an explorative tool that casts the Moot in a new light. But as a heuristic tool, it does not imply that the Moot always falls neatly into the ideal type. The conclusion of the study of the interaction between T. S. Eliot and Karl Mannheim suggests that it is only the latter who can be designated as a 'Programmatic Modernist' in any meaningful way. Mannheim's drive to construct a programme through his vision of 'Planning for Freedom' is prototypically Modernist. Conversely, while Eliot certainly acted upon the drive to build a new society, his rejection of blueprints renders any connotation with the Political Modernist tag less persuasive. This reading has nevertheless brought a fresh perspective on the underlying reasons for Eliot's apparent repudiation of Mannheim's ideas. That is, while they disagreed on the nature of culture and cultural transformation, Eliot ultimately came to disregard Mannheim's planning owing to his confidence in divine providence and God's grace.

The final chapter explores the ways in which the Moot took practical steps to establish a movement which would work towards the inauguration of a 'New Christendom'. The Moot actively participated in Oldham's strategic work to create the supportive structures for the intended movement. This involved founding the CCFCL and later the CFC, which would provide the necessary administrative backbone and co-ordination. The agent or the 'engine' of the hoped-for societal renewal was to be an 'Order', uniting individuals and groups in the commitment to spread and incarnate the ideals of the New Christendom throughout society. While the Order never materialized, Oldham's networking took these ideas into various groups within civil society and even caught the ears of those at the very top of the British political elite. It is thanks to this networking that several ideas originating in Moot papers played some role in shaping what became the 1944 Education Act. While no joint publications were issued by the Moot, many of the ideas discussed appeared in the publications of individual members in several media outlets. The *CNL* operated more or less as the mouthpiece of the group; its rationale and function featured as a topic in the Moot's agenda, its editorial group consisted of Moot members and a large number of its articles were written by members. The *CNL* had some measure of success as a Christian sociopolitical forum during the war and was recommended to Winston Churchill as a venture worth supporting. Furthermore, correspondence reveals how the Moot strategically used the BBC to their advantage, reaching an audience of millions. Finally, many of the members published books that at least partly resulted from their engagement with the Moot. These activities illustrate that the Moot was more than a 'think-tank' or 'discussion group', but rather can be categorized, in Anthony Wallace's terms, as an abortive revitalization movement. In fact, this framework offers the first comprehensive interpretation of the Moot's aims and development based on all the available archival documentation.

Theoretical gains

This study has also made theoretical gains. By framing the Moot as a Modernist movement, I have extended Erik Tonning's 'Modernism and Christianity Studies' beyond the arts into the sociopolitical field (although there can be no sharp demarcation between the two). Whether understood as a *nomos* to overcome or embrace, Tonning has argued that Modernism cannot be apprehended apart from its 'formative tension' with Christianity. No generalizations can be made from a single case study such as this; nevertheless, it does invite further investigation into the 'formative tension' between Christianity and 'Programmatic Modernist' movements. While starting from a different premise, Michel Lackey's study *The Modernist God State* can arguably be understood in this light. On his reading, National Socialism, far from being a secular movement, drew heavily upon Christian symbolism, derived its ideology from a Christian morality and relied on a religious episteme.[1]

My argument challenges Griffin's reading of Modernism as a secular and even anti-Christian phenomenon. In Griffin's conception, Christianity is depicted as an aspect of the defunct paradigm that the Modernists sought to overcome. What the Moot suggests is that although Christianity was clearly viewed as an obsolete paradigm for some among the British intellectual elite, for others, it provided the much-needed impetus – indeed the only viable means – to regenerate the Western world. The huge network of intellectuals that the Moot engaged with, who were essentially sympathetic with the aims of the group, is a further indication that Christianity was anything but a spent social force. Rather than a mere conservative agent, Christianity was considered to possess a vitality with the potency to bring about cultural renewal and rebirth.

Admittedly, Moot members regularly spoke of living in a secular age in the wake of the Enlightenment. Indeed, their endeavour cannot be understood without this premise. Fear of secularization and its consequences is a motivating factor behind its existence.[2] Oldham in his memorandum, 'The Problems and Tasks of the Council on the Christian Faith and the Common Life', expresses this well. Fearing that the demise of Christian beliefs, values and understanding of life's ultimate ends would have far-reaching consequences for the future, he pleaded for a Christian response that demanded a 'deep conversion of the Christian mind ... and new understanding of the function of the Church in modern society'.[3]

Despite their recognition of living in a secular age, the Moot still held that re-establishing the dominant position that Christianity had occupied for centuries in Western civilization was fully attainable. This confidence in the possibility of reversing secularization can be contrasted with Christian social thought advanced within the recent resurgence of political theology. Among Western theologians engaged in these questions today, there are few voices aspiring to a restoration of Christendom. In an emerging post-secular milieu characterized by an increased scepticism of the possibility of a strict secular/sacred and private/public divide, even some secular thinkers have conceded to the value of religious communities' contribution within the public sphere.[4] For theologians, this has presented the church with a renewed opportunity to have a public role. Former Archbishop of

Canterbury Rowan Williams has argued for a secular state that is neutral – not in the sense that it rejects any public religious contributions – but in the sense that it does not favour one religious group over another. For Christians, this means being content with accepting that the Church is but one of many communities that will be heard.[5] Ola Sigurdson also accepts this pluralistic premise. He is cautiously optimistic that the emerging post-secular world presents the church with the prospect of reflecting on its social embodiment while also recognizing that it 'constitutes one body among many religious and non-religious bodies'. Thus, the church 'no longer possesses any place from which panoptic control is possible'.[6] Similar ideas can be heard from Croatian-born Miroslav Volf who, while rejecting 'religious totalitarianism', asserts that religious communities ought not to be excluded from the public discourse. The cross implies that 'a faith that seeks to impose itself and its way of life on others through any form of coercion – is also a serious malfunctioning faith'.[7] Further, acknowledging the current pluralistic context, Volf argues that Christians should 'grant the same religious and political freedoms that they claim for themselves'.[8] Another example is the highly influential pacifist theologian Stanley Hauerwas' vigorous polemic against the hegemony of Christendom or 'Constantinianism'. According to Hauerwas, Constantinianism – a reference to the church's coveting of positions of power and influence – inevitably compromises the church's faithful witness to the crucified Christ. Drawing upon Michael de Certeau's distinction, Hauerwas favours a church of tactics (the art of the weak) over the Constantinian 'strategic' church.[9] Hauerwas' antipathy towards Constantinianism derives from a theological conviction of the crucifixion as an exemplary political act, but there is clearly also an affinity between his thought and the post-structuralist suspicion of power.

There are admittedly residues of the 'New Christendom' discourse of the first half of the twentieth century in contemporary political theologies that cannot be ignored. Oliver O'Donovan wishes to retain the language of Christendom in the church's mission. Nevertheless, he argues that the 'story-tellers of Christendom do not celebrate coercion; they celebrate the power of God to humble the haughty ones of the earth and to harness them to the purposes of peace'.[10] Another notable proponent is John Milbank, who buoyantly argues in *Beyond Secular Order* (2014) for a renaissance of Christendom.[11] In some sense he can be seen as the heir of Maurice Reckitt's Christendom Group. Milbank's dedication of his seminal *Theology and Social Theory* to the 'surviving members of the Christendom Trust' is an acknowledgment of its influence on his thinking. This influence can be seen not least in his appeal to 'a Christian socialist vision ... a recovery but transformation of an antique medieval political ontology'.[12]

Nevertheless, notwithstanding these last examples, there has been a shift, and any contemporary Christian social engagement has to reckon with today's pluralistic social context and begin from a position of weakness and marginality. The examples given are indicative of the fact that the historical context determines the strategies deployed by Christian thinkers. Accordingly, the Moot's commitment to the ideal of a renewed Christendom derives from their sense that their aims were realistic. There was simply little reason to believe that secularization was at this point in history an irreversible force. Eliot held that society was in a state of equilibrium, balancing between the renewal of either a Christian or pagan society. Choices had to be made.[13] As discussed in my introductory chapter, the Church of England during the 1930s and '40s enjoyed a strong position in the public debate; it carried significant political clout and church attendance remained high. Indeed, in his historiography *The Audit of War*, Cornelly Barnett maintains the 'cultural elite', whether politically conservative or liberal, busied themselves with plans for a 'New Jerusalem' after the war: '[s]elfish greed, the moral legacy of Victorian capitalism, would give way to Christian community, motivating to work hard for the good of all'.[14] This book, then, points to the Moot as a case study that adds to the growing literature that problematizes the discourse of secularization as a uniform and undisrupted process in modern society, that often conceives the nineteenth century as dominated by a 'crisis of faith' that rendered Christianity obsolete by the early twentieth century.

Legacy of the Moot

In the Moot's final years from 1944 to early 1947, meetings became less frequent and discussions more topical, thereby revolving less around the creation of a programme of action. Some of the early vigour of the Moot had been lost. The last Moot meeting took place from 10 to 13 January 1947, only days prior to the sudden death of Karl Mannheim. At the time it was not apparent that this tragic event would instigate the end of the Moot.[15] However, the minutes from the first meeting of the Moot's successor group, the St Julian's Group, in December 1947, clarifies the reason for the Moot's discontinuation. Oldham disclosed that the Moot had been brought to a close by 'common consent'. Commenting that there is a healthy cycle of death and rebirth as far as institutions are concerned, Oldham further suggested that what had brought the Moot to its natural end was indeed the death of Mannheim and a decline in attendance.[16] From correspondence in the Polanyi Papers, it is apparent that some form of gathering of intellectuals, nevertheless, continued under Oldham's leadership into the 1960s.[17]

It is difficult to assess the legacy of the Moot, since much will remain unquantifiable and hidden. Many of the members bore witness to the impact that the Moot had on their own thought and action. It is to this that Eliot alluded in an obituary for Mannheim, where he spoke of Mannheim's concealed influence on his friends that would 'not be immediately apparent to those who know both Mannheim and his friends only through their published works'.[18] While still at the Moot, H. A. Hodges professed that its 'concerns are always in the centre of my attention, and colour everything that I do'.[19] Much of the Moot's influence, therefore, was through individual members, their informal networking with other intellectuals and organizations, and their publications and radio broadcasting.

The impact of the Moot continued to shape the minds of its members well after its final gathering in 1947. In an interview with Ved Mehta in the 1960s, Alec Vidler spoke of the Moot as 'the best group I have been a member of, and the most high-powered'.[20] Vidler also acknowledged that the Moot was the inspiration for the formation of the 'Soundings' group that gathered a number of theologians in Cambridge in the 1960s. Furthermore, Oldham repeatedly referred to the Moot as a group of friends, and indeed it became a forum where lifelong creative friendships were formed; Oldham and Polanyi, for instance, corresponded regularly into the 1960s. This correspondence reveals the extent to which they mutually informed each others' thought.[21] As Oldham was approaching his 90th year, he wrote of Polanyi as 'one of my chief educators', and of their friendship as 'one of my most precious possessions'.[22] Another example is Adolf Löwe's letter written on the occasion of Geoffrey Vickers' 86th birthday in October 1980. Löwe wrote in appreciation of their lasting transatlantic friendship. Out of all Moot members, wrote Löwe, 'it is you and I who not only have survived but in our own manner carry on what was born there and then'.[23]

What is clear is that the Moot did not achieve the kind of impact that Oldham had desired. Part of the explanation for this lies in the direction of public discourse in the UK after the war, which took a decisive turn away from cultural questions towards economics and the welfare state. Hans Pfeifer makes this point in his review of *The Moot Papers*, where he suggests that the ideas of the Moot fell into oblivion after the war since 'material reconstruction was more in people's minds than cultural recovery; also, the East-West conflict soon attracted a great deal of attention, and a critical evaluation of the decline of Western values was not seen to be helpful'.[24] The war had provided a context for Christian intellectuals to participate in the public discourse as the war was often framed as a conflict between civilizations. In Britain, the war justification was built on the premise of the defence of the Judeo-Christian tradition in the face of the threat of pagan fascist regimes, and at least in the early phases of the war also of communist Russia. However, after the war, discussions on the demand for a stable socio-religious foundation for society subsided, and in its place the idea of the welfare state emerged as the new nation-building project. Furthermore, the fault line shifted from Judeo-Christian civilization versus neo-pagan totalitarianism, to capitalism versus communism and thereby towards a privileging of economics over and against religion and culture.

Nevertheless, modern societies are arguably still in a state of 'ambivalence' as experienced by the Moot and described by Zygmunt Bauman. As Milbank has suggested, postmodernism can be seen as an extensive footnote to Nietzsche. Milbank points to Nietzsche's nihilism in the light of his 'death of God' pronouncement and the way in which the twentieth century was subsequently plagued by attempts to fill the void of the demise of Christianity. If the earlier part of the century saw attempts to fill this void through numerous replacement religions, argues Milbank, the latter part is characterized by a utilitarianism and free market capitalism. Essentially, Milbank questions – as did the Moot – whether a society without religion can sustain deep values.[25]

Especially bearing in mind the current unrest in Europe, the questions that the Moot asked are thus likely to resurface. For with critical voices declaring the end of neoliberalism and capitalism in the wake of the latest financial turmoil; with the rise of the growing influence of far-right populism across the Western world and its rejection of liberal multi-culturalism; and with the fear of an impending environmental meltdown of apocalyptic proportions, the sense of liminality is yet again casting its shadow over Europe. This milieu is prone to revive enquiries into more fundamental questions of values, identity and transcendence. The question now, as then, is: if not Christianity, what alternative will provide Europe with a common vision?

Notes

1 Lackey, *Modernist God State*, ch. 6.
2 Secularization was primarily understood in terms of the veining public role of Christianity and the relegation of religion to the private sphere. Cf. John Middleton Murry, *The Price of Leadership* (London: SCM Press, 1939), 107; Dawson,

Judgement, 83; Karl Mannheim, 'Towards a New Social Philosophy: A Challenge to Christian Thinkers by a Sociologist', [1941], BA/5/22.

3   J. H. Oldham, 'The Problems and Tasks of the Council on the Christian Faith and the Common Life' [late 1938], OLD/13/8/73.

4   See for example Eduardo Mendieta and Jonathan Vanantwerpen, eds. *The Power of Religion in the Public Sphere* (New York: Columbia University Press, 2011); Jürgen Habermas, 'Religion in the Public Sphere', *European Journal of Philosophy* 14, no. 1 (2006), 1–25. It is naturally questionable whether religious communities have ever ceased to participate in the public sphere.

5   Rowan Williams, *Faith in the Public Square* (London: Bloomsbury, 2012).

6   Ola Sigurdson, 'Beyond Secularism? Towards a Post-Secular Political Theology', *Modern Theology* 26, no. 2 (2010), 193.

7   Miroslav Volf, *A Public Faith: How Followers of Christ Should Serve the Common Good* (Grand Rapids, MI: Brazos Press, 2011), xv–xvi.

8   Ibid., xvii.

9   Stanley Hauerwas, *After Christendom? How the Church Is to Behave If Freedom, Justice, and a Christian Nation Are Bad Ideas* (Nashville: Abingdon Press, 1999), 16–18. Hauerwas writes, 'I certainly do not long for a time when something called "Christianity" had hegemonic culture and political power. Indeed my presumption that when such hegemony has existed the possibility of the church to lead a the faithful is decisively compromised (ibid., 27f).'

10   Oliver O'Donovan, *The Desire of the Nations* (Cambridge: Cambridge University Press, 1996), 223.

11   John Milbank, *Beyond Secular Order: The Representation of Being and the Representation of the People* (Somerset: Wiley-Blackwell, 2013), ProQuest ebrary, 10.

12   There are a number of further correlations between Milbank's political theology and the 'New Christendom' discourse prevalent in Christian social thought during the 1920s and 1930s that would make for an interesting study.

13   Eliot, *Idea*, 13.

14   Correlli Barnett, *The Audit of War: The Illusion & Reality of Britain as a Great Nation* (London: Macmillan, 1986), 11.

15   In a letter to Oldham on 13 March 1947, Michael Polanyi hailed the previous meeting as a success in achieving a definite position after years of preparation (Michael Polanyi, 'Letter to J. H. Oldham', 13 March 1947, MPP/15/3). Oldham was more cautious, replying that 'I was perhaps less satisfied than you were that we had got there, but I agree that we made some progress along the road and I very much want to follow it further (J. H. Oldham, "Letter to Michael Polanyi", 17 March 1947, MPP/15/3).' Since no minutes from the meeting have been located, it is unclear what Polanyi was referring to, but it indicates that their lines of investigation had not been exhausted and that Oldham had yet reached the decision to close the Moot down.

16 'Minutes from the 1st meeting of the St Julian Group', 19–22 December 1947, OLD/13/3/47. The main purpose of the St Julian Group was to discuss the meaning of God in a dialogue between believers and nonbelievers and assist the *Christian News-Letter* in addressing these questions. The confusion of the actual closure of the Moot is compounded by fact of the minutes from the St Julian's Group being labelled as 'Moot Papers' (cf. 'Minutes from St. Julian's Weekend 17–20 December 1948', OLD/13/4/105).
17 See the appendix Mullins, 'Polanyi'.
18 Eliot, 'Professor Karl Mannheim'.
19 H. A. Hodges, 'Letter from H. A. Hodges', 6 November 1942, BA/05/26.
20 Ved Mehta, *The New Theologian* (London: Weidenfeld and Nicolson, 1966), 62.
21 Phil Mullins has investigated Oldham's significant editorial influences on Polanyi's *Personal Knowledge,* published in 1958 (Mullins, 'Polanyi', 185–7).
22 J. H. Oldham, 'Letter to Michael Polanyi', 19 August 1964, MPP/15/5.
23 As cited in Vickers, *Rethinking the Future*, 193.
24 Hans Pfeifer, 'Keith Clements (Ed.), the Moot Papers, Faith, Freedom and Society 1938–1944', *Theology* 114, no. 1 (2011), 63–4.
25 John Milbank, *The Myth of the Secular*, podcast audio, accessed 20 November 2016, 2012, http://www.cbc.ca/radio/ideas/the-myth-of-the-secular-part-6-1.2920704.

Appendix: List of the Moot Members

Regular members

John Baillie (1886–1960)
Reformed theologian at New College, Edinburgh.
Meetings attended: 1, 2, 3, 4, 5, 12, 13, 14, 15, 16, 20, 21

Cathleen Bliss (1908–1989)
The assistant editor and later editor (1945) of *Christian News-Letter*.
Meetings attended: 17, 18, 19, 20, 21

Sir **Fred Clarke** (1880–1952)
Director of the Institute of Education.
Meetings attended: 7, 8, 9, 11, 12, 13, 14, 17, 19, 21

Christopher Dawson (1889–1970)
Roman Catholic historian.
Meetings attended: 1, 10, 12

T. S. Eliot (1888–1965)
Poet and critic.
Meetings attended: 1, 2, 3, 4, 5, 8, 9, 10, 12, 13, 15, 17

H. H. Farmer (1892–1981)
Professor of systematic theology, Westminster College, Cambridge.
Meetings attended: 1, 5,

The details of the members provided here are largely based upon Keith Clements' *The Moot Papers*

Eric Fenn (1899–1995)
Assistant Director of Religious Broadcasting of the BBC.
Meetings attended: 1, 2, 3, 4, 5, 7, 9, 10, 12, 13, 14, 16, 17, 18, 19, 20

Sir **Hector Hetherington** (1888–1965)
Scottish philosopher and Principal of Glasgow University.
Meetings attended: 10, 11, 15, 16, 17

H. A. Hodges (1905–1976)
Professor in philosophy at Reading University.
Meetings attended: 1, 2, 3, 4, 8, 9, 10, 11, 12, 13, 14, 15, 16, 17, 18, 19, 20, 21

Eleanora Iredale (1892–1966)
Acted as Oldham's assistant on several of his ventures.
Meetings attended: 1, 2, 3, 4, 5, 8, 9, 10, 11, 13, 14, 15, 16, 17

Daniel Jenkins (1914–2002)
Student Christian Movement (SCM).
Meetings attended: 18, 19

Adolf Löwe (1893–1995)
German émigré, sociologist and economist.
Meetings attended: 1, 2, 3, 5, 7, 8

Donald M. MacKinnon (1908–1960)
Scottish theologian and philosopher.
Meetings attended: 21

Karl Mannheim (1893–1947)
Native Hungarian and sociologist.
Meetings attended: 2, 3, 4, 5, 7, 8, 9, 10, 11, 12, 13, 14, 15, 16, 17, 18, 19, 20, 21

Alexander Miller (1908–1960)
Presbyterian minister.
Meetings attended: 17, 18, 19, 20, 21

Sir **Walter Moberly** (1881–1974)
Educationist and the director of the Student Grants Committee.
Meetings attended: 1, 2, 3, 4, 5, 7, 8, 9, 10, 11, 12, 13, 14, 15, 16, 19, 20, 21

John Middleton Murry (1889–1957)
Christian communist, pacifist and literary critic.
Meetings attended: 1, 2, 3, 5, 7, 8, 9, 11, 13, 15

Sir **Walter Oakeshott** (1903–1987)
Educationist and the Head Master of St Paul's School.
Meetings attended: 2, 8, 9, 10, 12, 13

J. H. Oldham (1974–1969)
The chair and founder of the Moot. Influential ecumenist and key figure in the formation of the World Council of Churches.
Meetings attended: All

Mary Oldham (1877–1965)
Married to and assistant of J. H. Oldham (is listed as present at most of the Moot meetings, but is never recorded to have commented upon the discussion).
Meetings attended: 1, 2, 3, 4, 5, 7, 8, 9, 11, 13, 15, 17, 18, 19, 21

Michael Polanyi (1891–1976)
Hungarian-born scientist and philosopher.
Meetings attended: 20, 21

Gilbert Shaw (1886–1967)
Anglican clergy.
Meetings attended: 2, 3, 4, 5, 7, 8, 10, 11, 13, 14, 16, 18, 19

Oliver Tomkins (1908–1992)
Anglican clergy and ecumenist.
Meetings attended: 3, 4, 5

Sir **Geoffrey Vickers** (1894–1982)
Lawyer and social activist.[1]
Meetings attended: 5, 8

Alec Vidler (1899–1991)
Anglo-Catholic clergyman and the editor of *Theology* journal.
Meetings attended: 2, 3, 4, 5, 7, 8, 9, 10, 11, 12, 14, 15, 16, 17, 18, 19, 20, 21

Visitors

M. Chaning-Pearce (unknown)
Educationist and writer.
Meeting(s) attended: 13, 14

A. C. Craig (1886–1985)
Presbyterian minister and general secretary of the British Council of Churches (1942).
Meeting(s) attended: 5

O. S. Franks (1905–1992)
Professor of moral philosophy, Glasgow University, and civil servant during the Second World War.
Meeting(s) attended: 5

A. C. Goyder (1908–1997)
Businessman and director of British International Paper.
Meeting(s) attended: 5

W. D. L. Greer (1902–1972)
Anglican clergy and general secretary of SCM.
Meeting(s) attended: 5

Sir **Noel Hall** (1902–1983)
Economist and civil servant.
Meeting(s) attended: 4

E. Lampert (unknown)
Russian Orthodox theologian.
Meeting(s) attended: 14

Philip Mairet (1886–1975)
Editor of *New English Weekly*.
Meeting(s) attended: 5, 10, 20

Lesslie Newbigin (1909–1998)
Presbyterian theologian and missionary.
Meeting(s) attended: 2

Reinhold Niebuhr (1892–1971)
American theologian and political activist.
Meeting(s) attended: 5, 17

William Paton (1886–1943)
Leading ecumenist and founder of the British Council of Churches.
Meeting(s) attended: 2

Lord **Frank Pakenham** (1905–2001)
Political activist (Labour) and the assistant of William Beveridge during the war.
*Meeting(s) attended:*16

Gilbert Russell (unknown)
Medical missionary in China.
Meeting(s) attended: 11

W. G. Symons (unknown)
Civil servant.
Meeting(s) attended: 19

R. H. Tawney (1880–1962)
Professor of Economic History at the London School of Economics and a Christian socialist.
Meeting(s) attended: 5

Note

1   Adolf Löwe considered Vickers a 'member' although he only attended two meetings (see Jeanne Vickers, *Rethinking the Future: The Correspondence between Geoffrey Vickers and Adolph Lowe* (London: Transaction Publishers, 1991), 193).

Archives

BBC Written Archives Centre Caversham
Reference: GB 898 (BBC)
Collected by: Jonas Kurlberg

Bodleian Special Collections, Oxford University
Conservative Party Archives
Reference: GB 161 CRD (CPA)
Collected by: Jonas Kurlberg

Brotherton Special Collections, University of Leeds
Letters and papers concerning the lay Christian ecumenical society 'The Moot'
Reference: GB 1471 BC MS 20s Moot (LM)
Collected by: David Addyman

Centre for Research Collections, Edinburgh University Library
Papers of Professor John Baillie
Reference: GB 237 BAI (BA)
Collected by: David Addyman

Charles Deering McCormick Library of Special Collection, Northwestern University
T. S. Eliot Correspondence Collection
Reference: (NWE)
Collected by: Jonas Kurlberg

Church of England Archives
Lambeth Palace Library
Record Centre, Bermondsey
Reference: GB 105 (COE)
Collected by: Jonas Kurlberg

New College Library, University of Edinburgh
J. H. Oldham Archives
Reference: GB 238 MS OLD (OA)
Collected by: David Addyman

Institute of Education,
Records of the Moot
Reference: GB 366 DC/MOO (IOE/MOO)

Fred Clarke Papers
Reference: GB 366 DC/FC (IOE/FC)
Collected by: David Addyman & Jonas Kurlberg

Henry Ransom Humanities Research Center, University of Texas
T. S. Eliot Collection
Reference: (UTE)
Collected by: Erik Tonning

Houghton Library, Harvard University
T.S. Eliot Papers
(HLE)
Collected by: Jonas Kurlberg

King's College Library, University of Cambridge
The Hayward Bequest of T. S. Eliot Papers
Reference: GB 272 HB (HB)
Collected by: David Addyman and Jonas Kurlberg

New York Public Library
T.S. Eliot Collection of Paper (NYE)
Collected by: Jonas Kurlberg

Regenstein Library, University of Chicago
Michael Polanyi Papers (MPP)
Louis Wirth Papers (LWP)
Collected by: Jonas Kurlberg

University of Keele Library
A. D. Lindsey Papers
Reference: GB 172 LIN *(LP)*

Karl Mannheim Papers
Reference: GB 172 MAN *(KMP)*
Collected by: David Addyman

University of St. Thomas Library
Christopher Dawson Papers (CDP)
Collected by: Jonas Kurlberg

World Council of Churches Archives, Geneva
Reference: (WCC)
Collected by: Jonas Kurlberg

Bibliography

Ackroyd, Peter. *T. S. Eliot*. London: Hamish Hamilton, 1984.
Aquinas, Thomas. *Summa Theologica*. Cambridge: Cambridge University Press, 2006.
Arendt, Hannah. *The Origins of Totalitarianism*. 2nd ed. New York: Harcourt, Brace & World, 1958 [1951].
Arendt, Hannah, and Jerome Kohn. 'On the Nature of Totalitarianism: An Essay in Understanding'. In *Essays in Understanding: 1930–1954*, 328–60. New York: Harcourt Brace, 1994.
Aristotle. *The Art of Rhetoric*. Translated by H C Lawson-Tancred. London: Penguin Books, 2004.
Asher, Kenneth. *T. S. Eliot and Ideology*. Cambridge: Cambridge University Press, 1995.
Auden, W. H. 'The Public V. The Late Mr. William Butler Yeats'. In *The English Auden: Poems, Essays and Dramatic Writings 1927–1939*, edited by Edward Mendelson, 389–93. London: Faber & Faber, 1977.
Baillie, John. 'Does God Defend the Right'. *Christian News-Letter*, no. 53 (30 October 1940).
Baillie, John. *What Is Christian Civilization?* London: Oxford University Press, 1945.
Barber, Michael. *Making of the 1944 Education Act*. London: Continuum, 2000.
Barnett, Correlli. *The Audit of War: The Illusion & Reality of Britain as a Great Nation*. London: Macmillan, 1986.
Barré, Jean-Luc. *Jacques and Raïssa Maritain: Beggars for Heaven*. Translated by Bernard E. Doering. Notre Dame, IN: University of Notre Dame, 2005.
Barth, Karl. *A Letter to Great Britain from Switzerland*. London: The Sheldon Press, 1941.
Bauman, Zygmunt. *Legislators and Interpreters*. Cambridge: Polity Press, 1989.
Bauman, Zygmunt. *Modernity and Ambivalence*. Cambridge: Polity Press, 1991.
Bauman, Zygmunt. *Modernity and the Holocaust*. Cambridge: Polity Press, 1989.
Beebe, Maurice. 'Introduction: What Modernism Was'. *Journal of Modern Literature* 3, no. 5 (1974): 1065–84.
Belgion, Montgomery. 'The Germanization of Britain'. *New English Weekly* 26, no. 18 (15 February 1945): 137–8.
Berger, Peter L. 'The Desecularization of the World: A Global Overview'. In *The Desecularization of the World: Resurgent Religion and World Politics*, edited by Peter Berger, 1–18. Grand Rapids, MI: Eerdmans, 1999.
Berger, Peter L. 'Further Thoughts on Religion and Modernity'. *Sociology* 49 (2012): 313–16.
Berger, Peter L. *The Sacred Canopy*. Garden City, NY: Anchor Books, 1967.
Berger, Peter, and Thomas Luckmann. *The Social Construction of Reality – a Treatise in the Sociology of Knowledge*. London: Penguin Books, 1971.

Beveridge, William. *The Pillars of Security: And Other War-Time Essays and Addresses*. London: George Allen & Unwin, 1943.

Bewdley, Baldwin of, Marquess of Salisbury, Lord Amulree, Lord Birdwood, William Bragg, Earl of Clarendon, Earl of Cork and Orrery, et al. 'Moral Rearmament'. *The Times* (1938).

Blair, Sara. 'Modernism and the Politics of Culture'. In *Cambridge Companion to Modernism*, edited by Michael Levenson, 155–77. Cambridge: Cambridge University Press, 2011.

Bradbury, Malcolm, and James McFarlane. 'The Name and Nature of Modernism'. In *Modernism: 1890–1930*, edited by Malcolm Bradbury and James McFarlane, 19–55. Harmondsworth: Penguin Books, 1976.

Brown, Callum G. *The Death of Christian Britain*. 2nd ed. London: Routledge, 2009.

Bruce, Steve. *God Is Dead–Secularisation in the West*. Oxford: Blackwell Publishing, 2002.

Bruce, Steve. *Secularization: In Defence of an Unfashionable Theory*. Oxford: Oxford University Press, 2011.

Brunner, Emil, and Karl Barth. *Natural Theology*. Translated by Peter Fraenkel. London: The Centenary Press, 1946.

Buber, Martin. *I and Thou*. Edinburgh: T&T Clark, 1937.

Buchman, Frank N. D. *Remaking the World: The Speeches of Frank N. D. Buchman*. London: Blandford Press, 1947.

Carey, John. *The Intellectuals and the Masses: Pride and Prejudice among the Literary Intelligentsia, 1880–1939*. London: Faber & Faber, 1992.

Chadwick, Owen. *The Secularization of the European Mind in the Nineteenth Century*. Cambridge: Cambridge University Press, 1975.

Clarke, Fred. 'The Crisis in Education'. In *Church, Community, and State in Relation to Education*, edited by Fred Clarke, W. Zenkovsky, Paul Monroe, Charles R. Morris, J. W. D. Smith, PH. Kohnstamm, and J. H. Oldham, 3–27. London: George Allen & Unwin, 1938.

Clarke, Fred. *Education and Social Change: An English Interpretation*. Christian News-Letter Books. London: The Sheldon Press, 1940.

Clarke, Fred. *Freedom in the Educative Society*. London: University of London Press, 1948.

Clarke, Fred, W. Zenkovsky, Paul Monroe, Charles R. Morris, J. W. D. Smith, PH. Kohnstamm, and J. H. Oldham. *Church, Community, and State in Relation to Education*. London: George Allen & Unwin, 1938.

Clements, Keith. *Faith on the Frontier: A Life of J. H. Oldham*. Edinburgh: T&T Clark, 1999.

Clements, Keith. 'John Baillie and the Moot'. In *Christ, Church and Society: Essays on John Baillie and Donald Baillie*, edited by David Fergusson, 199–219. Edinburgh: T&T Clark, 1993.

Clements, Keith. *The Moot Papers: Faith, Freedom and Society 1938–1944*. London: T&T Clark, 2010.

Collini, Stefan. *Absent Minds: Intellectuals in Britain*. Oxford: Oxford University Press, 2006.

Collini, Stefan. 'The European Modernist as Anglican Moralist: The Later Criticism of T. S. Eliot'. In *Enlightenment, Passion, Modernity: Historical Essays in European Thought and Culture*, edited by Mark S. Micale and Robert L. Dietle, 207–29. Stanford: Stanford University Press, 2000.

Coupland, Philip M. *Britannia, Europa and Christendom: British Christians and European Integration*. New York: Palgrave Macmillan, 2006.

Coyle, M. 'T. S. Eliot on the Air: "Culture" and the Challenges of Mass Communication'. In *T. S. Eliot and Our Turning World*, edited by Jewel Spears Brooker. London: Macmillan, 2001.

Culleton, Claire A., and Karen Leick. 'Silence, Acquiescence, and Dread'. In *Modernism on File: Writers, Artists, and the FBI, 1920–1950*, edited by Claire A. Culleton and Karen Leick, 1–22. New York: Palgrave Macmillan, 2008.

Cunard, Nancy. *Authors Takes Side on the Spanish Civil War*. London: Left Review, 1937.

Cunningham, Valentine. *British Writers of the Thirties*. Oxford: Oxford University Press, 1988.

Curtis, Lionel. *Civitas Dei: The Commonwealth of God*. Edinburgh: R & R Clark, 1938.

Dancy, John. *Walter Oakeshott: A Diversity of Gifts*. Norwich: Michaell Russell, 1995.

Davie, Grace. *Europe: The Exceptional Case: Parameters of Faith in the Modern World*. London: Darton, Longman and Todd, 2002.

Davie, Grace. *Religion in Britain since 1945: Believing without Belonging*. Oxford: Blackwell, 1994.

Dawson, Christopher. *Beyond Politics*. London: Sheed & Ward, 1939.

Dawson, Christopher. *Christianity and the New Age*. London: Sheed & Ward, 1931.

Dawson, Christopher. *The Judgement of the Nations*. London: Sheed & Ward, 1943.

Dawson, Christopher. *Religion and the Modern State*. London: Sheed and Ward, 1935.

Dawson, Christopher. 'Religion and the Totalitarian State'. *The Criterion* 14, no. 54 (1934): 1–16.

Dawson, Christopher. 'What Is the Alternative to Totalitarianism'. *Christian News-Letter*, no. 107 (12 November 1941).

Dilworth, Thomas. 'David Jones and Fascism'. *Journal of Modern Literature* 13, no. 1 (1986): 149–62.

Durkheim, Emile. *The Elementary Forms of the Religious Life*. Translated by Joseph Ward Swain. London: George Allen & Unwin, 1964 [1915].

Edwards, M. T. '"God's Totalitarianism": Ecumenical Protestant Discourse During the Good War, 1941–45'. *Totalitarian Movements and Political Religions* 10, no. 3–4 (2009): 285–302.

Edwards, M. T. *The Right of the Protestant Left: God's Totalitarianism*. New York: Palgrave Macmillan, 2012.

Eisenstadt, Shmuel 'Multiple Modernities'. *Daedalus* 129 (2000): 1–30.

Eliot, T. S. *After Strange Gods: A Primer on Modern Heresy*. London: Faber & Faber, 1934.

Eliot, T. S. 'The Christian Conception of Education'. In *Malvern 1941: The Life of the Church the Order of Society*, 201–14. London: Longmans, 1941.

Eliot, T. S. 'Christianity and Communism'. *The Listener* 7, no. 166 (12 March 1932): 382–3.

Eliot, T. S. 'The Church and Society'. *New English Weekly* 6, no. 23 (21 March 1935): 482.

Eliot, T. S. 'The Church's Message to the World'. *The Listener* 17, no. 423 (17 February 1937): 293–4.

Eliot, T. S. 'The Class and the Élite'. *New English Weekly* 11, no. 6 (October 1945): 499–509.

Eliot, T. S. 'A Commentary'. *The Criterion* XVII, no. 66 (17 October 1937): 81–6.

Eliot, T. S. 'Editorial 3rd September'. *Christian News-Letter*, no. 97 (3rd September 1941).

Eliot, T. S. 'Editorial 8th July'. *Christian News-Letter*, no. 141 (8 July 1942).

Eliot, T. S. 'Editorial 14th August'. *Christian News-Letter*, no. 42 (14 August 1940).

Eliot, T. S. 'Editorial 21st August'. *Christian News-Letter*, no. 43 (21 August 1940).

Eliot, T. S. 'Editorial 28th August'. *Christian News-Letter*, no. 44 (28 August 1940).

Eliot, T. S. 'Education in a Christian Society'. *Christian News-Letter*, no. 20 (13 March 1940).

Eliot, T. S. 'Full Employment and the Responsibility of Christians'. *Christian News-Letter*, no. 230 (21st March 1945): 7–11.

Eliot, T. S. 'The Germanisation of Britain'. *New English Weekly*, 29 March 1945.

Eliot, T. S. *The Idea of a Christian Society*. London: Faber & Faber, 1939.

Eliot, T. S. 'Man and Society'. *The Spectator* (6 June 1940).

Eliot, T. S. 'The Modern Dilemma'. *The Christian Register* 102, no. 41 (19 October 1933): 675–6.

Eliot, T. S. *Murder in the Cathedral*. London: Faber & Faber, 1965 [1935].

Eliot, T. S. *Notes Towards the Definition of Culture*. 2nd ed. London: Faber & Faber, 1962 [1948].

Eliot, T. S. 'On Reading Official Reports'. *New English Weekly* 15 (11 May 1939): 61–2.

Eliot, T. S. 'Planning and Religion'. *Theology* XLVI, no. 275 (1943): 102–6.

Eliot, T. S. 'Professor Karl Mannheim'. *The Times* (25 January 1947): 7.

Eliot, T. S. 'Responsibility and Power'. *Christian News-Letter*, no. 196 (1 December 1943).

Eliot, T. S. *Thoughts after Lambeth*. London: Faber & Faber, 1931.

Eliot, T. S. 'Towards a Christian Britain'. In *The Church Looks Ahead*, edited by J. H. Oldham, 106–17. London: Faber & Faber, 1941.

Eliot, T. S. 'Towards a Christian Britain'. *The Listener* 25, no. 639 (1941): 524–5.

Eliot, T. S. 'Tradition and the Individual Talent'. *Egoist* VI (1919): 72–3.

Eliot, T. S., Valerie Eliot, and John Haffenden. *The Letters of T.S. Eliot Volume 3* [in English]. London: Faber & Faber, 2012.

Evans, Richard J. *In Defence of History*. London: Granta Publications, 2000 [1997].

Every, George. 'Planning within Limits'. *Christian News-Letter*, no. 160 (18 November 1942).
Eysteinsson, Astradur. *The Concept of Modernism*. Ithaca, NY: Cornell University Press, 1990.
Fenn, Erik. 'Dr. Asmussen Explains'. *Christian News-Letter*, no. 254 (20 February 1946).
Ferrall, Charles. *Modernist Writing and Reactionary Politics*. Cambridge: Cambridge University Press, 2001.
Forster, E. M. 'What I Believe'. In *Two Cheers for Democracy*, edited by E. M. Forster, 65–73. London: Edward Arnold, 1972 [1938].
Frank, Joseph. *Responses to Modernity: Essays in the Politics of Culture*. Bronx: Fordham University Press, 2012.
Gábor, Éva. 'Michael Polanyi in the Moot'. *Polanyiana* 1–2, no. 2 (1992): 120–6.
Gay, Peter. *Modernism: The Lure of Heresy from Baudelaire to Beckett and Beyond*. London: Vintage Books, 2009.
Gay, Peter. *Weimar Culture: The Outsider as Insider*. London: Secker & Warburg, 1968.
Gentile, Emilio *Politics as Religion*. Translated by George Staunton. Princeton, NJ: Princeton University Press, 2006.
Gore, Charles, et al. *The Return of Christendom*. London: George Allen and Unwin, 1922.
Griffin, Roger. *Modernism and Fascism: The Sense of a Beginning under Mussolini and Hitler*. Basingstoke: Palgrave, 2007.
Grimley, Matthew. *Citizenship, Community, and the Church of England: Liberal Anglican Theories of the State between the Wars*. Oxford: Clarendon Press, 2004.
Grimley, Matthew. 'Civil Society and the Clerisy: Christian Élites and National Culture, C. 1930–1950'. In *Civil Society in British History: Ideas, Identities, Institutions*, edited by Jose Harris, 231–47. Oxford: Oxford University Press, 2003.
Habermas, Jürgen. 'Religion in the Public Sphere'. *European Journal of Philosophy* 14, no. 1 (2006): 1–25.
Hague, René. *David Jones*. Cardiff: University of Wales Press, 1975.
Hauerwas, Stanley. *After Christendom? How the Church Is to Behave If Freedom, Justice, and a Christian Nation Are Bad Ideas*. Nashville: Abingdon Press, 1999.
Hayek, Fredrick A. *The Counter-Revolution of Science: Studies on the Abuse of Reason*. Glencoe: The Free Press, 1991 [1941].
Hayek, Fredrick A. *The Road to Serfdom*. Abingdon: Routledge, 2001 [1944].
Herf, Jeffrey. *Reactionary Modernism: Technology, Culture, and Politics in Weimar and the Third Reich*. Cambridge: Cambridge University Press, 1986.
Hocking, William Ernest. *The Lasting Elements of Individualism*. New Haven, CT: Yale University Press, 1937.
Hodges, H. A. 'Christianity in an Age of Science'. *Christian News-Letter*, no. 120 (11th February 1942).
Hodges, H. A. 'The Meaning of Moral Rearmament'. *Theology* 38, no. 227 May (1939): 322–32.

Hodges, H. A. 'The Problem of Archetypes'. *Christian News-Letter*, no. 183 (2 June 1943).

Hodges, H. A. 'Social Standards in a Mixed Society'. *Christian News-Letter*, no. 43 (21 August 1940).

Hodges, H. A. 'What Differences Does Christianity Make?'. *Christian News-Letter*, no. 27 (1 May 1940).

Holts, Ernest. *Three Faces of Fascism: Action Française, Italian Fascism and National Socialism*. Translated by Leila Vennewitz. London: Weidenfeld and Nicolson, 1965.

Hynes, Samuel. *The Auden Generation: Literature and Politics in England in the 1930's*. London: Faber & Faber, 1979. 1976.

Jackson, Eleanor M. *Red Tape and the Gospel: A Study of the Significance of the Ecumenical Missionary Struggle of William Paton (1886–1943)*. Birmingham: Phlogiston Publishing, 1980.

Jackson, Paul. 'Extremes of Faith and Nation: British Fascism and Christianity'. *Religion Compass* 4, no. 8 (2010): 507–17.

Jenkins, D. E., and Marjorie Reeves. 'Outside Ecclesiastical Organization: The Christian Frontier Council'. In *Christian Thinking and Social Order: Conviction Politics from the 1930s to the Present Day*, edited by Marjorie Reeves. London: Cassell, 1999.

Julius, Anthony. *T.S. Eliot, Anti-Semitism, and Literary Form*. Cambridge: Cambridge University Press, 1995.

Kermode, Frank. *Sense of an Ending: Studies in the Theory of Fiction*. New York: Oxford University Press, 2000.

Kettler, David, and Colin Loader. *Karl Mannheim: Social as Political Education*. New Brunswick: Transaction, 2001.

Kettler, David, and Volker Meja. *Karl Mannheim and the Crisis of Liberalism*. New Brunswick and London: Transaction, 1995.

Kettler, David, Volker Meja, and Nico Stehr. *Karl Mannheim*. Chichester: Ellis Horwood Tavistock, 1984.

Kirk, P. T. R. *The Church and Social Evils*. London: Industrial Christian Fellowship, 1937.

Kojecky, Roger. *T. S. Eliot's Social Criticism*. New York: Farrar, Straus and Giroux, 1972.

Ku, Hsiao-Yuh 'Education for Liberal Democracy: Fred Clarke and the 1944 Education Act'. *History of Education* 42, no. 5 (2013): 578–97. doi:10.1080/0046760X.2013.823627, http://dx.doi.org/10.1080/0046760X.2013.823627.

Kudomi, Yoshiyuki. 'Karl Mannheim in Britain: An Interim Research Report'. *Hitotsuabashi Journal of Social Studies* 28, no. 2 (1996): 43–56.

Kurlberg, Jonas. 'The Moot, the End of Civilization and the Re-Birth of Christendom'. In *Modernism, Christianity and Apocalypse*, edited by Erik Tonning, Matthew Feldman and David Addyman, 222–36. Leiden: Brill, 2014.

Kurlberg, Jonas. 'Resisting Totalitarianism: The Moot and a New Christendom'. *Religion Compass* 7, no. 12 (2013): 517–31.

Lackey, Michael. *The Modernist God State: A Literary Study of the Nazi's Christian Reich*. New York: Continuum, 2012.

Lackey, Michael. 'The Moot Papers: Faith, Freedom and Society 1938-1947'. *Modernism/Modernity* 17, no. 4 (2010): 959-61.

Landes, Richard Allen. *Heaven on Earth the Varieties of the Millennial Experience*. Oxford: Oxford University Press, 2011.

Lang, Cosmo, Cardinal Hinsley, Walter H. Armstrong, and William Temple. 'Foundations of Peace'. *The Times* (21 December 1940): 5.

Larsen, Timothy. *Crisis of Doubt: Honest Faith in Nineteenth-Century England* [in English]. Oxford; New York: Oxford University Press, 2006.

Lewis, Pericles. 'Modernism and Religion'. In *The Cambridge Companion to Modernism*, edited by Michael Levenson, 178-96. Cambridge: Cambridge University Press, 2011.

Lewis, Pericles. *Religious Experience and the Modernist Novel*. Cambridge: Cambridge University Press, 2010.

Livingstone, Richard. 'The Crisis of Civilisation'. In *The Deeper Causes of the War*, edited by Sydney E. Hooper, 94-115. London: George Allen and Unwin, 1940.

Loader, Colin. *The Intellectual Development of Karl Mannheim*. Cambridge: Cambridge University Press, 1985.

Luckhurst, Roger. 'Religion, Psychical Research, Spiritualism, and the Occult'. In *Oxford Handbook of Modernisms*, edited by Peter Brooker, Andrzej Gąsiorek, Deborah Longworth, and Andrew Thacker. Oxford: Oxford University Press, 2010.

Lukács, Georg. *The Meaning of Contemporary Realism*. London: Merlin Press, 1972 [1963].

MacKinnon, Donald. 'Surveys: Christian Social Thought'. *Theology* 38, no. 227 (May 1939): 378-82.

Maier, Hans. 'On the Interpretations of Totalitarian Rule 1919-89'. In *Totalitarianism and Political Religions, Volume III: Concepts for the Comparison of Dictatorship – Theory and History of Interpretation*, edited by Hans Maier, 3-21. Abingdon: Routledge, 2007.

Manganiello, Dominic. *Joyce's Politics*. London: Routledge & Kegan Paul, 1980.

Mannheim, Karl. 'The Democratization of Culture'. In *From Karl Mannheim*, edited by Kurt E. Wolf, 271-346. New York: Oxford University Press, 1971.

Mannheim, Karl. *Diagnosis of Our Time: Wartime Essays of a Sociologist*. London: Kegan Paul, 1943.

Mannheim, Karl. *Freedom, Power and Democratic Planning*. London: Routledge & Kegan Paul, 1951.

Mannheim, Karl. 'The Historical Political Task of Britain'. *Christian News-Letter*, no. 135 (27 May 1942).

Mannheim, Karl. *Ideology and Utopia*. New York: Harvest Books, 1968 [1936].

Mannheim, Karl. *Man and Society: In an Age of Reconstruction*. London: Kegan Paul, 1940.

Mannheim, Karl. 'The Meaning of Popularisation in a Mass Society'. *Christian News-Letter*, no. 227 (7 February 1945): 7-12.

Maritain, Jacques. *Christianity and Democracy*. London: The Centenary Press, 1945.
Maritain, Jacques. *The Philosophy of Art*. Translated by John O'Connor. Ditchling: S. Dominic's Press, 1923.
Maritain, Jacques. *The Rights of Man and Natural Law*. London: The Centenary Press, 1944.
Maritain, Jacques. *True Humanism*. London: The Centenary Press, 1938.
Martin, David. *A General Theory of Secularization*. Oxford: Blackwell, 1978.
Martin, David. *Pentecostalism: The World Their Parish*. Oxford: Blackwell, 2002.
Martin, David. 'Secularisation and the Future of Christianity'. *Journal of Contemporary Religion* 20, no. 2 (2005): 145–50.
Martin, David. 'Towards Eliminating the Concept of Secularization'. In *Penguin Survey of the Social Sciences*, edited by Julius Gould, 169–82. Harmondsworth: Penguin, 1965.
Maud, John. 'Full Employment and the Responsibility of Christians'. *Christian News-Letter*, no. 229 (14th March 1945).
McCulloch, Gary. *Educational Reconstruction: The 1944 Education Act and the Twenty-First Century*. Ilford: Woburn Press, 1994.
McDiarmid, Lucy. *Saving Civilization: Yeats, Eliot, and Auden between the Wars*. Cambridge: Cambridge University Press, 1984.
Mehta, Ved. *The New Theologian*. London: Weidenfeld and Nicolson, 1966.
Mendieta, Eduardo, and Jonathan Vanantwerpen, eds. *The Power of Religion in the Public Sphere*. New York: Columbia University Press, 2011.
Merkley, P. *Reinhold Niebuhr: A Political Account*. Montreal: MQUP, 1975. ProQuest ebrary.
Micklem, Nathaniel. *The Crisis and the Christian*. Crisis Booklet. Edited by Hugh Martin London: SCM Press, 1938.
Milbank, John. *Beyond Secular Order: The Representation of Being and the Representation of the People*. Somerset: Wiley-Blackwell, 2013. ProQuest ebrary.
Milbank, John. *The Myth of the Secular*. Podcast audio. Accessed 20th November 2016, 2012. http://www.cbc.ca/radio/ideas/the-myth-of-the-secular-part-6-1.2920704.
Milbank, John. *Theology and Social Theory: Beyond Secular Reason*. 2nd ed. Oxford: Blackwell, 2006.
Mitchell, F. W. *Sir Fred Clarke: Master Teacher 1880–1952*. London: Longmans, 1967.
Moberly, Walter. 'The Christian Frontier Council'. *Christian News-Letter*, no. 154 (7 October 1942).
Moberly, Walter. *The Crisis in the University*. London: SCM Press, 1949.
Moberly, Walter. *Plato's Conception of Education and Its Meaning for to-Day*. Oxford: Oxford University Press, 1944.
Moody, A. David. *Thomas Stearn Eliot: Poet*. 2nd ed. Cambridge: Cambridge University Press, 1994.
Mullins, Phil. 'Michael Polanyi and J. H. Oldham: In Praise of Friendship'. *Appraisal* 1, no. 4 (1997): 179–89.

Mullins, Phil, and Struan Jacobs. 'T.S. Eliot's Idea of the Clerisy, and Its Discussion by Karl Mannheim and Michael Polanyi in the Context of J.H. Oldham's Moot'. *Journal of Classical Sociology* 6, no. 2 (2006): 147–56.

Munton, Alan. 'Modernist Politics: Socialism, Anarchism, Fascism'. In *The Oxford Handbook of Modernisms*, edited by Peter Brooker, Andrzej Gąsiorek, Deborah Longworth, and Andrew Thacker, 477–500. Oxford: Oxford University Press, 2010.

Murry, John Middleton. *Adam and Eve: An Essay Towards a New and Better Society*. London: Andrew Dakers, 1944.

Murry, John Middleton. 'Apologia'. *Adelphi* 14, no. 6 (May 1938): 161–9.

Murry, John Middleton. 'Can Democracy Survive?'. *Christian News-Letter*, no. 274 (27 November 1946).

Murry, John Middleton. *The Defence of Democracy*. London: Jonathan Cape, 1939.

Murry, John Middleton. 'Democracy and the Totalitarian Ideal'. *Adelphi* 15, no. 4 (1939): 149–57.

Murry, John Middleton. *Europe in Travail*. Christian News-Letter Books. Edited by Alec R. Vidler London: The Sheldon Press, 1940.

Murry, John Middleton. 'The Free Society'. *Christian News-Letter*, no. 284 (30 April 1947).

Murry, John Middleton. *The Necessity of Communism*. London: Jonathan Cape, 1932.

Murry, John Middleton. *The Price of Leadership*. London: SCM Press, 1939.

Murry, John Middleton. 'The Task of Democracy'. *Adelphi* 15, no. 5 (Feburary 1939): 212–17.

Murry, John Middleton. 'Towards a Christian Society'. *Adelphi* 15, no. 1 (1938): 9–13.

Mussolini, Benito. *Fascism: Doctrine and Institutions*. New York: Howard Fertig, 1968 [1935].

Niebuhr, Reinhold. *The Nature and Destiny of Man: A Christian Interpretation: Vol I*. Louisville: Westminster John Knox Press, 1996.

Niebuhr, Reinhold. *Reflections on the End of an Era*. New York: Charles Scribner's Sons, 1936.

Nietzsche, Fredrich. *The Gay Science*. Translated by Josefine Nauckhoff. Cambridge: Cambridge University Press, 2001 [1882].

Nietzsche, Fredrich. *Human, All Too Human: A Book for Free Spirits*. Translated by R. J. Hollingdale. Cambridge: Cambridge University Press, 1996.

Norman, E. R. *Church and Society in England 1770–1970*. Oxford: Clarendon Press, 1976.

North, Michael. *The Political Aesthetic of Yeats, Eliot, and Pound*. Cambridge: Cambridge University Press, 1991.

Nurser, John S. *For All the Peoples and All Nations: The Ecumenical Church and Human Rights*. Washington, DC: Georgetown University Press, 2005.

O'Donovan, Oliver. *The Desire of the Nations*. Cambridge: Cambridge University Press, 1996.

Oldham, J. H. 'All Real Life Is Meeting'. *Christian News-Letter*, no. 112 (17 December 1941).

Oldham, J. H. 'Christian Humanism'. In *Humanism: Three B.B.C. Talks*, 15–20. London: Watts & Co., 1944.

Oldham, J. H. *Church, Community and State: A World Issue*. London: SCM Press, 1935.

Oldham, J. H, ed. *The Churches Survey Their Task: The Report of the Conference at Oxford, July 1937, on Church, Community, and State*. London: George Allen & Unwin, 1937.

Oldham, J. H. 'Diagnosis of Our Time'. *Christian News-Letter*, no. 174 (24 February 1943).

Oldham, J. H. 'Editorial 3rd April 1940'. *Christian News-Letter*, no. 23 (3 April 1940).

Oldham, J. H. 'Editorial 3rd January 1940'. *Christian News-Letter*, no. 10 (3 January 1940).

Oldham, J. H. 'Editorial 18th October 1939'. *Christian News-Letter*, no. 0 (18 October 1939).

Oldham, J. H. 'Freedom and Planning'. *Christian News-Letter* 104, Supplement (22 October 1941).

Oldham, J. H. 'The Idea of a Christian Society'. *Christian News-Letter*, no. 18 (28 Feburary 1940).

Oldham, J. H. 'Letter from Karl Mannheim'. *Christian News-Letter*, no. 135 (27 May 1942).

Oldham, J. H. 'Planning for Freedom'. *Christian News-Letter*, no. 104 (22 October 1941).

Oldham, J. H. *The Question of the Church in the World of to-Day*. London: Edinburgh House Press, 1936.

Oldham, J. H. *Real Life Is Meeting*. Christian News-Letter Books No. 14. London: Sheldon Press, 1942.

Oldham, J. H. *The Resurrection of Christendom*. London: Sheldon Press, 1940.

Oldham, J. H. 'The Roots of Our Troubles'. In *The Church Looks Ahead*, edited by J. H. [and others] Oldham, 17–41. London: Faber & Faber, 1941.

Oldham, J. H. 'The Way Out'. *Christian News-Letter*, no. 45 (4 September 1940).

Oldham, J. H. 'What Is a "Christian" News-Letter?'. *Christian News-Letter*, no. 0 (18 October 1939).

Oldham, J. H. 'Lessons of the Crisis'. *The Times* (5 October 1938): 15.

Oliver, Simon. 'Introducing Radical Orthodoxy: From Participation to Late Modernity'. In *Radical Orthodoxy Reader*, edited by Simon Oliver and John Milbank, 3–27. London: Routledge, 2009.

Overy, Richard. *The Morbid Age: Britain and the Crisis of Civilization, 1919–1939*. London: Penguin Books, 2010.

Perl, Jeffrey M. *The Tradition of Return: The Implicit History of Modern Literature*. Princeton, NJ: Princeton University Press, 1984.

Pfeifer, Hans. 'Keith Clements (Ed.), *the Moot Papers, Faith, Freedom and Society 1938–1944*'. *Theology* 114, no. 1 (2011): 61–4.

Polanyi, Michael. *Society, Economics, and Philosophy: Selected Papers*. New Brunswick: Transaction, 1997.
Pound, Ezra. *The Cantos of Ezra Pound*. London: Faber & Faber, 1964.
Quigley, Carroll. *Tragedy and Hope: A History of the World in Our Time*. New York: Macmillan, 1966.
Reckitt, Maurice. 'Editorial: Valedictory'. *Christendom* XVI, no. 80 (1950): 251–4.
Reckitt, Maurice. 'The Idea of Christendom in Relation to Modern Society'. In *The Return of Christendom*, edited by Charles Gore, et al., 19–40. London: George Allen and Unwin, 1922.
Redles, David. *National Socialist Millennialism*. Oxford: Oxford University Press, 2011.
Reeves, Marjorie, and Elaine Kaye. 'Tracts for Wartime: *The Christian News-Letter*'. In *Christian Thinking and Social Order: Conviction Politics from the 1930s to the Present Day*, edited by Marjorie Reeves, 49–79. London: Cassell, 1999.
Rhodes, James M. *The Hitler Movement: A Modern Millenarian Revolution*. Stanford, CA: The Hoover Institution, 1980.
Ritschel, Daniel. *The Politics of Planning: The Debate on Economic Planning in Britain in the 1930s* [in eng]. Oxford Historical Monographs. Oxford: Oxford University Press, 1997. doi:10.1093/acprof:oso/9780198206477.001.0001.
Roberts, David D. 'Fascism, Modernism and the Quest for an Alternative Modernity' [In English]. *Patterns of Prejudice* 43, no. 1 (2009): 91–102.
Robichaud, Paul. *Making the Past Present: David Jones, the Middle Ages, & Modernism*. Washington, DC: The Catholic University of America Press, 2006.
Rose, Nikolas, Pat O'Malley, and Mariana Valverde. 'Governmentality'. *Annual Review of Law and Social Science* 2 (2006): 83–104.
Saler, Michael. *The Avant-Garde of Interwar England: Medieval Modernism and the London Underground*. Oxford: Oxford University Press, 1999.
Sartori, Giovanni. *Parties and Party Systems: A Framework for Analysis*. Cambridge: Cambridge University Press, 1976.
Schloesser, Stephen. *Jazz Age Catholicism: Mystic Modernism in Postwar* Paris, *1919–1933* [in English]. Toronto: University of Toronto Press, 2005.
Schuchard, Ronald. 'Burbank with a Baedeker, Eliot with a Cigar: American Intellectuals, Anti-Semitism, and the Idea of Culture'. *Modernism/Modernity* 10, no. 1 (2003): 1–26.
Schuhard, Margret. 'T. S. Eliot and Adolf Lowe in Dialogue'. *Arbeiten aus Anglistik und Amerikanistik* 31, no. 1 (2006): 3–24.
Schumpeter, Joseph. *Capitalism, Socialism, and Democracy*. London: Routledge, 2003 [1943].
Scott, Christina. *A Historian and His World: A Life of Christopher Dawson, 1889–1970*. New Brunswick: Transaction Publishers, 1992.
Shorten, Richard. *Modernism and Totalitarianism*. Basingstoke: Palgrave, 2012.
Sigurdson, Ola. 'Beyond Secularism? Towards a Post-Secular Political Theology'. *Modern Theology* 26, no. 2 (2010): 177–96.

Silver, Harold. *Higher Education and Opinion Making in Twentieth-Century England*. London: Woburn Press, 2003.

Smith, Graeme. 'Christian Totalitarianism: Joseph Oldham and Oxford 1937'. *Political Theology* 3, no. 1 (2001): 32–46.

Smith, Graeme. *Oxford 1937: The Universal Christian Council for Life and Work Conference*. Frankfurt am Main: Peter Lang, 2004.

Spengler, Oswald. *The Decline of the West*. London: Allen & Unwin, 1961 [1926].

Spurr, Barry *'Anglo-Catholic in Religion' T.S. Eliot and Christianity*. Cambridge: Lutterworth Press, 2010.

Steele, Tom, and Richard Kenneth Taylor. 'Oldham's Moot (1938–1947), the Universities and the Adult Citizen'. *History of Education* 39, no. 2 (2010): 183–97.

Surette, Leon. *The Birth of Modernism: Ezra Pound, T.S. Eliot, W.B. Yeats, and the Occult* [in English]. Montreal: McGill-Queen's University Press, 1993.

Surette, Leon. *Dreams of a Totalitarian Utopia: Literary Modernism and Politics* [in English]. Montreal: McGill-Queen's University Press, 2011.

Surette, Leon. *A Light from Eleusis: A Study of Ezra Pound's Cantos* [in English]. Oxford; New York: Clarendon Press; Oxford University Press, 1979.

Taylor, Charles. *A Secular Age*. Cambridge: Harvard University Press, 2007.

Taylor, William. 'Education and the Moot'. In *In History and Education: Essays Presented to Peter Gordon*, edited by Richard Aldrich, 159–86. London: Woburn Press, 1996.

Temple, William. 'Begin Now'. *Christian News-Letter*, no. 41 (7 August 1940).

Temple, William. 'The Restoration of Christendom'. *Christendom* 1 (1936): 17–29.

Temple, William. 'What Christians Stand for in the Secular World'. *Christian News-Letter Supplement*, no. 198 (29 Dec 1943).

'T Hooft, W. A. Visser, and J. H. Oldham. *The Church and Its Function in Society*. London: George Allen & Allen, 1937.

Tillich, Paul. *My Travel Diary: 1936*. Translated by Maria Pelikan. London: SCM Press, 1970.

Tillich, Paul. *The Socialist Decision* [Die sozialistische Entscheidung]. Translated by Franklin Sherman. New York: Harper & Row, 1977.

Tillich, Paul. *Systematic Theology: Volume III*. Chicago: The University of Chicago Press, 1963.

Tollefson, Kenneth D. 'Titus: Epistle of Religious Revitalization'. *Biblical Theology Bulletin: A Journal of Bible and Theology* 30, no. 4 (November 1, 2000): 145–57.

Tonning, Erik. 'Introduction'. In *Modernism, Christianity, and Apocalypse*, edited by Erik Tonning, Matthew Feldman, and David Addyman. Leiden: Brill, 2014.

Tonning, Erik. *Modernism and Christianity*. Basingstoke: Palgrave Macmillan, 2014.

Vickers, Geoffrey. 'God and Politics'. *Christian News-Letter*, no. 260 (15 May 1946).

Vickers, Jeanne. *Rethinking the Future: The Correspondence between Geoffrey Vickers and Adolph Lowe* [in eng]. London: Transaction Publishers, 1991.

Vidler, Alec. 'Editorial: Planning for What'. *Theology* 44, no. 266 (1942): 65–70.

Vidler, Alec. 'Inquiries Concerning Natural Law'. *Theology* 44, no. 260 (1942): 65–73.

Vidler, Alec. 'The Obedience of a Christian Intellectual'. *Christian News-Letter*, no. 272 (30th October 1946).
Vidler, Alec. *God's Judgment on Europe*. London: Longmans, Green and Co., 1940.
Vidler, Alec. *Scenes from a Clerical Life*. London: Collins, 1977.
Vidler, Alec. *Secular Despair and Christian Faith*. London: SCM Press, 1941.
Villis, Tom. *British Catholics & Fascism: Religious Identity and Political Extremism between the Wars*. Basingstoke: Palgrave Macmillan, 2013.
Villis, Tom. *Reaction and the Avant-Garde: The Revolt against Liberal Democracy in Early Twentieth-Century Britain*. London: Tauris Academic Studies, 2006.
Voas, David, and Alasdair Crockett. 'Religion in Britain: Neither Believing nor Belonging'. *Sociology* 39, no. 1 (2005): 11–28.
Volf, Miroslav. *A Public Faith: How Followers of Christ Should Serve the Common Good*. Grand Rapids, MI: Brazos Press, 2011.
Wallace, Anthony W. C. 'Revitalization Movements'. *American Anthropologist* 58, no. 2 (1956): 264–81.
Webb, Sidney, and Beatrice. *Soviet Communism: A New Civilisation*. 3rd ed. London: Longman, Green and Co., 1944 [1935].
Weber, Max. *The Protestant Ethic and the Spirit of Capitalism*. Translated by Talcott Parsons. London: George Allen & Unwin, 1930.
Wells, H. G. *The Rights of Man or, What Are We Fighting For?* Harmondsworth: Penguin, 1940.
Wicht, Wolfgang. 'Eliot and Karl Mannheim: Cultural Reconstruction Vs. The Destruction of Culture'. *Zeitschrift für Anglistik und Amerikanistik* 36 (1988): 197–204.
Wilk, Christopher. 'Introduction: What Was Modernism'. In *Modernism: Designing a New World : 1914–1939*, edited by Christopher Wilk, 11–21. London: V&A Publications, 2006.
Williams, Raymond. *Culture and Society 1780–1950*. Hammondsworth: Pelican Books, 1971 [1958].
Williams, Raymond. *The Politics of Modernism: Against the New Conformists*. London: Verso Press, 1989.
Williams, Rowan. *Faith in the Public Square*. London: Bloomsbury, 2012.
Williamson, Philip. 'Christian Conservatives and the Totalitarian Challenge, 1933–40'. *English Historical Review* 115, no. 462 (2000): 607–42.
Wilson, Bryan. *Religion in Sociological Perspective*. Oxford: Oxford University Press, 1982.
Woldring, H.E.S. *Karl Mannheim: The Development of His Thought*. Assen: Van Gorcum, 1986.
Woolf, Virginia. *Three Guineas*. London: Hogarth Press, 1943 [1938].
Woolf, Virginia. 'Why Art Today Follows Politics'. In *Virginia Woolf: Selected Essays*, edited by David Bradshaw, 213–15. Oxford: Oxford University Press, 2008.

Ziffus, Sigrid. 'Karl Mannheim Und Der Moot-Kreis: Ein Wenig Beachteter Aspekt Seines Wirkens Im Englischen Exil'. In *Exil, Wissenshaft, Identität*, edited by Ilja Srubar, 206–23. Frankfurt am Main: Suhrkamp, 1988.

Žižek, Slavoj. *Did Somebody Say Totalitarianism?: Five Interventions in the (Mis)Use of a Notion*. London: Verso, 2001.

Index

Action Française 99–100, 101, 125 n.109, 151, 192
All Souls Group 187
anthropocentric humanism. *See* humanism
apocalypticism 6, 7, 9, 10, 17, 19, 29, 43, 49, 74, 134, 136–7, 226
Aquinas, Thomas 53, 55, 57, 61, 62–3, 64, 80 n.100. *See also* Thomism, neo-Thomism
Arendt, Hannah 90, 109, 111, 160 n.138
Aristotle 54, 62
Arnold, Matthew 128 n.171, 216 n.309
Arnold, Thomas 183
arts and crafts movement 53
Asher, Kenneth 151
Auden, W. H. 53, 87, 91
authoritarianism 87, 90, 95, 100, 111, 112, 115, 151, 152, 160 n.138

Baillie, John 2, 4, 10, 50, 89, 164, 197
    BBC 195
    Christian News-Letter 193
    communalism 38
    democracy 92
    Maritain, Jacques 55–6, 79 n.95, 197
    natural law 64, 79 n.95
    open Christian civilization 61
    theocracy 107
    values 64, 65–6
Baldwin, Stanley 32
Barker, Ernest 32
Barth, Karl 64–5, 80 n.111, 191
Bauman, Zygmunt 29, 74, 106, 113, 138, 226
BBC 193–6, 221
Beebe, Maurice 4, 6
Berger, Peter 13, 17, 26 n.81, 137, 156 n.36
Beveridge Report 110, 116, 191
Beveridge, William 3, 32, 80 n.117, 110, 116, 187
Blair, Sara 6

Bliss, Kathleen 3, 171, 193
Bloomsbury Group 53, 76 n.28, 172
Bradbury, Malcolm 5
Brave New World 72, 114, 184
Brown, Callum 15, 26 n.84
Bruce, Steve 13, 25 n.72
Brunner, Emil 55, 80 n.111
Buber, Martin 37, 46 n.59, 197
Buchman, Frank 31–2, 162
bureaucracy 39, 69, 92, 130
Butler, R. A. 178, 186–8, 197

capitalism 39, 41, 42–3, 46 n.67, 87, 91, 94, 99, 101, 102, 103, 111, 117, 118, 119, 121 n.3, 184, 199, 224, 226
centralization. *See also* 'Planning for Freedom'
    inevitability of 67–8, 71, 108, 111, 129 n.193, 192
    modern society 71–2, 109–10
    relation to totalitarianism 40, 60, 88, 101, 108–15
    resistance to 78 n.79
Christendom 11, 36, 50, 51–2, 56–7, 60–1, 63, 66, 73, 77 n.57, 99, 162, 220, 222, 223. *See also* New Christendom
Christendom Group 51, 101, 152, 162–3, 223
Christian Frontiers Council 168, 170–1, 187, 189, 207 n.80, 221
Christianization 15, 66, 86, 102, 104, 107, 119, 144, 169. *See also* in-depth Christianization
Christian Modernism 15–20, 221–2
Christian News-Letter 189–93, 213 n.236, 213 n.245, 221
Christian society 50–1, 85, 105, 138, 140, 172, 182, 190, 193, 197
    Christian secular society 55, 60–1
    church and state 60–1, 108
    education 142, 186, 192

medievalism 50, 56–7
modernity 51, 73
the Order 62, 173
pluralism 61
shared values 65
totalitarianism 108
Christian totalitarianism 86, 89–90, 107–8, 110, 118, 119, 120, 127 n.166, 128 n.167
Christian values 64–6, 105, 107, 182, 191, 202
church and state 60, 86, 90, 103–4, 108, 193
Churchill, Winston 90, 178, 191, 221
civilizational crisis
    anthropology 36–7
    economic causes 38–9
    interwar crisis discourse 10, 29–30
    Modernism 5–7, 29
    political threats 39–43
    spiritual roots 31–5
civil society 10, 68, 114, 172, 180, 221
Clarke, Fred 2
    BBC 195
    democracy 93
    education 183–5, 186–8, 192, 197
    Mannheim, Karl 70–1, 210 n.181
Clements, Keith 10, 20, 21 n.9, 22 n.14, 75 n.8, 86, 103, 169, 170, 191, 193
Cocteau, Jean 11
coercion 66, 86, 90, 94–5, 103–7, 117, 119, 201, 220, 223
Colerigde, Samuel 139, 144–5, 156 n.50
Collini, Stefan 101, 133, 134–5, 152, 160 n.139
commotive 38, 46 n.62, 179
communism 7, 32, 40, 41, 85, 87, 99–101, 102, 103, 116, 119, 121, 141, 161, 163, 220, 226
Community of Christians. *See* Eliot, T. S.
Comte, August 138, 139, 156 n.42
Council on the Christian Faith and the Common Life 78 n.68, 163, 165, 168–71, 175, 181, 182, 189, 190, 194, 221
Coupland, Phillip 15, 51–2
cultural transformation 146, 151, 153, 201, 202, 220
Cunningham, Valentine 87
Curtis, Lionel 32–3

dark age 6, 33, 142, 151
Davie, Grace 13, 14
Dawson, Christopher 2, 41, 163, 196
    bureaucratic society 39, 88
    Christendom 61
    democracy 88, 92, 94, 97–8, 109, 138
    desecularization 40
    ersatz religion 34, 88
    humanism 78 n.60, 78 n.62
    Kingdom of God as totalitarian 107
    Mannheim, Karl 69, 71, 72, 115, 120, 148–9, 152, 192
    modern state 33–4, 39, 40, 88
    the Moot 3, 99
    the Order 176, 177, 179, 180
    right-wing politics 99, 119
    spiritual versus political freedom 97–8
    Sword of the Spirit 173, 179
    totalitarianism 34, 40, 88, 90, 109–10
decadence 4, 35, 161, 162
'decadence and renewal' 1, 7, 9, 10, 12, 43, 49, 133, 134
    interwar decadence discourse 6, 29–30, 34, 49, 74, 87, 219
    Modernism 4, 7–8, 29, 133
decentralization 65, 78 n.79, 96, 124
Demant, V. A. 72, 96, 152, 163
democracy
    Christianity 98, 153, 181
    defence of 85, 93–4, 98, 102, 119, 123 n.39, 187, 189
    definitions 92–3, 98, 108, 120, 200–1
    education for a democratic culture 106, 141, 185, 188, 192
    militant democracy 68, 94–5, 96, 106
    misgivings of liberal democracy 36–7, 39, 85, 90–2, 100, 101, 107, 119
    Modernism 87
    planned democracy 68, 110, 112–15, 120, 139, 140, 153, 185, 186, 192, 196, 200
    reform of democracy 70–1, 93–4, 114
    totalitarian democracy 109, 110, 111, 114, 138, 156 n.39
    totalitarianism 33–4, 39
Dent, H. C., 171, 187
dictatorship 43, 103, 107, 110, 112, 113, 115, 118, 120, 130 n.221, 148, 160 n.137, 173, 200, 201

disenchantment 12, 18, 27 n.105
disintegration 31, 33, 34, 35, 36, 37, 41–2, 57, 60, 61, 78 n.79, 87, 89, 105, 110, 133, 137, 138, 147, 153, 173–4, 188, 220
Durkheim, Emilie 13, 82 n.136, 138

education 180, 182-9. *See also* 1944 Education Act
  as a means to re-Christianize 102
  centralization 183, 187
  character formation 97, 106, 112, 142, 182, 183–5, 188
  Christianity 184, 185, 192
  coercion 105, 188
  'education for life' (*see* education, character formation)
  Education Group 185–8, 211 n.204, 212 n.226
  equal opportunity 165, 182, 187, 192, 196
  experimental college 185–6
  for social cohesion 95, 102, 105, 106, 180
  religious education 185, 188
  societal transformation 182
  universities 184
  values 184, 187, 188
  vocational training 184–5, 188
Edwards, Mark 52, 86, 121
Eisenstadt, Shmuel 13
Eliot, T. S.
  anti-Semitism 100, 126 n.118
  authoritarianism 86–7, 115, 126 n.118, 151–2, 160 n.137
  BBC 34, 194, 195, 196
  Christian Frontiers Council 171
  Christian News-Letter 171, 190, 192–3
  Christian society 50, 55, 138, 140, 142, 149, 196, 224
  Christian totalitarianism 107–8
  class 61, 146–7, 150, 153
  clerisy 105, 144–5, 150 (*see also* elite(s))
  Community of Christians 173, 174
  conservatism 51, 100, 200
  conversion 19, 33, 55, 152
  crisis of modernity 33, 137–8, 153
  culture 139–40, 142–3, 145–7, 151, 153, 200

democracy 39, 87, 91–2, 100, 185
education 142, 184, 185, 186, 192, 196, 212 n.226
elite 143–7
eschatology 134, 142
future of Western societies 50, 138, 224
hierarchy 86–7, 119, 151, 152
imagination 138–9, 147–8
individualism 37, 74, 95
intellectuals 6–7, 90, 99–101, 102–3, 106, 120, 141, 144, 203, 225–6
intelligentsia (*see also* elite(s))
liberalism 36–8, 57–8, 105–6, 124 n.82, 137, 196, 200
Mannheim, Karl 11, 70, 72, 105, 115, 135–6, 141–2, 145, 146–51, 153, 196, 220
Maritain, Jacques 55, 60
Middle Ages 52–3
Modernism 16, 133, 136, 143–4, 154, 220
monarchy 102, 115, 160 n.137
the Moot 2, 118, 135–6, 144, 146, 167, 169, 196, 203, 225
natural law 63, 64, 65
the Order 177, 180, 209 n.144
original sin 105
planning 11, 105, 115, 141, 142, 143, 148, 149, 151, 153, 154, 157 n.65, 196, 220
pluralism 61, 146
providence 11, 150, 154, 220
right wing politics 7, 86–7, 99–101, 151–2
social function of religion 139–40, 147–8, 150, 153
totalitarianism and liberalism 99, 105, 109
totalitarianism 107–8, 115, 141, 151
tradition 23 n.38, 36, 51
'way of life' 105, 115, 139, 147 (*see also* Eliot, T. S., culture)
elite(s) 7, 10, 12, 14, 15, 29, 31, 53, 62, 68, 72, 93, 103, 105, 110, 113, 118, 119, 134–5, 141, 142, 143, 144–7, 153, 154, 173–4, 178, 179, 180, 181, 184, 185, 200, 202, 204, 219, 221, 222, 224

elitism 106, 111, 119
the Enlightenment 5, 7, 8, 16, 37, 38, 39, 58, 66, 74, 97, 98, 106, 134, 148, 150, 151, 222
epistemology 14, 35, 104
equality 91, 96, 105, 165, 172, 182, 188
equal opportunity. *See* education
eschatology 74, 105, 107, 134, 142
Evans, Richard 21
Every, George 99, 115, 192
Eysteinsson, Astradur 4, 5

Farmer, H. H. 2, 3, 89, 101–2
fascism 85, 151, 163, 202, 226
    admiration 102, 103
    Christian sympathisers 99–101, 151
    definition 95, 125 n.109
    Modernism 86–7
    modernity 73–4, 178
    the Moot 41, 85, 114
    quasi-religious 16, 32
    Programmatic Modernism 8, 9, 11, 87
    resistance to 15, 32, 34, 40, 101, 140, 141, 161, 163, 220, 226
    totalitarianism 93
Fenn, Eric 2, 3, 20, 31, 72, 89, 149, 182, 193–6
Ferrall, Charles 87
First World War 6
formalism 4, 5, 53, 54, 76 n.28
Forster, E. M. 123 n.39, 164, 172
Foucault, Michel 86, 103–4, 120
Fraternity of the Spirit. *See* the Order
freedom 112–15
    Christianity 32
    expression 71, 93, 95, 111
    humanistic conception 97
    individual 58, 93, 94–5, 97, 98, 111, 119, 173
    positive definition 97
    private property 118
    problem of freedom in modern society 39, 50
    responsibility 59, 64, 97, 112, 114, 119, 188
    self-determination 98
    spiritual 61, 73, 95, 96
    spiritual versus political 97–8

Gay, Peter 4–5, 133
Gentile, Emilio 40, 88–9
Gill, Eric 53, 55
Griffin, Roger 1, 4, 7–12, 15–20, 29, 30, 43, 49–50, 52, 73–5, 87, 133, 134, 154, 162, 219, 220, 222
Grimley, Matthew 10, 15, 121
Grisebach, Eberhard 37–8, 97
guild socialism 53, 55, 78 n.79

Hall, N. F. 176, 208 n.117
Hauerwas, Stanley 223, 227 n.9
Hayek, Fredrick 102, 110
hegemony 86, 121, 223, 227 n.9
Hetherington, Hector 2, 51, 71, 96, 117
historical materialism 42–3
Hitler, Adolf 7, 9, 32, 101–3, 161, 188
Hitlerjugend 102
Hocking, W. E. 22 n.15, 38, 46 n.62, 179
Hodges, H. A.
    archetypes 66, 159 n.124
    BBC 194
    common good 64–5, 107
    crisis of modern society 42–3
    education 183
    exploitation under industrialization 38
    freedom and responsibility 97
    Mannheim, Karl 71, 112, 114, 183
    Maritain, Jacques 56
    the Moot 2, 118, 167, 202, 203, 225
    natural law 62
    'new Summa' 77 n.58
    the Order 176, 177, 181
    planning 112
    secularization 35
    socialism 42–3, 116–18
    Thomism 57, 77 n.58
Holocaust 191
Hooper, Sydney E. 32
humanism 14, 57, 61, 78 n.60, 78 n.62, 82 n.132, 96, 97, 148, 149, 152, 154, 184
    anthropocentric humanism 57–9, 59
    integral humanism 54, 58, 60, 67
    theocentric humanism 55, 57, 58, 73
human rights 52, 79 n.95, 96, 97, 98
hylomorphism 54
Hynes, Samuel 87

impersonal forces 38, 39
inculturation 89
in-depth Christianization 86, 103–4. *See also* Christianization
individualism 37, 38, 39, 66, 74, 87, 95, 119
Industrial Christian Fellowship 32
industrialization 5, 8, 12, 37, 38–9, 43, 55, 68, 89, 110
Institute of Education 71, 183, 210 n.180
integral humanism. *See* humanism
intelligentsia 90–1, 103, 120, 134, 143, 145, 219. *See also* elite(s)
interwar period 9, 10, 11, 29, 30, 43, 49–50, 54, 74, 85, 87, 91–2, 99–101, 116, 134, 164, 219
Iredale, Eleanora 2, 3, 61, 89, 165, 169

Jackson, Paul 99
Jenkins, Daniel 3, 171
Jones, David 53, 102–3
Joyce, James 6, 7, 53
Julius, Anthony 100

Kafka, Franz 6, 8
Kenyon, Ruth 163
Kermode, Frank 1, 6, 7, 17, 29, 49, 86–7
Kettler, David 70, 115, 134
Kirk, P. T. R. 32
Kojecky, Roger 10, 72, 127 n.166, 133, 134, 135

Lackey, Michael 86, 103–5, 222
Lang, Cosmo 44 n.15, 168, 178, 194
Larsen, Timothy 14–15
left-wing politics 87, 103, 116. *See also* communism; socialism
Lewis, C. S. 3, 22 n.15
Lewis, Pericles 16–17, 30
Lewis, Windham 7, 23 n.41, 87
liberalism 31, 53, 104, 111, 188, 200. *See also* liberal values
  antipathy towards 58, 99, 199
  crisis of 90–1, 99, 109, 138, 197
  economic 98
  freedom 97
  laissez faire 8, 36, 40, 56, 68, 69, 98, 109, 111, 113, 120, 137, 140, 141, 153, 188

social disintegration 36, 38, 57, 105, 119, 137, 138, 153
liberal theology 60, 73
liberal values 37, 71, 94–7, 98, 220
Lindsey, A. D. 168, 171, 190
Livingston, (Sir) Richard 32, 187
Loader, Colin 70, 94
Lord Halifax 178
Löwe, Adolf
  BBC 194
  Christian dictatorship 107, 110–11, 120
  crisis of modern society 42
  education 184, 185–6, 197
  Mannheim, Karl 71
  the Moot 225
  the Order 175–6
Luckhurst, Roger 16
Lukács, Georg 6

McDiarmid, Lucy 52–3, 158 n.102
McFarlane, James 5
machine age 38, 42, 110
MacKinnon, Donald 3, 77 n.41
Maier, Hans 108
Mairet, Philip 3, 20, 72, 152, 162, 177, 190, 199
Manganiello, Dominic 6
manifesto 164–8, 195, 202, 220
Mannheim, Karl
  archetypes 66, 137
  BBC 215 n.303
  causes of Second World War 41
  Christianity 15, 36, 45 n.56, 69–70, 96, 106, 127 n.153, 137, 140, 150, 181
  crisis in modern societies 10, 36, 39, 40, 41, 136–8, 153
  crisis in valuation 36, 137–8
  culture 142–3, 147
  democracy 92, 93–5, 96, 119
  education 141, 183, 186, 187, 210 n.184
  Eliot, T. S. 11, 134, 145–6
  elites 141, 143, 144–7, 174
  freedom 95, 98, 112–14
  functionalist view of religion 69, 138–9, 147–8, 149–50, 154, 156 n.45, 197
  humanism 96, 134, 148, 149, 152
  intellectual 106, 141

liberal values 95, 96–7, 98
Maritain, Jacques 55, 56, 70
militant democracy 94–5, 96, 106
Modernism 74, 134, 220
modern society as intrinsically
  totalitarian 88, 109–10, 111, 141
the Moot 2, 4, 70–3, 111–15, 134, 136,
  155 n.24, 161, 165, 197, 198, 202,
  203, 224
natural law 63, 64
the Order 173–4, 175, 176, 177, 178–9,
  180–1, 200
planned democracy 112–13, 139–40,
  141, 153, 192, 200
planning (*see* 'Planning for Freedom')
Polanyi, Michael 20, 115, 130 n.224
propaganda 74, 102, 106, 119, 189, 192
reformism 199–200
revitalization 51, 112, 179, 180
secularization 14–15, 137, 138, 153
socialism 42, 116, 117
social techniques 74, 106, 113, 189
sociology of knowledge 14
totalitarianism 15, 40, 88, 111–15, 139,
  141
totalitarianism, learning from 102,
  161–2, 178
Maritain, Jacques 3, 11, 37, 52, 53–6,
  57–67, 70, 73, 77 n.57, 79 n.95, 88,
  100, 117, 172, 192, 196, 197, 220
Martin, David 13
Martin, Hugh 31
Marx, Karl 5, 13, 41, 42, 116
masses 9, 29, 40, 92, 102, 103, 106–7, 109,
  111, 113, 117, 123 n.50, 139, 141,
  162, 164
mass society 5, 39, 87, 92, 114, 141, 145,
  146, 147, 173
Maurras, Charles 7, 99–100, 151, 192
'mazeway' 49, 74, 167, 171, 220
mechanization 88, 96, 138, 139, 156 n.39,
  173
medieval 10, 11, 14, 15, 52, 54, 58, 61, 63,
  66, 72, 73, 162, 220, 223
medievalism 42, 51–2, 55, 56, 78 n.75, 161,
  164, 199, 220
medieval Modernism 53–6, 75
Mein Kampf 102, 164
Meja, Volker 70, 115, 134

Micklem, Nathaniel 31, 180
Middle Ages 51, 52–3, 54, 56, 57, 60, 62,
  73, 78 n.79
middle axiom 64, 205 n.41
Milbank, John 18, 223, 226, 227 n.12
millenarianism 17
Miller, Lex 3, 114, 117, 130 n.238
Moberly, Walter
  BBC 32, 195, 196
  Christian Frontier Council 170, 171,
    207 n.88
  Council of the Christian Faith and the
    Common Life 168, 169
  democracy 93
  education 183, 184–5, 188, 197
  Mannheim, Karl 71–2
  the Moot 2, 169
  natural law 63–4
  the Order 170, 176, 177, 181
  secularization 35
  totalitarianism 89, 107, 188
Modernism. *See also* medieval
  Modernism; Programmatic
  Modernism
  aesthetics 4, 5, 9, 11, 54, 87
  ahistorical 4, 5
  Christianity 11, 12, 18–20, 52, 221–2
    (*see also* Christian Modernism)
  definition 4–10
  epiphanic 8
  fascism 8, 11, 73–4
  the Moot 10–12, 15–16, 221–2
  politics 4–6, 86–7
  reaction against modernity 4, 5–6, 17,
    30, 43, 54, 133
  religion 5, 12, 16, 30
  scholasticism 53–6, 58
monarchy 87, 100, 101, 115, 160 n.137
monologism 37–8
the Moot
  failures 118, 166–7, 201–4
  history 2–4
  legacy 196–8, 204, 224–6
  meetings and procedures 3–4
  members 2–3, Appendix
  research groups 164, 176, 186, 205 n.15
Moral Re-Armament Movement 32, 162,
  204 n.11
Mosley, Oswald 100

Mott, J. R. 190
multiple modernities 13
Munich agreement 31, 33
Munton, Alan 6
Murry, John Middleton
   BBC 194, 195
   capitalism 39, 41, 101, 199
   Christian society 51, 56, 60, 108, 128 n.171, 198
   Christian totalitarianism 108, 128 n.167
   communism 33, 116, 119, 162, 163
   crisis in modern society 33, 36–7, 41
   decentralisation and local autonomy 78 n.79, 114, 198
   democracy 93–4, 117, 181
   education 183, 186
   guild socialism 78 n.79
   industrialized societies 39
   Mannheim, Karl 72, 78 n.79, 114, 181, 198
   the Moot 2, 135, 166, 198, 200, 203, 217 n.343
   natural law 64
   the Order 177, 180, 181
   revolution 33, 41
   totalitarianism 11, 93, 108, 109, 110, 111, 114
Mussolini, Benito 7, 9, 11, 32, 95, 103, 151
myth 4, 7, 9, 16, 33, 39, 53
mythic past 8, 11, 16, 50, 52, 60, 220

natural law 62–7, 79 n.95, 80 n.100, 104, 185
Nazism 1, 8, 9, 11, 31, 64, 69, 85, 91, 101–2, 109, 118, 119, 121, 178–9, 188, 191, 194, 220. *See also* fascism
neo-orthodoxy 73, 80 n.111
Neo-Scholasticism 53, 66. *See also* neo-Thomism
neo-Thomism 1, 54–5, 66, 220. *See also* Thomism
Newbigin, Lesslie 3
New Christendom 15, 50, 51–2, 55, 58–61, 67, 73, 119, 121, 168, 175, 181, 191, 197, 198, 220, 221, 223, 227 n.12
new era 7, 8, 73, 154
new man 9, 58, 138, 199
Niebuhr, Reinhold 3, 31, 44 n.12, 52, 55, 60, 76 n.20, 88, 104–5, 116, 117, 127 n.145, 177, 190, 191, 197
Nietzsche, Friedrich 5, 8, 18, 137, 156 n.54, 226
nihilism 8, 18, 42, 43, 150, 153, 226
1944 Education Act 186–9, 197, 204, 221
1937 Oxford Conference on Church, Community and State 2, 34, 50, 86, 88–90, 163, 173, 184
nominalism 18
nomos 17, 19, 30, 134, 137, 221
North, Michael 87
Nurser, John 52

Oakeshott, Walter 2, 149, 163, 168, 171, 176–7, 187, 199
O'Donovan, Oliver 223
Ogilvie, Fredrick W. 165, 193–4
Oldham, J. H.
   anthropology 37–8, 59, 64, 97, 112, 191, 197
   BBC 193–6
   centralization 71, 112
   Christian Frontiers Council 170–1, 221
   Christian societal renewal 2, 10, 49–51, 52, 161, 193, 222
   Christian values 65–6, 80 n.117, 81 n.121
   civilizational crisis 1, 33, 36, 37, 39, 43
   Council on the Christian Faith and the Common Life 78 n.68, 165, 168–70, 181, 221
   democracy 92, 93
   editor of the *Christian News-Letter* 189–90, 191, 193
   education 185, 186, 187, 188
   'essential rights' 96–7
   freedom 96–7, 98
   industrialized societies 39
   liberal values 37
   manifesto 59, 67, 73, 104, 164–8, 182, 198
   Mannheim, Karl 70, 71, 112, 115, 141, 192
   Maritain, Jacques 59, 82 n.132
   the Moot 2–4, 12, 73, 136, 163, 198, 202, 203, 221, 224–5
   natural law 64, 65, 185
   neo-orthodoxy 80 n.111

New Christendom 51, 191, 198
'open conspiracy' 104, 172
the Order 2, 161, 172, 174–5, 177, 178, 179–82
planning 40
revolution 198–9
secularization 35
totalitarianism 34, 40, 85, 86, 88–90, 97, 99, 102, 108, 112
oligarchy 39, 87, 91–2
the Order 1, 12, 61–2, 99, 161, 163, 172–82, 200, 209 n.144, 221
commitments 175–7, 182
political versus 'prophetic' purpose 175–6, 178–9
rationale 172, 177
suggested constitutions 174–5, 177, 179–80
original sin 104–6, 127 n.153, 149
Overy, Richard 6, 29, 30
Oxford Group Movement 32

paganism 1, 34, 35, 40, 41, 50, 51, 101, 107, 138, 142, 178, 224
Pakenham, Frank 3, 110
palingenesis 8, 11, 17, 162. *See also* rebirth
parliamentarianism 94, 96, 98, 112, 113, 118, 201
Paton, William 3, 170
Paul, Saint 74
Peace Aims Group 52
Perl, Jeffrey 52
'Planning for Freedom' 50, 67–70, 73, 79 n.79, 94–5, 102, 112–15, 120, 136, 141, 145, 152, 161, 163, 174, 183, 192, 200, 220
pluralism 61, 65, 95, 96, 113, 140, 179, 223, 224
Polanyi, Michael 3, 10, 20, 72, 115, 127 n.139, 145, 149, 150, 152, 159 n.119, 225, 227
Political and Economic Planning 22 n.13, 163
Political Modernism. *See* Programmatic Modernism
political religion 16, 69, 74, 88–9, 95
post-structuralism 104, 121, 223
post-war reconstruction 43, 51–2, 116, 148, 189, 192, 200, 225

Pound, Ezra 7, 9, 16, 53, 87, 100
power 6, 40–1, 72, 93, 101, 104, 108, 109, 110, 112, 113, 117–18, 120, 145, 152, 180–1, 186, 223
premodern 9, 11, 74
primordial 17, 18, 27 n.102, 154 n.7
Programmatic Modernism
Christianity 1, 17–20, 73–5, 219, 222
definition 7–10, 133–4, 154, 162
heuristic framework 1–2, 8, 12, 219
the Moot 1, 10–12, 49–50, 73–5, 90, 162, 219–20, 222
return to mythic past 52, 60, 73, 220
scholasticism 58–9
totalitarianism 87
progress 7, 38, 39, 43, 143, 200
propaganda 39, 40, 57, 74, 102, 103, 105, 106–7, 119, 180, 183, 192
providence 11, 72, 73, 134, 149, 150, 220

reactionary 9, 53, 87, 100, 101, 116, 152, 158 n.102, 199, 201
Read, Herbert 53, 135
realism (Christian) 52, 59–60, 104–5, 118, 197
rebirth 9, 10–11, 17, 52, 142, 161, 164, 181, 199, 222
Reckitt, Maurice 51, 152, 162, 223
Reeves, Marjorie 187
the Reformation 45 n.56, 58
renewal 9, 11, 16–17, 18, 30, 43, 49–50, 58, 59, 60, 66, 75, 94, 133, 140, 144, 147, 153, 172, 174, 182, 190, 194–5, 196, 222, 223
replacement religion 16, 17, 34, 40, 140, 226. *See also* political religion
revitalization 6, 9, 49–50, 51, 144, 174
revitalization movement 12, 17–18, 49–50, 73, 74, 84 n.177, 162, 163, 167, 171, 172, 189, 201, 203–4, 220–1
revival 50, 69, 139, 148
revolution 1, 6, 9, 33, 41, 57, 67, 86, 93, 118, 161, 162, 164, 172, 176, 177, 180, 181, 182, 188–9, 198–203, 219
Rhodes, Cecil 172
right wing 7, 8, 86–7, 91, 99–101, 115, 119, 226
Robichaud, Paul 53
Round Table Group 172, 202

Rousseau, Jean-Jacques 64
Royal Institute of International Affairs 22 n.14, 32

sacralization 16, 40, 88, 89, 90, 109, 110
sacred canopy 8, 17, 18, 74, 137, 140, 147, 154, 156 n.36
St Julian's Group 21 n.12, 77 n.41, 224, 228 n.16
Saler, Michael 53, 75
Sartori, Giovanni 200–1
Sayers, Dorothy 164, 190
Schloesser, Stephen 11, 54–5, 75
Schmitt, Carl 92
scholasticism 11, 57, 58, 63, 64, 73, 104. *See also* Neo-Scholasticism
Schumpeter, Joseph A 98
science 35, 42, 106, 113, 185, 191
scientism 38, 72, 115
Scotus, Duns 18
Second World War 4, 15, 41, 42, 177, 178, 193, 200, 202
secularization 5, 12–15, 25 n.72, 30, 34–5, 39, 40, 43, 74, 89, 109, 134, 137–8, 140, 153, 156 n.54, 219, 222, 224, 226 n.2
secularization theory 12–15, 16
Shaw, Gilbert 3, 118, 164, 167, 175, 199
Sigurdson, Ola 223
Smith, Graeme 86, 89–90, 97, 98, 108
Smith, W. H. 168, 171, 190
social construction 29, 148
socialism 6, 7, 42, 86, 103, 115–19, 223
Social Nationalism. *See* Nazism
social philosophy 36, 51, 58, 62, 64, 67, 69, 92, 96, 102, 107, 109, 113, 165, 182, 185, 202
social techniques 74, 94, 102, 103, 106, 113, 189
socio-political movement 1, 10, 59, 60, 66, 67, 71, 73, 104, 161, 163, 164, 165, 168, 172, 173, 176, 178–81, 191–2, 193, 198, 199, 203, 220, 221. *See also* revitalization movement
Spengler, Oswald 25 n.63
Spurr, Barry 135
Stalin, Joseph 32, 103, 118
subconscious 57, 66, 86, 103, 104, 139
Surette, Leon 5, 16, 87, 100, 101, 103, 124 n.82, 151

Tate, Allan 135
Tawney, R. H. 3, 177, 190
Taylor, Charles 14, 27 n.105
Temple, William 3, 22 n.15, 31, 52, 67, 81 n.130, 116–17, 167, 168, 173, 187, 190, 191, 194, 195
theocentric humanism 55, 57–9, 66, 73. *See also* humanism
theocracy 61, 107
third way 56, 61, 112, 120, 121, 181
Thomism 11, 54, 57, 58, 60, 62, 63, 73, 77 n.58, 79 n.95. *See also* neo-Thomism
Tillich, Paul 3, 94, 116, 159 n.118, 172–3, 182
Tonning, Erik 18–20, 30, 52, 74–5, 152, 221–2
totalitarian democracy. *See* democracy
totalitarianism 11, 119–21. *See also* totalitarian democracy
  admiration for 101–3, 119, 162, 220 (*see also* Christian totalitarianism)
  antithetical to Christianity 32, 40, 89, 101, 107
  centralization 40, 68, 72, 88, 109–11, 111–15, 118, 120
  Christian response 2, 50, 52, 97, 119, 139, 140, 153, 179
  definitions 108–11, 120, 128 n.177, 160 n.138
  freedom 32
  the Moot 11, 41, 85–6, 119–20
  outcome of modern societies 34, 40, 43, 72, 85, 88, 99, 105, 109–11, 113
  political religion 40, 88–9, 140, 153
  reaction to liberalism 57, 99
  repressive 38, 57, 68, 95, 98, 111, 119, 120, 141, 172
  resistance to 32, 34, 40, 42, 50, 85–6, 91, 93, 97, 104, 108, 111, 172, 179, 192, 220
Toynbee, Arnold 3, 30, 32, 34, 190, 194
tradition 4, 7, 18, 19, 23 n.38, 36, 50, 51, 62, 91, 96, 114, 116, 139, 140, 143, 146, 147, 148, 150, 152, 172, 174, 184, 200, 226
transcendence 30, 134, 138, 140, 150, 153, 219

universal suffrage 93, 98

Van Dusen, H. P. 52, 76 n.20
Vickers, Geoffrey 3, 96, 165, 180, 193, 225
Vidler, Alec
   anthropology 59–60
   Christian News-Letter 190, 193
   communalism 38
   democracy 93
   Mannheim, Karl 70, 72, 113–14
   Maritain, Jacques 55–6
   modern society 35, 38–9, 46 n.67, 109, 197
   the Moot 3, 196, 220, 225
   natural law 63, 64, 65, 79 n.97, 80 n.100
   New Christendom 56–7, 59
   the Order 176, 177, 180, 181
   propaganda and coercion 105
   St Deiniol's Koinonia 173
   socialism 116, 119
   totalitarianism 110, 113–14

Villis, Tom 91, 99
Voas, David 13
Volf, Miroslav 223

Wallace, Anthony 1, 12, 49, 74, 162, 167, 171, 189, 201, 204, 220, 221
Webb, Beatrice 103
Webb, Sybney 103
Weber, Max 12, 13, 39, 46 n.67, 139, 156 n.46
welfare state 116, 225, 226
Wells, H. G. 96
Wilk, Christopher 6, 22 n.18
Williams, Raymond 5–6, 86, 188, 196
Williams, Rowan 223
Wirth, Louis 85, 136
Woolf, Virginia 7, 172
World Council of Churches 3, 170

Yeats, W. B. 7, 16, 53, 87

www.ingramcontent.com/pod-product-compliance
Lightning Source LLC
Chambersburg PA
CBHW070024010526
44117CB00011B/1701